TABLE OF CONTENTS

ARGO BROTHERS

www.argobrothers.com

INTRODUCTION

The Specialized High Schools Admissions Test (SHSAT) is an exam that students take in order to gain admission into one of the New York Specialized High Schools. Out of the nine Specialized High Schools, eight of the schools admit students solely on the SHSAT score. Fiorello H. LaGuardia High School of Music & Art and Performing Arts (LaGuardia), is the only specialized high school which admits based on an audition and academic review.

Here is a list if the Specialized High Schools along with their contact information.

The Bronx High School of Science
75 West 205th Street, Bronx, New York 10468
Contact Number: (718) 817-7700
www.bxscience.edu

Brooklyn Technical High School
29 Fort Greene Place, Brooklyn, New York 11217
Contact Number: (718) 804-6400
www.bths.edu

The Brooklyn Latin School
223 Graham Avenue, Brooklyn, New York 11206
Contact Number: (718) 366-0154
www.brooklynlatin.org

High School for Mathematics, Science & Engineering at the City College of New York
240 Convent Avenue, New York, New York 10031
Contact Number: (212) 281-6490
www.hsmse.org

High School for American Studies at Lehman College
2925 Goulden Avenue, Bronx, New York 10468
Contact Number: (718) 329-2144
www.hsas-lehman.org

Queens High School for the Sciences at York College
94-50 159th Street,Jamaica, New York 11433
Contact Number: (718) 657-3181
www.qhss.org

Staten Island Technical High School
485 Clawson Street, Staten Island, New York 10306
Contact Number: (718) 667-3222
www.siths.org

Stuyvesant High School
345 Chambers Street, New York, New York 10282-1099
Contact Number: (212) 312-4800
stuy.enschool.org

Fiorello H. LaGuardia High School of Music & Art and Performing Arts
100 Amsterdam Avenue, New York, New York 10023
Contact Number: (212) 496-0700
www.laguardiahs.org

Ready for the NEW redesigned Specialized High Schools Admissions Test?

The NEW SHSAT is a 3 hour timed multiple choice test with two sections, ELA and Math.

Number of Questions	Content
20	5-8 stand-alone revising/editing questions and 2 passages with 6-8 questions each.
37	6 reading comprehension passages with 5-7 questions each.
52	Math multiple choice problems
5	Grid-in math questions

SHSAT 2017 CHANGES

The SHSAT is changing! If you are taking the Fall 2017 SHSAT Exam, you should be aware of the following changes so you can properly prepare for the exam. The old SHSAT test comprised of two sections: verbal and math. The verbal section included five scrambled paragraphs, followed by ten logical reasoning questions followed by 5 reading comprehension passages. The math section included 50 multiple choice questions. The time limit for the exam was 150 minutes.

So... what are the new changes you should be aware of?

- The new time limit for the SHSAT exam is now 180 minutes. (30 minutes more than the old SHSAT exam)
- NO MORE SCRAMBLED PARAGRAPHS.
- NO MORE LOGICAL REASONING QUESTIONS.
- Verbal section is renamed to the English Language Arts (ELA) section.
- There is 57 questions per section (57 questions for ELA and 57 questions for Math). 47 out of 57 questions in each section will be scored. 10 questions are field test items which will not count toward the students score. Students will not know which 10 questions are classified as field test items.
- The ELA section will include 20 revising and editing questions along with 6 reading passages.
- The math section will include 5 grid-in questions
- All multiple choice questions will have 4 answer choices instead of 5.

If you did not watch our video yet which outlines **EVERYTHING** you need to know regarding the new changes for the SHSAT exam, please watch our video here:
YouTube.com/ArgoBrothers

The Importance of Ranking Schools

When you take the SHSAT test, you will be required to rank the Specialized High Schools you want to attend. It is extremely important that you know ahead of time which schools you would like to attend. You will only be admitted into one school if your score meets the level. Acceptance is based on the score you get on the SHSAT exam followed by your choices of schools.

When making the decision to rank the schools, some important things to think about are:

- How far away is the school from you?
- Does the school have a program you are interested in?
- Is there a certain sport or activity you would like to do in high school?
- Is the school a good fit for you? Each school differs in class size and specialty.

What do I need on test day?

You will need to bring your signed Admission Ticket which will have your school choices. There are **no calculators** permitted on the exam. Have more than one number 2 pencil, an eraser and a watch to keep track of time. Water and snacks are allowed, however you must wait until your proctor gives you permission to eat the snacks. Most importantly, bring your confidence! If the exam seems difficult, do not stress. Give it your best shot and have fun!

How can I study for this exam?

The first thing you need to understand is to do well on this exam, you must put in the time and effort to study. This is a challenging exam, so here is a list of a few important tips.

- **Practice and PRACTICE!**
  Take as many practice exams as you can find. Taking simulated exams will give you a very good idea on the type of questions that will be asked during the exam and will make you more confident.
- **Read Books**
  The best way to raise your score in the English Language Arts section of the exam is to read books, articles and newspapers. You will develop a better vocabulary list and find it easier to read the passages provided in the exam.
- **Learn from your mistakes**
  When you go over your practice exams, make sure you understand **why** you got the question wrong. Did you read the corrections correctly? Was it a simple calculation error? Try to understand why you got the answer wrong.

Test Day Strategies

There is no penalty for wrong answers, so **do not** leave anything blank. If you do not know the answer to a question, then circle the question and move on. When you are done with all solvable questions, return to the circled questions. If you still do not know the answer, make an educated guess.

If you still have time after finishing all questions, then check your answers. While you practice, find roughly fifteen questions from throughout your practice that you believe to exemplify the test. You should know how to answer these questions perfectly. On test day, use these fifteen questions as a warmup. Make sure that you go through all steps when going through the question. You should be able to explain why each wrong answer is wrong.

You do not need to take the exam in the order that it is presented. Take the test in the order that you believe will maximize your time on those questions which you are most likely to get correct. It is better to spend time on questions you know you can get right than spending an excessive amount of time on questions that you find more difficult.

ENGLISH LANGUAGE ARTS

The new SHSAT now includes 20 revising/editing questions. Below is a basic overview about grammar rules that you should be familiar with. This review serves as a basic guide and should not be your only guide to fully prepare you for the SHSAT exam.

GRAMMAR

What is a sentence?

A proper sentence has, at the very least, a *subject* and a *verb*.

The *subject* is the person, place or thing that is causing an action to occur.
The *verb* is the action that is taking place by the subject.

For example, let's say we have the very simple sentence:

The boy kicks.

The subject in this sentence would be "the boy", and the verb would be "kicks". Simple enough, right?

There is one more part that, while it is <u>not</u> necessary, is usually found in a sentence: the *object*.
The *object* of a sentence is the person, place or thing that the subject performs the action on.

Let's look at the previous sentence with an object added:

<u>The boy kicks the ball.</u>

In this sentence, the subject is again "the boy," the verb is "kicks," and finally, the object is "the ball."

The sentence can also be broken down more roughly to just the *subject* and *predicate*. The *predicate* can be made up of just the verb, or both a verb and an object.

In the above sentence, "kicks the ball" would be the predicate.

Here are a few more examples of proper sentences:
- Henry loved to eat apples.
- Jenna and Margaret will get ready for the party.
- Moe needs a haircut.

Subject-Verb Agreement

As mentioned before, every subject must be connected to a verb. However, the conjugation (form of the verb) must also agree with the subject given.

The three friends <u>play</u> video games every Saturday and Sunday. (CORRECT)
The three friends <u>plays</u> video games every Saturday and Sunday. (INCORRECT)

The book on animals <u>provides</u> a good understanding on habitats. (CORRECT)
The book on animals <u>provide</u> a good understanding on habitats. (INCORRECT)

Depending on the sentence, this may or may not prove to be difficult. For all sentences, the subject of the sentence, whether it is a person, place or thing, can be changed to its appropriate *pronoun*.

A *pronoun* is a word that is used in place of a person, place or thing (noun).

Pronouns:

	Singular (ONE)	Plural (TWO OR GREATER)
1st Person	I	we
2ns Person	you	you
3rd Person	he, she, it	they

Example of Conjugated Verbs:

to eat	Singular (ONE)	Plural (TWO OR GREATER)
1st Person	I eat	we eat
2ns Person	you eat	you eat
3rd Person	he, she, it eats	they eat

The core idea is to be able to identify the subject of the sentence and then determine whether the verb agrees with the pronoun.

Looking back at the two previous examples for sentences, the subjects can be changed as such:

The three friends play video games every Saturday and Sunday.
They play video games every Saturday and Sunday.

The book on animals provides a good understanding on habitats.
It provides a good understanding on habitats.

Understanding how to change a subject to its appropriate noun is crucial in being able to grasp subject-verb agreement. The focus is mainly on *3rd-Person Singular (he, she, it)* and *3rd-Person Plural (they)*

Here are some examples of each:

- He: the boy, the man, the male cat, Tom
- She: the girl, the woman, the female cat, Ashley
- They: the boys, the girls, the men, the women, the cats, Tom and Ashley

Collective Nouns:

Collective nouns are subjects that refer to _groups_ of things. A collective noun can be a class of students, a team, or a committee. It can even be a collection of _ideas_.

Collective nouns can be both singular and plural.

It: singular collective nouns
They: plural collective nouns

Examples of singular collective nouns include:
• team
• squad
• audience
• analysis of reports
• interaction between two students

> _Note: For the last two examples, the grouping itself is the subject. The rest of the subject is a description of the group._

Example of plural collective nouns include:

• teams
• squads
• audiences
• analyses of reports
• interactions between two students

Individuals Among Groups

The opposite can be said for subjects that are considered to be individuals among collective nouns.

Such nouns are associated with the pronoun, _it_.

Examples of individual subjects include:

• each of the boys
• every teacher
• one of the women
• a member of the group

11

www.argobrothers.com

ENGLISH

Indefinite Pronouns (Singular or Plural)

Indefinite pronouns can be define as words that replace nouns without specifying the noun being replaced. There are a few words that can be used as *either* singular or plural.

Singular or Plural Pronouns:

- all
- any
- some
- more
- most
- none

Pronoun-Antecedent Agreement

In some examples, the pronoun in the sentence will be used later to refer to the subject that has already been introduced. These questions are easily answered using the principles of Subject-Verb agreement to identify the associated pronoun.

Some examples include:

Students must provide his or her homework at the beginning of class. (INCORRECT)
Students must provide their homework at the beginning of class. (CORRECT)

In the example above, the subject of the sentence is "Students" and as such, the pronoun associated to it would be "they" or "their," not the singular pronouns "his or her."

The person can pick up their bag on the way out. (INCORRECT)
The person can pick up his or her bag on the way out. (CORRECT)

The opposite idea is provided in this example. The "person" is the subject of the sentence, and the associated pronoun would be the 3rd - Person singular "his or her" and not 3rd - Person plural "their."

12

Subject vs. Object Pronouns

Since you can now identify and differentiate between subjects and objects, it is crucial to understand that there are significant differences in the pronouns used for both instances.

Subject Pronouns:

	Singular (ONE)	Plural (TWO OR GREATER)
1st Person	I	we
2ns Person	you	you
3rd Person	he, she, it	they

Object Pronouns:

	Singular (ONE)	Plural (TWO OR GREATER)
1st Person	mine, me, myself	mine, me, myself
2ns Person	your, yourself	your, yourself
3rd Person	his, her(s), its	his, her(s), its

I vs. me
One of the biggest mistakes that many test takers make is misusing "I" and "me." The first is used in the context of the subject of the sentence, and the second for the object of a sentence.

SUBJECT: I
OBJECT: me

The following two examples provide context to the misuse of the subject pronoun.

John and me are both extremely hungry. (INCORRECT)
John and I are both extremely hungry. (CORRECT)

The next two sentences provide examples of the misuse of the object pronoun.

Ms. Evergreen gave John and I failing grades this marking period. (INCORRECT)
Ms. Evergreen gave John and me failing grades this marking period. (CORRECT)

www.argobrothers.com

ENGLISH

Who vs. whom

The same context can be provided for who and whom:

SUBJECT: who
OBJECT: whom

Whom is going to open that door for me? (INCORRECT)
Who is going to open that door for me? (CORRECT)

Who are you going to the movies with? (INCORRECT)
Whom are you going to the movies with? (CORRECT)

Note that in the second pair of examples given, the subject of the sentence is "you." Thus, the object MUST be "whom." Another example of such has been provided below:

To whom is she writing that letter? (CORRECT)
Whom did he hire for the new position? (CORRECT)

Reflexive Pronouns

Reflexive pronouns are object pronouns that end in either "-self" or "-selves" and refer back to the subject of the sentence.

Object Pronouns:

	Singular (ONE)	Plural (TWO OR GREATER)
1ˢᵗ Person	myself	ourselves
2ⁿˢ Person	yourself	yourself
3ʳᵈ Person	himself, herself, itself	themselves

Here are a number of examples of reflexive pronouns in use:

- *I gave me a note to read in the near future. (INCORRECT)*
- *I gave <u>myself</u> a note to read in the near future. (CORRECT)*

- *You must give <u>yourself</u> some time to rest from the injury. (CORRECT)*

- *He cannot help <u>himself</u> out of bed. You should go aid him. (CORRECT)*

Ambiguous Pronouns

The word ambiguous itself means unclear, and an ambiguous pronoun is found in situations when it is unclear which noun the pronoun refers to.

Between <u>Ms. Jameson</u> and <u>Ms. Richard</u>, she gives the harder exams. (INCORRECT)
Among <u>Ms. Jameson</u> and <u>Ms. Richard</u>, <u>Ms. Richard</u> gives the harder exams. (CORRECT)

In the first sentence, who is "she" referring to in this sentence? Both the subjects are female, making it hard to differentiate between who the pronoun is referring to.

Christie loves <u>their</u> artwork. (INCORRECT)
Christie loves the <u>Metropolitan Art Students' artwork</u>. (CORRECT)

In the first example, who is "their" referring to? There is no indication of who the artists are.

SENTENCE STRUCTURE

While a basic sentence can be broken down to just a subject and predicate, most sentences are much more complex and are made up of two components: clauses and phrases.

Clause vs. Phrase

A *clause* is a part of a sentence that **contains both a subject and predicate**. There are two types of clauses:

1. **Independent clause**: a clause that can stand on its own as a sentence
   Example: Alicia eats two pies.

2. **Dependent clause**: a clause that cannot stand on its own as a sentence
   Example: When John jumps very high...

> *The most basic sentence consists of just a clause:*
>
> - *Cats meow.*
> - *Girl runs.*
> - *Jack cooks.*

A phrase is a part of a sentence **that lacks either a subject, predicate or both**.

Example: By the way...
Example: Without Jimmy...

Sentences can be comprised of all three of these concepts:

By the way, *when John jumps very high*, *Alicia eats two pies*.

    A. Phrase   B. Dependent clause   C. Independent clause

PUNCTUATION

Commas

Notice how in a previous example, commas were used to separate the clauses and phrase in the previous example:

By the way, when John jumps very high, Alicia eats two pies.

A *comma* **separates segments of a sentence**.

The use of a comma includes:

1. Separate two **independent clauses** when they are separated by the following words:
   a. and, but, or, nor, so, yet, for

   Amy is very hungry today, **but** *she does not have any food at home.*

2. Separate **dependent clauses**, **phrases**, and **words** that come before the **main independent clause**.

   However, before his mother could answer the phone, **John was out of the house**.

3. Separate three or more clauses, phrases or words that are written in a series.

   Jumping rope, climbing fences, and running on the track are all exercises.

   John likes to read comics written by Marvel, DC, and Image Comics.

Misuse of Commas

Unless in extreme cases, **commas are not needed for dependent clauses or phrases**.

I went to eat some apples, after swimming ten laps. (INCORRECT)
Tim does not want to see her, while he is eating. (INCORRECT)

ENGLISH

Semicolons

A *semicolon* **separates major sentence elements or independent clauses**.

In other words, a semicolon is used to separate two stand-alone sentences that are not already joined by a period or conjunction.

Hint: Consider semicolons to be almost identical to periods. If a period cannot fit in the sentence provided, neither can a semicolon.

Look at the following few examples, and just replace the periods with semicolons.

John loves snowballs. He eats them whenever there is a blizzard. (CORRECT)
Without any money. Tara cannot go to Florida to search for her missing pants. (INCORRECT)

↓

John loves snowballs; he eats them whenever there is a blizzard. (CORRECT)
Without any money; Tara cannot go to Florida to search for her missing pants. (INCORRECT)

In the first example, both "John loves snowballs" and "He eats them whenever there is a blizzard" are considered to be independent clauses: they can be read as complete sentences. Therefore, either a period or semicolon can separate the clauses.

*In the second example, "Without any money" is a **phrase**, and "Tara cannot go to Florida to search for her missing pants" is an independent clause. As such, the two parts should be separated by a **comma**, as was discussed in the previous section.*

Without any money, Tara cannot go to Florida to search for her missing pants. (CORRECT)

Colons

A *colon* **introduces quotations, examples or lists.**

A few examples of each are as follows:

Quotations:

- *I will recite the first sentence on the note: "Always remember to brush and floss."*
- *Never forget his final choice of words: "Live, laugh and love."*

Examples:
- *We all know who will win this fight: the dog.*
- *There are only two options right now: stand up or back down.*

Lists:
- *I want to visit a number of places while in Europe: London, Rome and Athens.*
- *Here is the full list of items needed from the store: eggs, milk, orange juice and double-stuffed chocolate cookies.*

Quotation Marks

Quotation marks are **used to indicate either dialogue or direct quotes**. While that is simple enough to understand, punctuation is a bit trickier to grasp.

The rules of punctuation in quotation marks are as follows:

1. If the quotation is at the start of the sentence and is followed by a clause, the first word is capitalized and ends in a comma inside the quotation marks. If the quote is a question, use a question mark in place of the comma.

- *"The door is open," said John.*
- *"One of these days, I will win," replied Ralph.*
- *"Where is the bathroom?" asked Brienne of Tarth.*

2. If a clause precedes a quotation, the ending punctuation is placed within the quotation marks. The first word of the quote is capitalized.

- Albert asked, "Are you hungry?"
- She replied, "I will always love basketball."
- Did he really ask, "Is that a tree?"

3. In some instances, the quotation may be separated with a clause in between. Separate such quotes with commas as such.

- "When you were walking," Ralph asked, "did you see a black dog?"
- "You can walk," Beth said uneasily, "if you are ready to walk."
- "One day," Mufasa told Simba, "this entire valley will be yours."

Question Marks and Periods

A *question mark* is **used at the end of a direct question**. A *period* is **used at the end of a direct statement**. Understanding the difference between a statement and question is the key to avoiding mistakes between the two.

Here are a few examples of differentiating between statements and questions.

- *Will Timothy run ten laps today. (INCORRECT)*
- *Renee will never be a great martial artist? (INCORRECT)*
- *I must write a hundred page paper tomorrow? (INCORRECT)*
- *Did the chicken come before the egg. (INCORRECT)*

- *Will Timothy run ten laps today? (CORRECT)*
- *Renee will never be a great martial artist. (CORRECT)*
- *I must write a hundred page paper tomorrow. (CORRECT)*
- *Did the chicken come before the egg? (CORRECT)*

Apostrophes

An *apostrophe* has two specific functions: **to indicate contractions and to show possessive form**.

Examples of contractions include:
- will not: won't
- cannot: can't
- I am: I'm
- he is: he's

Examples of possessive form include:
- Lisa's jacket
- Jeff's basketball
- The Yankees' field
- Ross' hat

Common Mistake: It's vs. Its

It is crucial to understand the difference between "it's" and "its"

Contraction: It's (it is)
- *It's* getting hot in here.
- *It's* almost time for bed.

Possessive: Its
- *Its* tail is now blue!
- *Can* you please give *its* hair back?

SENTENCE STRUCTURE ERRORS

Run-on Sentences

A run-on sentence is a combination of two or more independent clauses that are joined inappropriately.

Remember, there are four different ways to join or separate independent clauses. The following will be a review of the list, used to appropriately fix the given run-on sentences.

1. Combination of commas with the conjunctions: and, but, or, nor, so, yet, for

> *John loves to go skiing he cannot due to Pasadena's warm weather. (INCORRECT)*
> *John loves to go skiing,* **but** *he cannot due to Pasadena's warm weather. (CORRECT)*

2. Semicolons

> *John loves to go skiing he cannot due to Pasadena's warm weather. (INCORRECT)*
> *John loves to go skiing; he cannot due to Pasadena's warm weather. (CORRECT)*

3. Subordinate conjunctions and commas (although, if, since, while, after)

> *John loves to go skiing he cannot due to Pasadena's warm weather. (INCORRECT)*
> ***Although** John loves to go skiing, he cannot due to Pasadena's warm weather. (CORRECT)*

4. Periods

> *John loves to go skiing he cannot due to Pasadena's warm weather. (INCORRECT)*
> *John loves to go skiing. He cannot due to Pasadena's warm weather. (CORRECT)*

Sentence Fragments

Sentence fragments are otherwise known an incomplete sentence. An incomplete sentence **lacks either a subject, predicate, both, or is not a complete thought**.

Remember, just because a sentence is long and connected with a number of phrases and clauses does not mean that it is a complete sentence.

Examples of sentence fragments include:

Incomplete Thoughts:
- *Because his mother told him to **(...what did he do?)***
- *After the snowstorm ends. **(...what after?)***
- *If you are willing to buy a ticket from Expedia for a one-way trip to Alaska. **(...what will happen?)***

VERB TENSES

Grammatical tenses are forms taken to show the time of action.

Simple Tense:

Present	I eat
Past	I ate
Future	I will eat

22

ENGLISH

Perfect Tense

The perfect tense shows that the action has already been completed.

Perfect Present	I have eaten
Perfect Past	I had eaten
Perfect Future	I will have eaten

Example: *I <u>had eaten</u> by the time the news about Antonio reached me.*
Example: *Thank you, but I <u>have eaten</u> my share of food today.*

Progressive Tense

The progressive tense shows an action that is still continuing.

Present Progressive	I am eating
Past Progressive	I was eating
Future Progressive	I will be eating

Example: *I <u>am eating</u> right now.*
Example: *I <u>was eating</u> while they burned down my house.*

Perfect Progressive Tense

The progressive tense shows an action that is still continuing.

Perfect Present Progressive	I have been walking
Perfect Past Progressive	I had been eating
Perfect Future Progressive	I will have been eating

23

www.argobrothers.com

ENGLISH

ADJECTIVES VS. ADVERBS

Adjectives and adverbs are both used to describe words. It is essential to know the different uses of the two.

- Adjectives describe or modify pronouns and nouns.
  EXAMPLE: red ball, angry Jim, funny clown

- Adverbs describe or modify verbs, adjectives or other adverbs.
  EXAMPLE: hardly running, recklessly paint, drastically different

HINT: Most adverbs ends in "-ly".

Here are a few examples of the incorrect use of adverbs.

Driving <u>reckless</u> in the snow and ice is a very dangerous decision. (INCORRECT)
Driving <u>recklessly</u> in the snow and ice is a very dangerous decision. (CORRECT)

Amber finished her homework <u>quick</u>. (INCORRECT)
Amber finished her homework <u>quickly</u>. (CORRECT)

COMPARATIVES AND SUPERLATIVES

Comparatives and superlatives are adjectives used to compare different objects.

- Comparatives compare two objects.
  "-er" is added to the end of the adjective.
  If adding "-er" is inappropriate, the word "more" is added.

- Superlatives compare more than objects.
  "-est" is added to the end of the adjective
  If adding "-er" is inappropriate, the word "more" is added.

HINT: "More" and "most" is added to adjectives with three or more syllables (beautiful, important).

COMPARATIVES AND SUPERLATIVES		
Adjective	**Comparative**	**Superlative**
fast	faster	fastest
big	bigger	biggest
rich	richer	richest
ridiculous	more ridiculous	most ridiculous

In some instances, the entire structure of the adjective changes to suit the comparative and superlative.

IRREGULAR COMPARATIVES AND SUPERLATIVES		
Adjective	**Comparative**	**Superlative**
good	better	best
bad	worse	worst
much	more	most
little	less	least
far	farther	farthest

Remember that comparatives are used when comparing two nouns or pronouns, and superlatives are used for three or more nouns or pronouns.

Between Jacob and Edward, Jacob is the <u>strongest</u>. (INCORRECT)
Between Jacob and Edward, Jacob is the <u>stronger</u>. (CORRECT)

Among Harry, Ron and Hermione, Hermione is the <u>smarter</u>. (INCORRECT)
Among Harry, Ron and Hermione, Hermione is the <u>smartest</u>. (CORRECT)

Illogical Comparisons

When comparing two or more objects, the nouns or pronouns must be of the same entity. For instance, one cannot compare a painter to a painting, or an author to a book. Painters are compared with other painters, and books are compare with other books.

Satoshi's <u>test scores</u> are higher than <u>John</u>. (INCORRECT)
Satoshi's <u>test scores</u> are higher than <u>John's</u>. (CORRECT)

The <u>coffee from Starbucks</u> is much better than Dunkin Donuts. (INCORRECT)
The coffee from Starbucks is much better than <u>Dunkin Donuts coffee</u>. (CORRECT)

OTHER GRAMMATICAL TRAITS

Double Negatives

The use of two negative words can turn the sentence into a positive one, which may not be the intent of the writer. Double negatives are usually discouraged.

Don't say nothing. (INCORRECT)
Don't say anything. (CORRECT)

Redundancy

Unnecessary repetition makes writing more difficult to read and makes the sentence seem longer than it actually is. The objective is to remove any repeated information.

The meeting on Tuesday has been <u>postponed until later</u>. (INCORRECT)
The meeting on Tuesday has been <u>postponed</u>. (CORRECT)

The definition of "postpone" is to take place at a later time; "until later" is not needed.

The attack was an <u>unintentional mistake</u>. (INCORRECT)
The attack was a <u>mistake</u>. (CORRECT)

A "mistake" is something that is misguided and unintentional.

LIST OF MOST COMMONLY MISUSED WORDS

A, an
The article *a* is used before a consonant sound, and *an* is used before a vowel sound.
a car, an apple

Accept, except
Accept is a verb meaning to receive, and *except* means to leave out.
I accepted the gift.
Everyone went to the party <u>except</u> me.

Affect, effect
Affect is a verb meaning to influence, and *effect* is a noun that means result.
The disaster <u>affected</u> everyone in town.
The <u>effect</u> of the disaster was saddening.

Already, all ready
Already means by a certain time, and *all already* means completely ready.
I have <u>already</u> completed my homework.
My homework is <u>all ready</u> to be submitted.

Altogether, all together
Altogether means entirely, and *all together* means as an entire group.
He is <u>altogether</u> a very capable individual.
<u>All together</u>, there is a total of twenty members.

Among, between
Among is used in groups of three or more, whereas *between* is used for two individuals.
<u>Among</u> the three friends, Henry is the coolest.
<u>Between</u> the two friends, Henry is the uglier.

Amount, number
Amount is a numberless bulk, and *number* refers to a specific count.
The <u>amount</u> of homework I have is ridiculous.
The <u>number</u> of homework packets I have is ridiculous.

As, like
As is a conjunction that is followed by a verb, while *like* is a preposition and is not followed by a verb.
Please cook the recipe <u>as</u> I instructed.
This food looks <u>like</u> dung.

Beside, besides
Beside means next to, and *besides* means apart from.
The bird flew <u>beside</u> his fellow friends.
<u>Besides</u> watching birds fly, I enjoy eating pie.

Farther, further
Farther is used to compare distances that are measurable, and *further* is used to describe the advancement of an idea or object.
The boat is twenty miles <u>farther</u> than from here.
We must explore this experiment <u>further</u>

Fewer, less — *Fewer* applies to objects that can be counted, and *less* is used for degrees that cannot be measured.
There are five <u>fewer</u> cupcakes than there was yesterday.
I am <u>less</u> happy today.

Its, it's — *Its* is possessive, and *it's* is a contraction for it is.
Its horns are enormous.
It's quite enormous.

Principal, principle — *Principal* refers to the head of something, and *principle* refers to a fundamental truth.
The principal of the school laid down the rules.
The principle behind survival is to lay low at all times.

Than, then — *Than* is used to compare things, whereas *then* is used in reference to time.
I am smarter than you.
I will study for the test and then get a higher score than you.

Their, there, they're — *Their* is the possessive form of they, *there* is an indication of place, and *they're* is the contraction of they are.
I can't wait to go to their party.
Over there, you will find a list of party foods.
They're 30 minnutes away from the party.

CAPITALIZATION

Here is a list of nouns, otherwise known as "proper nouns" that must be capitalized in any sentence.

- Proper first and last names, names of organizations
  - Amanda Greenberg, Yankees, Wall Street
- Titles that precede names
  - Doctor Johnson, Mister Freddy, Aunt Jemima
- Days of the week and months in a year
  - Monday, January, Thursday
- Holidays
  - Fourth of July, Thanksgiving, Halloween, Memorial Day

The first word of a sentence or quotation must also be capitalized.

My name is Diane Johnson.
John replied, "The dog is blue."

READING PASSAGES ARE NOTHING TO BE WARY OF.

Reading questions can be intimidating and even overwhelming at times. Nonetheless, they are a large part of the SHSAT exam and cannot afford to be ignored.

Common Reading Comprehension Mistakes

Remember, the Reading section is not quizzing you on how well you read and understand the passage; rather, it tests you on how easily and swiftly you recognize the author's intended answer. Increasing your score by earning points is only achieved by arriving to the correct answer choice. The main focus should always be placed on spending as much time as possible on the reading questions provided. The best way to do so is by avoiding a few common reading mistakes:

• Studying all of the questions before the passage
• Reading the passage too closely
• Nitpicking sentences you have difficulty understanding

Notice how all of the main difficulties listed above center around one element: time management. The last two mistakes go hand in hand. Recall that the primary purpose is to gain only a general understanding of the passage to tackle the questions. You will be required to reread certain parts of the passage when attempting to answer the questions anyway, so why waste additional time fussing over specific details?

Tackling Reading Comprehension Questions
Phase I: Read the Passage

Phase II: Identifying the Question Types

Now that you've gained a good understanding of how to approach the passage itself, you can finally start to look at the most important part of the section: the questions themselves. Determining the type of question being asked is the first step; doing so will allow you to effectively read parts of the passage to answer appropriately.

A. Main Idea Questions
The main idea question focuses on summarizing the most important idea of the passage. It is helpful to understand that the main idea ties all of the paragraphs together and is the overall central theme.

Common Traps in Main Idea Questions. The main idea should be neither too narrow nor too broad. Too narrow of an answer choice tends to cover some details in the passage, but not all that were discussed. Adversely, an answer choice may cover all of the ideas in the passage, but may include others that were

not mentioned directly in the reading. Any answer covering unsupported or new information will be incorrect.

Examples of main idea questions can include:
- What is the main idea of this passage?
- What is the passage mainly about?
- A good title for this passage would be...?
- Which of the following most accurately describes the passage?
- What is the author's primary purpose in this passage?

B. Detail Questions

Detail questions are the most common form of questions found in the Reading Comprehension section. Thankfully, they are very easy to master and answer correctly; just consider them to be a part of an open book test. Whatever the question is asking, the passage must provide the details. Depending on what you are asked, you just have to locate that information in the passage.

It is always important to read information outside of the reference provided in the question. The questions most likely require some amount of context clues to fully answer, so reading the sentence before and after the following sentence can help. Identifying detail questions is simple enough. In some instances, a phrase in the question may refer to back to the passage: "According to the passage...".

Examples of detail questions can include:
- According to the passage, which of the following is true?
- John was best known for his ability to do what?
- During its final trip to the Atlantic Ocean, what did the ship come across?

C. Inference Questions

Inference questions mainly ask you to draw conclusions based on information provided directly in the passage. Note that the inference is never directly stated in the passage.

For example, a passage can discuss the travels of a character. It may describe in great detail surroundings of the area that the character is set in, but may not explicitly state the location. Take a look at the passage below.

"Hundreds of cars honked on the road as Jim walked down the littered streets. The view of the sky was completely blocked by the dozens of skyscrapers. The air was thick with smoke and smog. Jim felt sickened and disgusted; this was not what he had imagined at all."

From this excerpt, a number of details can be inferred. While it is not directly stated, it can be concluded that Jim is most likely visiting a city. It is most likely his first time stepping into the city as well, according to his

negative reaction to his experience. All of this can easily be interpreted without having any direct details on Jim's whereabouts or past travels.

Common Traps in Inference Questions. Remember, the answer to inference questions are never directly stated in the passage – answers that discuss the exact details are to be avoided.
Examples of inference questions can include:
• The character in this passage is most likely...
• This passage can most likely be found in a...

D. Vocabulary Questions
Vocabulary questions ask you to find synonyms of specific words that are to be found in the reading passage. The word provided may or not be a word that you recognize, but the key to answering such questions correctly lies in using context clues.

Answering vocabulary questions is very simple. Read the sentence that the word is located in, as well as the sentences that come both before and after for better reference. Once you have a general understanding of what the word is, replace the vocabulary word with each of the answer choices and select the word that best fits the definition of the word.

Examples of vocabulary questions can include:
• The word _____ most nearly means...
• According to the passage, which word most closely represents _____?

This concludes a basic review of the ELA section for the NEW SHSAT Exam. In this book you will find five full-length exams to practice and get a better understanding of the NEW SHSAT Exam.

SHSAT
MATH REVIEW

MATH

Math on the SHSAT

Let us explore the major concepts tested in each of the subject areas. Again, this is not a comprehensive list.

Arithmetic

- Real numbers including integers, prime numbers, rational numbers and irrational numbers
- Number sequences
- Factors and multiples
- Fractions and decimals
- Arithmetic operations
- Percentages, ratios, and rates
- Absolute value

Algebra

- Algebraic expressions
- Coordinate planes, slopes, and intercepts
- Functions and relations
- Linear equations
- Quadratic equations
- Inequalities
- Rules of exponents and Roots

Geometry

- Right, isosceles, and other special triangles
- Pythagorean theorem
- Properties and measurements of circles
- Polygons
- Perimeter, area, and volume
- Properties and measurements of three-dimensional figures

Data Interpretation

- Descriptive statistics
- Understanding data from charts and graphs
- Frequency distributions
- Probability
- Permutations
- Means and averages

Mathematical Conventions on the SHSAT

While math can be straightforward at times, there are many nuances that need to be considered when working with problems to determine how you interpret information. Here are some of the key conventions:

- All numbers on the exam are real numbers. There will be no questions relating to imaginary numbers.
- Geometric figures are **not** drawn to scale unless otherwise indicated.
- While you should not assume lengths based on how geometric figures look, you should assume that all lines in a figure are straight lines and that the figure lies on a plane unless otherwise indicated.
- Contrary to geometric figures, coordinate planes and numbers lines **are** drawn to scale.
- Graphs on the exam, including histograms, pie charts, and line graphs are drawn to scale and you can make assumptions based on the visual presentation of the data.
- π is assumed to represent the value 3.14.
- For geometry questions, the sum of the measure of the interior angles of a triangle equals 180°.

Arithmetic: The Basics

Arithmetic encompasses the fundamental building blocks of math. It includes basic concepts like the mathematical operations of addition, subtraction, multiplication and division. Almost all the questions you encounter on the exam will require you to apply principles of arithmetic in some capacity. You will need to understand the order of operations, real numbers, ratios, and fractions. The concepts discussed in this section will help you refresh your understanding of basic arithmetic and prepare you to navigate the more difficult exam concepts such as algebraic expressions and geometry.

Math Building Blocks

Before we dive into the specifics of arithmetic and the other concepts tested on the math section of the exam, let us review the fundamental building blocks of math, especially common symbols and types of numbers. These concepts will appear in some form on the exam and a clear understanding of these fundamentals is key to your success.

What's That Sign?

Math Symbol	Common Name	Description
<	Less than	Used to signify that the quantity to the left of the symbol is less than the quantity to the right.
>	Greater than	Used to signify that the quantity to the left of the symbol is greater than the quantity to the right.
≤	Less than or equal to	Used to signify that the quantity to the left of the symbol is less than or equal to the quantity to the right.
≥	Greater than or equal to	Used to signify that the quantity to the left of the symbol is greater than or equal to the quantity to the right.

MATH

Math Symbol	Common Name	Description
√	Square root	An irrational number that produces a specified quantity when multiplied by itself.
|x|	Absolute value	Reflects the positive distance of the expressed number from zero.
!	Factorial	The product of the whole numbers from 1 to a given number.
||	Parallel Lines	Signifies that two lines are parallel to each other and do not intersect at any point.
⊥	Perpendicular Lines	Signifies that two lines separated by this symbol intersect to form a right angle.
π	Pi	The geometric ratio of a circle's circumference to its diameter; the value used on the SHSAT is 3.14.

Real Numbers

You will encounter only real numbers on the SHSAT, so you need not concern yourself with studying concepts related to imaginary numbers. Real numbers are numbers found on the number line and are, with the exception of zero, either positive or negative. Several classes of numbers are included in the real numbers category and will appear on the exam. Let's look at the various types of real numbers you can expect to see.

Whole Numbers

Whole numbers are positive counting numbers including zero that contain no decimal or fraction parts.

> 0, 1, 2, 3, 4, 5...

Integers

Integers are all positive and negative whole numbers, including zero. Integers that occur in a sequence like the ones below are called consecutive integers.

> -2, -1, 0, 1, 2, 3...

Rational Numbers

Rational numbers are any numbers, positive or negative, that can be expressed as a ratio of two numbers. All integers and fractions are considered rational numbers.

$$\frac{1}{2} \quad \frac{3}{4} \quad \frac{1}{4}$$

Irrational Numbers

Irrational numbers are all numbers, positive or negative, that are not rational and cannot be expressed as a ratio.

$$\pi, \sqrt{5}$$

Prime Numbers

A prime number is a number that has only two positive divisors, 1 and itself. For example, 5 is a prime number because it is only divisible by 1 and itself. Prime numbers are tested often on the exam.

> It is best to familiarize yourself with the most common prime numbers, which are those that occur below 100:
> 2, 3, 5, 7, 11, 13, 17, 19, 23, 29, 31, 37, 41, 43, 47, 53, 59, 61, 67, 71, 73, 79, 83, 89, & 97

There are some other properties of prime numbers you should know:

- Neither 0 nor 1 is a prime number
- Only positive numbers can be prime numbers
- 2 is the only even prime number

Factors

A factor is an integer that divides into another integer evenly and has no remainder.

> Take the number 24 as an example:
>
> - 1, 2, 3, 4, 6, 8, 12, and 24 are all factors of 24 since they all divide evenly into the number and have no remainder. On the other hand, the number 5 is **not** a factor since when you divide 5 into 24, there **is** a remainder.

Greatest Common Factor

The greatest common factor of two numbers is the largest factor shared by both numbers.

Suppose you wanted to find the greater common factor of 48 and 60. You would first start by identifying the factors for each number:

- Factors of 48: 1, 2, 3, 4, 6, 8, **12**, 16, 24, 48
- Factors of 60: 1, 2, 3, 4, 5, 6, 10, **12**, 15, 20, 30, 60

The greatest common factor of 48 and 60 is 12. The least common factor—in this case, 1— is not likely to be tested on the exam.

Multiples

A multiple is essentially the opposite of a factor. Instead of division, multiples are determined by multiplication. A multiple of a number is the product of the number and any other whole number. Zero is a multiple of every number.

0, 8, 16, 24, 32, 40, 64, and 800 are all multiples of 8 because they are the product of multiplying 8 by another number. When any whole number is multiplied by 8, the product is a multiple.

Least Common Multiple

The least common multiple of two or more whole numbers greater than zero is the smallest whole number divisible by each of the numbers.

If you wanted to find the least common multiple of 5 and 6, for example, you would start by identifying the multiples of each.

- Multiples of 5: 10, 15, 20, 25, 30, 35, 40...
- Multiples of 6: 12, 18, 24, 30, 36, 42...

Since you are looking for the least common multiple, you want to select the smallest number that occurs in both lists. In the case, the least common multiple is 30. The greatest common multiple is not likely to be tested on the exam.

Numeric Operations

The SHSAT Math section includes problems that will require you to add, subtract, multiply, and divide real numbers, including fractions, decimals, roots, and algebraic expressions with non-numeric variables. There are key operations you should keep in mind when dealing with numbers in order to work more efficiently and minimize mistakes.

Laws of Operations

Commutative Property: Addition and multiplication are commutative operations; the order in which they are performed does not impact the answer.

$$a \cdot b = b \cdot a$$
$$a + b = b + a$$

www.argobrothers.com

Associative Property: Addition and multiplication are also associative; when written as an expression, they can be regrouped without impacting the final answer.

$$a + (b + c) = (a + b) + c$$
$$(a \cdot b) \cdot c = a \cdot (b \cdot c)$$

Distributive Property: The distributive property outlines how values in an expression should be distributed to the terms being added or subtracted. The distributive property can also be used in division.

$$a(b + c) = ab + ac$$
$$\frac{a + b}{2} = \frac{a}{2} + \frac{b}{2}$$

Order of Operations

The commutative, associative, and distributive properties outline some standard approaches to dealing with addition and multiplication. When other operations are involved, it is important to understand the proper order in which to solve each component of the problem.

The acronym **PEMDAS** outlines the correct order for mathematical operations. Performing operations out of order, specifically those dealing with more than addition and multiplication, will often lead you to the incorrect answer.

Parentheses: Complete anything in **parentheses** first.

Exponents: Next, calculate any **exponents.**

Multiplication/Division: Then attack **multiplication** and **division** elements from left to right.

Addition/Subtraction: Finally, attack **addition** and **subtraction** elements from left to right.

Not all equations will contain all these elements. However, be sure to still follow the order when attacking the elements that are present.

Let us look at an example:

$100 - 4(7 - 4)^3$	First, solve for the values in the parentheses
$100 - 4(3)^3$	Solve $(7 - 4)$ and replace the value in parentheses with 3
$100 - 4(3)^3 = 100 - 4(27)$	Solve the exponent
$100 - 4(27) = 100 - 108$	Multiply and divide
$100 - 108 = -8$	Solve addition and subtraction elements

The final answer is −8. Remember to work equations in the proper order and that multiplication, division, addition, and subtraction should be solved from left to right.

Absolute Value

Absolute value is the distance of a number from zero. The value is always expressed as a positive number. Absolute value is symbolized by a number being enclosed in two vertical bars.

$$|12|$$

The absolute value of a positive number is always just the number itself.

$$|12| = 12$$

The absolute value of a negative number is derived by dropping the negative sign in front of the number.

$$|-14| = 14$$

You may see absolute value appear in a number of ways on the exam, including as expressions where you must solve for a value. Here's an example:

$4 - 2 + |5 - 7| =$

$\quad |5 - 7| = |-2| = 2$ Solve what is in the brackets

$\quad 4 - 2 + 2 = 4$ Plug in the value to the rest of the expression and solve

Fractions

Now, let us look at a subset of rational numbers, namely fractions and ratios.

There is no shortage of fractions on the SHSAT. You will see them appear in word problems, as part of algebraic expressions, and in pure problem solving questions. The two main components of a fraction are the numerator and the denominator.

$$\frac{a}{b} \quad \begin{array}{l} \longrightarrow \text{ numerator} \\ \longrightarrow \text{ denominator} \end{array}$$

You will need to know how to perform various operations with fractions, including addition, subtraction, multiplication, division, simplifying, and converting them to mixed numbers. Let us look at some of the key facts about fractions and operations related to them.

Reciprocals

The reciprocal of a fraction is found simply by reversing the numerator and the denominator. For example, the reciprocal of $\frac{2}{3}$ is $\frac{3}{2}$. The product of any fraction and its reciprocal is always 1. All whole numbers except zero have a reciprocal where the reciprocal of a is $\frac{1}{a}$.

Equivalent Fractions

Since fractions represent the part of a given whole, increasing the whole and the part by the same amount does not change the relationship. Consider the fraction $\frac{1}{2}$. If you multiplied the numerator and denominator by 3, for example, you would end up with the equivalent fraction $\frac{3}{6}$.

Reducing Fractions

There are a number of instances in which you will need to reduce fractions on the exam; in fact, whenever you are able to do so, you should. When you reduce a fraction, you simply express the fraction in its lowest terms.

Let us suppose you have the fraction $\frac{40}{80}$. To reduce the fraction, identify the greatest common factor shared by the numerator and denominator. In this case, 40 and 80 share several factors:

Factors of 40: 1, 2, 4, 5, 8, 10, 20, **40**
Factors of 80: 1, 2, 4, 5, 8, 10, 20, **40**

The greatest common factor of the numerator and the denominator is **40**. To reduce the fraction, determine how many times the greatest common factor divides into both the numerator and the denominator.

Numerator: $\frac{40}{40} = 1$ Denominator: $\frac{80}{40} = 2$ Reduced fraction: $\frac{40}{80} = \frac{1}{2}$

Mixed Numbers

A mixed number is a fraction that is preceded by an integer. For example: $2\frac{3}{7}$.

It is often not possible to work with mixed numbers and perform operations like addition and subtraction. You must instead convert a mixed fraction into a standard fraction having just a numerator and a denominator. Converting a fraction is rather straightforward. First, you multiply the denominator and the integer, then add the product to the numerator. The denominator from the mixed fraction will remain the same.

$$2\frac{3}{7} = \frac{7 \cdot 2 + 3}{7} = \frac{17}{7}$$

Adding and Subtracting Fractions

Adding and subtracting fractions is a straightforward operation when the fractions have the same denominator. In these cases, you simply add or subtract the numerators; the denominator remains the same.

Examples: $\frac{2}{4} - \frac{1}{4} = \frac{1}{4}$ $\frac{8}{13} + \frac{23}{13} = \frac{31}{13}$

Adding and subtracting fractions that do not have the same denominator involves a bit more calculation. The most efficient way to approach adding and subtracting fractions is cross-multiplying. Let us take $\frac{11}{21}$ + $\frac{4}{11}$ as an example.

First, multiply the denominator of the second fraction by the numerator of the first fraction:

$$\frac{11}{21} \qquad \frac{4}{11} \qquad\qquad 11 \cdot 11 = 121$$

Then, multiply the denominator of the first fraction by the numerator of the second fraction:

$$\frac{11}{12} \qquad \frac{4}{11} \qquad\qquad 12 \cdot 4 = 48$$

The sum of these two operations is your new **numerator**: 48 + 121 = **169**. You are not done yet, however: to find your new denominator, multiply both denominators:

$$\frac{11}{12} + \frac{4}{11} = \frac{11(11) + 4(12)}{12(11)} = \frac{169}{132} \qquad \text{The sum of the fractions}$$

The process is the same for subtracting fractions, except that instead of adding the products of the cross-multiplication to get the new numerator, you will subtract.

Multiplying Fractions

When multiplying fractions, the process is the same regardless of whether or not the denominators are the same.

$$\frac{8}{11} \cdot \frac{7}{13} = \frac{8 \cdot 7}{11 \cdot 13} = \frac{56}{143}$$

Dividing Fractions

Dividing fractions is similar to the process of multiplying fractions since multiplication and division are inverse operations. To divide fractions, multiply the first fraction by the reciprocal or inverse of the second fraction.

$$\frac{1}{5} \div \frac{3}{7} = \frac{1}{5} \cdot \frac{7}{3} = \frac{7}{15}$$

Ratios

Ratios are often written as fractions and compare two quantities. Ratios, like fractions, deal with parts of the whole, but also express the relationship between two quantities that may not be part of the same whole.

Ratios can be written as fractions or using the common notation $x : y$. For example, if a word problem tells you that the ratio of girls to boys in the class is four boys for every three girls, you can write that as: $\frac{4}{3}$ or 4 : 3.

If a question asks you what the ratio of girls to boys is, whatever follows the term **of** is the numerator and whatever follows **to** is the denominator.

Ratios often appear on the exam in word problems. Be careful and make sure you understand what ratio the question is asking you to examine. Let us look at a few examples:

Nathan has 7 sodas and 4 bottles of water in his cooler. What is the ratio of sodas to bottles of water in the cooler?

Since you are looking for the ratio of sodas to bottles of water, your ratio would look like this:

$\dfrac{soda}{bottles\ of\ water}$ **or** sodas : bottles of water

$\dfrac{7}{4}$ or $7:4$ Once we know what our ratio looks like, we plug in the numbers.

$7:4:2$ Ratios are not always expressed with just two variables. Suppose Nathan has 7 sodas, 4 bottles of water, and 2 juice boxes. To express the ratio of the drinks in the cooler, add the juice boxes to the original ratio.

This is a fixed ratio, meaning that each portion of the ratio directly corresponds to a particular item in the cooler. So, if you reordered the ratio so that it read $4:7:2$, you no longer have the ratio of sodas to bottled waters to juice boxes. Instead, you had the ratio of bottled waters to sodas to juice boxes.

> Tori's soccer team loses 10 games out of every 30 games that it plays. What is the ratio of Tori's soccer team's wins to losses?

$\dfrac{wins}{losses}$ or wins : losses   You are looking for the ratio of wins to losses.

Be careful not to assume the ratio of wins to losses is $10:30$. While that is the order the parts are listed in the problem, the order does not correspond to the question. Further, the question does not explicitly tell you the number of wins. 30 is the number of games played, so we need to calculate the number of wins before we can determine the ratio.

$30 - 10 = 20$ Subtract the number of losses from the total number of games

$\dfrac{wins}{losses} = \dfrac{20}{10} = \dfrac{2}{1} = 2:1$ Insert the number of wins into your ratio formula

Proportions

Proportions are an extension of ratios. Proportions are equations that set two ratios equal to one another and are helpful to determine ratios when quantities in a specific ratio relationship increase or decrease.

> If Nathan has 7 sodas and 4 bottles of water, proportions tell us that if Nathan has 14 sodas, he would have 8 bottles of water. This proportion can be expressed as:
>
> $$\dfrac{14}{8} = \dfrac{7}{4}$$

Decimals

A decimal, like a fraction, expresses a part of a whole. Decimals are tested often on the SHSAT and it is important to understand the fundamentals of a decimal, including how the specific digits of the decimal are described. Take the decimal 123.456, for example. Each digit has its own mathematical label:

$$1\ 2\ 3\ .\ 4\ 5\ 6$$

1: Hundreds	3: Ones	5: Hundredths
2: Tens	4: Tenths	6: Thousandths

www.argobrothers.com

MATH

Fractions to Decimals

You may occasionally need to change either the expressions in the problem or your answer from fractions to decimals or decimals to factions.

> To change a fraction to a decimal, simply divide the denominator into the numerator.
>
> $$\frac{7}{20} = 7 \div 20 = 0.35$$

Decimals to Fractions

Suppose you have the decimal 54.67. To convert a decimal to a fraction, first remove the decimal point and make the resulting whole number your numerator and, for right now, make 1 your denominator:

$$54.67 = \frac{5467}{1}$$

Then, count the number of digits after the decimal point. In this case, .67 follows the decimal point. So, two digits follow the decimal point. Place a 0 after the 1 in the denominator for each digit that occurs after the decimal point in order to determine the fractional equivalent to your decimal.

$$54.67 = \frac{5467}{100}$$

In order to verify that you have the correct fraction, simply divide the denominator into the numerator--you will end up right back at 54.67.

Percentages

Percentages, like fractions and decimals, represent a portion of the whole and are heavily tested on the exam in a number of ways. Percentages are based on the whole of 100. 20% of something is essentially 20 parts of 100. Percentages can be written a number of different ways. For example, we can write 20% as follows:

$$20\% \text{ or } \frac{20}{100} \text{ or } .20$$

On the exam, you may be asked to calculate what percentage an integer is of another integer. For example, a problem solving question may ask you: *5 is what percentage of 20?*

$5 = ?\%(20)$	Write the problem as an equation
$5 = \frac{x}{100}(20)$	Since percentages are always based on 100, you can add more information to the equation to help you solve and substitute an unknown variable for the value we are missing.
$5 = \frac{20x}{100} = \frac{2x}{10} = \frac{x}{5}$	Reduce the fraction
$5 = \frac{x}{5}$	Cross-multiply
$25 = x$	5 is **25**% of 20

You solved the problem and got the correct answer, but it took a lot of steps, which translates to a lot of time. There are some common formulas you can use on the exam to help approach percentage problems of various types. Let us look at these in more detail.

44

Part of the Whole Formula

Problems involving percentages on the exam will normally, like the previous problem, give you two of the values and ask you to calculate the third. In the previous example, you had 5, the part, and 20, the whole. You were looking for the percentage. You can solve the problem with fewer steps by using a formula:

Formula: $percent = \frac{part}{whole}$

$percent = \frac{5}{20} = .25$ *or* 25%

Let us look at a few more examples:

Example 1:

What is 20% of 42?

$percent \cdot whole = part$ Percentage Formula

$.20 \cdot 42 = 8.4\%$ Solve

Example 2:

12 is 40% of what number?

$\frac{part}{percent} = whole$ Percentage Formula

$\frac{12}{.40} = 30$ Solve

Percent Increase and Decrease

The SHSAT commonly tests the percent of increase and decrease. While word problems are most common, questions are presented in a number of different ways and may ask you to determine, for example, a new price based on a price increase of a certain percentage, or the decreased percentage of revenue for one fiscal year compared to a previous year. Like the previous problems, you will be given some pieces of information and asked to find the missing element. Let us look at some common formulas to help you calculate percentage increase and decrease.

Example:

The staff at Salsa Kitchen was reduced from 40 to 29 employees. What is the percent decrease in staff?

To calculate the percentage decrease, use the following formula:

$percentage\ decrease = \frac{amount\ of\ decrease}{original\ whole} \cdot 100$

In order to calculate the *amount of decrease*, you must find the difference of the number of current employees and the number of original employees. In this case, Salsa Kitchen started with 40 employees and now has 29, for a difference of 11.

$percentage\ decrease = \frac{11}{40} \cdot 100$

$percentage\ decrease = .275 \cdot 100 = \mathbf{27.5\%}.$

ARGO BROTHERS
www.argobrothers.com

MATH

Example:
Ansley works in a bookstore for $12.00 per hour. If her pay is increased to $14.00, then what is her percent increase in pay?

To calculate percentage increase, use this formula:

$$\text{percentage increase} = \frac{\text{amount of increase}}{\text{original whole}}$$

In order to calculate the *amount of increase*, you must find the difference of Ansley's current hourly pay and her previous hourly pay. In this case, Ansley started off earning $12.00 an hour before her pay increased to $14.00 an hour. The amount of increase is $2.00.

$$\text{percentage increase} = \frac{2}{12} \cdot 100$$

$$\text{percentage increase} = \frac{1}{6} \cdot 100 = \textbf{16.66\%}$$

Combined Percentages

Sometimes questions on the exam will ask you to calculate more than one percentage. You may also be asked to find the percentage of a percentage. It is important to understand that you cannot compare percentages that are not part of the same whole. This is a common trap on the exam and you can count on an answer choice that matches the outcome of this mistake.

Example:
During the semi-annual sale, dresses were reduced by 20%. Then, the price was further reduced by 10%. If a dress was originally $200, what is the final price of the dress?

The dress was first reduced by 20% then by 10%. While it may be tempting to calculate the new final price by reducing the original price of $200 by 30%, that is not correct.

$.20 \cdot \$200 = \$40.00$	First, calculate the first price reduction of 20%
$\$200.00 - \$40.00 = \$160.00$	Subtract $40.00 from the original price

If the price of dress was reduced by 20%, there would be a $40.00 price difference from the original price. So, after the first reduction, the price of the dress would be $160.00.

$.10 \cdot \$160 = \$16.00$	Calculate the second price reduction
$\$160.00 - \$16.00 = \$144.00$	Reduce the dress by the new discount

If you had erroneously decreased the original price of $200 by 30%, you would have arrived at $140, which is incorrect.

Algebra: The Basics

Algebra involves many of the same concepts as arithmetic like absolute value, fractions, and numerical operations. Algebra often uses variables, which are letters used to represent an unknown quantity. Variables are incorporated into expressions and you will often be asked to solve equations to find their value. The concepts discussed in this chapter present themselves in various mathematical capacities on the exam. You will need to understand concepts like factoring, polynomials, algebraic expressions, exponents, roots, and inequalities. Let us start by reviewing some important vocabulary associated with algebra.

Essential Algebra Vocabulary

Coefficient: A multiplier in front of a variable that indicates how many of the variable there are. For example, for the term 5x, 5 is the coefficient. Whenever a term occurs without a coefficient in front of it, like x, the coefficient is 1.

Constant: A numerical quantity that does not change.

Equation: Equations are the building blocks of algebra. An equation is two expressions linked together with an equal sign where values of each expression can be solved or simplified. $2x + 1 = x - 10$ is an example of an equation.

Expression: An expression is made up of a single or multiple algebraic term(s), linked together by operations. $5x - 6$, $6xy$, and $x - 1$ are all expressions.

Term: A component of an algebraic equation that either represents the product or quotient of a constant and variable, or a specific value separated by arithmetic operations. In the expression $4x + 3b - 2$, $4x$, $3b$, and 2 are all terms.

Variable: A letter used to represent an unknown value. Any letter may be used for variables and you many not always need to or be able to find the specific value associated with the variable. In many cases on the exam, however, you will solve to find the value of variables.

Simplifying Algebraic Expressions

Before you dive into solving more complicated equations, you need to understand a few simplification tools that allow you to change algebraic expressions into simpler but equivalent forms.

Algebraic Laws of Operations

Like with arithmetic, algebra also has three basic properties for dealing with equations: commutative, additive, and distributive.

Commutative Property: Addition and multiplication are commutative operations; the order in which they are performed does not impact the answer. The commutative property does not hold for subtraction.

$$2a \cdot 3b = 3b \cdot 2a$$
$$2a + 3b = 3b + 2a$$

Associative Property: Addition and multiplication are also associative; when written as an expression, they can be regrouped, and like terms can be combined without impacting the final answer.

Addition:

$$= 2a - 3a + 5b + 2b$$
$$= (2a - 3a) + (5b + 2b)$$
$$= -a + 7b$$

Multiplication:

$$= (6a \cdot 5b) \cdot 4b$$
$$= 6a(5b \cdot 4b)$$
$$= 6a(20b^2)$$
$$= 120ab^2$$

Distributive Property: The distributive property outlines how values in an expression should be distributed when performing more than one operation (addition, subtraction, multiplication).

$$3a(4b - 6c) = (3a \cdot 4b) - (3a \cdot 6c)$$
$$= 12ab - 18ac$$

The associative, commutative, and distributive properties apply to many of the problems you will see on the exam. In some expressions and equations, you may need to combine the operations of the properties to arrive at your answer.

Combining Like Terms

Combining like terms is an effective approach to simplifying and solving algebraic expressions. As you work through the expression, using the appropriate law(s) of operation, look for terms that have the same characteristics and combine them into a single term. Any term that shares the same variable in the same form can be combined.

$x^3 + x^2 + 2x + 3x - 4$ In this case, $2x$ and $3x$ are like terms and can be combined.

$x^3 + x^2 + 5x - 4$ Notice that x^3 and x^2 cannot be combined. While they share the same base, the exponent x is different.

Substitution

Substitution is also another effective way to solve algebraic expressions or to express them in terms of other variables. Let us look at a sample question:

Evaluate $4x^2 - 8x$ when $x = 3$.

Here, you would substitute the value 3 for every x in the expression. Remember the order of operations; solve the parentheses and exponents first:

$4(3)^2 - 8(3) =$

$4(9) - 24 = 36 - 24$

$= 12$

Substitution may sometimes require you to replace non-mathematical symbols with values or operations. For example, you may see a question that uses a non-mathematical symbol instead of an operation sign. In this case, the question will always outline what the symbol represents.

Suppose $x \blacksquare \frac{8 - x}{x^2}$ where $x > 0$. Evaluate $3 \blacksquare$.

While it may appear confusing at first, this is simply a substitution question.

$\frac{8 - x}{x^2}$ x times $\blacksquare$ is equal to this expression

$3 \blacksquare = \frac{8 - 3}{3^2} = \frac{5}{9}$ $3 \blacksquare$ tells you that 3 is the value of x. You will need to substitute the value 3 wherever you see an x, then solve.

Factoring and Polynomials

Factoring is another approach to simplifying algebraic expressions and is essentially the opposite of distribution, though they are commonly used together. Factoring allows you to evaluate complex expressions by breaking it into simpler expressions, taking into consideration monomials, polynomials, binomials, and trinomials.

Monomials: A single term expression. For example, $3x$ or $4y$.

Polynomials: An expression with more than one term. For example, $3x^2 + 2y + 3$.

Binomials: A polynomial expression with exactly two terms. For example, $4x + 6$.

Trinomials: A polynomial expression with exactly three terms. For example, $4y^2 + 3x - 2$.

When there is a monomial factor common to all the terms in the polynomial expression, it can be factored out to create simpler expressions. Suppose you have the following expression:

$4x + 8xy$

$4x(1 + 2y)$ $\qquad\qquad$ $4x$ is the common factor and can be used to simplify the expression

Common Polynomial Equations

There are common polynomials that you may encounter on the exam. Knowing how to recognize and factor these can save you time on exam day.

The difference of squares can be factored out into the product of two simpler expressions.

$$a^2 - b^2 = (a - b)(a + b)$$

Some polynomials can be factored into two matching binomials.

$$a^2 - 2ab + b^2 = (a - b)(a - b)$$

Some polynomials are trinomials that are perfect squares.

$$a^2 + 2b^2 + b^2 = (a + b)^2$$

Since factoring is the opposite of distribution, these equations are all commutative.

Roots and Exponents

Exponents

You may have noticed that polynomials often involve exponents. While this is not always the case, exponents

are an important component of algebra and have their own set of rules you should be familiar with going into the exam.

An exponent tells you how many times to multiply a number by itself to find a particular value. If we have the exponent 3^2, the number 3 is called the base while the number 2 is referred to as the exponent or power.

To solve an exponent, multiply the base by itself the number of times expressed by the exponent. Take 5^3, for example. If you were to rewrite the expression without exponents and solve, it would look like this:

$$5 \cdot 5 \cdot 5 = 125$$

Any base with an exponent of 2 is commonly referred to as *squared* and any base with an exponent of 3 is referred to as *cubed*. It is helpful to be familiar with some of the common exponents you may see on the exam. The following chart outlines common squares and cubes that commonly appear in arithmetic and algebra problems.

Common Squares	Common Cubes
$1^2 = 1$	$1^3 = 1$
$2^2 = 4$	$2^3 = 8$
$3^2 = 9$	$3^3 = 27$
$4^2 = 16$	$4^3 = 64$
$5^2 = 25$	$5^3 = 125$
$6^2 = 36$	$6^3 = 216$
$7^2 = 49$	$7^3 = 343$
$8^2 = 64$	$8^3 = 512$
$9^2 = 81$	$9^3 = 729$
$10^2 = 100$	$10^3 = 1000$

Rules of Exponents

Working with exponents is pretty straightforward when you only have a base and a positive exponent like 3^2. But you will see exponents on the exam that include negative numbers and involve mathematical operations like multiplication and division. The following chart is a helpful tool to familiarize yourself with the rules of exponents and how to deal with various presentations of exponents on the exam.

Exponent Rule	Example
$x^0 = 1$	Any nonzero number to the zero power is equal to 1. Note that 0^0 has no defined value. *Example:* $5^0 = 1$
$x^1 = x$	Any nonzero number raised to the power of 1 is equal to the number itself. *Example:* $6^1 = 6$

Exponent Rule	Example
$(x^a)(x^b) = x^{a+b}$	When you multiply exponents with the same base, add the exponents to calculate the value of the expression. *Example:* $(4^2)(4^3) = 4^{2+3} = 4^5 = 1024$
$\frac{x^a}{x^b} = x^{a-b}$	When you divide exponents with the same base, subtract the exponents to calculate the value of the expression. *Example:* $\frac{4^3}{4^2} = 4^{3-2} = 4^1 = 4$
$(xy)^a = (x^a)(y^a)$	The product of two bases raised to a power can be simplified and solved by raising each number in the expressions to the same power. *Example:* $(4^2)(2^2) = 8^2 = 64$
$(x/y)^a = \frac{x^a}{y^a}$	The quotient of two bases raised to a power can be simplified and solved raising each number in the expressions to the same power. *Example:* $(3/4)3 = \frac{3^3}{4^3} = \frac{9}{64}$
$x^{-a} = \frac{1}{x^a}$	Any nonzero number raised to a negative power is equivalent to its reciprocal raised to a positive power. *Example:* $3^{-2} = \frac{1}{3^2} = \frac{1}{9}$
$(x^a)^b = x^{ab}$	When a power is raised to another power, multiply the exponents. *Example:* $(3^2)^3 = 3^{2\cdot3} = 3^6 = 729$

Exponents in Expressions and Equations

The exponent rules cover the basics of dealing with exponents that primarily involve multiplication. It is important to note that it is not possible to add and subtract exponents in an expression if they do not have the same base and the same exponent. Consider the following expression:

$2^9 + 2^7$

This expression is in its simplest form. You cannot add the terms to get a new expression of 2^{16}. Each part of the expression should be solved separately to arrive at your answer: $2^9 = 512$ and $2^7 = 128$. When you add the two together, you get 640. When you calculate 2^{16} you get 65,536. That's a vast difference in answers!

Exponents in these cases **must** be computed separately. The same goes for subtraction. However, when working with terms that share the same base and have the same exponents, you can add and subtract to simply the expression. Suppose you have the algebraic expression $3x^4 + 6x^4$. Here your base and exponent, x and 4, respectively, are the same. You can add the two terms together, keeping the base and exponents intact. Your new expression will be $9x^4$.

You may or may not have the information needed to fully solve the expression, but you can put it in its simplest terms.

www.argobrothers.com

MATH

Negative Numbers and Exponents

There is another possible situation involving exponents to keep in mind when a negative number is raised to a positive power.

When you raise a negative number to a positive power, the same rules apply for multiplying negative and positive numbers together. The product of a negative and positive number is a negative number, while the product of two negative numbers is a positive number. How does that relate to exponents? Since an exponent represents the number of times you multiply a number by itself, when you have a negative number raised to an exponent, whether it is an odd or even exponent will impact whether your final answer is positive or negative.

$$-4^2 = (-4)(-4)$$

In this case, the value of the expression $(-4)(-4)$ is 16. However, the value of -4^3 is calculated $(-4)(-4)(-4)$, which is -64.

When you raise a negative number to an even exponent, the result will be a positive number. When you raise a negative number to an odd exponent, the result will be a negative number.

Roots

Exponents are closely linked to roots, another mathematical concept that deals with the number of times a number goes into another number. Like exponents, roots appear on the exam in various forms, and an understanding of the basic principles of roots will help you simplify expressions and solve equations.

Roots are the inverse function of exponents. The roots you will encounter on the exam are generally confined to square roots and cube roots. You will need to either solve or simplify them. A root is symbolized by a figure that looks like a check mark with a trailing bar which extends over the number whose root is being taken: $\sqrt{4}$.

The above example is the standard notation for a square root. In this case, the expression is translated as "the square root of 4." To solve, you are looking for a number that, when squared equals 4. If you look back at the common exponents table you will find that $2^2 = 4$. So the square root of 4 is 2.

You may sometimes see the root symbol with an exponent in front of it: $\sqrt[3]{27}$.

In this case, you must take the *cubed* root of 27. You need to identify the number that when cubed, equals 27. Again, if you refer back to the chart of common squares and cubes, you will see that $3^3 = 27$. So the cubed root of 27 is 3.

The SHSAT will only ask you to find the square root of positive numbers. However, the square root may be negative or positive, because any real number squared will always yield a positive number. If you are comparing quantities, for example, and have the equation: $\sqrt{100} = x$, it is easy to assume $x = 10$. Yet x could also be -10, and must be considered.

Simplifying Roots

You cannot add or subtract roots that appear in equations or expressions. You can, however, multiply or divide them in order to solve or simplify. In some cases, you may be able to solve for the value regardless of the operation being performed. For example:

52

$$\sqrt{4} + \sqrt{16}$$

Here, you can take the root of each of the terms separately, so 2 and 4, then find the sum, 6. You are not adding the roots; instead, you are adding values of the solved roots. Solving for $\sqrt{20}$ would be incorrect.

You can multiply the same roots in a given expression. You cannot, however, multiply a square root by a cubed root. Consider this example:

$$\sqrt{2} \cdot \sqrt{8} \cdot \sqrt[3]{27}$$

$$\sqrt{16} \cdot \sqrt[3]{27} \qquad \text{Simplify}$$

$$\sqrt{16} = \pm 4 \quad \sqrt[3]{27} = 3 \qquad \text{Solve for roots}$$

$$4 \cdot 3 = 12 \textbf{ OR } -4 \cdot 3 = -12$$

You can also divide roots of the same type. Here, you can complete the division as you would without the roots to simplify the expression. Then, solve the new simplified root to determine your answer.

$$\frac{\sqrt{16}}{\sqrt{4}} = \sqrt{\frac{16}{4}} = \sqrt{4} = \pm 2$$

Using these general principles, you can also reduce numbers under the root sign to create smaller but equivalent expressions. You can simplify the original root and create a new expression that includes simpler terms and solve:

$$\sqrt{81} = \sqrt{9} \cdot \sqrt{9} = \pm 3 \cdot \pm 3 = \pm 9$$

Fractional Exponents

You may have a number raised to a fractional exponent. To simplify and solve, convert the exponent to a root.

$$4^{\frac{1}{2}} = \sqrt{4^1} = \pm 2$$

In these instances, the denominator tells you the type of root, while the numerator tells you what power to raise the base number or variable.

Solving Algebraic Equations

Equations are algebraic functions that set two expressions equal to each other. Equations consist of numbers, operations, variables, or non-mathematical symbols. Your goal is usually to isolate the variables and solve or simplify as much as possible.

Since equations set two expressions equal to each other, when you manipulate the equation, you must ensure that you perform all operations to **both** sides of the equation. This is the most fundamental principle of working with algebraic equations.

Equations can have any number of variables. On the exam, you will see equations with one variable, on up to four or five unique variables. Equations that do not contain any exponents are the most common on the exam and are referred to as **linear equations**.

$x + 20 = 45$ The equation is telling you that the sum of x and 20 is equal to 45.

$x + 20 - 20 = 45 - 20$ You want to isolate x in order to solve for its value. Subtract 20 from each side of the equation. This keeps x positive and isolates it at the same time.

$x = 25$

MATH

Equations with one variable on one side tend to be easier to solve than those with multiple variables or variables on both sides of the equation. Naturally, the latter requires more manipulation and computation. In a time crunch, seeking out one-variable equations may help you get to more questions in the time you have remaining.

Let us look at an equation with the same variable on both sides:

$5x - 7 = 3x + 10$ To solve for x, you still need to isolate the variable. Solve to get all the terms with the variable on one side of the equation. First, subtract $3x$ from both sides.

$5x - 3x - 7 = 10$ Next, finish isolating the variables by adding 7 to both sides. When you add 7 to the left side of the equation, it cancels out the -7 already there.

$5x - 3x = 17$ Calculate

$2x = 17$ Divide by 2

$x = 8.5$

To make sure you have the right answer, you can plug the value you have for x into the original equation.

$5(8.5) - 7 = 3(8.5) + 10$

$42.5 - 7 = 25.5 + 10$

$35.5 = 35.5$

Absolute Value Equations

Solving equations with absolute value expressions involves a little more work than equations that do not. Remember that the absolute value of a number is the positive distance from zero to that number on a number line. When you take absolute value of algebraic equations, you will have two answers: one where the expression between the absolute value brackets is positive and one where the expression in the absolute value brackets is negative. Here's an example:

If $|x + 3| = 10$, then $x = ?$

Just like you would in any other equation, you want to isolate the variable. You can worry about the implications of the absolute value later. In fact, write the equation out, without the absolute value notation:

$x + 3 = 10$

$x = 10 - 3 = 7$

You have solved for x, but you are not done yet. Since the expression on the left side asks you to take the absolute value of the expression, and absolute value is always expressed as a positive number, you need to consider that instead of 10, the expression can also yield an answer of -10. To do so, adjust the right side of the equation to -10 and solve.

$x + 3 = -10$

$x = -10 - 3 = -13$

54

You can plug your answers back in to the original equations to see if they are correct. Both these values are correct. It is important to consider both possibilities when dealing with absolute value although the question may not specifically prompt you to so.

Variables in the Denominator

When variables are in the denominator, they warrant special attention. You still want to isolate the variable and solve or simplify. Consider this example:

$$9 = \frac{1}{x + 3} + 5$$

$$4 = \frac{1}{x + 3}$$ Subtract 5 from both sides to try to isolate the variable

$$4(x + 3) = (x + 3) \cdot \frac{1}{(x + 3)}$$ Multiply each side by the expression in the denominator

$$4(x + 3) = 1$$ The expression $x + 3$ on the right side cancels out

$$x + 3 = \frac{1}{4}$$ You could distribute the 4, but you are trying to isolate the variable. Divide each side by 4 to further isolate the variable.

$$x = \frac{1}{4} - 3 = \frac{1}{4} - \frac{12}{4}$$ Subtract 3 from both sides to solve for x by turning the integer into a fraction with the same denominator

$$= -\frac{11}{4} = -2.75 = -2\frac{3}{4}$$

Equations with More than One Variable

Of course, the test creators won't let you slide with solving for just one variable. Sometimes you will see equations with two variables. As with one variable expressions, your goal is to either solve or simplify. You can do so using many of the methods previously discussed. Equations with more than one variable, as you might imagine, can be more challenging than their one variable counterparts, and often require more steps to arrive at the answer. Usually, you are also given two separate equations to help you arrive at the answer.

Example:
Solve for x and y if $2x + 5y = 7$ and $x + 4y = 2$

$$x + 4y = 2$$ Solve for one of the variables in terms of the other variable

$$x = 2 - 4y$$

$$2(2 - 4y) + 5y = 7$$ Now plug in the expression for x into the first equation and solve for y

$$4 - 8y + 5y = 7$$

$$4 - 3y = 7$$

$$-3y = 3$$

$$y = -1$$

$$x = 2 - 4(-1)$$ Now that you have the value for y, plug it in and solve for x

$$x = 2 + 4 = 6$$

Remember, plug in the values you calculated to check your answers. To determine which variable to try to solve for first, look for the equation where one variable is easier to isolate and start there.

www.argobrothers.com

MATH

Quadratic Equations

The quadratic equation is a special equation where specific polynomials are set to equal zero.

$$ax^2 + bx + c = 0$$

For the quadratic equation, $a \neq 0$, and a, b, and c are constants representing the coefficients that precede the variable x.

Earlier in this section, we reviewed factoring and binomials, which are key components to finding values in a quadratic equation. Consider the example:

$x^2 - 5x + 6 = 0$

$(x - 2)(x - 3) = 0$ To solve for x, first factor out the binomial terms:

Math Prep Tip: If you are unsure if you have factored properly and identified the correct binomials, check your work using distribution. As you multiply in order, write out the products; if you have factored correctly, your distribution should yield the original equation.

$(x - 2)x - (x - 2)3$	Distribute the first term in the first binomial into both terms in the second binomial
$((x)(x) - 2x) - (3x - 6)$	Next, do the same with the second term in the first binomial
$x^2 - 2x - 3x + 6 = x^2 - 5x + 6$	Now, combine the products to see if it matches your original equation

Everything looks good! Let us get back to solving the problem.

$x - 2 = 0$	$x - 3 = 0$	Quadratic equations **always** have two solutions. The two solutions may be the same number. To solve for the values of x, set each of the binomial factors to 0.
$x = 2$	$x = 3$	Both 2 and 3 are solutions to the equation. Plug in your answers to check if the values are correct.
$(2)^2 - 5(2) + 6 = 0$	$(3)^2 - 5(3) + 6 = 0$	
$4 - 10 + 6 = -6 + 6 = 0$	$9 - 15 + 6 = -6 + 6 = 0$	Solve

The values check out when plugged in. The solution for the quadratic equation is $x = 2$ **OR** $x = 3$.

Math Prep Tip: The quadratic equation may be rewritten to generate the quadratic formula:

$$x = \frac{-b \pm \sqrt{b} - 4ac}{2a}$$

The quadratic formula is not tested on the exam.

Inequalities

Inequalities are similar to equations. Instead of setting two expressions equal, however, inequalities describe their relative value. Inequalities express four quantity comparisons:

x greater than y: $x > y$
x less than y: $x < y$
x greater than or equal to y: $x \geq y$
x less than or equal to y: $x \leq y$

Solving Inequalities

Inequalities are approached using the same techniques as the equations in this section. Your goal is still to isolate the variables and solve for their value, if possible. As with equations, whatever function you perform on one side, you must perform on the other. Inequalities have one difference that can impact your answer choice if you are not careful. Whenever you divide or multiply both sides by a negative number, you must flip the inequality sign to ensure the inequality remains valid. Let's look at an inequality example:

$$3 - \frac{x}{4} \geq 2$$

$$-\frac{x}{4} \geq 2 - 3 = -\frac{x}{4} \geq -1 \qquad \text{First, isolate the variable}$$

$$(-4)\left(-\frac{x}{4}\right) \leq (-4)(-1)$$

$$x \leq 4 \qquad \text{Since we multiplied both sides by a negative number we changed the direction of the inequality sign. The negative signs cancel out.}$$

The expression reads x is less than or equal to 4. While you have solved for x, this is not your answer. The complete answer is all the values equal to or less than 4. Inequalities are sometimes represented on a number line. The above example on a number line would look like:

The filled-in point over the 4 indicates that 4 is included in the possible list of values. If the final answer was $x < 4$, the circle would **not** be filled in. The number line in that case would look like:

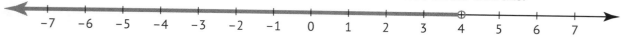

Coordinate Geometry

Coordinate geometry is the transition point from algebra to geometry and involves the use of algebraic expressions to create graphical displays on a coordinate plane. The coordinate plane is composed of a vertical and horizontal axis that run perpendicular to each other. All points on a coordinate plane can be plotted in reference to these axes, which intersect at zero. This meeting point is referred to as the **point of origin**.

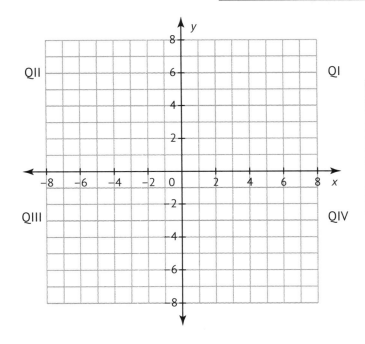

Quadrant	x-coordinate	y-coordinate
I	positive	positive
II	negative	positive
III	negative	negative
IV	positive	negative

The coordinate plane has four distinct quadrants when the origin is placed at the center. Quadrant I is in the upper right corner, quadrant II is in the upper left corner, quadrant III is in the lower left corner, and quadrant IV is in the lower right corner.

Points are plotted on a coordinate plane. Every point has two coordinates, one on the x-axis and one on the y-axis. The origin sits at the intersection of the two axes and has coordinates (0,0). The coordinates of points not at the center are determined by their positive or negative difference from the origin. Coordinates are always written with the x coordinate first: (x,y). You can determine whether the x and y coordinates are positive or negative based on the quadrant they fall in.

On the exam, it is helpful to know these quadrant locations for coordinates to save time and prevent you from having to plot the points on the coordinate plane each time.

Graphing Coordinates

Sometimes you need to either graph coordinates or determine the value of coordinates already on the graph. When given a set of coordinates, simply start at zero and plot the distance across (left or right) for the value of x, then up or down for the value of y.

Let us look at a set of coordinates and how to graph them on the coordinate plane. Suppose you are asked to identify a graph that has a point with the coordinates (3,2). Your graph would look like this:

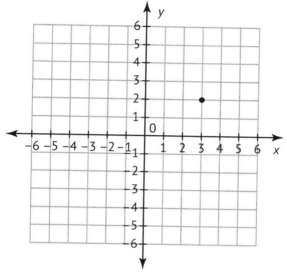

You can see the coordinates start at the point of origin, shift 3 spaces to the right, then shift 2 spaces up. If you refer back to the quadrant chart, you can see that it predicted our coordinates, which are both positive, would be in quadrant I.

Calculating Distance on the Coordinate Plane

You may be asked to calculate the distance between two points on a coordinate plane. If the points are in the same vertical or horizontal plane, you can simply count the spaces between the points. Distance is always positive.

You can also use the distance formula to plug in coordinates and calculate the distance between two points.

Distance Formula:
$$distance = \sqrt{(x_2 - x_1)^2 + (y_2 - y_1)^2}$$

To find the distance between two coordinates—let us say (5,−2) and (−4,9)—plug in the values in the equation and solve.

$$distance = \sqrt{(-4 - 5)^2 + (9 - (-2)^2}$$

$$distance = \sqrt{(-9)^2 + 11^2}$$

$$distance = \sqrt{202}$$

Midpoint

The midpoint is also a measure of distance between points on a coordinate plane. Instead of the distance from one point to another, the coordinates of the midpoint are the average of the endpoints. To find the midpoint of two points, take the average of your endpoints using the midpoint formula:

Midpoint Formula:
$$midpoint = \frac{x_1 + x_2}{2}, \frac{y_1 + y_2}{2}$$

Suppose you have the points (–1,2) and (3,–6). Plug in the coordinates to find the midpoint:

$$midpoint = \frac{-1 + 3}{2}, \frac{2 - 6}{2}$$

$$midpoint = (1,-2)$$

Slope

Points on a coordinate plane connect to form lines. The slope is the measure of how steep a line is in relation to the x-axis and y-axis. The equation of a line can be written as: $y = mx + b$, where m is the slope, b is the y-intercept, and x and y represent possible coordinate values. This equation is commonly referred to as **slope-intercept form**.

Slope-Intercept Form:
$$y = mx + b$$

The y-intercept is just another way of describing the point that falls directly on the y-axis. Likewise, the x-intercept describes the point that falls directly on the x-axis. All lines will have no more than one x and one y intercept.

The slope is the measure of *the rise over the run* of a line, or the change in the y-coordinate values (rise) and the change in x-coordinate values (run). You need two points to find the slope of a line.

Consider the coordinates (4,3) and (–2,–1). Calculate the change in x and y to find the slope, m.

$$m = \frac{\text{change in } y}{\text{change in } x} = \frac{3 - (-1)}{4 - (-2)} = \frac{4}{6} = \frac{2}{3}$$

You may sometimes be asked to find the slope of a line from an equation instead of coordinates. Suppose you have the equation $2x + y = 5$. To find the slope, put the equation in slope-intercept form, $y = mx + b$:

$$2x + y = 5$$
$$y = 5 - 2x \text{ OR in slope-intercept form: } y = -2x + 5$$

The slope of this line is –2.

Properties of Slopes

Knowing some of the common properties of slopes and what they look like graphically can help save you time and calculation on the exam.

- The slope of a line can be either positive or negative.
- Slopes do not have to be whole integers, they can be fractions as well.

- Parallel lines on the same coordinate plane will always have the same slope. For example, if the slope of line *a* is 3, **all** lines parallel to that line will also have a slope of 3.
- The slope of a line on the same coordinate plane that is perpendicular to another line is the **negative reciprocal**. If a line has a slope of 2, **all** lines perpendicular to that line will have a slope of $-\frac{1}{2}$.

A **positive** slope rises from left to right.   A **negative** slope falls from left to right.

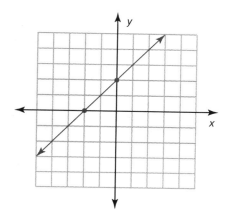

Any **horizontal** line has a slope of 0 since there is no change to the *y* value.

The slope of any **vertical** line cannot be defined because all of its points have the same *x*-coordinate.

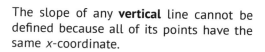

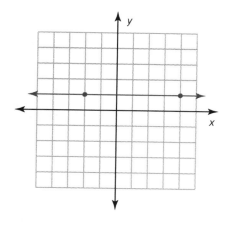

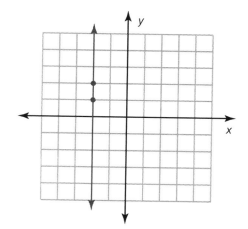

Functions

Algebraic functions can be expressed as a graph or as an equation and describe a relationship between corresponding inputs and outputs. Functions are typically represented by the notation *f(x)* and indicates calculations to be performed.

For example, you may see something similar to the following:

$$f(x) = 2x + 4$$

For the function above, f is the name of the function. Any letter can be used in place of f to name a function.

A question may present you with the above equation and ask you to solve $f(3)$. To solve, replace each x in the equation with the input of 3. For $f(3)$:

$$f(3) = 2(3) + 4$$

$$f(3) = 10$$

Functions can also be graphed on a coordinate plane. Depending on the equation, the graph may not always be a straight line. Instead, functions can be parabolas.

$$f(x) = -x^2 - 8x - 15 \qquad\qquad f(x) = -x^2 + 8x - 19$$

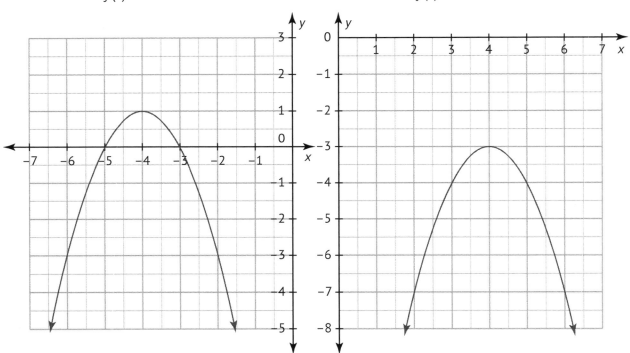

Geometry: The Basics

Geometry focuses primarily on the measurements of shapes, lines, angles, and planes. Several key areas of geometry are tested on the SHSAT. You will see problems that involve triangles, circles, and two-dimensional shapes of various sizes with different numbers of sides. This section will refresh your memory of the related formulas and concepts, outline key geometric concepts that occur frequently on the exam, and equip you with problem solving strategies to improve your accuracy.

Diagrams and Formulas

Most of the geometry questions on the exam will be accompanied by a diagram. In most cases, this works to your advantage. Often the diagrams contain useful information to help you answer the question. For example, if you have a diagram of a circle and the diameter is noted as 4 cm, you can calculate the radius of the circle, which is half the diameter.

It is important to note that geometry diagrams on the exam are typically **not** drawn to scale. You should not make assumptions based on how diagrams "look." Instead, you should use the information presented in the questions and any given measurements to calculate the information you are looking for to find a corresponding answer choice.

We will review key geometric formulas in this section. While the formulas are helpful to know, they are useless if you are unsure of how to use them. Questions on the exam, particularly those dealing with triangles, will require you to think beyond simply plugging numbers into a formula. Instead, you will have to critically analyze the given components to arrive at the correct answer.

Lines, Angles, Planes, and Shapes (L.A.P.S)

The building blocks of geometry are lines, angles, planes, and shapes. You will encounter one or more of these components in all the geometry questions on the exam. While geometry is a dense subject matter that includes some very complex principles, remember that the SHSAT is a test of your understanding of high-school level math and is primarily concerned with your basic math skills. As such, complex topics like differential geometry, model theory, and geometric proofs will not appear on the exam.

The exam will focus specifically on coordinate and plane geometry. Planes are two-dimensional flat surface areas that extend infinitely in all directions. The surfaces of geometric shapes like polygons, triangles, and hexagons all lie on planes; lines and points are also essential components of geometric planes. Using points, angles, and units of measurement, you can calculate critical information about a shape, plot coordinates on a plane, and draw conclusions about angle measurements. This section will cover the **L.A.P.S** fundamentals, including key definitions, formulas, and approaches to various problems.

Lines

A line is a one-dimensional figure on a plane. Lines are always straight and drawn with arrows at each end to indicate their infinite nature. Lines extend in both directions infinitely.

Lines are uniquely determined by two points. Points are found on all geometric shapes. They are not measurable units, although the distance between two points is a common calculation which you will be asked to perform. In the diagram below, **A** and **B** are points on the line. These points are unique and only one line runs through them. Remember that the line extends infinitely in both directions.

Instead of figures, you may see the common notation $\overleftrightarrow{AB}$ used. The notation indicates that you have a line, with no defined end, that crosses through points **A** and **B**.

Rays

A ray can be defined by two points where it begins at one of the points and passes through a second point while extending infinitely in one direction. The length of a ray cannot be determined and thus, neither can you find its mid-point.

MATH

In the diagram below, the ray begins at point **A**, passes through point **B**, and continues infinitely in one direction. As with a line, you can use a shorthand notation for this figure. The notation $\overrightarrow{AB}$ shows the points on the ray and that it continues infinitely in one direction.

Segments

A segment is a part of a line. However, segments have a measurable length. Unlike a line, segments do not continue infinitely. The annotation for a segment is written as $\overline{AB}$.

The key characteristics of a segment are its two end points and its midpoint. The end points mark finite ends of a segment while the midpoint is positioned at the center of a segment. Only segments have midpoints.

In the diagram below, **A** and **B** are the end points of the segment. **M** represents the midpoint or center of the segment.

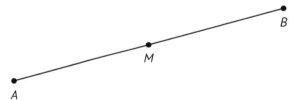

A and **B** are the same distance from the midpoint: $\overline{AM} = \overline{MB}$. If you have an exam question that tells you **M** is the midpoint of segment $\overline{AB}$ and that $\overline{MB}$ = 3, you can deduce that $\overline{AM}$ is also 3.

Parallel Lines

Parallel lines are two lines which exist on the same plane but do not intersect each other. You should not assume that because two lines are not touching in a diagram that they are parallel lines, since it is possible they may intersect at some point. For exam questions addressing parallel lines, the question will explicitly state the lines are parallel or will use the common notation for parallel lines.

$\overleftrightarrow{AB}$ and $\overleftrightarrow{CD}$ are parallel lines. Their relationship can be annotated as $\overleftrightarrow{AB} \parallel \overleftrightarrow{CD}$.

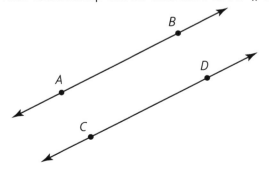

Perpendicular Lines

Perpendicular lines are two lines that intersect each other forming a 90° angle. We will discuss angles in more detail below. Just like with parallel lines, never assume you are dealing with perpendicular lines

unless the instructions specifically tell you so or you can identify the 90° angle. The standard notation for two lines that are perpendicular is $\overleftrightarrow{AB} \perp \overleftrightarrow{CD}$.

Intersection

An intersection, as its name implies, refers to the point where two lines, segments, or rays intersects. Perpendicular lines have an intersection point, but not all lines that intersect are perpendicular since they do not all form 90° angles.

Angles

Angles are formed when two lines intersect. The point of intersection is referred to as the **vertex** of the angle. Angles are measured in degrees and can be either acute, obtuse, right or straight. The measure of the angle determines its classification.

Type of Angle	Degree Measurement	Visual Representation
Acute	Acute angles are angles that measure less than 90°	
Right	Right angles measure **exactly** 90°	
Obtuse	Obtuse angles are angles that measure between 91° and 180°	
Straight	Straight angles are angles that measures **exactly** 180° and are equivalent to a straight line	

The typical naming convention for angles is to use the labels for the three points on the intersecting lines, segments, or rays, making sure to place the vertex in the middle. The common symbol to represent an angle is ∠.

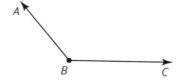

This angle can be written as ∠ABC or ∠CBA. This angle can also be simply named ∠B. However, only use this notation when there are no other angles that share B as the vertex.

Other Types of Angles

Any time a line intersects another line, at least one angle is formed. Questions will ask to you identify the

measures of angles. Knowing a few fundamentals about different type of angles occurring on the same line and how they relate to each other will help you save a lot of time. Let us look at the key angle relationships.

Supplementary and Complementary Angles

Two angles with a sum of 180° are called **supplementary angles**.

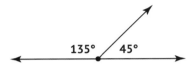

Two angles with a sum of 90° are called **complementary angles**.

Vertical Angles

Two lines or line segments that intersect form **vertical angles**. Vertical angles, or opposite angles, are congruent and have the same angle measurement.

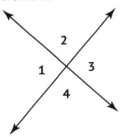

In the figure above, ∠2 and ∠4 are vertical angles. ∠1 and ∠3 are also vertical angles. If ∠4 = 50°, then ∠2 = 50° since they are vertical angles. Moreover, if ∠4 = 50°, then ∠1 = 130° because ∠4 and ∠1 are supplementary.

Adjacent Angles

Angles that share a common vertex and common side are called **adjacent angles**. Take a look at the following example.

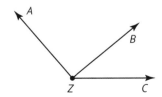

∠AZB and ∠BZC are adjacent angles because they share a common vertex, Z, and a common side, $\overrightarrow{ZB}$.

Transversals

A transversal is a line that intersects two or more lines at two or more points.

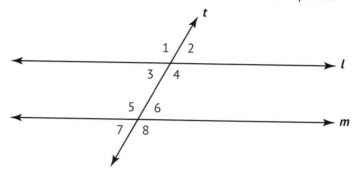

When a transversal intersects a pair of parallel lines, as in the above example, the resulting angles are related in some way:

- Angles 1, 4, 5, and 8 are equal.
- Angles 2, 3, 6, and 7 are equal.
- The sum of any two adjacent angles, such as 1 and 2 or 7 and 8, equals 180° since they form a straight angle on a line.
- The sum of any large angle + any small angle = 180° since the large and small angles in this figure combine into straight lines, all the large angles are equal, and all the small angles are equal.

You will see these concepts of angles appear again in the next sections where we will explore properties and measurements of polygons.

Shapes: Polygons

You will encounter a number of different types of polygons on the exam. A polygon is a two-dimensional enclosed figure with three or more straight sides. Polygons are named based on the number of sides they have.

Polygon Name	Number of Sides
Triangle	3
Quadrilateral	4
Pentagon	5
Hexagon	6
Heptagon	7
Octagon	8

MATH

Nonagon	9
Decagon	10
Dodecagon	12

Polygons can be either regular or irregular. Regular polygons have all sides of equal length and equal angles. Irregular polygons do not. It is important to understand the difference so that you do not make erroneous assumptions about the size of a figure that could lead you to an incorrect answer. The test questions will tell you if you are dealing with a regular or irregular polygon.

While all polygons are different in the number of sides they have, they do share some fundamental characteristics.

- The area of a polygon is the measure of the area of the region inside the polygon.
- A polygon with equal sides and equal interior angles is a regular polygon.
- The sum of the exterior angles of any polygon is 360°.
- The perimeter of a polygon is the sum of the lengths of its sides.

Geometry questions will focus primarily on finding various measurements, like volume, area, and circumference, of the polygons. A majority of the polygons on the exams will be triangle and four-sided polygons, also known as quadrilaterals.

This section will look at the basic properties of polygons, and the formulas used to calculate the measurement of the sides and angles. It will also discuss circles and how to approach figures that include more than one polygon or circle. Triangles have many properties, rules, and calculations and merit a deeper review given their complexity and popularity on the exam. First, let us look at some general principles of quadrilaterals.

Quadrilaterals

Quadrilaterals are four-sided polygons. Quadrilaterals can be regular or irregular and the sum of their interior angles is 360°. The most common quadrilaterals tested on the exam are squares and rectangles, but there are also several others.

Rectangles

A rectangle is a quadrilateral where the opposite sides are parallel and the interior angles are all right angles. The opposite sides of a rectangle are of equal length. The diagonals of a rectangle are also of equal length.

> **Formula for the Area of a Rectangle**
>
> *area = length · width*

MATH

www.argobrothers.com

Diagonals of a Rectangle

The two diagonals of a rectangle are always equal to each other. Both diagonals divide the rectangle into two equal right triangles. Since the diagonals of the rectangle form right triangles that include the diagonal and two sides of the rectangle, if you know two of the values, you can calculate the third with the Pythagorean equation (discussed below).

Square

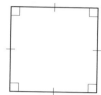

A square is a rectangle with four equal sides. All squares are rectangles but not all rectangles are squares.

> **Formula for the Area of a Square**
>
> *area = s²*
>
> In the formula, *s* is the length of a side.

Diagonals of a Square

The diagonals of a square bisect each other at right angles and have equal lengths. The diagonals also cut the square into two 45-45-90 triangles. If you know the length of one side of the square, you can calculate the length of the diagonal.

Parallelogram

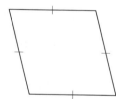

A parallelogram is a quadrilateral with two sets of parallel and equal sides. The length and width do not need to be the same in a parallelogram but the opposing sides will always be equal and the adjacent angles will be supplementary.

> **Formula for the Area of a Parallelogram**
>
> *area = base · height*

Diagonals of a Parallelogram

The diagonals of a parallelogram divide the figure into two congruent triangles.

Polygon Angles

The sum of the interior angles inside of a polygon is determined by the number of sides in the figure; this is true for both regular and irregular polygons. The figures you will see most often on the exam, triangles and quadrilaterals, both have set measures for their interior angles. Triangles will always total 180 degrees and quadrilaterals will total 360 degrees.

MATH

You can always figure out the total measurement of the internal angles of a polygon by using the formula:

$$(n - 2) \cdot 180$$

In the formula, n equals the number of sides.

Triangles

Triangles are three-sided polygons. The sum of the interior angles is 180°. The height of the triangle is the perpendicular distance from the vertex to opposite leg and can be found inside or outside of the triangle.

Formula for the Area of a Triangle

$area = \frac{1}{2}\ base \cdot height$

Equilateral Triangles

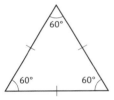

An equilateral triangle has three equal sides and three equal angles.

Once you know that you have two 60° angles, you can assume you are dealing with an equilateral triangle.

Isosceles Triangles

An isosceles triangle has two equal sides and two equal angles.

The two equal angles are opposite the two equal sides. The sides opposite equal angles are always equal, and the angles opposite equal sides are always equal.

Right Triangles

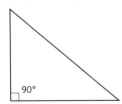

Right triangles are tested more than any other type of triangle on the exam. A right triangle is any triangle that contains a right angle. The side opposite the right angle is the hypotenuse. The other two sides are called legs. The remaining two angles add up to 90 degrees.

<u>Right Triangles and the Pythagorean Theorem</u>

The Pythagorean Theorem is one of the most tested theories on the exam, which makes sense as it applies to right triangles and right triangles are tested frequently. The theory establishes the relationship of a right triangle's legs to its hypotenuse.

Pythagorean Theorem

$$a^2 + b^2 = c^2$$

In this equation, **a** and **b** are the legs and **c** is the hypotenuse.

Since right triangles adhere to the Pythagorean Theorem, they rarely yield integers for the lengths of the legs. But a few integer triplets perfectly conform to the Theorem. These are referred to as **Pythagorean triples**. The ones you will see on the exam include:

- 3, 4, 5
- 5, 12, 13
- 7, 24, 25
- 8, 15, 17

Also note that any multiples of these triples conform. For example, 6, 8, 10 are multiples of the triples 3, 4, 5. Memorizing these will help you identify measurements and answer questions more quickly.

Shapes: Circles

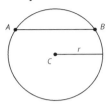

Circles are not polygons because they do not have straight sides. Circles are tested on the exam and you will mainly be asked to find some part of its measurements. Here are some quick facts about circles:

- All circles contain 360°
- The distance from the center to any point on the circle is called the radius. The radius of a circle is a critical piece: if you know a circle's radius, you can figure out all its other measurements.
- The diameter of a circle stretches between endpoints on the circle and passes through the center.
- A chord also extends from endpoint to endpoint on the circle, but it does not necessarily pass through the center.
- In the figure above, point C is the center of the circle, r is the radius, and $\overline{AB}$ is a chord.

Formula for the Circumference of a Circle

The circumference is the distance around the circle.

$$circumference = 2\pi r$$

The standard value for *pi* on the exam is 3.14.

Formula for the Area of a Circle

$$area = \pi r^2$$

In this formula, r is the radius. When you need to find the area of a circle, your real goal is to figure out the radius. For an added challenge, sometimes a question may give you the diameter or the circumference and you will need to calculate the radius (half the diameter) to solve for the area.

Shapes: Solids

Rectangular Solids

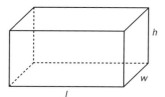

A rectangular solid is a prism with a rectangular base and edges that are perpendicular to its base.

A rectangular solid has three key dimensions: length, width, and height. If you know these three measurements, you can find the solid's volume and surface area.

Formula for the Surface Area

$A = 2 \cdot w \cdot l + 2 \cdot l \cdot h + 2 \cdot h \cdot w$

Formula for the Volume

volume $= l \cdot w \cdot h$

Cubes

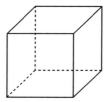

A cube is a rectangular solid with sides (s) that are all equal. Cubes have six faces, each of which is a square, meaning the length, width, and height of each are equal.

Formula for the Surface Area

volume $= 6s^2$

Formula for the Volume

volume $= s^3$

Right Circular Cylinders

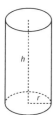

A right circular cylinder is a geometric solid that has two circular bases. A right circular cylinder has a lateral measurement, and its height forms a rectangle.

Formula for the Volume

The only measurement you will be asked to calculate for right cylinders is the volume.

volume $= \pi r^2 h$

Data Interpretation: The Basics

Data interpretation questions test your ability to derive information from graphs, charts, and other visual displays. Data interpretation questions are more of an extension of problem solving questions than a unique question type or concept. For these questions, you will interpret data from charts, graphs, and other images and use this information to solve for the correct answer(s).

This section will provide a brief overview of central tendency, probability, and frequency distributions.

Measures of Central Tendency

Measures of central tendency identify the distribution of certain values in an attempt to make data more understandable and allow for accurate interpretation. The three measures of central tendency are the mean, median, and mode.

Mean

The **mean** is commonly referred to as the average, and is the sum of all terms divided by the number of terms. To express the mean as an equation, set the mean equal to its relationship with the terms in the data set:

$$mean = \frac{sum\ of\ terms}{number\ of\ terms}$$

Suppose on your last four statistics exams, you received the following scores: 84, 92, 93, 87. If you wanted to find the mean of your scores, calculate using the equation for the mean:

$$mean = \frac{84 + 92 + 93 + 87}{4} = \frac{356}{4} = 89$$

Sometimes, instead of all the terms, a test question might provide you with the mean and ask you to identify the other values. You can rearrange, simplify, and substitute to arrive at your answer.

Median

The **median** of a set of data is the middle term when the numbers are written in ascending order. For example, to calculate the median of the group 7, 12, 14, 6, 4, 3, and 17, you would first list the numbers in order.

   3, 4, 6, 7, 12, 14, 17

Then find the middle number, which is in this case is 7. If, however, the number 21 was added to this set, you would have **two** numbers in the middle: 7 and 12. In this case, you average the two numbers (7 + 12, divided by 2) to reach a median of 9.5.

Mode

The **mode** is simply the number that occurs the most. In the group 1, 2, 3, 3, 3, 3, 4, and 7, the mode is 3 since it appears the most frequently in the group.

Range

The **range** of a data set is the difference between the largest term and the smallest term. For example, the range of 12, –24, 13, 2, and 4 is 13 – (–24) = 37.

Probability

Probability is the measure of the number of specific outcomes compared to the number of possible outcomes:

$$p = \frac{\#\ of\ specific\ outcomes}{\#\ of\ possible\ outcomes}$$

If you have 10 cookies in a bag—3 chocolate chip, 2 oatmeal, 4 lemon, and 1 peanut butter—the probability of your reaching into the bag and selecting a lemon cookie is $\frac{4}{10}$ or $\frac{2}{5}$. Probability can be written as a fraction or a decimal.

You may be asked to determine multiple-event probability, such as the probability of reaching into the bag of cookies a second time and grabbing a lemon cookie. In these instances, you must find the probability for each event and then multiply them.

Frequency Distribution

A **frequency distribution** is a table used to describe a data set. It also lists intervals or ranges of data values—called **data classes**—together with the number of data values or **frequency** from the set that are in each class.

Suppose that the exam scores of 20 psychology students are as follows:

97, 92, 88, 75, 83, 67, 89, 55, 72, 78, 81, 91, 57, 63, 67, 74, 87, 84, 98, 46

You can construct a frequency table with classes 90–99, 80–89, 70–79 etc., by counting the number of grades in each grade range.

Class	Frequency (f)
90–99	4
80–89	6
70–79	4
60–69	3
50–59	2
40–49	1

Note that the sum of the frequency column is equal to 20, the total number of test scores that you were given.

This concludes your review for the math section. In the following pages you will find 5 full-length exams to practice with. Good luck!

SHSAT
PRACTICE TESTS

You Tube

VIDEO EXPLANATIONS
YouTube.com/ArgoBrothers

www.argobrothers.com

Practice Test 1
SHSAT

This exam is 3 hours long. Try to take this full exam in one sitting to simulate real test conditions.

While taking this exam, refrain from hearing music or watching T.V.

Please note, calculators are not permitted! You are permitted to answer questions in any order you see fit.

Allocate your test time accordingly.

Concentrate and GOOD LUCK!

SHSAT PRACTICE TEST 1
ANSWER SHEET

ENGLISH LANGUAGE ARTS	MATHEMATICS

ENGLISH LANGUAGE ARTS

1 Ⓐ Ⓑ Ⓒ Ⓓ
2 Ⓐ Ⓑ Ⓒ Ⓓ
3 Ⓐ Ⓑ Ⓒ Ⓓ
4 Ⓐ Ⓑ Ⓒ Ⓓ
5 Ⓐ Ⓑ Ⓒ Ⓓ
6 Ⓐ Ⓑ Ⓒ Ⓓ
7 Ⓐ Ⓑ Ⓒ Ⓓ
8 Ⓐ Ⓑ Ⓒ Ⓓ
9 Ⓐ Ⓑ Ⓒ Ⓓ
10 Ⓐ Ⓑ Ⓒ Ⓓ
11 Ⓐ Ⓑ Ⓒ Ⓓ
12 Ⓐ Ⓑ Ⓒ Ⓓ
13 Ⓐ Ⓑ Ⓒ Ⓓ
14 Ⓐ Ⓑ Ⓒ Ⓓ
15 Ⓐ Ⓑ Ⓒ Ⓓ
16 Ⓐ Ⓑ Ⓒ Ⓓ
17 Ⓐ Ⓑ Ⓒ Ⓓ
18 Ⓐ Ⓑ Ⓒ Ⓓ
19 Ⓐ Ⓑ Ⓒ Ⓓ
20 Ⓐ Ⓑ Ⓒ Ⓓ
21 Ⓐ Ⓑ Ⓒ Ⓓ
22 Ⓐ Ⓑ Ⓒ Ⓓ
23 Ⓐ Ⓑ Ⓒ Ⓓ
24 Ⓐ Ⓑ Ⓒ Ⓓ
25 Ⓐ Ⓑ Ⓒ Ⓓ
26 Ⓐ Ⓑ Ⓒ Ⓓ
27 Ⓐ Ⓑ Ⓒ Ⓓ
28 Ⓐ Ⓑ Ⓒ Ⓓ
29 Ⓐ Ⓑ Ⓒ Ⓓ

30 Ⓐ Ⓑ Ⓒ Ⓓ
31 Ⓐ Ⓑ Ⓒ Ⓓ
32 Ⓐ Ⓑ Ⓒ Ⓓ
33 Ⓐ Ⓑ Ⓒ Ⓓ
34 Ⓐ Ⓑ Ⓒ Ⓓ
35 Ⓐ Ⓑ Ⓒ Ⓓ
36 Ⓐ Ⓑ Ⓒ Ⓓ
37 Ⓐ Ⓑ Ⓒ Ⓓ
38 Ⓐ Ⓑ Ⓒ Ⓓ
39 Ⓐ Ⓑ Ⓒ Ⓓ
40 Ⓐ Ⓑ Ⓒ Ⓓ
41 Ⓐ Ⓑ Ⓒ Ⓓ
42 Ⓐ Ⓑ Ⓒ Ⓓ
43 Ⓐ Ⓑ Ⓒ Ⓓ
44 Ⓐ Ⓑ Ⓒ Ⓓ
45 Ⓐ Ⓑ Ⓒ Ⓓ
46 Ⓐ Ⓑ Ⓒ Ⓓ
47 Ⓐ Ⓑ Ⓒ Ⓓ
48 Ⓐ Ⓑ Ⓒ Ⓓ
49 Ⓐ Ⓑ Ⓒ Ⓓ
50 Ⓐ Ⓑ Ⓒ Ⓓ
51 Ⓐ Ⓑ Ⓒ Ⓓ
52 Ⓐ Ⓑ Ⓒ Ⓓ
53 Ⓐ Ⓑ Ⓒ Ⓓ
54 Ⓐ Ⓑ Ⓒ Ⓓ
55 Ⓐ Ⓑ Ⓒ Ⓓ
56 Ⓐ Ⓑ Ⓒ Ⓓ
57 Ⓐ Ⓑ Ⓒ Ⓓ

MATHEMATICS

1 Ⓐ Ⓑ Ⓒ Ⓓ
2 Ⓐ Ⓑ Ⓒ Ⓓ
3 Ⓐ Ⓑ Ⓒ Ⓓ
4 Ⓐ Ⓑ Ⓒ Ⓓ
5 Ⓐ Ⓑ Ⓒ Ⓓ
6 Ⓐ Ⓑ Ⓒ Ⓓ
7 Ⓐ Ⓑ Ⓒ Ⓓ
8 Ⓐ Ⓑ Ⓒ Ⓓ
9 Ⓐ Ⓑ Ⓒ Ⓓ
10 Ⓐ Ⓑ Ⓒ Ⓓ
11 Ⓐ Ⓑ Ⓒ Ⓓ
12 Ⓐ Ⓑ Ⓒ Ⓓ
13 Ⓐ Ⓑ Ⓒ Ⓓ
14 Ⓐ Ⓑ Ⓒ Ⓓ
15 Ⓐ Ⓑ Ⓒ Ⓓ
16 Ⓐ Ⓑ Ⓒ Ⓓ
17 Ⓐ Ⓑ Ⓒ Ⓓ
18 Ⓐ Ⓑ Ⓒ Ⓓ
19 Ⓐ Ⓑ Ⓒ Ⓓ
20 Ⓐ Ⓑ Ⓒ Ⓓ
21 Ⓐ Ⓑ Ⓒ Ⓓ
22 Ⓐ Ⓑ Ⓒ Ⓓ
23 Ⓐ Ⓑ Ⓒ Ⓓ
24 Ⓐ Ⓑ Ⓒ Ⓓ
25 Ⓐ Ⓑ Ⓒ Ⓓ
26 Ⓐ Ⓑ Ⓒ Ⓓ

27 Ⓐ Ⓑ Ⓒ Ⓓ
28 Ⓐ Ⓑ Ⓒ Ⓓ
29 Ⓐ Ⓑ Ⓒ Ⓓ
30 Ⓐ Ⓑ Ⓒ Ⓓ
31 Ⓐ Ⓑ Ⓒ Ⓓ
32 Ⓐ Ⓑ Ⓒ Ⓓ
33 Ⓐ Ⓑ Ⓒ Ⓓ
34 Ⓐ Ⓑ Ⓒ Ⓓ
35 Ⓐ Ⓑ Ⓒ Ⓓ
36 Ⓐ Ⓑ Ⓒ Ⓓ
37 Ⓐ Ⓑ Ⓒ Ⓓ
38 Ⓐ Ⓑ Ⓒ Ⓓ
39 Ⓐ Ⓑ Ⓒ Ⓓ
40 Ⓐ Ⓑ Ⓒ Ⓓ
41 Ⓐ Ⓑ Ⓒ Ⓓ
42 Ⓐ Ⓑ Ⓒ Ⓓ
43 Ⓐ Ⓑ Ⓒ Ⓓ
44 Ⓐ Ⓑ Ⓒ Ⓓ
45 Ⓐ Ⓑ Ⓒ Ⓓ
46 Ⓐ Ⓑ Ⓒ Ⓓ
47 Ⓐ Ⓑ Ⓒ Ⓓ
48 Ⓐ Ⓑ Ⓒ Ⓓ
49 Ⓐ Ⓑ Ⓒ Ⓓ
50 Ⓐ Ⓑ Ⓒ Ⓓ
51 Ⓐ Ⓑ Ⓒ Ⓓ
52 Ⓐ Ⓑ Ⓒ Ⓓ

MATHEMATICS (GRID IN)

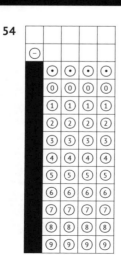
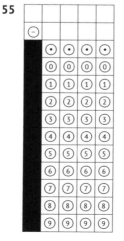
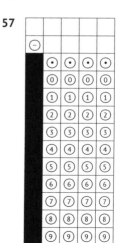

53   54   55   56   57

ARGO
BROTHERS
www.argobrothers.com

DIRECTIONS: For questions 1 to 5, you will be asked to recognize and correct errors in sentences or short paragraphs.

1. Read this sentence.

> The Space Race which began in 1955, was a memorable part of the Cold War between the United States and the Soviet Union.

Which edit should be made to correct this sentence?

A. Insert a **comma** after **Race**
B. Insert a **comma** after **part**
C. Insert a **comma** after **War**
D. Insert a **comma** after **States**

2. Read this sentence.

> From 1952 to 1988, the United States and Soviet Union engaged in a legendary Olympic rivalry, during which the Soviets capture over a thousand medals, while the Americans won 774.

Which edit should be made to correct the sentence?

A. Change **engaged** to **engage**
B. Change **which** to **that**
C. Change **capture** to **captured**
D. Change **won** to **win**

3. Read this paragraph.

> (1) It's easy to see that the magnificent pets in a dog show are cute, but it's much harder to understand how they are actually judged. (2) Each animal in a dog show is rated based on its adherence to breed standards, which are established guidelines for how dogs of a particular type are supposed to look and behave. (3) First, judges determine which dog at the show is the finest example of each breed. (4) Then, those dogs compete in groupings of similar dogs, including working dogs, sporting dogs, toy dogs, and terriers. (5) Again, the goal is to be the dog that best represents its breed's ideals. (6) Finally, the winners of the group stages compete to see which of them is the best example of its breed in the show.

Which sentence is the least related to the main ideas of the paragraph and could be removed?

A. Sentence 1
B. Sentence 2
C. Sentence 3
D. Sentence 4

CONTINUE ON TO THE NEXT PAGE →

4. Read this paragraph.

(1) Walt Disney's name is synonymous with outstanding cartoons, but few people appreciate how many iconic characters Disney created himself. (2) His most iconic creation, Mickey Mouse, was born in 1928, alongside his love interest Minnie Mouse. (3) Disney created Pluto and Goofy in 1930 and 1932, respectively. (4) Appearing in over 150 cartoons between 1934 and 1959, Mickey's grouchy pal Donald Duck was introduced in 1934. (5) In addition to this core of favorites, Disney created a robust supporting cast that made his cartoons feel as though they occurred in a rich, fully inhabited world.

Which sentence needs to be revised to correct a dangling participle?

A. Sentence 2
B. Sentence 3
C. Sentence 4
D. Sentence 5

5. Read this sentence.

After the assassination of Abraham Lincoln, the civil war continued for almost two months before the last Confederate forces surrendered in Oklahoma, ending the war.

Which edit should be made to correct the sentence?

A. Change **civil war** to **Civil War**
B. Change **Confederate** to **confederate**
C. Change **forces** to **Forces**
D. Change **ending the war** to **ending the War**

CONTINUE ON TO THE NEXT PAGE ➔

DIRECTIONS: Read the passage below to answer questions 6 to 13. The questions will focus on improving the writing quality of the passage to follow the conventions of standard written English.

Salmonella

(1) Salmonella is a rod-shaped bacterium that can cause the illness commonly known as "food poisoning" in humans. (2) According to the Centers for Disease Control and Prevention (CDC), Salmonella sickens more than a million Americans every year and causes as many as 380 deaths. (3) People infected with Salmonella typically experience abdominal pain, fever, and diarrhea. (4) Most healthy adults can fight off the infection in less than a week, but Salmonella can be deadly for infants, senior citizens, and people with compromised immune systems.

(5) Salmonella infections usually come from consuming food infected with the bacteria. (6) Meat (especially poultry) and eggs are the most common sources of Salmonella infections in the United States. (7) It can be difficult for chicken farmers to ensure their products are completely free of Salmonella because the bacteria does not make chickens sick. (8) When infected hens lay eggs, they pass along one or two bacteria into the yolk, where they can reproduce quickly under the right conditions.

(9) The CDC provides a variety of strategies for preventing Salmonella infection. (10) Refrigerating foods that may contain Salmonella prevents the bacteria from reproducing, lowering the chance that a sickening load of the bacteria will form. (11) All meat, poultry, and eggs should be cooked fully to an internal temperature of at least 160° F. (12) This guarantees that any existing bacteria will be killed before the food is eaten. (13) Finally, anybody handling or processing food should wash their hands and any surfaces touched by food frequently to prevent cross-contamination.

6. In sentence 2, why is the parenthetical note "(CDC)" necessary?

   A. When discussing a government agency, it is required to give both its formal name and initials.

   B. It explains the meaning of an acronym that is used later in the passage.

   C. It establishes a formal tone for the passage.

   D. It's not necessary. It can be removed.

CONTINUE ON TO THE NEXT PAGE →

7. What information could be added to sentence 4 to best improve clarity?

   A. What percentage of adults comprises "Most healthy adults..."
   B. An explanation of how the immune system fights Salmonella
   C. Age limits defining the terms "infant" and "senior citizen"
   D. An example of a situation in which somebody might have a compromised immune system

8. How could sentence 6 be rewritten to eliminate the use of parentheses?

   A. Meat, especially poultry, and eggs are the most common sources...
   B. Meat especially poultry and eggs are the most common sources...
   C. Meat – especially poultry – and eggs are the most common sources...
   D. A or C

9. What kind of major error can be found in sentence 7?

   A. Subject-verb agreement
   B. Spelling
   C. Capitalization
   D. Punctuation

10. Which change would best clarify the repeated use of the pronoun "they" in sentence 8?

    A. When infected hens lay eggs, those hens pass along one or two bacteria into the yolk, where they can reproduce quickly under the right conditions.
    B. When infected hens lay eggs, they pass along one or two bacteria into the yolk, where the eggs can reproduce quickly under the right conditions.
    C. When infected hens lay eggs, they pass along one or two bacteria into the yolk, where Salmonella can reproduce quickly under the right conditions.
    D. When infected hens lay eggs, Salmonella passes along one or two bacteria into the yolk, where they can reproduce quickly under the right conditions.

11. Which transition word would make the most sense at the beginning of sentence 11?

    A. However
    B. Additionally
    C. Subsequently
    D. Unfortunately

12. In sentence 11, how many commas should be used in the list?

    A. One
    B. Two
    C. Three
    D. Either two or three is correct

CONTINUE ON TO THE NEXT PAGE ➡

13. What kind of sentence would best follow sentence 13?

    A. An explanation of the concept of cross-contamination
    B. A summary of the entire passage
    C. An explanation of how to measure food temperatures
    D. Contact information for the CDC

CONTINUE ON TO THE NEXT PAGE →

ENGLISH LANGUAGE ARTS
Practice Test 1

DIRECTIONS: Read the passage below to answer questions 14 to 20. The questions will focus on improving the writing quality of the passage to follow the conventions of standard written English.

The Human Heart

(1) The heart is the most important organ inside the human body. (2) Located in the chest between vertebrae T5 and T8, the English physician William Harvey first explained the role of the heart in the circulatory system in 1628. (3) Harvey correctly identified that the heart was a pump whose primary purpose was to distribute blood throughout the body. (4) Harvey's work fundamentally changed the understanding of the human body and created the foundation of modern cardiology, the study of the heart.

(5) The human heart is divided into four chambers named the left atrium, right atrium, left ventricle, and right ventricle. (6) Fish, however, have a two-chambered heart. (7) The chambers of the heart are separated by one-way valves that ensure blood flows through the heart in the correct manner. (8) Oxygen-poor blood from the body flows into the right atrium, where it is pumped into the right ventricle. (9) The right ventricle sends that blood to the lungs, where it is enriched with oxygen. (10) That oxygen-rich blood reenters the heart through the left atrium and travels into the left ventricle, which distributes the blood to the rest of the body.

(11) There are many medical conditions which can affect the human heart. (12) The valves between chambers can become weak, leaky, or overly tight over time, decreasing heart function and causing weakness in patients. (13) Buildup of fatty deposits in the vessels of the heart, known as coronary artery disease, can also decrease the efficiency of the heart. (14) Left untreated, this can lead to a myocardial infarction, better known as a "heart attack." (15) During a heart attack, blood flow to one or more chambers of the heart is cut off, interrupting the normal function of the body and potentially causing irreversible damage or even death.

---

14. Which phrase should be removed from sentence 2 to clarify and strengthen it?

    A. Located in the chest between vertebrae T5 and T8...

    B. ...the English physician...

    C. ...in the circulatory system...

    D. ...in 1628.

CONTINUE ON TO THE NEXT PAGE →

15. If the author of this passage wanted to remove the word "named" from sentence 5, which of the following revisions would be correct?

A. The human heart is divided into four chambers, the left atrium, right atrium, left ventricle, and right ventricle.

B. The human heart is divided into four chambers; the left atrium, right atrium, left ventricle, and right ventricle.

C. The human heart is divided into four chambers: the left atrium, right atrium, left ventricle, and right ventricle.

D. The human heart is divided into four chambers (the left atrium, right atrium, left ventricle, and right ventricle).

16. Which sentence would best fit between sentence 5 and sentence 6?

A. This structure is identical for most other animals, including all mammals and birds.

B. Each of these chambers plays a unique role in the function of the heart.

C. Who'd have thought the heart was so complex?

D. Without all four chambers, the heart could not pump properly.

17. How could the author rewrite sentence 7 to avoid the use of passive voice?

A. The chambers of the heart are separated by one-way valves, ensuring blood flows through the heart in the correct manner.

B. The chambers of the heart get separated by one-way valves to ensure blood flows through the heart correctly.

C. To ensure the correct flow of blood, the chambers of the heart are separated by one-way valves.

D. One-way valves separate the chambers of the heart, ensuring blood flows through the heart in the correct manner.

18. Which edit is needed to correct sentence 11?

A. Change **are** to **is**

B. Change **which** to **that**

C. Change **affect** to **effect**

D. Change **the** to **a**

CONTINUE ON TO THE NEXT PAGE →

19. What is the best way to combine sentences 13 and 14 to clarify the relationship between ideas?

A. Buildup of fatty deposits in the vessels of the heart, known as coronary artery disease, can also decrease the efficiency of the heart, and left untreated, this can lead to a myocardial infarction, better known as a "heart attack."

B. When fatty deposits build up in the vessels of the heart, this is known as coronary artery disease, and it can cause a myocardial infarction, which is also known as a "heart attack."

C. Coronary artery disease, a buildup of fatty deposits in the vessels of the heart, can lead to a myocardial infarction, better known as a "heart attack."

D. A myocardial infarction, also known as a "heart attack" can occur as the result of coronary artery disease, a buildup of fatty deposits in the vessels of the heart.

20. Which of the following sentences would provide the best conclusion following sentence 15?

A. Since heart problems are often transferred through genes, doctors encourage anybody with a family history of cardiac issues to work closely with their physician to monitor their health.

B. According to the Centers for Disease Control and Prevention, more than 700,000 Americans have a heart attack each year.

C. Most heart attacks can be prevented through diet, exercise, and proper medication, however.

D. These and other cardiac conditions prove that, while the heart is crucial, it is not perfect.

CONTINUE ON TO THE NEXT PAGE →

DIRECTIONS: Analyze the passages below, and answer the commensurate questions. Only use information provided within the passage for your answers. There is only one answer for each question.

The opinion that absolute power is essential to the state is very prevalent among statesmen and publicists. They disagree, however, as to who should be invested with this absolute power, the executive or the people; but they agree in the 5 opinion that it should be lodged somewhere.

Without absolute power, they say, there is no peace, no unity in the state, no authority which is either final or supreme. Absolute power and sovereignty are sometimes called synonymous. There are 10 whole families of nations, with which a high respect for absolute power seems to be a natural tendency, which submit to it willingly and without reserve. It is not simply those today with less power that have submitted to an absolute ruler, 15 but rather members of nations of all time. The democratic Greeks believed that the authority of the people was absolute, just as the Romans understood the Caesars to ultimately have absolute power. 20

Individuals of great energy and superior intellect, when at the head of the government, are most apt to be provoked to resistance by any limit imposed to their universal authority, and seek to justify their action whenever they overstep the 25 limit imposed, by an appeal to the necessity of absolute power. The history of modern European states is filled with examples of rulers trying to claim absolute power, which provoked a great

30 many conflicts. And it is not always bad men who incline toward absolutism.

What is the meaning of absolute power? Absolute, in the full sense of the word, means freedom from all limitation. Really, there is nothing absolute but 35 what is without beginning and end; a beginning and an end are limitations. The truly absolute, therefore, can be predicated only of a being unlimited and infinite, that is, only of God. Hence, absolute power, in the real sense of the word, can 40 be conceived only as divine omnipotence.

21. What is the main idea of this passage?

    A. The nature of absolute power in states.
    B. To illustrate that even those who mean well will abuse power
    C. To show that there can never be a fair state.
    D. To prove that only democratic nations, in which absolute power is lodged in the people, are legitimate.

CONTINUE ON TO THE NEXT PAGE →

22. The author compares the absolute power desired by historical political leaders to what?

    A. The Greek power
    B. The power of European leaders
    C. An omnipotent deity
    D. The power of a parent over his/her child .

23. What does the author imply about those who try to seize absolute power?

    A. They are evil.
    B. They always lead to war.
    C. They believe themselves as great as the gods.
    D. They do not always have bad intentions.

24. What is the example, provided by the author, of absolute power lodged in an executive?

    A. The Greeks.
    B. Democratic Italy.
    C. Caesar
    D. The president of a contemporary nation.

25. Based on the passage, what might a leader attempting to gain absolute power argue so as to gain power?

    A. The ruler may argue that without absolute power he/she cannot obtain wealth.
    B. The ruler may argue that without absolute power he/she cannot invade neighboring territories.
    C. The ruler may argue that without absolute power he/she cannot prevent a civil war.
    D. The ruler may argue that without absolute power he/she cannot rule effectively.

26. What word does the author claim to be similar to absolute power?

    A. Constitutional power
    B. Sovereignty
    C. Executive power
    D. People power

CONTINUE ON TO THE NEXT PAGE →

The bar is a term applied collectively to all who give professional assistance to others in legal controversies, and are licensed by some competent authority to do so. The term in this sense is variously ascribed to the fact that the 5 space occupied by advocates in a court of justice is separated by a rail or bar from that which is appropriated to spectators.

As soon as a people emerge from barbarism, a body of people who make it their business to expound 10 the law and assist those who may need assistance in legal matters is always observed to make its appearance. As one of the requisites of civilization and legal order, the state confers upon its members special and peculiar privileges 15 by law and, at the same time, places them under regulations more or less strict for the protection of the public and of those who may place their interests in their care. In the earliest accounts we have of judicial investigations, the litigants are 20 brought into court in person and are permitted to give their own account of the controversy, and the judges, after inquiring further, proceed to give judgment. This places the ignorant and simple at the mercy of the cunning, crafty and designing, 25 and it is easily made the means of perverting justice and clothing wrong with the forms of law.

In the famous description of the shield wrought by Hephæstus for Achilles, the picture 30 of a judicial trial is given, and we perceive, immediately, that the most persuasive voice is expected to succeed, whatever may be the merits, unless perhaps the clamor of partisans, who are active and noisy about the court, shall 35 sway the action of the judges in the other direction.

That this would be so is by no means unlikely in any case in which popular sympathy is aroused or popular prejudice strongly excited, or even where 40 money or family influence was able to produce the appearance of strong popular feeling. In Athens, there seems to have been no distinct class of men who made advocacy their business, and causes were expected to be managed by someone 45 interested therein.

However, friends sometimes appeared to support the cause of those who lacked the ability or the eloquence to speak on their own behalf, and sometimes a public prosecutor was appointed for 50 a particular case, as Pericles was called upon by the people to prosecute Cimon, when the latter was accused of having been bribed to abandon the invasion of Macedon.

27. What is the main idea of this passage?

A. To discuss the historical origin and necessity of legal representation.
B. To discuss the origin of the beer bar.
C. To discuss the Greek origins of legal representation.
D. To argue for a buffering of the legal apparatus.

CONTINUE ON TO THE NEXT PAGE ➡

28. What is the origin of the term"bar?"

   A. The place people would go following a case.
   B. The gavel used to signal an end to a case.
   C. The tool used to adjudicate punishment to defendents.
   D. The railing separating those involved in the case from the public.

29. A member of the bar is both assigned special legal rights and _____ ?

   A. Responsibilities
   B. Payments
   C. Must be older than sixteen years of age.
   D. All of the above

30. What is Hephæstus shielding Achilles from?

   A. Popular opinion
   B. Arrows
   C. Trojans
   D. The plaintiff

31. What does the author imply about Pericles?

   A. He was a bully.
   B. He was ahead of his time.
   C. He was a god.
   D. He was very good at arguing his legal case.

32. Under what conditions would an Athenian call upon a friend for legal support?

   A. When their friend was a lawyer.
   B. When their friend was more persuasive than they were.
   C. When their friend was Pericles.
   D. When their friend could bribe the judges.

CONTINUE ON TO THE NEXT PAGE ➡

The congress of the revolution and the confederacy was peripatetic and, at various times in its history, held meetings at Philadelphia, Baltimore, Lancaster, York, Princeton, Annapolis, Trenton and New York. On June 21, 1783, a [5] handful of insubordinate and unpaid militia marched into Philadelphia, where congress was sitting and, unchecked by any efforts of the state or city authorities to keep the peace, broke up the session of congress by jeering the [10] members and pointing muskets at the windows. This, among other incidents, gave an impulse to the desire to obtain a permanent home for the national Legislature.

On October 7, 1783, congress resolved that [15] a building for its use should be erected at some place near the falls of the Delaware. This was soon after modified, in deference to sectional jealousy, by requiring the erection of a suitable building near the falls of the Potomac, so that the [20] meetings of congress might alternate between the two places. After long and warm debate, congress returned to its first resolution, and decided that there should be but one capital, and commissioners were appointed to lay out a federal town near the [25] falls of the Delaware.

December 23, 1784, it was resolved to meet regularly in New York city until the new town was completed. But, while money was wanting for more pressing demands, congress was unable to [30] go any further than the plan. The commissioners made their report, but no action was taken upon it.

The successful establishment of the Constitution, with the prospect of a federal government whose wealth and resources would surpass any previous [35] experience in America, revived the notion of a federal town. Objection was made to New York city as a permanent capital by many of the delegates from agricultural districts, who considered a [40] commercial metropolis very ineligible because of the direct influence which the moneyed interest might exert on congress; and objections were also made to Philadelphia by many of the southern members, who were affronted by the assiduity [45] of the Quakers in preparing and presenting to congress propositions for the abolition of slavery.

When the new congress also came to the conclusion to fix the location of the federal town in the north, placing it this time on the banks of [50] the Susquehanna, the decision roused intense anger among the southern delegates, and Madison declared that if this action had been foreseen, his state might never have entered the Union. As a compromise, it seemed probable that congress [55] would drift back again to the plan of two capitals and of alternate meetings north and south, an arrangement excellently adapted for preserving the two sections in their separate integrity, and for facilitating their ultimate separation.

33. What is this passage mostly about?

A. Why the Capital was in New York City.
B. Why there were arguments over the location of the nation's capital.
C. How special interests threatening the federal government was a concern at the nation's founding.
D. The history of the U.S. Capital prior to its locationing in Washington, D.C.

CONTINUE ON TO THE NEXT PAGE ➡

34. Which of the locations was not listed as a potential location for the Capital?

   A. Falls of the Delaware
   B. New York City
   C. Boston
   D. Philadelphia

35. New York City was rejected most fiercely as the location of the Capital by what group?

   A. Confederates
   B. Yankees
   C. Agriculturists
   D. Bankers

36. At the end of the passage, how many capitals does the author suggest were likely be built?

   A. One
   B. Two
   C. Three
   D. Four

37. What was the main reason noted by the author for why southerners rejected Philadelphia as the location of the Capital?

   A. It was in the north.
   B. It was a center of commerce .
   C. It was not owned by the United States of America.
   D. The abolitionist beliefs held by Quakers.

38. What does the author imply about the relationship between the north and south at the time directly following the American Revolution?

   A. The north and south were strong allies.
   B. Southern leaders did not trust Northern leaders.
   C. People did not consider a difference between the north and south.
   D. There were no ideological differences between the leading figures in the north and south.

CONTINUE ON TO THE NEXT PAGE →

The division of employments is a natural consequence of the life of man in society. It is, moreover, an element of productive power and of intellectual development. In the infancy of society, each individual, each family, manufactures, 5 with difficulty and in an imperfect manner, the objects it needs; the wisest, the old man of the tribe, preserves in his head the treasure, as yet very meagre, of acquired knowledge, which he endeavors to transmit by word of mouth to those 10 who are to survive him. But as tribes grow larger and improve, they come to sanction and maintain the right of the individual property of each man in the fruit of his labor; they come to understand the utility of exchanges freely consented to; and 15 henceforth, each man can devote himself to the special occupation for which he feels himself peculiarly fitted.

He achieves greater results in the branch of labor to which he thus devotes himself, and produces 20 more than is personally necessary to him; he lacks, on the other hand, everything that his individual labor is unable to supply, and exchange provides him with the means of establishing an equilibrium between what he produces himself and what he 25 wants but cannot produce; he gives his surplus in return for what he requires, and thus barters the services which he renders for those which he himself has occasion for.

When nations become greater and more 30 developed, the division of labor becomes more marked. Certain individuals now devote themselves to hunting, to fishing, to the cultivation of the soil; others to manufactures; others there are again who devote themselves 35 exclusively to the culture of the mind: these latter discover the laws of nature which God

has placed at the service of man, whom he has charged to discover them and turn them to 40 useful account. Thus they effectively help in the production of the wealth, upon the aggregate of which society subsists.

39. What is the main idea of this passage?

    A. To detail the many professions available to humans.

    B. To give a historical background of today's industrialized society

    C. To introduce the idea of a division of labor, and discuss its historical origins

    D. To justify the professions of those who do not work with their hands.

40. Why does the author imply it is more productive to focus on an individual trade?

    A. People will naturally trend towards professions they are most apt to perform.

    B. As people perform an individual skill more, they will continue to perfect that skill.

    C. When producing more of a single item, you can create techniques permitting one to scale the operation successfullsy.

    D. Less time is wasted changing actions when a worker continues to perform one task.

CONTINUE ON TO THE NEXT PAGE →

41. What is an example of the division of labor becoming "more marked" in modern society?

   A. A teacher who teaches the whole village from youth until adulthood.

   B. A political leader who knows all the laws and tales of the tribe by memory

   C. A neuroscientist studying the brains response to pain.

   D. A parent who must know what a good diet is for his/her child, how to teach the child language, and how to ensure a good future for that child.

42. What would be an example of how a surplus of goods can be used to exchange for other goods?

   A. A hunter turning their hides into clothing.

   B. A chef cooking for someone else.

   C. A lottery ticket winner exchanging his/her ticket for cash.

   D. A blacksmith trading a horseshoe for a loaf of bread.

43. What is the "treasure" that the old man holds?

   A. Gold
   B. Silver
   C. Food
   D. Knowledge

44. Which profession would the author consider a worker creating the "culture of the mind?"

   A. Hunter
   B. Theologist
   C. Wall builder
   D. Farmer

CONTINUE ON TO THE NEXT PAGE ➡

The large standing army was concentrated on the frontier and defended the interior of the empire against foreign invasions.

As far as was possible, the Roman imperial administration attempted to make the Roman armies as productive as possible. Some units operated brick factories, tile manufactories, lead and iron smelters, and many other enterprises. They were often allowed to remain headquartered in the same garrison town almost permanently and often drew their recruits from the local population. Someone who had joined the Roman army had decided upon his life's work, since the standard enlistment was for twenty-five years.

Since many recruits came from poor and isolated regions far from the centers of Roman life, the army literally taught them from the bottom up. They learned to dress properly, to speak Latin, to practice personal hygiene, as well as learning at least one, and perhaps more than one, trade. Along with this, however, it was even more important that they learn of the greatness of Rome and of the majesty of its institutions. Their year was marked off by great rituals in which they honored Roma, a goddess who was the exemplification of Rome, and made offerings for the peace of the imperial family, its security, the loyalty that bound the army to the service of the emperor, and so on.

Indeed, in times when Rome itself fell in disorder or when the imperial administration had fallen into the depths of corruption or ineffectiveness, the army's reverence for the ideal of Rome remained undiminished even though they might acclaim their general as emperor and march upon Rome to clear up the mess there. Consequently, they invested their spare time and effort in turning the

towns that sprang up along their fortresses into little Romes, or at least close to what the soldiers believed the essence of Rome to be. Stationed on the frontier, they were set to the task of creating the transportation and communication networks – roads, bridges, beacons, canals, ports, aqueducts – as well as numerous other public works throughout the empire.

45. What is the main idea of this passage?

  A. To inform readers of the many trades known by members of the Roman army
  B. To illustrate why the Roman army was so powerful
  C. To demonstrate the ways by which Rome generated loyalty amongst its population
  D. To illustrate the myriad ways that the Roman army supported both the infrastructure and idea of Rome

---

46. What was not a task noted in the passage as one performed by members of the Roman army?

  A. Creating bricks
  B. Creating canals
  C. Creating bridges
  D. Forging iron

CONTINUE ON TO THE NEXT PAGE →

47. What is implied about the standard recruit to the Roman army?

    A. They did not grow up knowing Latin.
    B. They were trained in combat from an early age.
    C. They always knew that they wanted to be members of the Roman army.
    D. They were skilled in a trade before joining the army.

48. In what way was the Roman army's reverence for the idea of Rome beneficial to the continuation of the Empire?

    A. It allowed for the center of power – the army – to maintain integrity in the face of nefarious political happenings.
    B. It permitted the members of the army to fight ferociously.
    C. It spread the romance languages.
    D. The Roman emperor was often at one time a member of the army.

49. What was the name of the god to whom many Roman soldiers prayed?

    A. Athena, the goddess of wisdom
    B. Mars, the god of war
    C. Roma, the god of Rome
    D. Belona, goddess of war and conquest

50. Roman soldiers were located on the frontier to protect the homeland and ____.

    A. Spread the technology and ideas of Rome.
    B. To more readily invade neighboring territories.
    C. To keep the military, mostly comprising of non-Romans, out of the capital.
    D. To keep them near their homeland.

CONTINUE ON TO THE NEXT PAGE ➡

A house should be built with the summer in view. In winter, one can live anywhere, but a poor dwelling in summer is unbearable. Deep water does not give a cool sensation. Far cooler is a shallow running stream. A room with sliding ⁵ doors is lighter than one with doors on hinges. When the ceiling is high, the room is cold in winter and difficult to light. As for construction, people agree in admiring a place with plenty of spare room as being pleasing to the eye and, at ¹⁰ the same time, useful for all sorts of purposes.

There is a charm about a neat and proper dwelling house, although this world, it is true, is but a temporary abode. Even the moonshine, when it strikes into the house where a good man lives in ¹⁵ peaceful ease, seems to gain in friendly brilliancy. The man is to be envied who lives in a house, not of the modern, garish kind, but set among venerable trees, with a garden where plants grow wild and yet seem to have been disposed with ²⁰ care, verandas and fences tastefully arranged, and all its furnishings simple but antique.

A house which multitudes of workmen have devoted all their ingenuity to decorate, where rare and strange things from home and abroad are set ²⁵ out in array, and where even the trees and shrubs are trained unnaturally – such is an unpleasant sight, depressing to look at, to say nothing of spending one's days in there. Nor, gazing on it, can one but reflect how easily it might vanish in a ³⁰ moment of time.

The appearance of a house is in some sort an index to the character of its occupant.

Once in the month of September, I passed over the plain of Kurusu and sought out a certain village ³⁵ among the hills beyond, when, threading my way

far down a narrow moss-grown path, I came upon a lonely hut. There was never a sound to greet me, save the dripping of water from a pipe buried ⁴⁰ in fallen leaves, but I knew that someone lived there, for sprays of chrysanthemum and maple leaves bestrewed the shelf before the shrine, and "Ah!" thought I, "In such a place a man can spend his days." But as I stood and gazed in wonder, ⁴⁵ I perceived in the garden beyond a great orange tree, its branches weighted down with fruit. It was strongly closed in on all sides by a fence. This broke the spell, and I thought to myself, "If only that tree had not been there!"

51. What is this passage mainly about?

    A. The author's distaste for modern architecture.

    B. The author's belief that orange trees are a detriment to one's dwelling.

    C. What makes for a good house.

    D. The author's belief that open-space is necessary for a good house.

---

52. Home design should be structured based on one's experience in which season?

    A. Winter

    B. Summer

    C. Fall

    D. Spring

CONTINUE ON TO THE NEXT PAGE →

53. What is a listed reason for why people like open spaces in homes?

   A. It is a sign of wealth.
   B. The space can be used for a multitude of purposes.
   C. It can allow you to put up more decorations.
   D. People should not have open spaces in their home.

54. The author would most likely prefer to live in what type of habitat?

   A. Urban environment with many cultural activities.
   B. Suburban environment with a nice lawn.
   C. Rural environment with wild trees.
   D. Rural environment with a nice lawn.

55. What reason does the author provide as to why one should not fully manicure one's residency?

   A. It will remind them of the temporal nature of their existence.
   B. It will be too costly.
   C. It will not allow for new things to be put on display.
   D. It is too time consuming.

56. What would have made the house noted at the end of the passage more preferable to the author?

   A. More trees
   B. More space
   C. Better location
   D. The removal of the orange tree and fence.

57. When the author of the passage writes, "The appearance of a house is in some sort an index to the character of its occupant" (lines 32-33), what point is he or she making about people and their houses?

   A. Houses are important characters in the lives of their owners.
   B. Houses often reflect their owners' personalities.
   C. A good house is the most important part of a satisfying life.
   D. The most important aspect of a house is its appearance.

CONTINUE ON TO THE NEXT PAGE ➡

ARGO
BROTHERS
www.argobrothers.com

90 MINUTES • 57 QUESTIONS

Select the best answer from the choices given by carefully solving each problem. Bubble the letter of your answer on the answer sheet. Please refrain from making any stray marks on the answer sheet. If you need to erase an answer, please erase thoroughly.

Important Notes:

1. There are no formulas or definitions in the math section that will be provided.
2. Diagrams may or may not be drawn to scale. Do not make assumptions based on the diagram unless it is specifically stated in the diagram or question.
3. Diagrams are not in more than one plane, unless stated otherwise.
4. Graphs are drawn to scale, therefore, you can assume relationships according to the graph. If lines appear parallel, then you can assume the lines to be parallel. This is also true for right angles and so forth.
5. Simplify fractions completely.

Practice Test 1 (Questions 1-57)

1. Convert $\frac{7}{20}$ to decimal form.

    A. 0.0035
    B. 0.035
    C. 0.35
    D. 3.50

2. The value of 500,000 + 400 + 5 is

    A. 500,450
    B. 540,005
    C. 540,500
    D. 500,405

3. If $x = 4$ and $y = 3$, what is $(x + y)^2$?

    A. 25
    B. 32
    C. 7
    D. 49

4. $(\sqrt{144})(\sqrt{16}) =$

    A. 16
    B. 48
    C. 12
    D. 32

CONTINUE ON TO THE NEXT PAGE →

Explanations to each problem on:
Youtube.com/ArgoBrothers

MATHEMATICS
TEST 1

ARGO
BROTHERS
www.argobrothers.com

5.   1 Knot = 3 Vines
      2 Shings = 4 Knots

How many Shings are in 9 Vines?

A. $\frac{4}{5}$

B. $\frac{2}{3}$

C. $\frac{5}{4}$

D. $\frac{3}{2}$

6. What number is halfway between $2 \cdot (\frac{3}{6})$ and 4 ?

A. 2
B. 2.5
C. 3
D. 1.5

7.

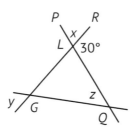

In the figure shown above LGQ is a triangle.
What is z in terms of y?

A. $30 - y$
B. $y + 150$
C. $2y + 30$
D. $2y - 30$

8. $-2 + 5(-18 \div 3 + 9) - 13 =$

A. 3
B. -4
C. 13
D. 0

9. The area of a square is equal to the area of a circle, whose diameter is 10. What is the length of a side of the square?

A. $\pi r \sqrt{5}$
B. $25\pi r$
C. $5\sqrt{\pi}$
D. $25\sqrt{\pi r}$

10. $4a(3b - 6)$

A. $7ab - 2a$
B. $12ab - 6$
C. $12b - 24$
D. $12ab - 24a$

11. $\frac{(-39)^2}{13^3} =$

A. -3
B. $\frac{-1}{13}$
C. $\frac{9}{13}$
D. 3

CONTINUE ON TO THE NEXT PAGE ➡

Explanations to each problem on:
Youtube.com/ArgoBrothers

MATHEMATICS
TEST 1

ARGO
BROTHERS
www.argobrothers.com

12. In a scaled diagram, 1 inch represents 20 feet. How many square inches on the diagram represent 1 square foot?

   A. 0.0025
   B. 0.04
   C. .4
   D. 400

13. What is the greatest common factor of 2,240 and 3,360?

   A. 105
   B. 280
   C. 1,120
   D. 2,240

14. If 50% of $2y$ is 12, what is y^2 ?

   A. 36
   B. 6
   C. 16
   D. 144

15.

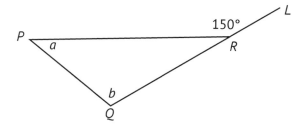

In the figure above ∢PRL is 150°. What is $\dfrac{a^2 - b^2}{(a - b)}$?

   A. 30°
   B. 120°
   C. 150°
   D. 160°

16. If $y = \dfrac{3}{4}$ and $xy^2 = \dfrac{9}{16}$, what is $(x - 4)$?

   A. −3
   B. $\dfrac{-13}{4}$
   C. $\dfrac{-9}{16}$
   D. −4

CONTINUE ON TO THE NEXT PAGE ➡

17. If P is an odd integer, which of the following must be an even number?

A. $\dfrac{P^2 - (\frac{P}{4})}{(a - b)}$

B. $\dfrac{P - 2P^2}{2P + 5}$

C. P^2

D. $\dfrac{2P^2 - 2P^3}{2P}$

---

18. If the diameter of a circle is P, and $\dfrac{P^2}{4} = 2$ what is the area of the circle?

A. 4π
B. 8π
C. $2\pi\sqrt{2}$
D. 2π

---

19. If a regular polygon has $(N - 10)$ sides, where, $N = (\frac{40}{10})^2$, what is the measure of one of its angles?

A. 120°
B. 160°
C. 240°
D. 720°

20.

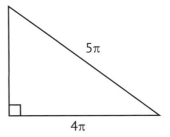

If the perimeter of the triangle shown above is the circumference of a circle, then what is the radius of the circle?

A. 9π
B. 4
C. 6
D. 6π

---

21. If $\overset{...}{x} = \dfrac{7}{x}$, what is the value of $\overset{...}{14}$ $(\overset{...}{14})$

A. 0.25
B. 0.50
C. 7
D. 14

---

22. What is the least common multiple of 4, 16, 25 and 30?

A. 160
B. 240
C. 480
D. 1200

CONTINUE ON TO THE NEXT PAGE ➡

Explanations to each problem on:
Youtube.com/ArgoBrothers

MATHEMATICS
TEST 1

ARGO
BROTHERS
www.argobrothers.com

23. How many positive integers are between $\frac{-7}{3}$ and $\frac{5}{2}$?

   A. 0
   B. 1
   C. 2
   D. 3

24. The perimeter of a rectangle is 80 inches. If the width is 18 inches, what is the area of the rectangle?

   A. 22 sq. in
   B. 324 sq. in
   C. 396 sq. in
   D. 6,400 sq. in

25. $7|-x-3| = b$. If $x = -3$, what is b?

   A. 24
   B. 40
   C. 42
   D. 0

26. $1 + 2 + 3 + 4 + 5 + ... + 100 =$

   A. 1010
   B. 5050
   C. 5000
   D. 1000

27. After a 10% increase, a population was 55. What was the population before the increase?

   A. 44
   B. 50
   C. 40
   D. 45

28. The length of a rectangular solid is 10. The width, w and the height, h follow the relationship, $w^3h^3 = 27$. What is the volume of the rectangular solid?

   A. 270
   B. 30
   C. 90
   D. 60

29.

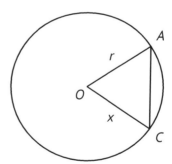

Figure not drawn to scale.

$\overline{AC}$ has a length of 10 and r, the radius, is 7. What is x?

   A. 5
   B. 7
   C. $7\sqrt{2}$
   D. 10

CONTINUE ON TO THE NEXT PAGE →

Explanations to each problem on:
Youtube.com/ArgoBrothers

MATHEMATICS
TEST 1

ARGO
BROTHERS

www.argobrothers.com

30.

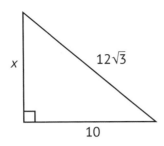

Figure not drawn to scale.

Find the length of x?

A. $\sqrt{83}$
B. $2\sqrt{83}$
C. $2\sqrt{332}$
D. 332

---

31. If $A = 3r^2h^2$, and (rh) increases by 100%, then the new A is how many times greater than the old A?

A. 2
B. 3
C. 4
D. 12

---

32. If $x^a = \sqrt[q]{x^p}$, what is $\dfrac{p^2}{q^2}$?

A. $\sqrt{a}$
B. $a^{1/3}$
C. a^2
D. a

---

33. Set $A = \{1, 2, 3, a\}$
Set $B = \{2, 4, 5, a^2, b\}$
What is $A \cap B$?

A. $\{2, a^2, b\}$
B. $\{2, \dfrac{b}{a}\}$
C. $\{2\}$
D. $\{2, \dfrac{a}{b}\}$

---

34. $2\sqrt{75} - (\sqrt{25})(\sqrt{3})$

A. $5\sqrt{3}$
B. $10\sqrt{3}$
C. $2\sqrt{3}$
D. 5

---

35. Express $\dfrac{0.0345}{10}$ in scientific notation.

A. 3.45×10^{-2}
B. $.0345 \times 10^{-2}$
C. 3.45×10^{-3}
D. 0.345×10^{-3}

---

36. ☆ × ☆ = $3x$, if x is even and negative **OR**
☆ × ☆ = $4x$, if x is odd.
Following the rule above, what is the value of ☆ − 23 ☆ ?

A. 92
B. −92
C. 529
D. −529

CONTINUE ON TO THE NEXT PAGE ➡

Explanations to each problem on:
Youtube.com/ArgoBrothers

MATHEMATICS
TEST 1

ARGO
BROTHERS
www.argobrothers.com

37. $y = x^3$

The only possible values of x are those in the set $\{\frac{-1}{3}, \frac{1}{2}, \frac{1}{3}\}$. What is the maximum value of y?

A. $\frac{-1}{27}$

B. $\frac{1}{4}$

C. $\frac{1}{8}$

D. $\frac{1}{6}$

38. What is $\dfrac{x^3 y^2 z^4}{z^3 y^3}$ equal to

A. $\dfrac{x^3}{3}$

B. $x^3 y z^2$

C. $\dfrac{x^3 z}{y}$

D. $\dfrac{x^3 y}{z}$

39.

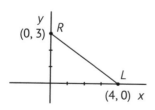

What is the length of $\overline{RL}$?

A. 6

B. 5

C. 4

D. 7

40. In a triangle, the sum of two angles equals the third. Find the measure of the third angle.

A. 45°

B. 60°

C. 90°

D. 30°

41. If Anthony and Bridget take turns watching T.V. every 4 hours and Anthony's third watch was at 10:00 P.M. and Bridget was the first to watch T.V., then when did Bridget begin her second watch?

A. 6:00 P.M.

B. 10:00 A.M.

C. 10:00 P.M.

D. 6:00 A.M.

42. There are a total of 9 bicycles and unicycles in a path. There are 13 wheels in total. If x is the number of bicycles, what is x^2?

A. 16

B. 12

C. 23

D. 13

CONTINUE ON TO THE NEXT PAGE →

43. A boy moves 4 miles south. Then he turns 90°
to the left. He moves forward 6 miles. He turns
90° to the left. He moves forward 4 miles. How
far is he now than from his starting point?

    A. 4 miles
    B. 3 miles
    C. 6 miles
    D. 5 miles

44.

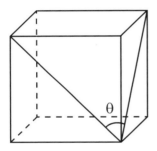

Note: The angle is between the two diagonal
lines of the cube.

In the figure above, what is the angle, θ?

    A. 45°
    B. 56°
    C. 60°
    D. 30°

45.

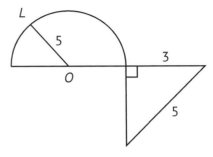

Figure not drawn to scale.

$\overline{OL}$ is the radius. What is the perimeter of the
figure above?

    A. $12 + 25\pi$
    B. $12 + 5\pi$
    C. $22 + 5\pi$
    D. $22 + 25\pi$

46. What is $0.\overline{53} - 0.\overline{36}$?

    A. $\dfrac{7}{50}$

    B. $\dfrac{7}{99}$

    C. $\dfrac{17}{99}$

    D. $\dfrac{7}{9}$

CONTINUE ON TO THE NEXT PAGE →

47. The sum of two positive numbers is 6 times their difference. What is the reciprocal of the ratio of the larger number to the smaller?

A. $\dfrac{5}{7}$

B. $\dfrac{7}{5}$

C. $\dfrac{5}{2}$

D. $\dfrac{2}{5}$

48. The mean weekly salary of 9 teachers in a school is \$1,000. If there are 9 teachers and 11 assistant principals and the mean weekly salary for assistant principals and teachers is \$1,275, what is the mean salary of the assistant principals?

A. \$1,100
B. \$1,500
C. \$1,137.50
D. \$1,300

49. Given $x_n = x_{n-1} + x_{n-2}$, what is $\dfrac{x_6}{x_5}$, knowing that $x_4 = 3$ and $x_3 = 2$?

A. $\dfrac{3}{2}$

B. $\dfrac{5}{8}$

C. $\dfrac{8}{5}$

D. $\dfrac{2}{3}$

50. $f(x) = \dfrac{1-x}{1-x}$, which of the following set is not a possible domain for the given function?

A. $\{2, 3, 5\}$
B. $\{1, 0, 6\}$
C. $\{\pi, 2.17, 10\}$
D. $\{2\pi, \pi^2, 0.65\}$

CONTINUE ON TO THE NEXT PAGE →

51. The new video game console was priced at $400 when it was released last year. This year, the price decreased by 15% during the holiday sale period. The game manufacturer recently announced that the same console will be re-released with new updates and expanded functionality. The retail price will be 25% greater than the previous sale price. When the game console is re-released, what will be the retail price?

   A. $360
   B. $425
   C. $380
   D. $415

52. Jimmy stands at the window of an apartment which is 40 feet above the ground. He releases a glider which flies a straight path to his friend, who catches the glider 10 feet above the ground in the neighboring building. If the buildings are 40 feet apart, what is the distance traveled by the glider?

   A. $10\sqrt{17}$ feet
   B. $10\sqrt{41}$ feet
   C. $40\sqrt{2}$ feet
   D. 50 feet

GRID IN

Directions: The following five questions are grid-in problems. On the answer sheet, please be sure to write your answer in the boxes at the top of the grid. Start on the left side of each grid.

53. After a 20% discount at the book store, a recipe book sells for $10. What was the original price of the book?

<table>
<tr><td></td><td></td><td></td><td></td></tr>
<tr><td>⊖</td><td></td><td></td><td></td></tr>
<tr><td></td><td>⊙</td><td>⊙</td><td>⊙</td><td>⊙</td></tr>
<tr><td></td><td>⓪</td><td>⓪</td><td>⓪</td><td>⓪</td></tr>
<tr><td></td><td>①</td><td>①</td><td>①</td><td>①</td></tr>
<tr><td></td><td>②</td><td>②</td><td>②</td><td>②</td></tr>
<tr><td></td><td>③</td><td>③</td><td>③</td><td>③</td></tr>
<tr><td></td><td>④</td><td>④</td><td>④</td><td>④</td></tr>
<tr><td></td><td>⑤</td><td>⑤</td><td>⑤</td><td>⑤</td></tr>
<tr><td></td><td>⑥</td><td>⑥</td><td>⑥</td><td>⑥</td></tr>
<tr><td></td><td>⑦</td><td>⑦</td><td>⑦</td><td>⑦</td></tr>
<tr><td></td><td>⑧</td><td>⑧</td><td>⑧</td><td>⑧</td></tr>
<tr><td></td><td>⑨</td><td>⑨</td><td>⑨</td><td>⑨</td></tr>
</table>

CONTINUE ON TO THE NEXT PAGE ➡

Explanations to each problem on:
Youtube.com/ArgoBrothers

MATHEMATICS
TEST 1

ARGO
BROTHERS
www.argobrothers.com

54. If the measure of angle P of triangle PQR is 3x, the measure of angle Q is 5x, and the measure of angle R is 4x, what is the value of x?

55. If Katie scored an 80, 83, and an 88 on her first three tests, what must she score on her fourth test if she wants an average of 85? Enter your answer in the text box below.

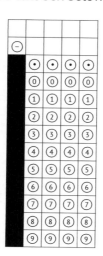

56. Suppose $2(a - 3) + 9 = 4a - 7$. What is the value of a?

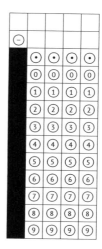

57. Solve the equation: $\dfrac{n + 4}{10} = \dfrac{n - 8}{2}$

THIS IS THE END OF THE TEST. IF THERE IS TIME REMAINING, YOU MAY CHECK YOUR ANSWERS TO PART 1 OR PART 2

SHSAT PRACTICE TEST 1
ANSWER KEY

Revising/Editing

1. **A**
2. **C**
3. **A**
4. **C**
5. **A**
6. **B**
7. **D**
8. **D**
9. **A**
10. **C**
11. **B**
12. **C**
13. **A**
14. **A**
15. **C**
16. **A**
17. **D**
18. **B**
19. **C**
20. **D**

Reading Comprehension

21. **A**
22. **C**
23. **D**
24. **C**
25. **D**
26. **B**
27. **A**
28. **D**
29. **A**
30. **A**
31. **D**
32. **B**
33. **C**
34. **C**
35. **C**
36. **B**
37. **D**
38. **B**
39. **C**
40. **A**

41. **C**
42. **D**
43. **D**
44. **B**
45. **D**
46. **D**
47. **A**
48. **A**
49. **C**
50. **A**
51. **C**
52. **B**
53. **B**
54. **C**
55. **A**
56. **D**
57. **B**

Math

1. **C**
2. **D**
3. **D**
4. **B**
5. **D**
6. **B**
7. **A**
8. **D**
9. **C**
10. **D**
11. **C**
12. **A**

13. **C**
14. **D**
15. **C**
16. **A**
17. **D**
18. **D**
19. **A**
20. **C**
21. **A**
22. **D**
23. **C**
24. **C**

25. **D**
26. **B**
27. **B**
28. **B**
29. **B**
30. **B**
31. **C**
32. **C**
33. **C**
34. **A**
35. **C**
36. **B**

37. **C**
38. **C**
39. **B**
40. **C**
41. **B**
42. **A**
43. **C**
44. **C**
45. **C**
46. **C**
47. **A**
48. **B**

49. **C**
50. **B**
51. **B**
52. **D**
53. **$12.50**
54. **15°**
55. **89**
56. **5**
57. **11**

1. **A** The phrase "which began in 1955" is a nonessential phrase whose main job is to provide extra information about "The Space Race." Nonessential phrases appearing in the middle of sentences should be separated with a comma on each side. Therefore, the sentence should read "The Space Race, which began in 1955, was a memorable part of the Cold War between the United States and the Soviet Union," making Answer A correct. Answers B, C, and D are all incorrect because each answer would create a sentence that was improperly spliced by commas.

2. **C** This sentence is consistently written using past tense verbs, which makes Answer C correct. Using a past tense verb is additionally important in this sentence because it clearly establishes that the events in question are matters of history and occurred in the definite past. For this reason, answers A and D are both incorrect because they would bring inconsistent present tense verbs into the sentence, creating confusion for the reader. Answer B is also incorrect because "that" and "which" are not interchangeable in this context, an error that could be quickly discovered by reading (or imagining reading) the sentence out loud.

3. **A** Even though it appears first, Sentence 1 is actually minimally related to the other sentences in the paragraph. Sentences 2 through 5 explain the process of dog show judging, describing it in a systematic way that immediately negates Sentence 1's assertion that the topic is hard to understand. A topic sentence like Sentence 1 undermines the reader's confidence that they'll explain an upcoming topic and should therefore be removed. Sentences 2, 3, and 4 all clearly connect to the same overarching topic (explaining how dog show judging works), and do so in a systematic, logical way so that removing any of them would weaken the paragraph overall.

4. **C** A dangling participle occurs when a modifying phrase at the beginning of a sentence has an unclear subject, creating reader confusion. The phrase "Appearing in over 150 cartoons between 1934 and 1959" in Sentence 4 is a dangling participle because it could be unclear to the reader that the phrase is describing Donald Duck, its intended subject who is not mentioned until later in the sentence. As written, the phrase could be interpreted by the reader to be describing any of the four characters previously mentioned (Mickey, Minnie, Pluto, and Goofy). Answer C is correct because Sentence 4 contains the dangling participle.

5. **A** Answer A is correct because, when speaking of the American Civil War in Standard American English, "Civil War" is considered a proper noun and therefore needs to be capitalized. Answer B is incorrect because "Confederate" is a proper adjective (meaning an adjective created from a proper noun, in this case "Confederacy" or "Confederate States of America"), and therefore must be capitalized. Answer C is incorrect because the term "forces" is a common noun referring to military troops generally, not any particular units, battalions, or agencies. Answer D is incorrect because "war" is a common noun when no particular war is specified. If the sentence read "... ending the Civil War," then that would be citing a specific, named war, creating a situation in which a proper noun is used. Since the sentence simply says "the war" in a nonspecific way, the common, non-capitalized form is used.

6. **B** "CDC" is used in sentence 9. Without the note at the beginning of the passage, readers unfamiliar with public health might not understand the meaning of the acronym.

7. **D** Of all the ideas in sentence 4, the concept of a "compromised immune system" is the most advanced and most likely for a reader to have questions about. Additionally, the writer would only have to add a few words to the existing sentence to provide an example. Answer A would provide the reader with interesting information, but it's not the best way to clarify the main ideas of the sentence. Answer B is incorrect because an explanation of immune function would require its own sentence (or paragraph). Answer C is incorrect because "infant" and "senior" are both commonly used terms that most readers would understand at least generally.

8. **D** Answer A is correct because two commas can be used to separate out a nonessential clause ("bonus information" that the sentence would be correct without). Answer C is also correct because dashes can be used to separate parenthetical information.

9. **A** "Bacteria" is a plural noun (the singular "bacterium" appears in sentence 1), so it takes the plural verb "do."

10. **C** The first use of "they" clearly refers to the word "hens," which immediately precedes it, making answers A and D incorrect. Answer C is the best choice because it clarifies that it is the Salmonella bacteria that are reproducing.

11. **B** "Additionally" is the best choice because the author is providing the reader with additional information about CDC guidance. "However" is incorrect because it implies the main idea in sentence 11 is contrary to that of sentence 10. "Subsequently" is incorrect because it implies a causal connection between sentences 10 and 11. "Unfortunately" is incorrect because there is nothing negative or bad about the temperature to which meat should be cooked.

12. **C** In isolation, answer D is correct because the sentence can be written with or without the Oxford comma. However, given the lists in sentences 3 and 4, it's been established that the author has chosen to use the Oxford comma, and sentence 11 should include it as well for consistency.

13. **A** Given that the author has stressed the need to prevent cross-contamination, it's important for the reader to understand what that means.

14. **A** "Located in the chest between vertebrae T5 and T8" should be moved from the sentence because it is a dangling modifier. Dangling modifiers occur when a sentence opens with a modifying phrase whose subject is unclear or easily misunderstood. When the sentence is read as written, it seems like the author is saying that William Harvey is located in the chest between vertebrae T5 and T8 rather than the heart. By eliminating the dangling modifier, the author can clarify his or her meaning and prevent confusion. While the wording of the rest of the sentence could be tightened generally, no other set of words is fundamentally incorrect, confusing, or erroneous.

15. **C** The colon is the appropriate punctuation mark to introduce a list, making Answer C correct. Answer A is wrong because the first comma in the sentence is used incorrectly. Answer B is wrong because, while a semicolon can be used to separate items in a list, it cannot be used to introduce a list.

Answer D is incorrect because by putting the chambers of the heart in parentheses, the author has downgraded the importance of that information to the sentence, making it seem optional. Since identifying the four chambers is one of the main goals of the sentence, that information should not be presented parenthetically.

16. A If the paragraph is read as written, there is a noticeable jump from discussing the structure of the human heart to discussing fish. Answer choice A provides a logical bridge between the two ideas, elaborating on the structure of the heart and providing context for the introduction of fish. Answer choices B and D are both relevant to the passage and the paragraph, but do not serve to smoothen the transition towards fish. Answer C is incorrect because it does not match the formal tone of the passage. The opening words "Who'd have thought" are informal and more aligned to conversational English than written English.

17. D Passive voice occurs when the subject of the sentence is having action done to it rather than performing the action. The use of passive voice is discouraged in formal writing. "The chambers of the heart are separated by one-way valves" is an example of passive voice because the subject ("The chambers of the heart") is being acted upon ("separated") by the valves. Answers A and B cannot be correct because they do not address this passive voice construction. Answer C simply moves the same passive voice error to a later point in the sentence. Answer D is correct because it makes "one-way valves" the subject of the sentence as well as the actor of the verb "separate," creating an active voice construction.

18. B The sentence should read: "There are many medical conditions that can affect the human heart." "Which" should only be used to introduce information that is optional or additional to a sentence (for example: "That fire hydrant, which is red, saved my life.") Since the main idea of the sentence is that these medical conditions affect the heart, "that" must be used. Answer A is incorrect because "There is many" would create a subject-verb agreement error. Answer C is incorrect because "affect" (meaning "to produce a change") is the correct verb form in this context. Answer D is incorrect because either "the" or "a" would make the sentence correct, so no change is necessary.

19. C Answer C represents the best combination of sentences 13 and 14 because it reduces wordiness and establishes a clear cause-and-effect relationship between coronary artery disease and a heart attack. Answer A is a lengthy sentence that uses a large number of commas, which many readers may find hard to follow. Answer B, while shorter, contains a number of excess words including "this is," "it can," and "which is." These unnecessary short words decrease the flow and smoothness of the sentence. Answer D explains the process backwards, beginning with the concept of a heart attack and then working towards its cause. Answer C provides a superior explanation of the cause-and-effect relationship between the two ideas by presenting them in the most natural order.

20. D Answer D sums up the content of the third paragraph (the idea that the heart is susceptible to a variety of diseases and conditions) and connects it to the main idea explored earlier in the passage (the key role of the heart in the body), providing a strong conclusion. Answer A is a true statement, but it does not connect logically and smoothly to sentence 15. Answer B is a relevant fact, but it does not provide a conclusion in any way. Answer C is a relevant detail as well, but it

does not provide a conclusion for either the paragraph or the passage as a whole.

READING COMPREHENSION

Passage 1 ("The opinion that absolute power is essential..."):

21. **A** This passage as a whole is an examination of the concept of absolute power in politics. Therefore, Answer A is the best choice. Answer choice B is not the best answer because, although the idea of power being abused is implied throughout the text, it is not explicitly explored. Answer C is incorrect because the passage does not in any way pass judgment on whether or not a fair state can exist. Answer D is incorrect because, as the text suggests in Lines 31-32, "...It is not always bad men who incline towards absolutism," meaning systems other than democracy can be fair and just.

22. **C** Answer C is correct because the final paragraph of the passage establishes that only a god can have real omnipotence. Lines 37-41 present this idea the most clearly. Answer A is incorrect and represents a misunderstanding of the text because the Greeks put power in the people, not politicians, as is explained in Lines 16-18. Answer B represents a misunderstanding of the text, as European rulers are mentioned as examples of power-hungry leaders, not the ultimate ideal of power. Answer D has no basis in the text because parents and children are never mentioned.

23. **D** Answer D is correct because Lines 31-32 clearly state: "...It is not always bad men who incline towards absolutism." The same lines mean that Answer A cannot be correct, because it assumes all people who seek absolutely power are fundamentally evil, which contradicts the actual content of the passage. Answer B is not the best answer because, while war is mentioned as a possibility in the passage, it is not established as the necessary end of power. Answer C represents a misunderstanding of the final paragraph, which discusses how a god is the only possible being with absolute power. There is nothing in the text itself that suggests people are actually trying to become gods.

24. **C** Lines 16-20 clearly establish that the Roman Caesar was a ruler with absolute power, making Answer C correct. Answer A is incorrect because Lines 17-18 establish that the Greeks were democratic and placed power in the people. Answer B is incorrect and has no basis in the text because there is no mention of "Democratic Italy" anywhere in the passage. Answer D is also incorrect the passage mostly focuses on concepts of government throughout history and does little to discuss contemporary examples.

25. **D** Answer D is the correct choice because Lines 21-27 establish that power-hungry leaders often suggest they need absolute power to rule effectively. This is most clearly reflected by the phrase "...by an appeal to the necessity of absolute power" in Lines 26-27. Answer A is incorrect because the idea of wealth or economics is not mentioned anywhere in the passage. Answer B is incorrect because the passage fails to explain how invading a neighboring country would be

advantageous to the people or a leader. Answer C has no textual basis because, while the idea of a conflict between rulers and citizens is heavily implied in the passage, there is not actual direction mention of civil war.

26. **B**   Lines 9-10 state that "Absolute power and sovereignty are sometimes called synonyms," making Answer B correct. The phrases "Constitutional Power," "Executive Power," and "People Power" never appear in the text, meaning Answers A, C, and D are all incorrect because they have no textual basis.

Passage 2 ("The bar is a term applied collectively..."):

27. **A**   Answer A is the best answer because the passage emphasizes the importance of representation and its earliest recorded appearances. Paragraph 2 explores this idea the fullest, particularly in lines 19-28, which explain that legal advocates were necessary to prevent innocent people from falling victim to unfair trials simply because they were less intelligent or eloquent than their opponent. Answer B is incorrect and has no textual basis because beer is not mentioned in the passage. Answer C is a good answer, but not the best answer because Paragraph 1 has nothing to do with Greeks specifically. Although the Greeks are used to provide examples throughout the rest of the passage, the main idea of the text is to explain the origins of the legal system and trace its growth over time. Answer D is also incorrect because the passage is not arguing for any changes in legal proceedings, simply discussing their history.

28. **D**   Answer D represents the correct explanation of the term "bar," as clearly described in Lines 4-8. Gavels, tools, and places of punishment are never mentioned in the passage, making Answers A, B, and C all incorrect because they have no textual basis.

29. **A**   Answer A is the best answer because it represents a correct interpretation of the role of bar members, as laid out in Lines 13-19. The phrases "confers...special and peculiar privileges" and "places them under regulations" should have been the biggest hints to the reader. The concept of money or payment for lawyers is not addressed in the passage, making Answer B correct because it has not textual basis. Answer C is similarly incorrect because the passage makes no mention of age. Of course, since Answers B and C are both incorrect, Answer D (which assumes they are both correct) must be wrong as well.

30. **A**   Answer A is the best choice because Lines 34-36 describe how the "clamor of partisans who are noisy and active around the court shall sway the action of the judges." These "partisans" represent people with agendas who try to stir up public opinion to sway a case. Answer B is incorrect because there is no mention of arrows anywhere in the passage, meaning Answer B has no textual basis. Similarly, although Achilles was a key figure in the Trojan War, the Trojans are never mentioned in the passage, meaning Answer C has no textual basis either. Answer D is not the best answer, although it is at least grounded in the text in that it focuses on legal issues. Lines 34-36 establish that it is outside voices who can influence the court, however, making Answer A the best choice.

31. **D**   Answer D is the best choice because Lines 46-51 establish that Pericles was chosen because he was considered an especially skilled and eloquent prosecutor. Answer A is incorrect because

there is nothing about Pericles' behavior or manner, as discussed in the text, that would suggest he was a bully. Answer B might be true, but there's nothing in the text to specifically back it up, so it cannot be the best answer. Answer C is incorrect because the only god mentioned in the passage, Hephaestus, is not connected to Pericles in any way.

32. **B** Answer B is the best choice because Lines 46-48 establish that "...friends sometimes appeared to support the cause of those who lacked the ability or the eloquence to speak on their own behalf..." Answer A is incorrect because the text does not specifically state that someone had to be a lawyer to represent a person in court, just that they had to be eloquent. Answer C is incorrect because Pericles is actually used as an example of a special prosecutor, not a defense advocate in the passage. Answer D is also incorrect because there's no mention of bribery anywhere in the passage.

Passage 3 ("The congress of the revolution...")

33. **C** Answer C is the best choice because Paragraph 4 clearly outlines how a variety of interests, from agriculture to Southern slaveholding interests, were all pulling the federal government in different directions as it tried to search for a permanent home. Lines 37-46 most clearly articulate this idea. The first paragraph also reinforces this concept, with the unpaid militia acting as another interest group that threatened the stability of government. Answer A is incorrect because, while the capital may have been in New York for a while, lines 37-38 clearly establish New York was not seen as a permanent capital. Answer B is a good answer because the passage discusses many arguments about the location of the capital; however, a close reading reveals competing interest groups to be the reason for these arguments, making Answer C the better answer. Answer D is a reasonable answer but fails to hit on the main ideas of special interests and in-fighting that dominate the passage.

34. **C** Answer C is correct because Boston is not mentioned anywhere in the passage. Answer A is incorrect because the Falls of the Delaware are mentioned as a potential location in Line 17. Answer B is incorrect because New York is mentioned as a temporary capital in Line 28. Answer D is incorrect because Philadelphia is mentioned as a congressional meeting place in Line 7.

35. **C** Answer C is correct because Lines 37-42 clearly establish that agriculturalists were opposed to New York City as a capital because it was a "commercial metropolis" that they believed was succeptable to bribery and corruption ("the direct influence which the moneyed interest might exert on congress..."). Answer A is incorrect because there were no Confederates in the 1780s and the term "Confederacy" is only mentioned in Paragraph 1. Answer B is incorrect because the term "Yankee" is never used in the passage, so it has no textual basis as an answer. Answer D is incorrect because bankers are not mentioned anywhere in the passage either, so the answer has no textual basis.

36. **B** Answer B is the correct choice because Lines 53-56 from the final paragraph clearly state: "As a compromise, it seemed probable that congress would drift back again to the plan of two capitals, and of alternating meetings north and south..." Answer A has no textual basis but probably reflects the reader's understanding that there's one capital now. Answers C and D are probably arrived at

by trying to count the number of possible locations mentioned in the text, but are both incorrect.

37. D Answer D is correct because Lines 42-46 clearly establish the abolitionist beliefs of Quakers as a major point of contention with slave-holding southerners. Answer A is incorrect because the northern-ness of Philadelphia is not described as being problematic in the passage. Answer B is incorrect and represents an issue people had with New York as the capital, according to the passage. Answer C is incorrect because it has no basis in the text and is factually incorrect.

38. B Answer B is correct because tensions between North and South are hinted at throughout the passage, including Lines 42-46, 50-53, and 56-59. Answer A is incorrect because the previously mentioned lines indicate that the North and South were, in fact, not strong allies, but rather treated each other in an adversarial manner. Answers C and D are both wrong because they are factually incorrect statements that depict the exact opposite of what is described in the passage.

Passage 4 ("The division of employments...")

39. C Answer C is the best choice because the first paragraph introduces the concept of division of labor and each subsequent paragraph adds to that idea or expands on it. Answer A is not the best choice because the passage doesn't get overly specific about different jobs but rather focuses on the general skills that a "tribe" requires. Answer B is not the best answer because, while the passage focuses on the idea of people refining specific skills, the idea of practice or repetition to increase skill is not a main feature of the passage. Answer D is also incorrect because the passage contains no justification or apology for any profession but rather asserts that they are all equally valuable, complementary pursuits.

40. A Answer A is correct because Lines 11-18 establish that as societies grow and develop, people begin to specialize in the jobs they are best at. This idea is reinforced by Lines 19-21 and 30-36. Answer B is incorrect because the concept of practice is not explored in depth throughout the passage. Answer C is also incorrect because the concept of industrialization or "scaling up" is not mentioned anywhere in the passage. Answer D is also incorrect because saving time is not one of the advantages of dividing labor that is mentioned in the passage.

41. C Answer C is the best choice because a neuroscientist is a highly specialized doctor who only focuses on one area of study. In an earlier, less developed society, someone might simply have been a "doctor," but as the division increases over time, each profession is broken down into a number of more specific jobs. Answer A is incorrect because, if the teacher is teaching everybody in the village, they are not very specialized. An 8th grade English teacher, for example, would be a modern specialized professional. Similarly, Answer B is incorrect because someone who knows all the laws isn't specialized. A labor law expert, for example, would be a modern specialized professional. Answer D is incorrect because a parent would need all of those skills to be successful, regardless of the complexity of their society or division of labor.

42. D Answer D is correct because it is the only choice that depicts a specialized professional (the

blacksmith) trading his/her wares (the horseshoe) for the wares (a loaf of bread) of another specialized professional (a baker). Answer A is incorrect because it shows a single professional expanding upon their own work. Answer B is incorrect because it does not establish that the chef is getting anything back in return. Answer C is incorrect because the lottery winner did not create the lottery ticket themself and trade it for something of equal value, but rather won a prize at random.

43. **D** Answer D is correct because Lines 7-9 state: "...the old man of the tribe, preserves in his treasure, as yet very meagre, of acquired knowledge..." A close reading of the sentence clearly reveals the treasure and knowledge that are mentioned to be one in the same. Answers A and B are both incorrect and have no textual basis because precious metals are never mentioned in the passage. Answer C is also incorrect because food is not mentioned at all in the first paragraph, which contains the explanation of the old man's "treasure."

44. **B** Answer B is correct because, when describing the work of those creating the "culture of the mind" in Lines 35-40, the passage states: "...these latter discover the laws of nature which God has placed at the service of man..." These words are essentially describing the role of a theologist, someone who ponders the existence of god(s) and their potential laws and ways. Answers A, C, and D are all incorrect because hunters, builders, and farmers all do manual work that has palpable, physical results. The theologist is the only of the included jobs whose main work is done with the mind rather than the hands.

Passage 5 ("The large standing army...")

45. **D** Answer D is correct because the passage explains how the army supported infrastructure in Lines 7-9 and 42-45 and describes how they supported the idea of Rome in Lines 16-29 and 36-40. Answer A is not the best answer because, while the passage does discuss some of the trades soldiers learned, that is not the main idea of the entire passage. Answer B is incorrect because, while the organization of the army hints at some of the reasons for Rome's might, there is no discussion of tactics or armaments in the passage, so military power is not the main idea. Answer C is not the best choice either because the passage only focuses on members of the army and does little to explain how Rome encouraged loyalty in common citizens.

46. **D** Answer D is the best answer because while the passage references the soldiers "smelting" iron in Line 8, forging is a completely different process. Answer A is incorrect because the passage clearly describes brickmaking in Line 7. Answers B and C are both incorrect because building canals and bridges is mentioned in Line 43.

47. **A** Answer A is the best choice because the phrase "They learned to dress properly, to speak Latin..." in line 19 implies strongly that the soldiers did not speak Latin before joining the Roman army. Answer B is incorrect because Lines 12-15 imply that the recruits were adults, since it states that 25 years would most likely be the rest of their lives. Answer C cannot be the best answer because there is no specific evidence in the text that suggests children grew up eager to join the army. Answer D is not the best answer because, if anything, the passage implies that the soldiers had

ARGO BROTHERS
www.argobrothers.com

minimal skills before enlisting and typically learned trades through the army.

48. A   Answer A is the best choice because the passage specifically discusses how the army was often a watchdog used to "clean up the mess" (Line 36) in Rome. Lines 32-36 as a whole describe a scenario in which the army might replace or challenge a corrupt emperor in the name of the Empire, preserving Rome's integrity. Answer B is not the best answer because the article emphasizes the army's cultural significance to Rome, not just their ability to fight. Answer C is also incorrect because, while the passage states that the soldiers learned Latin, it does not say anything about them passing it on to other locals in the new territories, spreading their language. Answer D is incorrect because the passage (especially lines 32-36) emphasizes the role of the army as a check-and-balance to the power of the emperor rather than a complement to it.

49. C   Answer C is correct because, in Lines 24-27, the passage clearly states that "...they honored Roma, a goddess who was the exemplification of Rome..." Answers A, B, and D are all incorrect because Athena, Mars, and Belona all go unmentioned in the passage, meaning those choices have no textual basis and cannot be the answer.

50. A   Answer A is correct because the passage provides specific examples of Roman technology (the foundries and factories mentioned in Lines 7-9 and the structures described in Lines 43-44) and Roman ideas (the Latin language mentioned in Line 19, the religious traditions mentioned in lines 24-29, and the political ideals discussed in Lines 30-36). Answer B is incorrect because the passage contains no information about actual Roman army strategy or tactics. Answer C is incorrect because the passage specifically discusses the value of the army returning to Rome in Lines 30-36. Answer D is incorrect because there is minimal mention of anybody's "homeland" in the passage.

Passage 6: ("A house should be built with the summer...")

51. C   Answer C is the best choice because, throughout the passage, the author discusses different qualities that make a home either comfortable and charming or off-putting. Although the author mentions his or her distaste for modern houses in Lines 17-22, modernism is not the main focus of the passage, so Answer A is incorrect. Answer B is also incorrect because, while the orange tree is a fault that the author finds in one particular house, it is far from the overall idea of the passage. Similarly, Answer D is incorrect because, while the author favors open space, that is just one of several points that he or she makes about what makes a "good house."

52. B   Answer B is correct because the opening sentence of the passage (Lines 1-2) clearly establishes that a house's construction should keep the summer "in view." Answer A is incorrect because, according to the author, "In winter, one can live anywhere" (Line 2). Answers C and D are both incorrect because no mention of the spring or autumn is made anywhere in the passage, so those answers have no textual basis.

53. B   Answer B is the best answer because the versatility of open spaces is described in Lines 8-11

when the author writes, "people agree in admiring a place with plenty of spare room, as being pleasing to the eye and at the same time useful for all sorts of purposes." Answer A is incorrect because the concepts of wealth or trying to look rich are not mentioned anywhere in the text. Answer C is not the best answer because Lines 23-29 explain how an over-decorated house is not good, according to the author. Answer D is incorrect because it is completely contrary to the content of Lines 8-11.

54. C   Answer C is the best choice because Lines 17-22 state: "The man is to be envied who lives in a house, not of the modern, garish kind, but set among venerable trees, with a garden where plants grow wild and yet seem to have been disposed with care..." These words show a clear preference for a rural setting with wild, natural-looking plant life. Answer A is incorrect because the above lines clearly demonstrate the author's preference for a quiet, pastoral setting over an urban city. Answers B and D are both incorrect as well because the author clearly states that he or she prefers "...a garden here plants grow wild," rather than a tamed, manicured lawn.

55. A   Answer A is correct because Lines 24-31 establish that the author feels over-tended gardens are an "unpleasant sight, depressing to look at" because they are a reminder of how life is temporary. In Lines 30-31, the author says that by tending plants, a homeowner can only be reminded of "how easily it might vanish in a moment of time." Answer B is incorrect because the author is not concerned with finances or expense at any point in the passage, but rather prefers to focus on philosophy. Answer C is incorrect because the author is not impressed with the idea of displaying "new things," but rather believes a home should be a simple place where one can contemplate life and the world. Answer D is incorrect because the author clearly does not believe in rushing or a "city pace" to life, so something being time consuming would be of no concern to him or her.

56. D   Answer D is correct because the domesticated fruit tree in the fenced garden is specifically mentioned as offensive to the author in Lines 44-49. The author even ends by saying "If only that tree had not been there!" Answers A, B, and C are all incorrect because they have no basis in the text. Since the author specifically finds fault with the fruit tree, Answer D is the only choice that makes sense based on the text.

57. B   Answer B is correct because the author clearly believes homes reflect their owners. A reader could deduce this because the word "character" in Line 33 is a synonym for "personality" in Answer choice B. Answer A is a decent choice, but certainly not the best answer, because it fails to access the idea that people and their houses are often similar. Answer C is also a decent choice because the author spends so much time stressing what makes a good home, but Lines 32-33 in particular focus on the similarities between houses and their owners, making Answer B a better choice. Answer D is incorrect because the author is consistently more interested with the spirit or feel of a place than its physical appearance throughout the passage.

Explanations to each problem on:
Youtube.com/ArgoBrothers

MATHEMATICS

ARGO
BROTHERS
www.argobrothers.com

Practice Test 1 (Answers and Explanations)

1. **C** $(\frac{7}{20}) \cdot (\frac{5}{5}) = (\frac{35}{100}) = 0.35$

2. **D** $500{,}000 + 400 + 5 = 500{,}405$

3. **D** Substitute and perform the respective operations.
$x = 4$
$y = 3$
$(4 + 3)^2 = (7)^2 = 49$

4. **B** $(\sqrt{144})(\sqrt{16}) = (12)(4) = 48$

5. **D** One approach to this type of problem is to look at the two equations and see what is common. Both equations have the word **Knot** in common.

Manipulate the equation so that both equations have the same number of Knots. You can do this by dividing the second equation by 4, to get $\frac{1}{2}$ Shings = 1 Knot.

Therefore, 3 Vines = $\frac{1}{2}$ Shings.

Since you are trying to find out how many Shings are in 9 Vines, simply multiply the equation by 3 to get 9 Vines = $\frac{3}{2}$ Shings.

6. **B** Simplifying the first number gives us 1. So, the question is asking for what number is between 1 and 4. As a general rule for these types of problems, we must divide the difference of the numbers by 2 and add that value to the original number. This gives us:
$(\frac{4 - 1}{2}) + 1 = (\frac{1.5}{2}) + 1 = 2.5$

7. **A** $\measuredangle GLQ = 150°$ since angles on a straight line add up to 180°.

$\measuredangle LGQ = y$ since vertical angles are always equal. Using this and the fact that the interior angles of a triangle add up to 180°, find z in terms of y.

$y + 150° + z = 180°$ and by solving for z, you get
$z = 30 - y$, which is answer choice A.

8. **D** Use PEMDAS (Parenthesis, Exponents, Multiplication, Division, Addition, Subtraction).

9. **C** You must remember the formula for the area of a circle and square. Given that the side of the square is, "*s*" and the radius and diameter of the circle are "*r*" and "*D*" respectively, we have:

A square = s^2

A circle= $(\pi)(r^2) = (\pi)(\frac{D^2}{4})$, since the radius is half the diameter (substitute the radius for $(\frac{D}{2})$.

We are given that the diameter is 10, and the areas are equal, so after setting both areas equal to each other, we have:

$s^2 = (\pi)(\frac{10^2}{4}) = 25\pi$, and solving for *s*, we get:

$s = 5\sqrt{\pi}$, which is answer choice C.

10. **D** Use distributive property
$4a(3b - 6) = 12ab - 24a$

11. **C** The trick here is to realize that 39 is the product of 13 and 3. Using that, we have:

$(\frac{(-3 \cdot 13)^2}{13^3}) = (\frac{(-3)^2 \cdot (13)^2}{13^3}) =$

$9 \cdot (\frac{13^2}{13^3}) = \frac{9}{13}$, which is answer choice C.

12. **A** If 1 inch represents 20 ft, you can square both sides to get 1 square inch equals 400 ft squared. We want to find how many square inches are in one square foot. Using this information, we can write a proportion:

$(\frac{1in^2}{400ft^2}) = (\frac{x in^2}{1ft^2})$

and solving for *x*, we get:

$x = \frac{1}{400} = 0.0025$, which is answer choice A.

13. **C** List the prime factors for each number

$2240 : 2^6 \cdot 5 \cdot 7$

$3360: 2^5 \cdot 3 \cdot 5 \cdot 7$

Multiply the factors that are common in both sets.

$2^5 \cdot 5 \cdot 7 = 1,120$, which is answer choice C.

14. **D** 50% of 2*y* is half of 2*y*, which is just *y*. So we have: *y* = 12, so then the square of y is 144. The answer choice is D.

15. C We know that:

$(a + b) = 150°$ because of the rule that an exterior angle of a triangle is equal to the two opposite interior angles (a and b). And, simplifying:

$$\left(\frac{a^2 - b^2}{a - b}\right) = \left(\frac{(a - b)(a + b)}{a - b}\right) = (a + b) = $$

$150°$, which is answer choice, C.

16. A If $y = \left(\frac{3}{4}\right)$ then $y^2 = \left(\frac{9}{16}\right)$ which means x must equal 1 for xy^2 to equal $\left(\frac{9}{16}\right)$.

Now we have to solve for $(x - 4)$. Since we know the value of x is 1, we can substitute the value of x in to get $(1-4)$ which is equals to -3.

The answer choice is A.

17. D One way to solve this problem would be to use hypothetical values and test which answer choice always results in an even number. Another way to solve the problem is by realizing if an integer is divided or multiplied by 2, it will always result in an even number. If you look carefully at answer choice D, the variable P is being multiplied by 2 and in this case also being divided by 2. Try to plug in any value for P, and using the expression in answer choice D will always result in an even integer.

18. D If the diameter is P, then we know that the radius is $\left(\frac{P}{2}\right)$ and using the given information, we can substitute and

find that the area is just:

$$A = \pi\left(\frac{P}{2}\right)^2 = \pi\left(\frac{P^2}{4}\right) = 2\pi,$$

which is answer choice D.

19. A We must find what N is first.

Simplifying, we find that $N = 16$ and so the polygon has $(16 - 10)$ sides or 6 sides. Now we need to find the total number of degrees in this hexagon, and then divide by 6. We can use the formula:

Total number of Degrees = $(N - 2)180°$, and so when $N = 6$, this simplifies to $720°$. Dividing this by 6, gives us:

$120°$ for each interior angle. The answer is A.

20. C It is important to note that this is a variation of a 3, 4, 5 right triangle. The fact that there is π multiplied with 4 and 5 does not change this relationship. Knowing this, the perimeter is 12π. This perimeter equals to the circumference of a circle, which gives way to this equation:

$12\pi = 2(\pi)r$, where r is the radius. Solving for the radius gives: $r = 6$, so the answer choice is C.

21. **A** In this problem, we just need to plug into the formula. We get:

$$\left(\frac{7}{14}\right) \cdot \left(\frac{7}{14}\right),$$

which simplifies to a quarter, which is 0.25, or answer choice A.

22. **D** Since 25 can only go into 1200, K is the answer choice.

23. **C** We can simplify each fraction to a mixed number. Then, we are just looking for the positive integers that are bigger than $-2\frac{1}{3}$ and less than $2\frac{1}{2}$. If we wrote all the integers between those two numbers, we would get −2, −1, 0, 1, 2. Eliminating the negative ones gives us: 1 and 2, which is 2 integers giving us answer choice C.

24. **C** The formula of the perimeter of a rectangle is $2l + 2w$, where l and w are the length and width respectively. They give us the width as 18 inches and the perimeter at 80 inches. Which means when we solve for the length, we get 22 inches.

To get the area, we just need to multiply the length and width together, so we get 18in × 22in, which is 396 sq. inches or answer choice C.

25. **D** All we need to do is plug in $x = -3$ in the first expression. We then get $b = 7 \cdot |0|$, which is just 0.

The answer is D.

26. **B** Here, we need to find the sum: $1 + 2 + 3 + 4 + ... + 100$.

Well, if we take the first and last number and add them, we get 101. If we take the 2nd and 99th number and add them, we get 101. If we continue this pattern, we will always get 101. So, we have 50 pairs of numbers that add up to 101 and we are adding them all up. So the answer is:

$50 \cdot 101 = 5050$, or answer choice B.

27. **B** Let's say that the original population was Y. Then we have that $1.1Y = 55$ because we increase Y by 10%.

Solving for Y gives us 50, or answer choice B.

28. **B** The volume of a rectangular solid is the product of the length, the width and the height.

$V = lwh$. We are given $l = 10$, so all we need is, wh. We can find this by taking the cube root of both sides of the equation below which is given to us:

$w^3h^3 = 27$ becomes $wh = 3$, so then:

$lwh = 30$, which is answer choice B.

You Tube

Explanations to each problem on:
Youtube.com/ArgoBrothers

MATHEMATICS
ANSWERS & EXPLANATIONS

ARGO
BROTHERS

www.argobrothers.com

29. **B** The key here is to realize that there are two radii of the circle drawn, OA and OC. All radii are equal, so $x = 7$. The answer is B.

30. **B** Using the Pythagorean Theorem, we get,

$x + 100 = 432$

$x = 332$

$x = \sqrt{332} = 2\sqrt{83}$, which is answer choice B.

31. **C** Another way of writing A is $A = 3(rh)^2$, and if we increase (rh) by 100%, we are actually doubling it. We can label the new A as A'. Since we doubled (rh) we can represent A' now as $A' = 3(2rh)^2 = 3 \cdot 4(rh)^2 = 12(rh)^2$ which is 4 times as large as the original A. The answer is C.

32. **C** We have,

$x^a = x^{\frac{p}{q}}$, which means $a = \frac{p}{q}$ so then,

$\frac{p^2}{q^2} = (\frac{p}{q})^2 = a^2$

The answer is C.

33. **C** The only common value(s) in both sets is 2. So the answer is {2} which is answer choice C.

34. **A** This can be simplified to

$2\sqrt{75} - \sqrt{25}\sqrt{3} = 10\sqrt{3} - 5\sqrt{3} = 5\sqrt{3}$

The answer is A.

35. **C** This can be reduced to 0.00345, which in scientific notation is 3.45×10^{-3}.

The answer is C.

36. **B** Since -23 is odd, we must use the second rule. The answer is $4(-23) = -92$.

The answer is B.

37. **C** The maximum value for y occurs when x is positive and large. This value of x is $(\frac{1}{2})$ giving us $y = (\frac{1}{8})$.

The answer is C.

38. **C** By simplifying, we get, $\frac{x^3 z}{y}$ or answer C.

39. **B** This is a special 3, 4, 5 right triangle. The length of RL must be 5. The answer is B.

40. **C**   If the sum of 2 angles equals the third, then the only value of the third angle that is possible is 90°.

One way of thinking of this is to realize that the sum of the third angle and the sum of the other two angles must be 180°.

The answer is C.

41. **B**   Bridget and Anthony take turns watching T.V. with 4 hour intervals. We progress in the order of Bridget (B), Anthony (A), Bridget (B), Anthony (A), etc. We can write a list where we know that Anthony's 3rd turn is at 10PM.

B-
A-
B-
A-
B-
A-10PM

Now, we can work backwards to find Bridget's time for her second turn. That turns out to be at 10 AM.

The answer is B.

42. **A**   We can write a system of two linear equations. The first represents the number of bikes and unicycles as x and y respectively as a sum. The second represents the number of wheels for each bike and unicycle as a sum.

$x + y = 9$
$2x + y = 13$

Solving these equations by either substitution or addition, we get that $x = 4$. So, $x^2 = 16$

The answer is A.

43. **C**   The direction of his path is shown below.

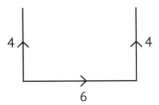

He is 6 miles from his starting point, which is answer choice C.

44. **C**   Since all the diagonals of a cube are equal, the angle is part of an equilateral triangle. So the angle measure is 60°.

The answer is C.

45. **C**   We must know the equation for the circumference of a semi-circle, which is simply half the circumference of a circle. We must also realize that the triangle is a special 3, 4, 5 right triangle. Adding the circumference of the semicircle, with the diameter of the semicircle and the perimeter of the triangle, we get the perimeter as $22 + 5\pi$.

The answer is C.

46. **C**   You must know that these repeating decimals can be simplified to, $\frac{53}{99}, \frac{36}{99}$ respectively. Subtracting these two repeating decimals, we get, $\frac{17}{99}$, which is answer choice C.

47. **A**   We can set up equation as follows, $(x + y) = 6(x - y)$ and solving for the ratio gives us: $\dfrac{x}{y} = \dfrac{7}{5}$

The question asks for the reciprocal of the ratio of the larger number to the smaller number. Therefore, the reciprocal of $\dfrac{7}{5}$ is $\dfrac{5}{7}$. The answer is A.

48. **B**   We are given the mean weekly salary for the 9 teachers as \$1,000. If x is the total for the salary of the teachers, then we have:

$$\dfrac{x}{9} = 1000$$

Now let's let y equal the total salary of the 11 assistant principals.

Then we have:

$$\dfrac{x + y}{9 + 11} = \dfrac{x + y}{20} = \dfrac{9000 + y}{20} = 1275$$

and solving for y, we get, $y = 16,500$. The mean weekly salary of the 11 assistant principals is just y divided by 11, giving \$1,500 or answer choice B.

49. **C**   The recursion formula just requires us to take the two previous terms to get the next. So the 5th term is the sum of the 4th and 3rd terms, or 5. The 6th term is the sum of the 5th and 4th terms or 8.

The 6th term divided by the 5th term is $\left(\dfrac{8}{5}\right)$ or answer C.

50. **B**   We cannot divide by 0, so the set that is not a possible domain is any set with the value 1 in it, or answer B.

51. **B**   This problem tests your understanding of increasing and decreasing percentages. You are given an initial value of \$400, followed by a decrease of 15%, which is then followed by an increase of 25%. You need to provide the final value. To calculate a change by percentage, use the formula: *initial value • (1 - percentage change)* Your two changes are −15% and −25%, respectively, so you can write out the entire expression as:

$$\$400 \times (1 - 15\%) \times (1 - 25\%) =$$
$$\$400(.85)(1.25) = \$425.$$

The answer choice is B.

52. **D**   This problem tests your ability to set up a geometric word problem. The given data lays out the dimensions of a right triangle. The clue you are given is that the start of the glider is 40 feet above the ground (distance to the ground is **always** measured along a line perpendicular to the ground). The glider starts its journey 40 feet above the ground and ends 10 feet above ground. Therefore, the height of the triangle is 30 feet. You are given the distance between the two buildings as 40 feet. You thus have the two legs of the triangle at 30 and 40. You should recognize this as a multiple of the Pythagorean Theorem proportions

of 3:4:5 and so arrive at 50 for the last side. The calculation is:

$$a^2 + b^2 = c^2 \text{ Pythagorean Theorem}$$
$$30^2 + 40^2 = c^2 \text{ substitution}$$
$$900 + 1600 = c^2 \text{ calculate}$$
$$2500 = c^2 \text{ simplify}$$
$$\sqrt{2500} = c = 50 \text{ calculate}$$

The correct answer is D. REMEMBER: The negative result of the square root can be ignored in this instance because we are looking for a distance, which will always be a positive number.

53. **$12.5**

This problem tests your understanding of how to work with percentages. A 20% discount is calculated as 100% − 20% = 80%. You are therefore being told that the sale price of $10.00 is **80%** of the original price (n). 80% is represented as .80 in decimal form. You can set up the calculation as:

$$\$10.00 = .80 \times n \qquad \text{given}$$
$$\frac{\$10.00}{.80} = n = \$12.50 \qquad \begin{array}{l}\text{divide both}\\\text{sides by .80}\\\text{and calculate}\end{array}$$

54. **15°**

If you draw a diagram you can see that the interior angles of triangle *PQR* is 3*x*, 5*x* and 4*x* respectively. We know that the sum of the interior angles in a triangle is 180 so we can set up an equation:

$$3x + 5x + 4x = 180. \quad \text{simplify like terms}$$
$$12x = 180. \quad \text{solve for } x$$
$$x = 15°$$

55. **89**

This problem tests your ability to set up an average calculation. In order to find the average of the test scores, use the formula:

$$\frac{\text{sum of test scores}}{\text{number of tests}} = \text{test score average}$$

The number of tests is 4 and the desired average is 85. You have 3 of the test scores, and are asked to find the fourth to achieve this average. So let *x* be the fourth test score.

Now write your equation:

$$\frac{x + 80 + 83 + 88}{4} = 85 \qquad \text{given}$$
$$x + 80 + 83 + 88 = 85(4) \qquad \begin{array}{l}\text{multiply both}\\\text{sides by 4}\end{array}$$
$$x + 251 = 340 \qquad \text{calculate}$$
$$x = 340 - 251 = 89 \quad \text{solve for } x$$

The answer is 89.

56. **5**

This problem tests your skills at algebraic manipulation.

$$2(x - 3) + 9 = 4x - 7 \quad \text{given}$$
$$2x - 6 + 9 = 4x - 7 \quad \text{distributive}$$
$$-6 + 9 + 7 = 4x - 2x \quad \begin{array}{l}\text{isolate your } x\\\text{terms by adding}\\7 - 2x \text{ to both}\\\text{sides}\end{array}$$
$$10 = 2x \qquad \text{simplify}$$
$$5 = x \qquad \begin{array}{l}\text{divide both sides}\\\text{by 5}\end{array}$$

The correct answer choice is **5**. NOTE: Be sure to substitute 5 as the value of x back into the original equation in order to verify your work.

57.   **11**

This problem asks you to solve the given equation for the value of n.

$$\frac{n + 4}{10} = \frac{n - 8}{2} \qquad \text{given}$$

$n + 4 = 5(n - 8)$ multiply both sides by 10

$n + 4 = 5n - 40$ distribute

$44 = 4n$ simplify by adding $40 - n$ to both sides

Practice Test 2
SHSAT

This exam is 3 hours long. Try to take this full exam in one sitting to simulate real test conditions.

While taking this exam, refrain from hearing music or watching T.V.

Please note, calculators are not permitted! You are permitted to answer questions in any order you see fit.

Allocate your test time accordingly.

Concentrate and GOOD LUCK!

SHSAT PRACTICE TEST 2
ANSWER SHEET

ENGLISH LANGUAGE ARTS

1. Ⓐ Ⓑ Ⓒ Ⓓ
2. Ⓐ Ⓑ Ⓒ Ⓓ
3. Ⓐ Ⓑ Ⓒ Ⓓ
4. Ⓐ Ⓑ Ⓒ Ⓓ
5. Ⓐ Ⓑ Ⓒ Ⓓ
6. Ⓐ Ⓑ Ⓒ Ⓓ
7. Ⓐ Ⓑ Ⓒ Ⓓ
8. Ⓐ Ⓑ Ⓒ Ⓓ
9. Ⓐ Ⓑ Ⓒ Ⓓ
10. Ⓐ Ⓑ Ⓒ Ⓓ
11. Ⓐ Ⓑ Ⓒ Ⓓ
12. Ⓐ Ⓑ Ⓒ Ⓓ
13. Ⓐ Ⓑ Ⓒ Ⓓ
14. Ⓐ Ⓑ Ⓒ Ⓓ
15. Ⓐ Ⓑ Ⓒ Ⓓ
16. Ⓐ Ⓑ Ⓒ Ⓓ
17. Ⓐ Ⓑ Ⓒ Ⓓ
18. Ⓐ Ⓑ Ⓒ Ⓓ
19. Ⓐ Ⓑ Ⓒ Ⓓ
20. Ⓐ Ⓑ Ⓒ Ⓓ
21. Ⓐ Ⓑ Ⓒ Ⓓ
22. Ⓐ Ⓑ Ⓒ Ⓓ
23. Ⓐ Ⓑ Ⓒ Ⓓ
24. Ⓐ Ⓑ Ⓒ Ⓓ
25. Ⓐ Ⓑ Ⓒ Ⓓ
26. Ⓐ Ⓑ Ⓒ Ⓓ
27. Ⓐ Ⓑ Ⓒ Ⓓ
28. Ⓐ Ⓑ Ⓒ Ⓓ
29. Ⓐ Ⓑ Ⓒ Ⓓ

30. Ⓐ Ⓑ Ⓒ Ⓓ
31. Ⓐ Ⓑ Ⓒ Ⓓ
32. Ⓐ Ⓑ Ⓒ Ⓓ
33. Ⓐ Ⓑ Ⓒ Ⓓ
34. Ⓐ Ⓑ Ⓒ Ⓓ
35. Ⓐ Ⓑ Ⓒ Ⓓ
36. Ⓐ Ⓑ Ⓒ Ⓓ
37. Ⓐ Ⓑ Ⓒ Ⓓ
38. Ⓐ Ⓑ Ⓒ Ⓓ
39. Ⓐ Ⓑ Ⓒ Ⓓ
40. Ⓐ Ⓑ Ⓒ Ⓓ
41. Ⓐ Ⓑ Ⓒ Ⓓ
42. Ⓐ Ⓑ Ⓒ Ⓓ
43. Ⓐ Ⓑ Ⓒ Ⓓ
44. Ⓐ Ⓑ Ⓒ Ⓓ
45. Ⓐ Ⓑ Ⓒ Ⓓ
46. Ⓐ Ⓑ Ⓒ Ⓓ
47. Ⓐ Ⓑ Ⓒ Ⓓ
48. Ⓐ Ⓑ Ⓒ Ⓓ
49. Ⓐ Ⓑ Ⓒ Ⓓ
50. Ⓐ Ⓑ Ⓒ Ⓓ
51. Ⓐ Ⓑ Ⓒ Ⓓ
52. Ⓐ Ⓑ Ⓒ Ⓓ
53. Ⓐ Ⓑ Ⓒ Ⓓ
54. Ⓐ Ⓑ Ⓒ Ⓓ
55. Ⓐ Ⓑ Ⓒ Ⓓ
56. Ⓐ Ⓑ Ⓒ Ⓓ
57. Ⓐ Ⓑ Ⓒ Ⓓ

MATHEMATICS

1. Ⓐ Ⓑ Ⓒ Ⓓ
2. Ⓐ Ⓑ Ⓒ Ⓓ
3. Ⓐ Ⓑ Ⓒ Ⓓ
4. Ⓐ Ⓑ Ⓒ Ⓓ
5. Ⓐ Ⓑ Ⓒ Ⓓ
6. Ⓐ Ⓑ Ⓒ Ⓓ
7. Ⓐ Ⓑ Ⓒ Ⓓ
8. Ⓐ Ⓑ Ⓒ Ⓓ
9. Ⓐ Ⓑ Ⓒ Ⓓ
10. Ⓐ Ⓑ Ⓒ Ⓓ
11. Ⓐ Ⓑ Ⓒ Ⓓ
12. Ⓐ Ⓑ Ⓒ Ⓓ
13. Ⓐ Ⓑ Ⓒ Ⓓ
14. Ⓐ Ⓑ Ⓒ Ⓓ
15. Ⓐ Ⓑ Ⓒ Ⓓ
16. Ⓐ Ⓑ Ⓒ Ⓓ
17. Ⓐ Ⓑ Ⓒ Ⓓ
18. Ⓐ Ⓑ Ⓒ Ⓓ
19. Ⓐ Ⓑ Ⓒ Ⓓ
20. Ⓐ Ⓑ Ⓒ Ⓓ
21. Ⓐ Ⓑ Ⓒ Ⓓ
22. Ⓐ Ⓑ Ⓒ Ⓓ
23. Ⓐ Ⓑ Ⓒ Ⓓ
24. Ⓐ Ⓑ Ⓒ Ⓓ
25. Ⓐ Ⓑ Ⓒ Ⓓ
26. Ⓐ Ⓑ Ⓒ Ⓓ

27. Ⓐ Ⓑ Ⓒ Ⓓ
28. Ⓐ Ⓑ Ⓒ Ⓓ
29. Ⓐ Ⓑ Ⓒ Ⓓ
30. Ⓐ Ⓑ Ⓒ Ⓓ
31. Ⓐ Ⓑ Ⓒ Ⓓ
32. Ⓐ Ⓑ Ⓒ Ⓓ
33. Ⓐ Ⓑ Ⓒ Ⓓ
34. Ⓐ Ⓑ Ⓒ Ⓓ
35. Ⓐ Ⓑ Ⓒ Ⓓ
36. Ⓐ Ⓑ Ⓒ Ⓓ
37. Ⓐ Ⓑ Ⓒ Ⓓ
38. Ⓐ Ⓑ Ⓒ Ⓓ
39. Ⓐ Ⓑ Ⓒ Ⓓ
40. Ⓐ Ⓑ Ⓒ Ⓓ
41. Ⓐ Ⓑ Ⓒ Ⓓ
42. Ⓐ Ⓑ Ⓒ Ⓓ
43. Ⓐ Ⓑ Ⓒ Ⓓ
44. Ⓐ Ⓑ Ⓒ Ⓓ
45. Ⓐ Ⓑ Ⓒ Ⓓ
46. Ⓐ Ⓑ Ⓒ Ⓓ
47. Ⓐ Ⓑ Ⓒ Ⓓ
48. Ⓐ Ⓑ Ⓒ Ⓓ
49. Ⓐ Ⓑ Ⓒ Ⓓ
50. Ⓐ Ⓑ Ⓒ Ⓓ
51. Ⓐ Ⓑ Ⓒ Ⓓ
52. Ⓐ Ⓑ Ⓒ Ⓓ

MATHEMATICS (GRID IN)

53.
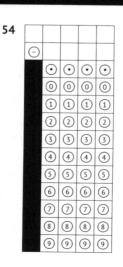
54.
55.
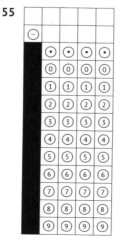
56.
57.

DIRECTIONS: For questions 1 to 5, you will be asked to recognize and correct errors in sentences or short paragraphs.

1. Read this sentence.

> Try not to become a man of success Einstein said, but rather try to become a man of value.

Which revision uses proper punctuation to format the quotation?

A. "Try not to become a man of success" Einstein said, "but rather try to become a man of value.

B. "Try not to become a man of success Einstein said," but rather "try to become a man of value."

C. "Try not to become a man of success" Einstein said, "but rather try to become a man of value."

D. "Try not to become a man of success," Einstein said, "but rather try to become a man of value."

2. Read this sentence.

> Although he was considered handsome and athletic in his youth, King Henry VIII of England become overweight because he enjoyed huge meals of many courses made from exotic ingredients.

Which edit should be made to correct the sentence?

A. Change **was considered** to **is considered**

B. Change **become** to **became**

C. Change **enjoyed** to is **enjoying**

D. Change **made from** to **make from**

3. Read this paragraph.

> (1) Sir Isaac Newton made a number of key discoveries in the seventeenth century that earned him a reputation as the father of modern physics. (2) In 1687, he publishes his three laws of motion, which formed the foundation for the study of mechanics. (3) His first law stated that an object at rest will tend to stay at rest until acted upon by an outside force, while an object in motion will tend to stay in motion until acted upon by an outside force. (4) Newton's second law explained for the first time how to calculate the amount of force an object generates. (5) The often-quoted third law established that for every action, there is an equal and opposite reaction.

Which sentence in the paragraph should be revised for verb tense consistency?

A. Sentence 1

B. Sentence 2

C. Sentence 3

D. Sentence 4

CONTINUE ON TO THE NEXT PAGE ➡

4. Read this paragraph.

> (1) The tale of Grover Cleveland's secret surgery is one of the most notorious stories about any American president. (2) Shortly after beginning his second term, Cleveland took a fishing trip on a private boat from New York to Cape Cod with a group of friends. (3) A secret kept from almost the entire country, Cleveland had a cancerous tumor in his mouth that needed to be removed. (4) A team of six surgeons worked to excise the mass below the deck of the moving ship. (5) Although the procedure was a total success, most Americans didn't hear the true reason for Cleveland's bizarre fishing trip for more than twenty years.

Which sentence in the paragraph should be revised to correct a dangling modifier?

A. Sentence 1
B. Sentence 2
C. Sentence 3
D. Sentence 4

5. Read this sentence.

> The fifteenth century Danish astronomer Tycho Brache was famous for both the accuracy of his planetary observations and his artificial nose, which he needed because of a dueling injury.

Which revision of this sentence eliminates the use of "to be" verbs?

A. The fifteenth century Danish astronomer Tycho Brahe was well known for both the accuracy of his planetary observations and his artificial nose, which he needed because of a dueling injury.

B. The fifteenth century Danish astronomer Tycho Brache was famous for the accuracy of his planetary observations as well as his artificial nose, which he needed because of a dueling injury.

C. Fifteenth century Danish astronomer Tycho Brahe's accurate planetary observations and artificial nose, which he needed because of a dueling injury, both made him a well-known figure.

D. Fifteenth century Danish astronomer Tycho Brahe's accurate planetary observations and artificial nose, which he needed because of a dueling injury, were both features that made him a well-known figure.

CONTINUE ON TO THE NEXT PAGE ➡

ENGLISH LANGUAGE ARTS
Practice Test 2

DIRECTIONS: Read the passage below to answer questions 6 to 13. The questions will focus on improving the writing quality of the passage to follow the conventions of standard written English.

William Shakespeare

(1) Even though he's been dead more than 400 years, William Shakespeare remains one of the most famous Englishmen in history. (2) He also remains one of the most widely read authors in the world, and his plays are still performed regularly. (3) Although much of the details of his personal life are lost to history, his 38 plays and 154 sonnets suggest that Shakespeare was a sensitive, witty man filled with love for life and language. (4) Many of his most famous plays and poems are still taught in schools around the world, so most people have at least some experience reading Shakespeare.

(5) Shakespeare's comedies often dealt with cases of mistaken identity, including situations where poor characters were mistaken for rich characters and female characters were mistaken for male characters. (6) To Shakespeare's audience, these storylines were funny because the social structure of the time was very rigid, and there was a common belief that people needed to know and stay in their place. (7) Shakespeare also explored how human flaws and weaknesses can create sadness and misery in his tragedies. (8) The main characters in Shakespeare's tragedies were generally short-sighted, vain, jealous, or mean-spirited, and those traits most often lead to their death or ruin. (9) Shakespeare's histories told romanticized versions of the lives of the English monarchs, which gave his audience a sense of history and national pride at a time when many common people could not read.

(10) Many of Shakespeare's plays were originally performed for the first time in London's Globe Theatre, which was built in 1599. (11) The Globe was one of the few places in England where people of different social classes were entertained together. (12) Middle and upper class patrons could buy cushioned seats that were protected from the rain, while the poor could afford to stand on the floor under the stage. (13) Even Queen Elizabeth I, arguably the most powerful figure of Shakespeare's time, enjoyed his plays. (14) Out of respect to his wide audience, Shakespeare ensured there were jokes and situations in his plays that people of all social classes and professions could relate to. (15) This ability to reach people of all different backgrounds and circumstances is one of the qualities that has kept Shakespeare's work relevant for so many centuries.

CONTINUE ON TO THE NEXT PAGE ➡

6. What is the best way to combine sentences 1 and 2 to avoid repetition?

   A. Even though he's been dead more than 400 years, William Shakespeare remains one of the most famous Englishmen in history, and he also remains one of the most widely read authors in the world, and his plays are still performed regularly.

   B. Even though he's been dead more than 400 years, William Shakespeare remains one of the most famous Englishmen in history; he also remains one of the most widely read authors in the world, and his plays are still performed regularly.

   C. Even though he's been dead more than 400 years, William Shakespeare remains one of the most famous Englishmen in history as well as one of the most widely read authors in the world, with plays that are still performed regularly.

   D. Even though he's been dead more than 400 years, William Shakespeare remains one of the most famous Englishmen in history, and in spite of the fact that he is dead, he is one of the most widely read authors in the world, and his plays are still performed regularly.

7. Which edit is needed to correct sentence 3?

   A. Change **much** to **many**
   B. Change **are** to **is**
   C. Change **suggest** to **suggests**
   D. Change **was** to **is**

8. Which revision of sentence 4 eliminates the use of passive voice?

   A. Many of his most famous plays and poems are still taught in schools around the world, so most people have read Shakespeare.

   B. Most people have at least some experience reading Shakespeare because his plays and poems are still taught in schools around the world.

   C. Most people have at least some experience reading Shakespeare because his most famous plays and poems are staples of high school literature classes.

   D. Most people have at least some experience reading Shakespeare because they are taught his most famous plays and poems in school.

9. Which sentence would best precede sentence 5 to serve as a topic sentence?

   A. Shakespeare's comedies are regarded as some of the funniest plays of all time.

   B. Throughout his career, Shakespeare wrote many different plays.

   C. All of Shakespeare's plays are widely regarded as works of genius.

   D. Shakespeare focused on three different kinds of plays: comedies, tragedies, and histories.

CONTINUE ON TO THE NEXT PAGE ➡

10. How could sentence 7 best be revised to clarify ideas and prevent reader confusion?

   A. Shakespeare explored how human flaws and weaknesses can create sadness and misery throughout his tragic plays.

   B. In his tragedies, Shakespeare explored how human flaws and weaknesses can create sadness and misery.

   C. At the same time, Shakespeare explored how human flaws and weaknesses can create sadness and misery in his tragedies.

   D. Another group of Shakespeare plays explored how human flaws and weaknesses can create sadness and misery: the tragedies.

11. Which edit is needed to correct sentence 8?

   A. Change **were** to **are**

   B. Change **those** to **these**

   C. Change **lead** to **led**

   D. Change **their** to **they're**

12. Which revision best corrects the wordiness of sentence 10?

   A. Many of Shakespeare's plays were performed for the first time in London's Globe Theatre, which was built in 1599.

   B. Many of Shakespeare's plays were originally performed in London's Globe Theatre, which was built in 1599.

   C. Many of Shakespeare's plays were originally performed for the first time in London's Globe Theatre, built in 1599.

   D. Many of Shakespeare's plays were originally performed in London's Globe Theatre, built in 1599.

13. Which sentence is least related to the main idea of the third paragraph and should be removed?

   A. Sentence 11

   B. Sentence 12

   C. Sentence 13

   D. Sentence 14

CONTINUE ON TO THE NEXT PAGE →

ENGLISH LANGUAGE ARTS
Practice Test 2

DIRECTIONS: Read the passage below to answer questions 14 to 20. The questions will focus on improving the writing quality of the passage to follow the conventions of standard written English.

The California Gold Rush

(1) The California Gold Rush, one of the most important chapters in American history, began with a carpenter inspecting a ditch in 1848. (2) James W. Marshall, who was supervising the construction of a sawmill about forty miles northeast of Sacramento, noticed a few bright flakes in a channel that workers had dug to carry water away from the mill's paddlewheel. (3) After testing the material, Marshall determined it was gold and contacted his employer, the frontier trader John Sutter. (4) Sutter confirmed the find, and word spread quickly that there was gold in California.

(5) Initially, most of the people searching for gold in the area around Sutter's Mill were native Californians, many of whom were Spanish-speaking. (6) This makes sense because when gold was first discovered, California was still a Mexican territory. (7) As word of the gold spread, people begun flocking to California from all around the world. (8) Many Americans traveled in wagon trains across the country to try and strike in rich in California. (9) Other prospectors came from as far as China, Hawaii, Latin America, and Europe. (10) By the end of the Gold Rush in 1855, over 300,000 people had come to California. (11) Very few of those people ever struck it rich by finding gold, but the immigration wave made California one of the most diverse and dynamic places in North America.

(12) The California Gold Rush still has a powerful legacy. (13) Most importantly the Gold Rush fast-tracked California to statehood and made San Francisco one of the most important cities in North America. (14) To this day, California is known as "The Golden State," and the signs for California state highways are shaped like a miner's spade to commemorate the important role the Gold Rush had in first bringing people to the area. (15) The NFL team that is based in San Francisco is even known as the 49ers, a common nickname for the prospectors who flooded the region in 1849.

14. How could sentence 2 be revised to communicate all the same main ideas with fewer words?

   A. James W. Marshall noticed a few bright flakes in a freshly dug channel near the sawmill he was building outside Sacramento.
   B. A sawmill supervisor outside Sacramento was the first person to find gold.
   C. Gold was first discovered by James W. Marshall near Sacramento.
   D. James W. Marshall was supervising the construction of a sawmill near Sacramento.

CONTINUE ON TO THE NEXT PAGE ➡

15. Which of the following sentences would best follow sentence 4?

A. The mill Marshall and Sutter were building was ultimately never used, although it is now a California Historical Landmark.

B. Marshall and Sutter tested the gold by washing it with lye, which would have dissolved so-called "fool's gold."

C. Although neither Marshall nor Sutter ever profited from the gold rush, their discovery began a chain of events that changed American history.

D. Ironically, even though he started the Gold Rush, Marshall eventually died in poverty.

16. What is the best way to combine sentences 5 and 6 to reduce wordiness and ensure clarity?

A. Initially, most of the people searching for gold in the area around Sutter's Mill were native Californians, many of whom were Spanish-speaking since California was part of Mexico at the time.

B. Most of the people searching for gold in the area around Sutter's Mill were native Californians, many of whom were Spanish-speaking, which makes sense because when gold was first discovered, California was still a Mexican territory.

C. When Marshall first discovered gold at Sutter's Mill in 1848, many of the first people to search for gold were Spanish-speaking native Californians.

D. Initially, most of the people searching for gold in the area around Sutter's Mill were native Californians, many of whom were

Spanish speaking, which makes sense because when gold was first discovered, California was still a Mexican territory.

17. Which edit is required to correct sentence 7?

A. Change **spread** to **was spreading**
B. Change **begun** to **began**
C. Change **flocking** to **flocked**
D. Change **around** to **throughout**

18. Which transition would fit best at the beginning of sentence 12?

A. As you can see
B. Over 150 years later
C. In conclusion
D. However

19. How should sentence 13 be revised to ensure correct comma usage?

A. No corrections are necessary.
B. Most importantly the Gold Rush fast-tracked California to statehood and made San Francisco one of the most important cities in North America.
C. Most importantly, the Gold Rush fast-tracked California to statehood, and made San Francisco one of the most important cities in North America.
D. Most importantly, the Gold Rush fast-tracked California to statehood and made San Francisco one of the most important cities in North America.

CONTINUE ON TO THE NEXT PAGE →

20. Which would make the best conclusion to follow sentence 15?

    A. The 49ers are one of the most successful teams in NFL history, continuing the impressive legacy of the Gold Rush.

    B. The Gold Rush also grew San Francisco from a town of 200 people to a booming metropolis of over 35,000.

    C. The 49ers' cheerleaders are even called the "Gold Rush Girls."

    D. If not for the Gold Rush, California would clearly have a very different cultural identity.

CONTINUE ON TO THE NEXT PAGE ➡

READING COMPREHENSION
Practice Test 2

DIRECTIONS: Analyze the passages below, and answer the commensurate questions. Only use information provided within the passage for your answers. There is only one answer for each question.

This text derives from an article authored in 1899.

The origin of the term caucus is obscure. It has been derived from the Algonquin word kaw-kaw-wus – to consult, to speak – but the more probable derivation makes it a corruption of "caulkers". In the early politics of Boston, and ⁵ particularly during the early difficulties between the townsmen and the British troops, the seafaring men and those employed about the ship yards were prominent among the towns-people, and there were numerous gatherings which may have ¹⁰ very easily come to be called by way of reproach a meeting of caulkers after the least influential class who attended them, or from the caulking house or caulk house in which they were held. What was at first a derisive description came to ¹⁵ be an appellation, and the gatherings of so-called caulkers became a caucus.

A caucus, in the political vocabulary of the United States, is primarily a private meeting of voters holding similar views, held prior to an election ²⁰ for the purpose of furthering such views at the election. With the development of parties and the rule of majorities, the caucus or some equivalent has become an indispensable adjunct of party government, and it may now be defined as a ²⁵ meeting of the majority of the electors belonging to the same party in any political or legislative body held preliminary to a meeting thereof, for the purpose of selecting candidates to be voted ³⁰ for, or for the purpose of determining the course of the party at the meeting of the whole body.

The candidates of each party are universally selected by caucus, either directly or indirectly through delegates to conventions chosen in ³⁵ caucuses. In legislative bodies, the course of each party is often predetermined with certainty in caucus, and open discussion between parties has been, in consequence, in some degree superseded. The caucus system is, in short, the basis of a ⁴⁰ complete electoral system which has grown up within each party, side by side with that which is alone contemplated by the laws. This condition has in recent years attracted much attention, and has been bitterly denounced as an evil. It was, ⁴⁵ however, early foreseen. John Adams, in 1814, wrote in the "Tenth Letter on Government": "They have invented a balance to all balance in their caucuses. We have congressional caucuses, state caucuses, county caucuses, city caucuses, district ⁵⁰ caucuses, town caucuses, parish caucuses, and Sunday caucuses at church doors; and in these aristocratical caucuses elections have been decided."

CONTINUE ON TO THE NEXT PAGE →

21. What is this passage predominantly about?

   A. The origin and political importance of caucuses in American politics.
   B. The origin of the American Revolution
   C. The etymological origin of the word caucus.
   D. The origin of congressional caucuses

22. What is not provided as a possible etymological origin of the term "caucus?"

   A. Algonquin roots.
   B. The name given to shipmen.
   C. The name given to the places where shipmen would meet.
   D. A Latin word meaning, "to discuss."

23. According to the passage, at what point in the election process does a caucus occur?

   A. A caucus is an election.
   B. A caucus occurs following an election, so that people may celebrate.
   C. A caucus occurs before an election.
   D. A caucus has no relevancy to an election.

24. What does John Adams imply to be an issue with caucuses?

   A. They involve only the most low class of citizens.
   B. They are time consuming.
   C. They allow aristocratic circles to decide elections.
   D. They are an outdated vestige of the revolution.

25. What would be an example of a caucus?

   A. A group of senators from one party meeting to discuss how they should vote on a bill.
   B. A group of people from different parties meeting so as to come to consensus.
   C. A group of people visiting a voting booth.
   D. A group of sailors on a ship.

26. How frequently are presidential candidates of a party selected by caucus, according to the passage?

   A. Never
   B. Sometimes
   C. Only when the primary votes are inconclusive.
   D. Always

CONTINUE ON TO THE NEXT PAGE ➡

According to Denizart, a duel is a combat between two or more individuals for reasons of a personal nature at a place indicated in a challenge. According to Cauchy, a duel is a private war, preceded by a challenge, by which each of the belligerent parties is warned to be on his guard and to resist force by force. John Reynaud describes a duel as a combat agreed upon in advance between two individuals who, by this fact, place themselves without the pale of all social laws. Dupin is more severe, and his definition strongly resembles a judgment without appeal. According to him, "dueling is the savage state; it is not the right but the argument of the stronger and more adroit, and sometimes of the more insolent."

Little is known of the origin of dueling, and we shall not trace it back to Cain, who, according to some, was but a fortunate duelist. We find the first traces of it in Germany, whose inhabitants, says Montesquieu, "made war upon one another for murder, theft and injury. This custom was modified by subjecting these wars to rules. They were engaged in by order of the magistrate; this was preferable to a general license to fight." Gondebaud, king of the Burgundians, was the first to introduce into the code the judicial duel. A law called the Gombette law, promulgated in 501, regulated it. Charlemagne imitated this example, and this barbarous legislation can scarcely be said to have been seriously altered until during the reign of Philip the Fair in 1296. Duels properly so called, that is, duels to which any of the definitions given above may be applied, date from the period when tournaments and the judicial duel ceased.

The discourse of Brantome on duels furnishes us some curious information as to the rules which duelists recognized in the sixteenth century. The combatants, if they followed the advice of the malicious chronicler, should take good care not to fight without witnesses, first, in order not to deprive the public of a fine spectacle, and then, not to expose themselves to be prosecuted as murderers. "It is not necessary, in these matters, to speak of courtesy," says the author of Dames Galantes. "The man who enters the lists should propose to himself to conquer or die, and above all, never to surrender; for the vanquisher disposes of the vanquished as he pleases. He may drag him over the field, hang him, burn him, hold him as a prisoner, or dispose of him as a slave. A soldier may fight his captain, provided he has served two years and asked to leave the company. If a father accuses his son of any crime by which he might be dishonored, the son may justly challenge his father to a duel, since the father has done him a greater injury by dishonoring him than he did him good by bringing him into this world and giving him life."

27. What is this passage mostly about?

A. The historical origins of duels.
B. A discussion of the judicial system in early Germany.
C. A meditation on ways that the criminal justice system has changed in the last two millennia.
D. A discussion of the definition of war.

CONTINUE ON TO THE NEXT PAGE →

28. Cauchy defines a duel as:

   A. A "savage state".
   B. A "private war".
   C. Two people fighting to the death.
   D. A method for deciding issues.

29. What is one reason provided as to why duels would always have witnesses?

   A. So that participants could show everyone their strength.
   B. Witnesses were needed to make the proceedings legal.
   C. So as to avoid being prosecuted for murder.
   D. Witnesses will be the following contestants.

30. Gondebaud is important in the history of the duel because:

   A. He was the first leader to recommend duels as a way of resolving conflict.
   B. He was the first to condemn it as savage
   C. He was the first to practice a duel.
   D. He was the first to introduce a judicial code associated with dueling.

31. Duels originated in which country?

   A. France
   B. Britain
   C. Germany
   D. Italy

32. Dupin is most Likely to prefer what modification to dueling practices?

   A. For them to be outlawed.
   B. For them to be modified such that death does not occur.
   C. For them to have stricter judicial codes.
   D. For them to only be used in the most severe cases.

CONTINUE ON TO THE NEXT PAGE ➡

President Andrew Jackson's early opportunities for education were very limited, and the unceasing action of his later years left him little time to remedy this defect. He is said, on very good authority, to have believed that the earth was flat. 5 His familiar letters are disfigured by grammatical and other mistakes. His public papers were always carefully revised, and often entirely written, by trusted subordinates. When forced to rely altogether upon his own pen, he was apt to slip. It is 10 an open secret that his nullification proclamation was the work of Edward Livingston, and his bank veto that of Amos Kendall; nevertheless, in all cases, it is equally certain that Jackson allowed his subordinates only the privilege of expressing 15 his ideas and policy, and that he expected from them a certain mechanical skill of expression, not the inception of a policy. Any influence upon him by subordinates was only obtained by indirection or by force of sympathy. 20

In temper, Jackson was arbitrary, forceful, persistent, not at all impulsive but willing to yield to his naturally hot temper. In brief, he was force personified, not aggressive force merely, but the force of self-control as well. According to the 25 necessity of the case, he could either maintain equanimity against any exasperation or pass into a fit of passion more demoniacal than human. In politics, he was the self-anointed successor of Jefferson as the assertor of individual rights 30 against the tendency to class formation, but with this difference: that in Jefferson's time, individualism claimed only recognition, while in Jackson, it had advanced to more active life.

35 Under Madison, Monroe and Adams, features had become powerful in the government which, for Jackson, seemed evil from the individual point of view: the incorporation of a bank to do government work, the protection of various 40 classes of manufactures by tariff taxation, and the expenditure of public money upon roads and canals. Against all these, Jackson fought as actively as Jefferson did passively. On the other hand, Jackson's individualism did not prevent 45 him, as it did Jefferson, from being a thoroughly national man, for in Jackson's time, individualism had taken a place as a co-ordinate factor in the national development.

It is easy to mark the points in Jefferson's teachings 50 from whose unhealthy development arose the Calhoun idea of nullification, but it would be impossible to imagine such a process in Jackson's case. Jefferson and Jackson had the same ultimate goal, but a different immediate object: the former 55 to protect the individual through the states; the latter to protect the individual through the nation. Jefferson would have opposed nullification in 1831-1832, but not with the heat and sense of personal antipathy which Jackson exhibited.

CONTINUE ON TO THE NEXT PAGE →

33. What is this passage mostly about?

    A. Biographical details of Andrew Jackson.
    B. Andrew Jackson 's upbringing.
    C. Andrew Jackson's opinion on individuality.
    D. Andrew Jackson's differences from Jefferson.

34. The author notes Jackson's belief that the earth was flat as an example of:

    A. Popular opinions of Jackson's time.
    B. Evidence that Jackson was not well learned.
    C. Evidence that Jackson did not believe in science.
    D. Evidence that the Earth was flat.

35. Jackson had a naturally ____ temper.

    A. Calm
    B. Arrogant
    C. Capricious
    D. Hot

36. According to the passage, Jackson was similar to Jefferson in his concern over the ____ ?

    A. Individual
    B. State
    C. Nation
    D. National bank

37. According to the passage, Jackson was more passionately supportive of the ____ than Jefferson?

    A. Individual
    B. Revolution
    C. Nation
    D. Rights of the President

38. Which of the following was not, according to Jackson, an assault on individual rights?

    A. Industry tariffs.
    B. The use of public funds on roads.
    C. The use of public funds on canals.
    D. The use of public funds on the military.

CONTINUE ON TO THE NEXT PAGE ➡

The following is an excerpt of an essay, written by an economist, from 1899.

Even the ablest and most conscientious management is not always able to maintain a balance between the resources and the expenses of a country. No country is insured against accidents which may decrease its income or 5 cause unforeseen expense. An event, a period of scarcity, for instance, or a revolution, may produce both a decrease of income and a great increase of expense. Again, the suddenness of a national want, its extent and its urgent character, are 10 such as to prevent providing for it with a rapidity corresponding to its suddenness: wealthy England herself attempted this in vain during the Crimean war. Finally, enterprises of evident usefulness, but the introduction of which demands time and are 15 very costly, may outweigh the current resources of the state, and necessitate for a longer or shorter period of additional revenue.

In the absence of actual resources furnished by taxation, and those which result from state 20 savings in the past, recourse must be had to the future. The state, like the private man, discounts the future: it borrows. Much has been said of the advantages of credit in private business: its usefulness in public affairs is not less than in 25 private. There is no essential difference between the national demand for credit and the demand for credit made by individuals. In both cases, the borrower appeals to the capitalist and for time within which to return the value he received. 30 These are the two constituent elements of every credit operation. As to the use the loan is put to and the results of the operation, the state which borrows can be compared only to the individual who borrows for purposes of consumption. In 35

fact, the state rarely asks money for productive investment; it borrows mostly because its disposable or prospective funds are insufficient for the present or the near future.

40 Credit is a marvelous instrument of action, one of the most powerful springs of the material and even moral progress of society. Its development, therefore, should be favored in every way; its uses and the forms it assumes cannot become 45 too numerous. But, in order to be really profitable, they should be in keeping with the very essence and real end of credit. This end is, as all know, in the first place, to keep capital from lying idle for a longer or shorter time, as the case may be, and in 50 the second, always to place capital in the hands of those who, at a given moment, may make the most productive use of it. Credit thus assures the continued circulation and fruitful employment of a nation's capital and adds to the motive 55 and protective power of this mighty instrument of labor.

39. What is this passage mostly about?

    A. The nature of credit.
    B. The use of credit by countries.
    C. How credit is used.
    D. Why credit should be used by individuals.

CONTINUE ON TO THE NEXT PAGE →

40. What is not provided as a reason a country may seek credit?

A. A country may need money to deal with a natural disaster.

B. A country may need to make a long term investment, but does not have the funds to create the invest ment.

C. A country may need to pay its military extra in war time.

D. To rebuild following a revolution.

41. The economist makes which claim in the second paragraph?

A. A country will never take on debt so as to make an investment.

B. A country will normally take on debt to pay for a good as opposed to an investment.

C. A country will only take on debt if it is for the sake of investing.

D. A country will never take on debt.

42. What situation does the author claim to be the second principle by which capital will be used most profitably?

A. If an individual uses it.

B. If a corporation uses it.

C. If no one uses it.

D. If the entity that can make the most use of the capital gains the capital.

43. Does the author believe public debt to be as important as personal debt?

A. The author is indifferent.

B. The author clearly favors individual use of debt.

C. The author clearly favors national use of debt.

D. The author believes the two uses to be of equal usefulness.

44. What would be an example of an item with "evident usefulness, but the introduction of which demands time and are very costly?"

A. A bridge connecting two urban centers

B. Back pay on pensions

C. A new law

D. Military expenses

CONTINUE ON TO THE NEXT PAGE ➡

Fermiers generaux was the name given in France, under the old monarchy, to a company which farmed certain branches of the public revenue, that is to say, contracted with the government to pay into the treasury a fixed yearly sum, taking 5 upon itself the collection of certain taxes as an equivalent. The system of farming the taxes was an old custom of the French monarchy. Under Francis I, the revenue arising from the sale of salt was farmed by private individuals in each 10 town. This was, at the time, a monopoly of the government.

The government reserved to itself the power of providing the people with salt, which it collected in its stores and sold to the retailers at 15 its own price. This monopoly was first assumed by Philippe de Valois in 1350. Other sources of revenue were likewise farmed by several individuals, most of whom were favorites of the court or of the minister of the day. Sully, the able 20 minister of Henry IV, seeing the dilapidation of the public revenue occasioned by this system by which, out of one hundred and fifty million dollars paid by the people, only thirty million reached the treasury, opened the contracts for farming 25 the taxes to public auction, giving them to the highest bidder, according to the ancient Roman practice. By this means, he greatly increased the revenue of the state.

But the practice of private contracts through 30 favor or bribing was renewed under the following reigns. Colbert, the minister of Louis XIV, called the farmers of the revenue to a severe account, and by an act of power, deprived them of their enormous gains. In 1728, under the regency, 35 the various individual leases were united into

a ferme generale, which was lent to a company, the members of which were henceforth called fermiers generaux.

40 In 1759, Silhouette, minister of Louis XV, quashed the contracts of the farmers general and levied the taxes by his own agents. But the system of contracts revived: for the court, the ministers and favorites were all well-disposed to them, 45 as private bargains were made with the farmers general by which they paid large sums as douceurs. In the time of Necker, the company consisted of forty-four members, who paid a rent of one hundred and eighty-six million of 50 livres, and Necker calculated their profit at about two millions yearly—no very extraordinary sum, if correct.

But independent of this profit there were the expenses of collection and a host of subalterns 55 to support: the company had its officers and accountants, receivers, collectors, etc., who, having the public force at their disposal, committed numerous acts of injustice toward the people, especially the poorer class, by distraining their 60 goods, selling their chattels, etc. The "gabelle" or sale of salt, among others, was a fruitful source of oppression.

CONTINUE ON TO THE NEXT PAGE →

**READING
COMPREHENSION**

45. What is this passage mostly about?

  A. How salt was extracted for sale in 18th century France.
  B. Methods monarchs used to oppress the peasants of France.
  C. A history of agricultural farmers in France.
  D. Methods of tax collection in monarchal France.

46. What word and/or phrase would most closely mean Fermiers generaux?

  A. General farmers
  B. Privatized tax collectors
  C. Fermented generals
  D. Farmers

47. Based on the passage, what is the most likely reason a farmer would be given his position in 1350?

  A. Family history of farming.
  B. Merit
  C. Farmers were appointed by lottery.
  D. The individual was politically aligned with the monarch.

48. Tax collection is discussed as a means to do all of the following except what?

  A. Gain funds for the state
  B. Reward those who are favored by the monarch
  C. Build roads
  D. Oppress the poor

49. Sully implemented a method for determining tax collectors based on which previous empire?

  A. Rome
  B. Britain
  C. Athens
  D. Earlier French empires

50. How many members were in the company during the time of Nekter?

  A. 1350
  B. 1728
  C. 44
  D. 89

CONTINUE ON TO THE NEXT PAGE ➡

We hear it maintained by people of more gravity than understanding that genius and taste are strictly reducible to rules, and that there is a rule for everything. So far is it from being true that the finest breath of fancy is a definable thing, that the plainest common sense is only what Mr. Locke would have called a mixed mode – subject to a particular sort of acquired and an definable tact. It is asked, "If you do not know the rule by which a thing is done, how can you be sure of doing it a second time?" And the answer is, "If you do not know the muscles by the help of which you walk, how is to you do not fall down at every step you take?"

In art, in taste, in life, in speech, you decide from feeling and not from reason; that is, from the impression of a number of things on the mind, which impression is true and well founded, though you may not be able to analyze or account for it in the several particulars. In a gesture you use, in a look you see, in a tone you hear, you judge of the expression, propriety, and meaning from habit, not from reason or rules; that is to say, from innumerable instances of like gestures, looks, and tones in innumerable other circumstances, variously modified, which are too many and too refined to be all distinctly recollected, but which do not therefore operate the less powerfully upon the mind and eye of taste.

Shall we say that these impressions (the immediate stamp of nature) do not operate in a given manner till they are classified and reduced to rules, or is not the rule itself grounded upon the truth and certainty of that natural operation? How then can the distinction of the understanding as to the manner on which they operated be necessary to their producing their due and uniform effect upon the mind? If certain effects did not regularly arise out of certain causes in mind as well as matter, there could be no rule given for them: nature does not follow the rule, but suggests it.

Reason is the interpreter and critic of nature and genius, not their law-giver and judge. He must be a poor creature indeed whose practical convictions do not in almost all cases outrun his deliberate understanding, or does not feel and know much more than he can give reason for. Hence the distinction between eloquence and wisdom, between ingenuity and common sense. A man may be dexterous and able in explaining the grounds of his opinions, and yet may be a mere sophist because be only sees one half of a subject. Another may feel the whole weight of a question, nothing relating to it may be lost upon him, and yet he may be able to give no account of the manner in which it affects him, or to drag his reasons from their silent lurking places.

51. What is this passage mostly about?

  A. Why people need to discuss their feelings using reason.
  B. The importance of reason in explaining one's emotions.
  C. Why feelings should have priority over reason.
  D. Why it is important to be in touch with one's feelings.

CONTINUE ON TO THE NEXT PAGE →

52. What does the author imply about Mr. Locke?

    A. He does not give priority to feelings over rules.
    B. He is in agreement with the author.
    C. He is very intelligent.
    D. He is very unintelligent.

53. What does the author believe to be the relationship between feelings and reason?

    A. The author believes that reason comes before feelings.
    B. The author believes that reason and feelings are distinct.
    C. The author believes that reason is used to provide explanation for one's feelings.
    D. The author does not believe in reason.

54. What would be an example of how the author believes the relationship between feelings and reason to operate?

    A. A person believes he should feel happy for a friend and then feels happy.
    B. A person is taught that he should hate someone else and develops hatred for that person.
    C. A person feels ill at the thought of hurting an animal and then becomes a vegetarian.
    D. A person hates math but learns it anyway.

55. What does the author imply about an individual who does not use reason adeptly?

    A. He/She is more intelligent than one who does use reason adeptly.
    B. He/She is less intelligent than one who does use reason adeptly.
    C. He/She has greater common sense than one who uses reason adeptly.
    D. He/She is not necessarily wrong in his/her beliefs.

56. What does the author imply about the man who "may be able to give no account of the manner in which it affects him?"

    A. He can be wiser than the person who is able to argue their point effectively.
    B. The person is wiser than someone who can argue their point correctly.
    C. The person would understand his position more closely if he could discuss it using rules.
    D. The man could feel stronger about his belief.

57. How does the author feel about a person "whose practical convictions do not in almost all cases outrun his deliberate understanding" (lines 36-37)?

    A. He thinks that person is very wise.
    B. He thinks that person will live a very fulfilling life.
    C. He thinks that person would agree with Locke.
    D. He thinks that person is pathetic.

90 MINUTES • 57 QUESTIONS

Select the best answer from the choices given by carefully solving each problem. Bubble the letter of your answer on the answer sheet. Please refrain from making any stray marks on the answer sheet. If you need to erase an answer, please erase thoroughly.

Important Notes:

1. There are no formulas or definitions in the math section that will be provided.
2. Diagrams may or may not be drawn to scale. Do not make assumptions based on the diagram unless it is specifically stated in the diagram or question.
3. Diagrams are not in more than one plane, unless stated otherwise.
4. Graphs are drawn to scale, therefore, you can assume relationships according to the graph. If lines appear parallel, then you can assume the lines to be parallel. This is also true for right angles and so forth.
5. Simplify fractions completely.

Practice Test 2 (Questions 1-57)

1. $(\sqrt{100})(\sqrt{64})$

   A. 10
   B. 18
   C. 80
   D. 164

2.
   7.2 aliens = 1 monster
   1 monster = 15.5 oranges

   Using the conversion above, how many oranges are equal to 1 alien?

   A. 0.46
   B. 1.95
   C. 2.15
   D. 22.7

CONTINUE ON TO THE NEXT PAGE →

3. What is the greatest common factor of 147 and 98?

A. 3
B. 7
C. 14
D. 49

4. If $x = 7$ and $y = 0$, what is the value of $\dfrac{11x}{x - y}$?

A. 0
B. 7
C. 10
D. 11

5. Lucy scored a 85, 64 and 76 on her math exams. What score must Lucy obtain on the next math test to have an average of exactly 80?

A. 93
B. 97
C. 94
D. 95

6. Helga has 4 dogs, 3 cats and 2 birds. If she closes her eyes and picks one animal, what is the probability that it does not have 4 legs?

A. $\dfrac{2}{7}$

B. $\dfrac{7}{9}$

C. $\dfrac{2}{9}$

D. $\dfrac{4}{7}$

7. If $y = x^2 \cdot x^x$, what is y when $x = 2$?

A. 16
B. 8
C. 4
D. 32

8. Train A, traveling at 200mph, leaves station A at 1P. M. Train B, traveling at 300mph, leaves station B at 3P.M. Both stations are directly across from each other and X miles away. If the trains meet at 4P.M., what is X?

A. 900mi
B. 700mi
C. 600mi
D. 400mi

CONTINUE ON TO THE NEXT PAGE →

9. Bernard is now *y* years old. Luis is 8 years older than Bernard. In terms of *y*, how old was Luis 5 years ago?

A. $8y - 5$
B. $y + 3$
C. $y + 13$
D. $y - 5$

10.

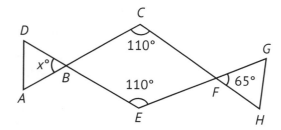

In the figure above, *ABC, DBE, EFG* and *CFH* are straight line segments. What is the value of *x*?

A. 45°
B. 65°
C. 70°
D. 75°

11. Which of the following shows the fraction $\frac{13}{3}$, $\frac{37}{8}$ and $\frac{19}{4}$ in order from greatest to least?

A. $\frac{37}{8}, \frac{19}{4}, \frac{13}{3}$

B. $\frac{37}{8}, \frac{13}{3}, \frac{19}{4}$

C. $\frac{19}{4}, \frac{13}{3}, \frac{37}{8}$

D. $\frac{19}{4}, \frac{37}{8}, \frac{13}{3}$

12. If *x* and *y* are integers, which is always even?

A. $\frac{x + y}{2}$

B. $2(\frac{x + y}{x})$

C. $2(x + y)$

D. $x^2 + y^2$

CONTINUE ON TO THE NEXT PAGE ➡

13.

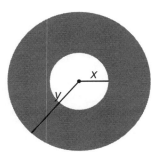

What is the probability that a point chosen will be in the shaded region?

A. $\dfrac{y^2}{x^2}$

B. $\dfrac{(x + y)^2}{y^2}$

C. $\dfrac{x^2}{y^2 - x^2}$

D. $\dfrac{y^2 - x^2}{y^2}$

14. If $q = x + y$ and $x = y + z$, what is z in terms of y and q?

A. $q - 2x$
B. $q - 2y$
C. $2x - q$
D. $2y + q$

15. What is $\dfrac{(5!)!}{5!}$?

A. 1
B. 5
C. 120
D. None of the above

16. What is $\dfrac{a^2 + 2ab + b^2}{(a + b)^3}$?

A. $(a + b)$

B. $a^2 + b^2$

C. $\dfrac{1}{a + b}$

D. $\dfrac{1}{(a + b)^2}$

17. It takes 3 cats 3 minutes to catch 3 mice. How many cats are needed to catch 99 mice in 99 minutes?

A. 3
B. 11
C. 33
D. 99

18. The sum of seven consecutive odd integers is 749, what is the largest of the seven integers?

A. 101
B. 103
C. 113
D. 115

CONTINUE ON TO THE NEXT PAGE →

Explanations to each problem on:
Youtube.com/ArgoBrothers

MATHEMATICS
TEST 2

ARGO
BROTHERS
www.argobrothers.com

19. $V = \pi r^2 h$

Using the formula above, if r is doubled and h is divided by 2, what is the ratio of the original volume to the new volume?

A. 1:4
B. 1:2
C. 1:1
D. 2:1

20. A yellow cab has a base fare of $3.50 per ride plus $0.20 for each $\frac{1}{4}$ of mile ridden. If a yellow cab costs $22.50, how many miles long was the ride?

A. 23.75 miles
B. 42.5 miles
C. 47.5 miles
D. 112.5 miles

21. John works 40 hours a week, and his monthly salary in June was $4,000. In the month of July, John got a 4% raise on his monthly salary. In the month of July, what was John's hourly rate? (Note: Assume there are four weeks in July)

A. $25
B. $26
C. $40
D. $100

22. If $8{,}575 = 5^x \cdot 7^y$, what is $(xy) - 5$?

A. 1
B. 3
C. 6
D. 7

23. When d is divided by 8, the remainder is 3. What is the remainder when $d + 3$ is divided by 8?

A. 1
B. 3
C. 4
D. 6

24. Tommy is making a 6 Letter password using only the letters A, B, C, D, E and F. How many different codes can Tommy make, if every letter can only be used once in each code?

A. 6
B. 120
C. 720
D. 46,656

25. $-5(x - 3) \geq 20$

What is the solution to the inequality shown above?

A. $x \geq -1$
B. $x \geq 7$
C. $x \leq -1$
D. $x \geq 1$

CONTINUE ON TO THE NEXT PAGE ➡

26. Which number line below shows the solution to the inequality $-2 < \dfrac{x}{3} \le 2$?

A.

B.

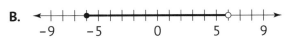

C.

D.

27.

Favorite Genres of Movies amongst Teens

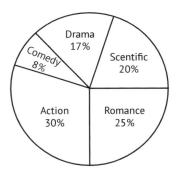

There are 15,000 teens whose favorite genre is comedy. How many teens have a favorite genre of action?

A. 30
B. 41,250
C. 52,500
D. 56,250

28. A computer originally priced at $550.50 is on sale for 20% off. Jamie used a 5% discount coupon which was applied to the sales price. How much did Jamie pay for the computer? (Assume there is no tax.)

A. $412.88
B. $418.38
C. $440.40
D. $522.98

29. Given the following value 4,760.

Solve the following, $\dfrac{x^2}{y}$, if x represents the smallest prime factor of the given value, and y represents the greatest prime factor of the given value.

A. $\dfrac{119}{4}$

B. $\dfrac{4}{17}$

C. $\dfrac{2}{119}$

D. $\dfrac{4}{119}$

30. An adult male Diptera has a mass of 11.5 milligrams. What is the Diptera's mass in grams?

A. 0.0115 g
B. 0.115 g
C. 1.15 g
D. 11.5 g

CONTINUE ON TO THE NEXT PAGE ➡

31. Michael has a project due in exactly 83 hours. It is currently 8:30 on a Monday morning. What time is his project due?

    A. 6:30 PM Friday
    B. 7:30 PM Friday
    C. 7:30 AM Thursday
    D. 7:30 PM Thursday

32. $\left(\dfrac{2}{3} + \dfrac{1}{4}\right) \div 2 =$

    A. $\dfrac{22}{12}$

    B. $\dfrac{1}{12}$

    C. $\dfrac{11}{24}$

    D. $\dfrac{1}{3}$

33. Michelle bought a dress that costs $103.00, a pair of shoes that costs $73.00 and a bag that costs $111.00. There is a 7% sales tax on all items priced at $90.00 and higher. There is no sales tax on items under $90.00. How much did Michelle spend on the following items, including tax?

    A. $287.00
    B. $295.49
    C. $300.60
    D. $301.98

34. How many terms are in the sequence, 0, 3, 6, … , 57, 60?

    A. 20
    B. 21
    C. 23
    D. 60

35. The larger of two consecutive even integers is two times the smaller. What is their sum?

    A. 2
    B. 3
    C. 4
    D. 6

36. $3^x = 27^{a+b}$ and $\dfrac{a^2 - b^2}{(a - b)} = 5.$ What is x?

    A. 6
    B. 9
    C. 12
    D. 15

37. In Mr. Farmer's class there are 30 kids. If there are twice as many boys as there are girls in the English club, then what percentage of the English club are boys?

    A. 33.3%
    B. 30%
    C. 20%
    D. 66.6%

CONTINUE ON TO THE NEXT PAGE ➡

38. $a \star b = a^3 - 3a^2b + 3ab^2 - b^3$

$a \oplus b = (a - b)(a - b)$

What is $\dfrac{a \star b}{a \oplus b}$

  A. $a^2 + b^2$
  B. $(a - b)$
  C. $a^2 + 3b^2 + 3ab$
  D. $a^2 - b^2$

39. What is the prime factorization of 752?

  A. $2^3 \cdot 48$
  B. $2^3 \cdot 49$
  C. $2^4 \cdot 47$
  D. $3^4 \cdot 47$

40. If x can be any integer, what is the least possible value of the expression $4x^2 - 10$?

  A. -10
  B. -4
  C. 4
  D. ∞

41. There are a total of 5 bicycles and tricycles in a park. There are 12 wheels. How many tricycles are there?

  A. 2
  B. 3
  C. 6
  D. 7

42. What is least possible value of $\dfrac{x^2 - 1}{x^2}$ if $x \geq 1$

  A. -1
  B. 0
  C. 3
  D. $\dfrac{3}{4}$

43. What is the maximum number of points in which a circle and triangle can intersect?

  A. 3
  B. 5
  C. 6
  D. ∞

44.

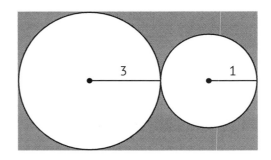

Figure not drawn to scale.

What is the area of the shaded region?
  A. $48 - 10\pi$
  B. $64 - 22\pi$
  C. $48 - 6\pi$
  D. 16π

CONTINUE ON TO THE NEXT PAGE →

45. There are 45 plastic ducks in a bag. If there are black, green, blue, and purple plastic ducks and $\frac{1}{3}$ of the plastic ducks are black, $\frac{1}{5}$ of the plastic ducks are blue, one third of the number of black plastic ducks are green, then how many purple plastic ducks are in the bag?

A. 6
B. 15
C. 16
D. 21

46.

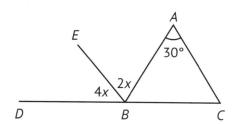

Figure not drawn to scale.

In the figure above, point *B* is on line segment *DC*. If *AB* = *BC*, what is the measure of angle *ABE*?

A. 20°
B. 40°
C. 80°
D. 90°

47.

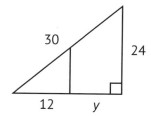

According to the figure above, what is the value of *y?*

A. 3
B. 6
C. 12
D. 15

48. A painter needs 4 gallons of paint to paint each room. If a house has 8 rooms in total, how many quarts of paint is he going to need?

A. 12
B. 32
C. 128
D. 200

49. A rectangle is inscribed in a circle. The rectangle is tangent at the points *A*, *B*, *C* and *D*. If the diagonal of the rectangle is 20 inches long, what is the area of the circle?

A. 10π
B. 15π
C. 20π
D. 100π

CONTINUE ON TO THE NEXT PAGE →

50.

Gas Prices	
Regular	$2.00
Premium	$2.25
Unloaded	$2.50

The prices in the table above show the different types of gas offered at a gas station and the prices of the gas per gallon. If Emily has $50, what is the least amount of gas, in gallons, she can purchase subtracted from the greatest amount of gas, in gallons, she can purchase?

A. 2 gallons
B. 3 gallons
C. 5 gallons
D. 20 gallons

---

51. A survey was conducted to determine the age at which the members of the Youth Advisory Committee started their first job.

Age at First Job

Age	Frequency
14	1
15	3
16	3
17	4
18	1
19	2
21	1

What was the median age reported by the Youth Advisory Committee?

A. 15.5
B. 16
C. 17.5
D. 17

52. Use the following frequency chart to answer the following question.

Item	Cost	Number
Oatmeal Cookies	$1.76	4
Whole Milk	$3.99	2
Sugar Cured Ham	$4.54	2
7 Grain Bread	$3.27	3
CFL Light bulbs	$2.00	5
Ginger Soda	$0.67	6
Chocolate Candy Bar	$1.15	?

How many Chocolate Candy Bars must Cindy purchase in order to end up with a median price of $1.88?

A. 0
B. 1
C. 2
D. 3

CONTINUE ON TO THE NEXT PAGE →

You Tube
Explanations to each problem on:
Youtube.com/ArgoBrothers

MATHEMATICS
TEST 2

ARGO BROTHERS
www.argobrothers.com

GRID IN

Directions: The following five questions are grid-in problems. On the answer sheet, please be sure to write your answer in the boxes at the top of the grid. Start on the left side of each grid.

53. If *A*, *B*, *C*, *D*, and *E* are points on a plane such that line *CD* bisects ⊰ *ACB* and line *CB* bisects right angle ⊰ *ACE*, then ⊰ *DCE* = ?

54. A truck traveled 130 miles using 4 gallons of diesel fuel. What distance would the same truck cover using 6.7 gallons of diesel fuel? (Round your answer to the nearest whole number)

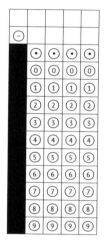

55. $||-10 - 18| - 20| =$

CONTINUE ON TO THE NEXT PAGE →

56. What is the perimeter of a rectangular garden that is 16 units wide and has the same area as a rectangular garden that is 10 units wide and 32 units long?

THIS IS THE END OF THE TEST. IF THERE IS TIME REMAINING, YOU MAY CHECK YOUR ANSWERS TO PART 1 OR PART 2.

57. For the equation: $-1 - \dfrac{2}{5} \cdot \dfrac{5m - 10}{2 + 3m} = 1$, solve for m. Enter your answer in the grid below, rounded to the nearest whole number.

SHSAT PRACTICE TEST 2
ANSWER KEY

Revising/Editing

1. **D**
2. **B**
3. **B**
4. **C**
5. **C**
6. **C**
7. **A**
8. **C**
9. **D**
10. **B**
11. **C**
12. **D**
13. **C**
14. **A**
15. **C**
16. **A**
17. **B**
18. **B**
19. **D**
20. **D**

Reading Comprehension

21. **A**
22. **D**
23. **C**
24. **C**
25. **A**
26. **D**
27. **A**
28. **B**
29. **C**
30. **D**
31. **C**
32. **A**
33. **A**
34. **B**
35. **D**
36. **A**
37. **C**
38. **D**
39. **B**
40. **C**
41. **B**
42. **D**
43. **D**
44. **A**
45. **D**
46. **B**
47. **D**
48. **C**
49. **A**
50. **C**
51. **C**
52. **A**
53. **C**
54. **C**
55. **D**
56. **A**
57. **D**

Math

1. **C**
2. **C**
3. **D**
4. **D**
5. **D**
6. **C**
7. **A**
8. **A**
9. **B**
10. **D**
11. **D**
12. **C**
13. **D**
14. **B**
15. **D**
16. **C**
17. **A**
18. **C**
19. **B**
20. **A**
21. **B**
22. **A**
23. **D**
24. **C**
25. **C**
26. **D**
27. **D**
28. **B**
29. **B**
30. **A**
31. **D**
32. **C**
33. **D**
34. **B**
35. **D**
36. **D**
37. **D**
38. **B**
39. **C**
40. **A**
41. **A**
42. **B**
43. **C**
44. **A**
45. **C**
46. **A**
47. **B**
48. **C**
49. **D**
50. **C**
51. **D**
52. **C**
53. **67.5°**
54. **218 miles**
55. **8**
56. **72**
57. **0**

1. **D** Answer D is correct because it correctly punctuates both halves of the sentence. First, "Try not to become a man of success" must go into quotation marks because it is part of what Einstein is saying. Similarly, "but rather try to become a man of value" also requires quotation marks because it is part of what is being said. Each half of the quotation also requires a comma for formatting. In the first half of the sentence, the comma goes inside the quotation mark before the attribution. In the second half of the sentence, the comma comes after the attribution and before the second set of quotation marks. Answer A is incorrect because there is no closing quotation mark at the end of the sentence. Answer B is incorrect because there is no comma following "rather." Answer C is incorrect because there is no comma following "success."

2. **B** This sentence is consistently written in the past tense and talks about historical events, so using the past tense verb "became" is the best correction that can be made to this sentence, making Answer B correct. Answers A, C, and D are all incorrect because each of them would introduce an inconsistent, confusing present tense verb to the sentence.

3. **B** Sentences 1, 3, 4, and 5 are written consistently in the past tense, which is appropriate because they discuss events from the historical past (as indicated by "...in the seventeenth century..." and "In 1687..."). Answer B is correct because Sentence 2 contains the present tense verb "publishes." This should be corrected to "published" to correctly indicate when the action occurred (in the past) and to make Sentence 2 consistent with the tense of the rest of the paragraph.

4. **C** A dangling modifier occurs when a sentence begins with a modifier whose subject is unclear or easily mistaken. "A secret kept form almost the entire nation," which comes at the beginning of Sentence 3, is a dangling modifier, making Answer C correct. "A secret kept..." is a dangling modifier because at point those words appear on the page, it's unclear what the secret is. The reader could mistakenly infer that the fishing trip itself was the secret rather than the cover story for the actual secret (the surgical procedure). Sentence 3 should be revised to clarify the relationship between these ideas.

5. **C** "To be" verbs (is, am, are, was, were, will be, etc.) are generally discouraged from use in formal writing. In this sentence, the only "to be" verb is "was" in the phrase "...was famous for..." Answer C is correct because it rearranges the sentence to eliminate the need for the "to be" verb. Answer choice A is incorrect because it maintains "was" and simply substitutes "well known" for "famous." Answer choice B is incorrect because it substitutes "as well as" for "and" without addressing the "to be" verb issue. Answer choice D is incorrect because it removes the "to be" verb was, but inserts the equally incorrect "were."

6. **C** Answer C is the best combination of the two sentences because it includes all relevant information without repeating key phrases. Answers A and B cannot be correct because both repeat the verb "remains," which is unnecessary. Similarly, Answer D is repetitive because it states the fact that Shakespeare is dead twice. Only Answer C communicates that Shakespeare has been dead for

more than 400 years, is one of history's most famous Englishmen, and is still widely read and performed without repeating phrases.

7. **A**   The adjective "much" is used to describe singular nouns. The adjective "many" is used to describe plural nouns. (For example, you have "much electricity" but "many light bulbs.") Since the adjective in question is modifying the plural noun "details," then "many" must be used. Answer B cannot be correct because the plural noun "details" takes the plural verb "are," so "is" would be incorrect. Answer C cannot be correct because the plural nouns "plays" and "sonnets" take the plural verb "suggest." Answer D cannot be correct because it's already been established that Shakespeare is dead, so he cannot exist in the present tense.

8. **C**   Passive voice occurs when the subject of a sentence or clause is having action performed on them rather than performing the action themselves. The original sentence states that Shakespeare's plays and poems "are still taught," which is a passive voice construction because the plays and poems are not the ones doing the teaching. Answers A, B, and D do not correct this error and are therefore all incorrect. Only Answer C creates an active voice construction by stating that the "plays and poems are staples."

9. **D**   Answer D provides the best topic sentence because it provides a clear preview of the paragraph's main ideas (the three types of plays Shakespeare focused on). Answer A would not make a good topic sentence because it only focuses on comedies. Answer B provides a relevant topic sentence for the paragraph, but it is somewhat vague and non-specific, so it cannot be the "best" answer. While Answer C makes tangential reference to Shakespeare having written a variety of plays, it is focused more on judgment or appraisal of his work than describing it.

10. **B**   As written, sentence 7 waits until its last word to identify that it is talking about the tragedies. Readers could easily become confused and think that Shakespeare "explored how human flaws and weaknesses can create sadness and misery" in his comedies, based on the fact that the comedies were the topic of the previous two sentences. Answer B eliminates this issue by providing a clear, signposted transition to discussing the tragedies. Answer A cannot be correct because it is simply a rewording of the original sentence with the same confusing structure intact. Answer C attempts to provide a transition from one idea to the next by using the phrase "At the same time," but the concept of tragedy is still not introduced until the last word of the sentence, leaving the reader to wonder whether the early content of the sentence is referring to the comedies or something else. Answer D attempts to create a transition towards the tragedies, but it is not the best answer because it still waits until the end of the sentence to name the tragedies, using the colon for a "dramatic reveal" rather than using clear signposting.

11. **C**   Paragraph 2 is consistently written using past tense verbs (dealt, were, was, explored, told, etc.). Answer C is correct because "lead" is a present tense verb, so it must be replaced for consistency. Answer A cannot be correct because "are" is a present tense verb, and therefore also inconsistent with the rest of the paragraph. Answer B is incorrect because either "these" or "those" would be acceptable in the sentence, so neither is wrong. Answer D is incorrect because "they're" is a contraction of "they are," which would not make sense in the sentence.

12. **D** Sentence 10 contains both repetitive language ("originally performed for the first time") and unnecessary to-be verb wordiness ("which was"). Answer D is the best revision because it addresses both these issues, creating a sentence that communicates all main ideas succinctly. Answer choices A and B are both incorrect because they maintain the unnecessary "which was" in the final phrase of the sentence. Answer C is incorrect because it maintains the repetitive "were originally performed for the first time."

13. **C** This set of sentences generally emphasizes how people of all different social classes and means came together at the Globe Theatre to enjoy Shakespeare's plays. Sentences 11, 12, and 14 all directly reflect this main idea, talking about different groups of people in general terms. Sentence 13, while tangentially related (and interesting), is the least connected to the others because it focuses on an individual (Queen Elizabeth). By focusing on the importance of Queen Elizabeth, Sentence 13 (Answer C) distracts from the main ideas of the paragraph and is therefore the best candidate to be removed.

14. **A** The main ideas of sentence 2 are James W. Marshall's name, the general location of the find (near Sacramento), and how Marshall first found the gold (by looking in a drainage channel). Answer A is correct because it includes all three of these elements. Answer B is incorrect because it does not introduce Marshall's name, which is referred to later in the paragraph. Answer C is incorrect because it doesn't give any information about how Marshall found the gold. Answer D is incorrect because it doesn't mention the discovery of gold (which is central to the entire passage) at all.

15. **C** Answer C is the best choice because it wraps up the discussion of Sutter and Marshall (neither of whom are mentioned again in the passage) and transitions into the discussion of the historical importance of the Gold Rush, which is the main topic of paragraphs 2 and 3. By wrapping up the content of paragraph 1 and preparing the reader for paragraph 2, Answer C is the ideal closing sentence for the first paragraph. Answers A, B, and D all provide additional interesting information, but they do nothing to help the passage flow or transition.

16. **A** Answer A is the best combination of the two sentences because it clearly explains the cultural makeup of most Californians at the beginning of the Gold Rush without adding extra words or including unnecessary information. Answer B unnecessarily mentions the mill and uses the cumbersome, expositional phrase "which makes sense because," adding meaningless length to the sentence. Answer C, while shortened, omits the important main idea that California was a part of Mexico at the time of Marshall's discovery. Answer D is a lengthy sentence that many readers might find confusing due to its high number of commas and also uses the wordy, unnecessary "which makes sense because" phrase.

17. **B** "Begun" and "began" are both past forms of "begin," but "begun" requires a helping verb to be used correctly (For example, "They had begun work the previous week" or "We have only just begun!"). Answer B is correct because there is no helping verb in the sentence. Answer A is incorrect because either the simple past or past progressive tense would be acceptable in this situation, so there is nothing wrong with "spread." Answer C is incorrect because neither "begun flocked" nor "began flocked" is grammatically correct (which can be demonstrated easily by saying either out

loud). Answer D is incorrect because either word would make the sentence correct, so the author's word choice does not need to be changed.

18. **B** Answer B is the best transition for the beginning of the final paragraph because it encourages the reader to consider today's world, which is the topic of the third paragraph, while also providing historical context for the reader. Answer A is incorrect because the use of the second person pronoun "you" is generally discouraged in formal writing and has not been used in the passage to this point. Answer C is incorrect because "In conclusion" is a self-referential transition that is discouraged in mature writing. Answer D is incorrect because the word "however" implies that the following information is contrary to what was previously presented, which is not the case in sentence 12.

19. **D** "Most importantly" should be separated from the rest of the sentence by a comma because it is an introductory phrase, which is one of the primary uses of commas. Answer D is correct because it adds this comma without including any unnecessary ones. Answer B is incorrect because it does not include a comma after the introductory phrase. Answer C is incorrect because it adds an unnecessary comma before "and," treating the sentence as though it were a compound sentence, when it is not. The Gold Rush is the subject of both the verbs "fast-tracked" and "made," so it should not be separated from the second half of the sentence with a comma. Answer A is obviously incorrect because sentence 13 is missing one necessary comma and includes one unnecessary one.

20. **D** Answer D provides the best conclusion sentence because it sums up both the final paragraph and the passage as a whole in a clear, succinct statement. It focuses on the main topic of the Gold Rush as well as the idea that the Gold Rush significantly changed California, which is explored throughout the passage. Answers A and C focus only on the last point mentioned (the 49ers football team), and as such, do not provide adequate conclusion to either the paragraph or the passage as a whole. Answer choice B is an interesting supporting detail, but it would be better served in the body of paragraph 2 rather than at the end of paragraph 3.

READING COMPREHENION

Passage 1 ("The origin of the term caucus..."):

21. **A** Answer A is the best choice because the entirety of the passage explores the origin of the caucus and its political importance. Answer B is incorrect because, while the Revolution is tangentially connected to the content of the passage, it is clearly not the main focus. Answer C demonstrates that the reader was paying close attention to the first paragraph of the passage, but it is not the best answer because the rest of the passage explores the history and function of caucuses rather than continuing to explore the word's root. Answer D is not the best answer because it limits the scope of the passage to "congressional caucuses," while the passage actually establishes that caucuses are used on a variety of levels throughout American government, not just in Congress.

175

22. **D** Answer D is the best choice because there is no mention of the Latin language in the passage whatsoever. Answer A cannot be correct because the possible Algonquin origins of "caucus" are explored in Lines 1-4. Answer B cannot be correct either because Lines 4-13 explain how the caucus may have gotten its name from shipmen. Answer C cannot be correct either because Lines 13-17 discuss how the term "caucus" could come from the name of the building where the shipmen met.

23. **C** Answer C is the best choice because Lines 18-22 clearly describe the role of the caucus before an election. Line 20 clearly says, "...held prior to an election." Answer A is not the best answer because, while caucuses are part of the greater election process, it is not correct to say a caucus "is" an election. Answer B is incorrect because there is no mention of celebrating anywhere in the passage, so that choice has no textual basis. Answer D is incorrect because the passage clearly ties the idea of a caucus to an election in Lines 18-31.

24. **C** Answer C is correct because Lines 45-53, in particular lines 51-53, explain that Adams felt "...in these aristocratical caucuses elections have been decided," meaning that the caucuses of wealthy and upper-class people had unfair influence on elections. Answer A is incorrect because the passage indicates throughout that all people caucus regardless of social class. Selecting Answer A most likely represents a misunderstanding of the word "aristocratical" in Line 52. Answer B has no textual basis because the procedure for caucusing is never specifically explained in the passage, meaning the reader would have no way of knowing the timeframe involved. Answer D is also incorrect because John Adams was himself a figure of the Revolutionary War, so he would be unlikely to see practices from the Revolution as "outdated" like someone today might. Furthermore, there is no textual evidence in Adams' words (Lines 45-53) that he felt caucusing was outdated.

25. **A** Answer A is correct because, according to Lines 19-21, a caucus is "primarily a meeting of voters holding similar views, held prior to an election for the purpose of furthering such views." Answer A matches this description because it establishes that everybody caucusing is in the same party ("voters holding similar views") and that they are strategizing on how to vote (deciding how to "[further] such views"). Answer B is incorrect because the passage states that caucuses are held within groups with similar views, so it would not make sense for members of opposing party to be caucusing together. Answer C is incorrect because the act of voting is not itself caucusing. Answer D is incorrect because it misapplies the information about sailors in Lines 4-17 to apply to all caucuses.

26. **D** Answer D is correct because Lines 32-35 state that "The candidates of each party are universally selected by caucus, either directly or indirectly through delegates to conventions chosen in caucuses." This sentence means that a caucus is always involved in the presidential election process. Answers A, B, and C are all incorrect because the text does not support them. The word "universally" in Line 32 should have been a major hint to the reader.

ARGO BROTHERS
www.argobrothers.com

Passage 2 ("According to Denizart...")

27. A Answer A is correct because the entirety of the passage focuses on the topic of dueling and its history. Answer B is incorrect because, while the passage states that organized dueling probably began in Germany, Germany is not the primary focus of the passage overall. Answer C is incorrect because the passage does not contain any "compare and contrast" element or other method of tracing change in the judicial system over time. Answer D is incorrect because, while the word "war" is used in the passage to describe dueling, traditional warfare is not the subject of the passage.

28. B Answer B is the correct answer because Lines 4-5 plainly state, "According to Cauchy, a duel is a private war preceded by a challenge..." Answer A is incorrect because it was Dupin who said dueling is a "savage state," not Cauchy (Lines 11-16). Answers C and D are both also incorrect because there is nothing in Cauchy's words (Lines 4-7) that supports either answer.

29. C Answer C is correct because in Lines 39-44, which explain the concept of the witness, it says, "The combatants... should take good care... not to expose themselves to be prosecuted as murderers." Answer A is incorrect because while the text does say duels are "a fine spectacle" (Line 42), it does not say anything about duelists showing off their strength against each other. Answer B is also incorrect because there is no mention in the passage of witnesses being a legal necessity; it is simply a practical consideration and a good idea to have one. Answer D is also incorrect because there is nothing in the passage to suggest that the witnesses would also duel, so there is no textual support for Answer D.

30. D Answer D is correct because Lines 25-26 plainly state, "Gondebaud, king of the Burgundians, was the first to introduce into the code the judicial duel." Answer A is incorrect because the passage identifies Germany as the earliest site of duels (Line 19), not Burgundy, where it is clearly established Gondebaud was from. Answer B is also incorrect because it was Dupin (Line 13), not Gondebaud who said dueling was "savage." Answer C is also incorrect because there is nothing in the text specifically stating that Gondebaud ever participated in a duel himself.

31. C Answer C is correct because Lines 18-19 plainly state, "We find the first traces of it in Germany..." Answers A, B, and D are all incorrect because there is no specific mention of France, Britain, or Italy anywhere in the passage. Since Germany is the only one of those countries mentioned by name anywhere in the passage, it is the only answer that can possibly be correct.

32. A Answer A is correct because it's clearly established in Line 13 that Dupin believes dueling is a "savage state," suggesting he would probably support its elimination. Answer B is incorrect because, even if death was removed from the equation, Dupin would still believe dueling was a silly, unreasoned way of settling disputes that simply favored the better duelist (Lines 13-15). Answer C cannot be correct because there is nothing in the passage to suggest that Dupin advocated for stricter laws, so there is no textual basis for the answer. Answer D is also incorrect because Dupin's words straightforwardly state that he is against dueling in general as a manner of solving disputes and would prefer not to see it any situation.

177

ARGO
BROTHERS
www.argobrothers.com

ENGLISH
ANSWERS & EXPLANATIONS

Passage 3 ("President Andrew Jackson's early opportunities..."):

33. **A** Answer A is the best choice because the passage presents a large number of details and ideas about different aspects of Jackson's life, habits, and beliefs, making it the closest to a general biography. Answer B is incorrect because only the first sentence of the passage makes reference to his childhood and early life, while the rest focuses on his work and ideas. Answer C is incorrect because, while individuality is a major feature of the passage's second half, it is far from the only point made in the passage. Answer D is similarly incorrect because, while comparing and contrasting Jefferson and Jackson is one of the author's concerns, it is not the general focus of the entire passage.

34. **B** Answer B is correct because the sentence stating Jackson believed the world to be flat (Line 5) immediately follows the sentence that says his "opportunities for education were very limited" (Lines 1-2), providing a direct connection between the two ideas. Answer A is incorrect both because the world was generally accepted as round by educated people of Jackson's time and because the author of the passage makes no mention of others believing this idea as well. Answer C is incorrect because the concept of science isn't explored in the passage at all, and the author does not discuss Jackson as an enemy of science. Answer D is incorrect because the author of the passage is not trying to convince the reader that the earth was flat at all, but rather using Jackson's belief as an example to illustrate his lack of educational sophistication.

35. **D** Answer D is correct because Lines 21-23 clearly state, "In temper, Jackson was arbitrary, forceful, persistent, not at all impulsive but willing to yield to his naturally hot temper." Answers A, B, and C are all incorrect because each represents the reader's inability to locate the appropriate lines to answer the question.

36. **A** Answer A is correct because the third and fourth paragraphs of the passage both discuss Jackson and Jefferson's individualistic attitudes at length. Lines 53-56's statement "Jefferson and Jackson had the same ultimate goal, but a different immediate object: the former to protect the individual through the states; the latter to protect the individual through the nation," should be a major indicator to readers, as should "Jackson's individualism did not prevent him, as it did Jefferson, from being a thoroughly national man" (Lines 44-46). Answers B, C, and D are all incorrect because they show a lack of understanding of the second half of the passage, which focuses extensively on comparing Jackson to Jefferson.

37. **C** Answer C is correct because Lines 44-46 clearly state: "Jackson's individualism did not prevent him, as it did Jefferson, from being a thoroughly national man." Additionally, Line 56 asserts that Jackson wanted to "protect the individual through the nation," demonstrating his difference from Jackson who protected "the individual through the states" (Line 55). Answers A, B, and D are all incorrect because they fail to acknowledge the key distinction made between the two presidents in the second half of the passage.

38. **D** Answer D is correct because military spending is not mentioned as a concern of Jackson's in the passage, whereas each other the other three answers is. Answer A cannot be correct because Line 40 establishes that Jackson was against tariffs. Answer B cannot be correct because Line 41

178

establishes that Jackson was opposed to federal funding being used for roads. Answer C cannot be correct because Line 42 establishes that Jackson was opposed to federal funding being used for canals. Answers A, B, and C all represent a misunderstanding of Lines 35-48.

Passage 4 ("Even the ablest and most conscientious..."):

39. **B**   Answer B is the best choice because the entirety of the passage discusses how credit can be useful to countries in times of need. Each of the three paragraphs explores this idea, making it the clear main idea of the passage. Answer A is not the best answer because, while credit is the main topic, the passage focuses specifically on the use of credit by countries, making Answer B a better selection. Answer C is incorrect because the passage doesn't just explore the general use of credit; it explores how countries use credit, making Answer B a better, more specific choice. Answer D is incorrect because the use of credit by individuals is only used in the passage as an analogy to show that the state's use of credit is similar to that of an individual, making Answer B the best answer.

40. **C**   Answer C is correct because the passage does not make any reference to paying soldiers. Answer A cannot be correct because a natural disaster would fall under the umbrella of "accidents which may decrease its income or cause unforeseen expense," which are established as reasons credit might be needed in Lines 5-6. Answer B cannot be correct because the author identifies long term investments as worthwhile uses of credit when he/she writes, "Finally, enterprises of evident usefulness, but the introduction of which demands time and are very costly, may outweigh the current resources of the state, and necessitate for a longer or shorter period of additional revenue" in Lines 14-18. Answer D cannot be correct because a "revolution" is specifically mentioned as a situation that may necessitate credit in Line 7.

41. **B**   Answer B is the best choice because Lines 35-39 state, "In fact, the state rarely asks for money for productive investment; it borrows most because its disposable or prospective funds are insufficient for the present or near future," establishing that the state is unlikely to borrow simply for investment. Answers A and C are both incorrect because they represents a faulty, "backwards" reading of Lines 35-39, which establish that the state rarely borrows to invest. Answer D cannot be correct because the author's whole thesis is that countries can and should borrow money, so arguing not to take on debt would be contradictory to the rest of the passage.

42. **D**   Answer D is correct because Lines 49-52 state: "...the second [principle], always to place capital in the hands of those who, at a given moment, may make the most productive use of it." Answers A, B, and C are all incorrect because they fail to identify the section of the passage (Lines 47-56) in which the author lays out his or her main ideas about the use of capital. Answers A and B both fail to recognize that the author is talking primarily about the state throughout the passage, not individuals or institutions. Answer C is especially wrong, because the idea of no one using capital is directly contradictory to the entire tone of the passage, which is about countries using credit effectively.

43. **D**   Answer D is correct because Lines 23-28 state: "Much has been said of the advantages of credit in private business: its usefulness in public affairs is not less than in private. There is no essential difference between the national demand for credit and the demand for credit made

by individuals." These lines demonstrate that the author considers public and private credit to be fundamentally the same. Answer A is incorrect because the author is clearly an advocate for the use of credit and not indifferent on this issue in any way. Answers B and C cannot be correct because the author does not prioritize one or the other or rank them in a hierarchy.

44. **A** Answer A is correct because a bridge has "evident usefulness" (increased ease of transportation, travel, etc.) but also takes tremendous time and money to construct. Answer B is incorrect because, while back pay on pensions is useful to those who are owed, it is not an evidently useful project for the overall common good. Answer C is incorrect because each government already has avenues by which laws are created, and borrowing money just to pass a new law would likely not provide a clear benefit to the majority of people. Answer D is also incorrect because, while the author defends the use of credit in times of war, the goal of borrowed money laid out in the passage is for the public good of citizens, not to expand the military prowess of a nation.

Passage 5 ("Fermiers generaux was the name given…")

45. **D** Answer D is the best choice because the passage as a whole explores how the French monarchy collected taxes for many years using a system of "farming them out." Each paragraph of the passage contributes to this idea, making it the clear overall focus. Answer A is not the best choice because, although the passage mentions salt as one of the goods farm taxed by the French government, salt is not the main focus of the passage in total. Answer B is incorrect because, while the concept of over-taxing is heavily implied at certain points in the passage, the author focuses simply on the methodology of tax collection rather than moralizing about it. Answer C is incorrect because it fails to identify that the words "farm" and "farming" in the passage do not carry their traditional agricultural meanings.

46. **B** Answer B is the best choice because it translates the idea of "Fermiers generaux" rather than just the words. The "fermiers" were not traditional agricultural farmers at all, but actually contracted tax collectors. Answer A is incorrect because it translates the words literally but doesn't provide any explanation as to what the term actually means. A reader relying on Answer A might not understand that the passage is not talking about agricultural farmers. Answer C is incorrect because it ties Fermiers generaux to fermentation and the military, neither of which are mentioned anywhere in the passage, meaning Answer C has no textual basis. Answer D is incorrect because it also fails to recognize that the "farming" taking place in the passage is not literal agriculture.

47. **D** Answer D is the correct choice because Lines 16-20 clearly establish that, beginning in 1350, Philippe de Valois distributed farming rights to people who "were favorites of the court or the minister of the day," establishing favoritism and corruption as the methods of gaining the farming contracts. Answer A is incorrect because there is no mention of family history anywhere in the passage. Answer A once again suggests that the reader does not understand the figurative use of the term "farming" throughout the passage. Answer B is incorrect because Line 19 clearly states that "favorites" were chosen rather than deserving applicants. Answer C is also correct because there is no mention of a lottery anywhere in the passage.

48. C Answer C is the correct choice because there is no mention of building roads anywhere in the passage. Answer A is incorrect because Lines 28-29 specifically establish that one of the main goals of taxation was that it "greatly increased the revenue of the state." Answer B is incorrect because Lines 17-20 clearly establish that the system benefitted the favorites of nobles and ministers. Answer D is also incorrect because Lines 53-62 detail how the farming system was used to oppress the poor.

49. A Answer A is correct because Lines 20-27 clearly state that Sully set up the tax collection system "according to the ancient Roman practice." Answers B and C are both incorrect (with no textual basis) because neither Britain nor Athens is mentioned anywhere in the text. Answer D is also incorrect because, as far as the reader knows from the passage, the earlier French empires only used the favoritism system to determine who collected taxes.

50. C Answer C is correct because Lines 47-48 clearly state: "In the time of Necker, the company consisted of forty-four members..." Answers A and B are both dates mentioned in the passage, so a reader who selected either of these answers was most likely just scanning the passage for numbers. Answer D is incorrect because it appears nowhere in the passage and, therefore, has no textual basis.

Passage 6 ("We hear it maintained by people..."):

51. C Answer C is the best choice because, throughout the passage, the author explores the idea that feelings should be trusted over intellectualization because it's possible to feel something strongly without understanding it. In Lines 11-14, for example, the author establishes that knowledge is less important than feeling because you can walk without understanding the anatomy behind the process. Answer A is incorrect because in Lines 15-20, the author establishes that, oftentimes, reason is insufficient to explain feelings. Answer B is similarly incorrect because the author contends that emotions are not always governed by reason, and therefore cannot be explained using that language (Lines 15-29). Answer D is also incorrect because, while the passage talks a great deal about feelings, it also focuses on reason. Answer D is not a complete answer because it does not address the issue of reason in the passage.

52. A Answer A is the best choice because the author identifies Locke as siding with "common sense" (Lines 4-8), which the author feels is overly general, didactic, and not true to each individual's feelings. Answer B is incorrect because the author squarely places Locke on the side of common sense and reason, which he is arguing against over-reliance on. Answers C and D are both incorrect because there isn't enough information to conclude that the author is assessing Locke's intelligence.

53. C Answer C is the best choice because the author clearly states in Lines 33-34: "Reason is the interpreter and critic of nature and genius," establishing that reason's role is to provide understanding and context for feelings. Answer A is incorrect because one of the author's main points throughout the passage is that reason should not come before feelings. Answer B is incorrect because Lines 33-34 clearly show that the author believes reason and feeling go hand-in-hand and both are necessary to be a full, thinking person. Answer D is also incorrect because Lines 33-34 clearly establish a need for reason, even in a world where people are more sensitive to their feelings.

54. **C** Answer C is the best choice because it shows a feeling leading a person to make a reasoned choice. This aligns with the author's assertion in Lines 31-32 that "nature does not follow the rule, but suggests it." Answer C shows someone making a rule (to become a vegetarian) based on nature's suggestion (their feeling of unease about animal cruelty). Answer A goes directly against what the author says, because it shows someone feeling happy because a societal rule tells them they ought to. Similarly, Answer B provides an example of a way of thinking that has been indoctrinated by society, which is clearly contrary to the way the author believes things should be. Answer D is incorrect because it shows a situation in which someone has directly circumvented or ignored their feelings, which the author would argue against.

55. **D** Answer D is the best choice because in Lines 15-29, the author establishes that reason is not the be-all, end-all, and that people can reach reasonable beliefs using only feelings. The author writes: "In a gesture you use, in a look you see, in a tone you hear, you judge of the expression, propriety, and meaning from habit, not from reason or rules" (Lines 20-23), establishing that people do not need reason to be correct. Answers A, B, and C are all incorrect because the author is not making judgments about intelligence or common sense, but rather urging people to use feeling in conjunction with those abilities.

56. **A** Answer A is correct because the author clearly establishes that one does not need to explain things using logic or reason to be wise. This is explored in the final paragraph, particularly Lines 44-54 when the author explains "the distinction between eloquence and wisdom, between ingenuity and common sense." Answer B is incorrect because the man who cannot explain himself is not necessarily wiser than the man who can; it's just a possibility. Answer C is incorrect because, throughout the passage, the author argues against the over-use of rules and logic. Answer D is incorrect because the author does not question the strength or validity of anybody's beliefs anywhere in the passage.

57. **D** Answer D is correct because the sentence in question begins on Line 44 with the phrase, "He must be a poor creature indeed," establishing that the author believes this kind of thinker to be pathetic or pitiable. Answer A is incorrect because the author would say someone who relies too much on deliberate understanding is a fool for not appreciating the nuances of life. Answer B is also incorrect because the author's characterization of the person in question as a "poor creature" strongly implies the person will not have a fulfilling life. Answer C is incorrect because Locke is only mentioned once in the passage tangentially, and the author never fully expounds where he or she believes Lock would fall on this spectrum of reason and feeling.

Explanations to each problem on:
Youtube.com/ArgoBrothers

MATHEMATICS

ARGO
BROTHERS
www.argobrothers.com

Practice Test 2 (Answers and Explanations)

1. **C** $(\sqrt{100})(\sqrt{64}) = (10)(8) = 80$

2. **C** 7.2 aliens = 1 monster = 15.5 oranges

$(\frac{1}{7.2})$ monster = 1 alien = $(\frac{15.5}{7.2})$ oranges

= 2.15 oranges.

3. **D** Factor each value, then chose all copies of the factors and multiply.

147: 3 • 7 • 7
98: 2 • 7 • 7
GCF: 7 • 7 = 49

4. **D** $\frac{11x}{x-y} = \frac{11(7)}{7-0} = \frac{77}{7} = 11$

5. **D** Lucy's average is the sum of all of her test scores divided by the total number of tests which is 4.

$\frac{85 + 64 + 76 + x}{4} = 80$

$\frac{225 + x}{4} = 80$

320 = 225 + x
x = 95

6. **C** There are 7 animals that have 4 legs out of 9 animals. So, there are 2 animals that do not have 4 legs out of 9.

$\frac{2}{9}$

7. **A** $y = (x^2)(x^x) = x^{2+x}$
if $x = 2$, then $y = 2^{2+2} = 2^4 = 16$

8. **A** By 4pm, train A has been traveling at 200 mph for 3 hours. Train A has traveled 600 miles. By 4pm, train B has been traveling 300 mph for 1 hour. Train B traveled 300 miles.

600 miles + 300 miles = 900 miles

9. **B**

Present Age	Age 5 years ago
Bernard: y	y − 5
Luis: y + 8	y + 3

10. **D** ∢CBE = ∢DBA due to vertical angles.

The sum of the integer angles of BCFE is 360° and ∢CBE can be found as followed.

Knowing that ∢CFE = ∢GFH, it follows

360° − (110° + 110° + 65° + ∢CBE) = 0
360° − 285° = ∢CBE = x°
x° = 75°

11. **D** $(\frac{19}{4})(\frac{2}{2}) = \frac{37}{8}$. This means $\frac{19}{4} > \frac{37}{8}$

Using cross multiplication, for $\frac{13}{3}$ and $\frac{37}{8}$, it follows

(8)(13) < (3)(37)

104 < 111, so $\frac{13}{3} < \frac{37}{8}$

Therefore: $\frac{19}{4} > \frac{37}{8} > \frac{13}{3}$

12. **C** Two times any integer is even always. Thus, this leaves our choices to probably **B** or **C**.

Since $(\frac{x+y}{x})$ is not always an integer, and $x + y$ is, the answer is C.

13. **D** The probability of a point being chosen if the shaded region is

$$\frac{\text{Average of shaded region}}{\text{Total Area}} = \frac{\pi y^2 - \pi x^2}{\pi y^2}$$

This simplifies to $\frac{y^2 - x^2}{y^2}$

14. **B** $q = x + y$ and $x = y + z$
so, $q = y + z + y = 2y + z$
$q - 2y = z$

15. **D** Let $x = 5!; \frac{(5!)!}{5!} = \frac{x!}{x} = (x - 1)!$
$(x - 1)! = (5! - 1)!$ This answer is huge relative to the rest of the answers, therefore the answer is non of the above.

16. **C** $(a + b)(a + b) = a^2 + 2ab + b^2 = (a + b)^2$
$\frac{a^2 + 2ab + b^2}{(a + b)^3} = \frac{(a + b)^2}{(a + b)^3} = \frac{1}{a + b}$

17. **A** If it takes 3 cats 3 minutes to catch 3 mice, then it will take 3(1) cats $3x$ minutes to catch $3x$ mice, as long as x is an integer.

$3x = 99$

$x = 33$. Since x is an integer, it will take 3(1) = 3 cats.

18. **C** Seven consecutive odd integers may be expressed as:

1st 2nd 3rd 4th 5th
$x + (x + 2) + (x + 4) + (x + 6) + (x + 8) +$

6th 7th
$(x + 10) + (x + 12) = 7x + 42 = 749$

$7x = 707$
$x = 101$

The largest is $x + 12$ or
$101 + 12 = 113$

19. **B**   Original Volume= $\pi r^2 h$

New Volume = $\pi(2r)^2(\frac{h}{2}) = \pi(4r^2)(\frac{h}{2})$
$= 2\pi r^2 h$

$\cancel{\pi r^2 h} : 2\cancel{\pi r^2 h}$
1:2

20. **A** $\$3.50 + \$0.20(4x) = \$22.50$
Where x is the number of miles ridden.

Solving for x:
$\$0.20(4x) = \$19$
$4x = 95$
$x = 23.75$ miles

21. **B**   Assuming there are 4 weeks in July, John's hourly rate can be calculated as follows:

$$\frac{\$(1.04)(4000)}{4 \text{ weeks}} = \frac{\$1040}{\text{week}}$$

$$\frac{\$1040}{\cancel{\text{week}}} \cdot \frac{1 \cancel{\text{week}}}{40 \text{ hours}} = \frac{\$26}{\text{hours}}$$

22. **A** $8575 = 5^2 \cdot 7^3$
$x = 2, y = 3; (xy) - 5 = (6) - 5 = 1$

23. **D**   Since d is not specified, the value can be chosen to be 43.

When 43 is divided by 8, there is a remainder of 3.

$d + 3 = 46$.

When 46 is divided by 8, there is a remainder of 6.

24. **C**   Permutations can be used. For 6 letters,
$6! = 6 \cdot 5 \cdot 4 \cdot 3 \cdot 2 \cdot 1 = 720$

25. **C** $-5(x - 3) \geq 20$
$(x - 3) \leq -4$
$x \leq -1$

26. **D** $-2 < \frac{x}{3} \leq 2$
$-6 < x \leq 6$

27. **D**   If there are x teens in total, then
$15,000 = 0.08x$
$x = 187,500$

Now, to find the number of teens whose favorite genre is action:
$(.30)(187,500) = 56,250$

28. **B**   With the 20% sale, the price becomes
$(0.8)(\$550.50) = \$440.40$

Applying the 5% coupon: (0.95)
$(\$440.4) = \$418.38$

29. **B** $4760 = 2^3 \cdot 5 \cdot 7 \cdot 17$
$x = 2, y = 17$
$\frac{x^2}{y} = \frac{4}{17}$

30. **A**   11.5 milligrams $= (\frac{11.5}{1000})$ grams $=$
0.0115 grams

31. **D** 83 hours = (24 + 24 + 24 + 11) hours. Each 24 hours is a full day. So three days and eleven hours passes. Thus, this leaves the project due at 7:30PM Thursday.

32. **C** $(\frac{2}{3} + \frac{1}{4}) \div 2 = (\frac{8}{12} + \frac{3}{12}) \cdot \frac{1}{2}$

$\frac{11}{12} \cdot \frac{1}{2} = \frac{11}{24}$

33. **D** The dress and the bag are the only items taxed with 7% sales tax. All the items cost:

1.07($103 + $111) + ($73)
$228.98 + $73 = $301.98

34. **B** There are $(\frac{60 - 0}{3}) + 1$ numbers.

35. **D** The two numbers are x and $(x + 2)$.
$x + (x + 2)$. The larger is $(x + 2)$.
So, $(x + 2) = 2x$
$x = 2$
$x + (x + 2) = 2 + (2 + 2) = 6$

36. **D** $3^x = 27^{a+b} = (3^3)^{a+b} = 3^{3a+3b}$
$x = 3a + 3b$ and $\frac{a^2 - b^2}{(a - b)} = \frac{(a - b)(a + b)}{(a - b)}$
$= a + b = 5$
$x = 3(a + b) = 3(5) = 15$

37. **D** Let x = # of boys
Let y = # of girls
$x = 2y$; $x + y = 2y + y = 30$
$3y = 30$
$y = 10$

The percentage of boys is
$\frac{x}{30} = \frac{2y}{30} = \frac{2(10)}{30} = \frac{20}{30} = \frac{2}{3} = 66.66\%$

38. **B** $a \star b = (a - b)^3$
$a \oplus b = (a - b)^2$
$\frac{a \star b}{a \oplus b} = \frac{(a - b)^3}{(a - b)^2} = a - b$

39. **C** $752 = 2^4 \cdot 47$

40. **A** Squaring any integer results in a positive integer.

The least value of $4x^2 - 10$ occurs when $4x^2$ is the lowest it can be, which happens at $x = 0$.

Then $4(0)^2 - 10 = -10$

41. **A** Let x = # of bicycles
Let y = # of tricycles
$x + y = 5$
$2x + 3y = 12$
$x = 5 - y$
$2(5 - y) + 3y = 10 - 2y + 3y = 12$
$10 + y = 12$
$y = 2$.
So, there are 2 tricycles.

42. **B** x^2 can never be negative for $x \geq 1$

So, the lowest value of x^2 is chosen, to make $\dfrac{x^2 - 1}{x^2}$ the lowest.

That occurs at $x = 1$

$$\frac{x^2 - 1}{x^2} = \frac{1^2 - 1}{1^2} = \frac{1 - 1}{1} = 0$$

43. **C**

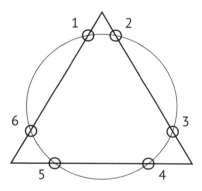

44. **A** The area of the rectangle is
$(3 + 3 + 1 + 1) \cdot (3 + 3) = 48$

      Length   Width

The area of the two circles is
$9\pi + \pi = 10\pi$

The area of the shaded region is
$48 - 10\pi$

45. **C** There are $\dfrac{1}{3}(45) = 15$ black ducks

and $\dfrac{1}{5}(45) = 9$ blue ducks

and $\dfrac{1}{3}(15) = 5$ green ducks.

$45 = 15 + 9 + 5 +$ purple, where
purple = # of purple ducks.
purple = 16.

46. **A** $\sphericalangle ABC + 2x + 4x = \sphericalangle ABC + 6x$,
then $6x + \sphericalangle ABC = 180°$.

$\sphericalangle ABC = 180° - 120° = 60°$,
since $\triangle ABC$ is isosceles.
So, $4x + 2x + 120° = 180°$

$6x = 180° - 120°$
Solve for x and you get $x = 10°$
So $2x = 2(10°) = 20°$

47. **B** This is a triangle with a 3, 4, 5 special right triangle proportion.

$$\frac{30}{6} = 5, \frac{24}{6} = 4$$

$$\frac{12 + y}{6} = 3$$

$12 + y = 18$

$y = 6$

48. **C** 1 gallon = 4 quarts
The painter needs
(4 gallons)(8 rooms) = 32 gallons

of paint= 32 ~~gallons~~ $\cdot \dfrac{4 \text{ quarts}}{1 \text{ gallon}}$

= 128 quarts.

Explanations to each problem on:
Youtube.com/ArgoBrothers

MATHEMATICS
ANSWERS & EXPLANATIONS

ARGO
BROTHERS
www.argobrothers.com

49. D

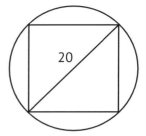

The radius is half of the diagonal length.

Circle Area = $\pi(r)^2 = \pi(10)^2 = 100\pi$

50. C Divide $50 by the unloaded price and regular price respectively.

Thus, this comes out to 20 gallons and 25 gallons, which gives a difference of 5 gallons.

51. D This problem tests your understanding of median value. First, organize the data in numerical order, remembering to put in each value the number of times it is listed in the frequency column.

Your data set will be: {14,15,15,15,16, 16,16,17,17,17,17,18,19,19,21}

The median is 17.

52. C This problem asks you to add Chocolate Candy Bars to the table in order to achieve a median price of $1.88. Recall that the median value is dependent on the count of entries in a set: it will be the value of the middle item by count. If there is an even number of entries in

the set, then the median value will be the average of the two middle values. Looking over the chart, you can see that there are no items in the data set with a value of $1.88. This tells you that the median must be an average of two values. You can see that $1.88 lies between $1.76 (Oatmeal Cookies) and $2.00 (CFL Light Bulbs). Sort the set of values from lowest to highest, remembering to have an entry for each count of each value. Your data set will look like this:

{.67, .67, .67, .67, .67, .67, 1.76, 1.76, 1.76, 1.76, 2, 2, 2, 2, 2, 3.27, 3.27, 3.27, 3.99, 3.99, 4.54, 4.54}

Count the number of entries greater than $1.88 and the number of entries lower than $1.88. In this case you find 12 entries above $1.88 and 10 entries below. So you will need to add 2 entries below $1.88. Chocolate Candy Bars are $1.15 so you will need to add 2 Chocolate Candy Bars in order to reach a median value of $1.88. The correct answer choice is C.

53. 67.5°

You are given that *CB* bisects the right-angle ⋆ *ACE*. So, ⋆ *ACB* = ⋆ *BCE* = $\frac{⋆\,ACE}{7.2}$ = $\frac{90°}{2}$ = 45°.

Since *CD* bisects ⋆ *ACB*, ⋆ *ACD* = ⋆ *DCB* = $\frac{⋆\,ACB}{2}$ = $\frac{45°}{2}$ = 22.5°.

Since ⋆ *DCE* = ⋆ *DCB* + ⋆ *BCE* = 22.5° + 45° = 67.5°.

54. **218** This problem tests your ability to set up a ratio equation. Given the distance of 130 miles travelled on 4 gallons of fuel, you are to find the number of miles the same truck could travel on 6.7 gallons of fuel. Write the equation:

$$\frac{130}{4} = \frac{x}{6.7} \quad \text{the given ratio}$$

$$\frac{130(6.7)}{4} = x \quad \text{multiply both sides by 6.7}$$

$$217.75 = x \quad \text{calculate}$$

The nearest whole number is 218, which is the correct answer.

55. **8** Solve the innermost absolute value expression first, then solve the outmost absolute value expression:

$$|-10 - 18| = |-28| - 20 = 8.$$

56. **72** This problem tests your ability to set up a word problem, as well as your understanding of the perimeter of a rectangle. You are asked to find the perimeter of a garden with a width of 16 units and an area equal to that of a 10-unit × 32-unit garden. Start by calculating the area of the second garden: 10 × 32 = 320. Next, divide the width of the first garden into the area of the second. This will give you the depth of the first garden: 320 ÷ 16 = 20. Now find the perimeter by substituting this value into the formula for Perimeter:

$$2 \times (width + depth) = Perimeter$$
Perimeter Formula

$$2 \times (16 + 20) = 72 = Perimeter$$
subtitute and calculate

The perimeter is 72.

57. **0** This problem asks you to solve a single variable equation:

$$-1 - \frac{2}{5} \cdot \frac{5m - 10}{2 + 3m} = 1 \quad \text{given}$$

$$-\frac{10m - 20}{10 + 15m} = 2 \quad \text{add 1 to both sides and simplify the fraction}$$

$$-(10m - 20) = 2(10 + 15m) \quad \text{multiply both sides by } (10 + 15m)$$

$$-10m + 20 = 20 + 30m \quad \text{simplify}$$

$$-40m = 0 \quad \text{simplify}$$

$$m = 0 \quad \text{solve for } m$$

The value of m is 0.

www.argobrothers.com

Practice Test 3
SHSAT

This exam is 3 hours long. Try to take this full exam in one sitting to simulate real test conditions.

While taking this exam, refrain from hearing music or watching T.V.

Please note, calculators are not permitted! You are permitted to answer questions in any order you see fit.

Allocate your test time accordingly.

Concentrate and GOOD LUCK!

You Tube
MATH VIDEO
EXPLANATIONS
YouTube.com/ArgoBrothers

SHSAT PRACTICE TEST 3
ANSWER SHEET

ENGLISH LANGUAGE ARTS

1 Ⓐ Ⓑ Ⓒ Ⓓ
2 Ⓐ Ⓑ Ⓒ Ⓓ
3 Ⓐ Ⓑ Ⓒ Ⓓ
4 Ⓐ Ⓑ Ⓒ Ⓓ
5 Ⓐ Ⓑ Ⓒ Ⓓ
6 Ⓐ Ⓑ Ⓒ Ⓓ
7 Ⓐ Ⓑ Ⓒ Ⓓ
8 Ⓐ Ⓑ Ⓒ Ⓓ
9 Ⓐ Ⓑ Ⓒ Ⓓ
10 Ⓐ Ⓑ Ⓒ Ⓓ
11 Ⓐ Ⓑ Ⓒ Ⓓ
12 Ⓐ Ⓑ Ⓒ Ⓓ
13 Ⓐ Ⓑ Ⓒ Ⓓ
14 Ⓐ Ⓑ Ⓒ Ⓓ
15 Ⓐ Ⓑ Ⓒ Ⓓ
16 Ⓐ Ⓑ Ⓒ Ⓓ
17 Ⓐ Ⓑ Ⓒ Ⓓ
18 Ⓐ Ⓑ Ⓒ Ⓓ
19 Ⓐ Ⓑ Ⓒ Ⓓ
20 Ⓐ Ⓑ Ⓒ Ⓓ
21 Ⓐ Ⓑ Ⓒ Ⓓ
22 Ⓐ Ⓑ Ⓒ Ⓓ
23 Ⓐ Ⓑ Ⓒ Ⓓ
24 Ⓐ Ⓑ Ⓒ Ⓓ
25 Ⓐ Ⓑ Ⓒ Ⓓ
26 Ⓐ Ⓑ Ⓒ Ⓓ
27 Ⓐ Ⓑ Ⓒ Ⓓ
28 Ⓐ Ⓑ Ⓒ Ⓓ
29 Ⓐ Ⓑ Ⓒ Ⓓ

30 Ⓐ Ⓑ Ⓒ Ⓓ
31 Ⓐ Ⓑ Ⓒ Ⓓ
32 Ⓐ Ⓑ Ⓒ Ⓓ
33 Ⓐ Ⓑ Ⓒ Ⓓ
34 Ⓐ Ⓑ Ⓒ Ⓓ
35 Ⓐ Ⓑ Ⓒ Ⓓ
36 Ⓐ Ⓑ Ⓒ Ⓓ
37 Ⓐ Ⓑ Ⓒ Ⓓ
38 Ⓐ Ⓑ Ⓒ Ⓓ
39 Ⓐ Ⓑ Ⓒ Ⓓ
40 Ⓐ Ⓑ Ⓒ Ⓓ
41 Ⓐ Ⓑ Ⓒ Ⓓ
42 Ⓐ Ⓑ Ⓒ Ⓓ
43 Ⓐ Ⓑ Ⓒ Ⓓ
44 Ⓐ Ⓑ Ⓒ Ⓓ
45 Ⓐ Ⓑ Ⓒ Ⓓ
46 Ⓐ Ⓑ Ⓒ Ⓓ
47 Ⓐ Ⓑ Ⓒ Ⓓ
48 Ⓐ Ⓑ Ⓒ Ⓓ
49 Ⓐ Ⓑ Ⓒ Ⓓ
50 Ⓐ Ⓑ Ⓒ Ⓓ
51 Ⓐ Ⓑ Ⓒ Ⓓ
52 Ⓐ Ⓑ Ⓒ Ⓓ
53 Ⓐ Ⓑ Ⓒ Ⓓ
54 Ⓐ Ⓑ Ⓒ Ⓓ
55 Ⓐ Ⓑ Ⓒ Ⓓ
56 Ⓐ Ⓑ Ⓒ Ⓓ
57 Ⓐ Ⓑ Ⓒ Ⓓ

MATHEMATICS

1 Ⓐ Ⓑ Ⓒ Ⓓ
2 Ⓐ Ⓑ Ⓒ Ⓓ
3 Ⓐ Ⓑ Ⓒ Ⓓ
4 Ⓐ Ⓑ Ⓒ Ⓓ
5 Ⓐ Ⓑ Ⓒ Ⓓ
6 Ⓐ Ⓑ Ⓒ Ⓓ
7 Ⓐ Ⓑ Ⓒ Ⓓ
8 Ⓐ Ⓑ Ⓒ Ⓓ
9 Ⓐ Ⓑ Ⓒ Ⓓ
10 Ⓐ Ⓑ Ⓒ Ⓓ
11 Ⓐ Ⓑ Ⓒ Ⓓ
12 Ⓐ Ⓑ Ⓒ Ⓓ
13 Ⓐ Ⓑ Ⓒ Ⓓ
14 Ⓐ Ⓑ Ⓒ Ⓓ
15 Ⓐ Ⓑ Ⓒ Ⓓ
16 Ⓐ Ⓑ Ⓒ Ⓓ
17 Ⓐ Ⓑ Ⓒ Ⓓ
18 Ⓐ Ⓑ Ⓒ Ⓓ
19 Ⓐ Ⓑ Ⓒ Ⓓ
20 Ⓐ Ⓑ Ⓒ Ⓓ
21 Ⓐ Ⓑ Ⓒ Ⓓ
22 Ⓐ Ⓑ Ⓒ Ⓓ
23 Ⓐ Ⓑ Ⓒ Ⓓ
24 Ⓐ Ⓑ Ⓒ Ⓓ
25 Ⓐ Ⓑ Ⓒ Ⓓ
26 Ⓐ Ⓑ Ⓒ Ⓓ

27 Ⓐ Ⓑ Ⓒ Ⓓ
28 Ⓐ Ⓑ Ⓒ Ⓓ
29 Ⓐ Ⓑ Ⓒ Ⓓ
30 Ⓐ Ⓑ Ⓒ Ⓓ
31 Ⓐ Ⓑ Ⓒ Ⓓ
32 Ⓐ Ⓑ Ⓒ Ⓓ
33 Ⓐ Ⓑ Ⓒ Ⓓ
34 Ⓐ Ⓑ Ⓒ Ⓓ
35 Ⓐ Ⓑ Ⓒ Ⓓ
36 Ⓐ Ⓑ Ⓒ Ⓓ
37 Ⓐ Ⓑ Ⓒ Ⓓ
38 Ⓐ Ⓑ Ⓒ Ⓓ
39 Ⓐ Ⓑ Ⓒ Ⓓ
40 Ⓐ Ⓑ Ⓒ Ⓓ
41 Ⓐ Ⓑ Ⓒ Ⓓ
42 Ⓐ Ⓑ Ⓒ Ⓓ
43 Ⓐ Ⓑ Ⓒ Ⓓ
44 Ⓐ Ⓑ Ⓒ Ⓓ
45 Ⓐ Ⓑ Ⓒ Ⓓ
46 Ⓐ Ⓑ Ⓒ Ⓓ
47 Ⓐ Ⓑ Ⓒ Ⓓ
48 Ⓐ Ⓑ Ⓒ Ⓓ
49 Ⓐ Ⓑ Ⓒ Ⓓ
50 Ⓐ Ⓑ Ⓒ Ⓓ
51 Ⓐ Ⓑ Ⓒ Ⓓ
52 Ⓐ Ⓑ Ⓒ Ⓓ

MATHEMATICS (GRID IN)

53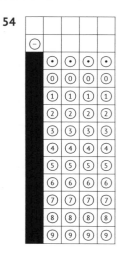
54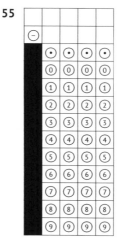
55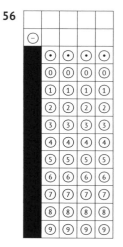
56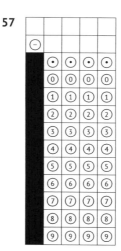
57

DIRECTIONS: For questions 1 to 5, you will be asked to recognize and correct errors in sentences or short paragraphs.

1. Read this paragraph.

(1) The Academy Awards, informally known as the Oscars, have taken place in Hollywood, California every year since 1929. (2) The goal of the yearly ceremony is to distribute awards for the best movies, greatest performances by actors, and most impressive technical achievements. (3) The Academy of Motion Picture Arts and Sciences presents awards for each of 24 different categories, ranging from "Best Actress in a Leading Role" to "Best Sound Mixing." (4) Elaborate, often memorable acceptance speeches are given by the winners of each award.

Which sentence in the paragraph should be revised to correct the use of passive voice?

A. Sentence 1
B. Sentence 2
C. Sentence 3
D. Sentence 4

2. Read this sentence.

In tennis, the ball is hit back and forth across the net by two players trying to score points.

How could this sentence be rewritten to eliminate the use of passive voice?

A. In tennis, two players hit a ball back and forth across a net to score points.
B. In tennis, the ball is hit by two players, who knock it back and forth to try and score points.
C. In tennis, the ball is hit by two players who try to score points by knocking the ball back and forth.
D. In tennis, points are scored when players hit the ball back and forth across the net.

CONTINUE ON TO THE NEXT PAGE →

3. Read this paragraph.

(1) George Gershwin was arguably the most influential American composer of the twentieth century. (2) Gershwin broke into the music industry in 1913 as a "song plugger," a public performer and salesman who promoted new music. (3) By the age of 20 Gershwin had written several hit songs. (4) Throughout his twenties, Gershwin wrote songs for Broadway musicals as well, partnering with his brother Ira, who was a lyricist. (5) Later in his career, Gershwin began focusing more on classical arrangements and opera. (6) Although he only lived 38 years, Gershwin left behind an impressive catalogue of songs, musicals, and film scores.

Which sentence in the paragraph should be revised to correct comma use?

A. Sentence 2
B. Sentence 3
C. Sentence 4
D. Sentence 5

4. Read this sentence.

A secret government program known as the Manhattan project developed the nuclear weapons that helped end World War II.

Which revision is most necessary to correct the sentence?

A. Change **government** to **Government**
B. Change **project** to **Project**
C. Change **nuclear weapons** to **Nuclear Weapons**
D. Change **World War II** to **world war II**

5. Read this paragraph.

(1) One of my happiest childhood memories is baking pies with my grandmother every fall. (2) My mother also baked, but I always felt a strong connection to the pies my grandma and I would make with the apples from her back yard. (3) The process would start with us picking the sweetest, most delicious-looking apples from their Golden Delicious tree. (4) Then, I would wash and peel the apples while my grandmother made the dough for our crust. (5) When the pie was ready to be filled, my grandmother would always let me put the cinnamon on top of the apples, which was my favorite part.

Which sentence is least relevant and should be removed from the paragraph?

A. Sentence 2
B. Sentence 3
C. Sentence 4
D. Sentence 5

CONTINUE ON TO THE NEXT PAGE →

ENGLISH LANGUAGE ARTS
Practice Test 3

DIRECTIONS: Read the passage below to answer questions 6 to 13. The questions will focus on improving the writing quality of the passage to follow the conventions of standard written English.

The Early Years of Baseball

(1) Baseball is hailed as a uniquely American sport, even though it is truly an international game. (2) One of the most fascinating aspects of baseball is its long, complex history. (3) Baseball evolved gradually from European bat-and-ball games, particularly cricket and rounders, which were popular schoolyard games in England during the colonial period. (4) People first began calling a variation of bat-and-ball "base-ball" or "bass-ball" in the south of England in the 1740s. (5) American colonists put their own spin on the games they brought with them from Europe and by the 1790s baseball had become popular throughout the United States.

(6) Early American baseball was a game of local variations. (7) The number of bases, the construction of the ball, and the methods of making outs could be different from town to town. (8) In 1845, Alexander Cartwright, a member of the New York Knickerbocker Club, created "The Knickerbocker Rules," the closest direct ancestor of the modern game. (9) The Knickerbocker Rules introduce the modern concept of a "force play," meaning the fielders could make an out by throwing the ball to the base a runner was approaching. (10) Previously, fielders had to "soak," or hit the runner with a thrown ball. (11) The Knickerbocker rules were significantly different from today's baseball in several key ways, however. (12) These official rules were used to play the earliest professional baseball games, beginning a long American tradition.

(13) For many years, these historical origins of baseball were clouded in myth. (14) In 1905, a group called the Mills Commission declared that Civil War General Abner Doubleday had invented baseball in Cooperstown, New York in 1839, which the commission most likely knew wasn't entirely true, but they wanted to provide baseball with a uniquely American back-story to distance the game from its European origins. (15) This kind of dishonesty provides a significant challenge to historians trying to discover the truth. (16) Furthermore, Doubleday was a decorated war hero, which made the game's invention seem more grandiose. (17) Over 100 years later, the Doubleday myth is still told by some historians, obscuring the incredible true history of baseball.

6. Which sentence could be eliminated from the first paragraph without detracting from the main ideas of the paragraph?

   A. Sentence 2
   B. Sentence 3
   C. Sentence 4
   D. Sentence 5

CONTINUE ON TO THE NEXT PAGE ➡

7. Which revision of sentence 5 makes proper use of commas?

   A. American colonists put their own spin on the games they brought with them, from Europe, and by the 1790s baseball had become popular throughout the United States.

   B. American colonists put their own spin on the games they brought with them from Europe, and by the 1790s baseball had become popular throughout the United States.

   C. American colonists put their own spin on the games they brought with them from Europe and by the 1790s, baseball had become popular throughout the United States.

   D. American colonists put their own spin on the games they brought with them from Europe, and by the 1790s, baseball had become popular throughout the United States.

8. What is the best way to combine sentences 6 and 7 to clarify the relationship between ideas and reduce wordiness?

   A. Early American baseball was a game of local variations because the number of bases, the construction of the ball, and the methods of making outs could be different from town to town.

   B. The number of bases, the construction of the ball, and the methods of making outs could all be different from town to town, making early American baseball a game of variations.

   C. Early American baseball was a game of town-to-town variations, including the number of bases, the construction of the ball, and the methods of making outs.

   D. Early American baseball was different from town to town, making it a game of variations.

9. Which transition word should be added to sentence 8?

   A. However

   B. Consequently

   C. Moreover

   D. Unfortunately

10. Which edit is needed to correct sentence 9?

   A. Change **Rules** to **Rule**

   B. Change **introduce** to **introduced**

   C. Change **meaning** to **meant**

   D. Change **approaching** to **approached**

11. Which of these would best follow sentence 11 to provide support?

   A. There was no such thing as a "strikeout," and the ball had to be pitched underhand.

   B. Alexander Cartwright is often referred to as "the Father of Modern Baseball."

   C. There are recreational leagues around the country today in which people still play Knickerbocker Rules games.

   D. The rules introduced the concept of a foul ball, which is still used in today's game.

CONTINUE ON TO THE NEXT PAGE →

12. How could sentence 14 best be split into two sentences to group related ideas together?

A. In 1905, a group called the Mills Commission declared that Civil War General Abner Doubleday had invented baseball in Cooperstown, New York in 1839, which the commission most likely knew wasn't entirely true. They wanted to provide baseball with a uniquely American back-story to distance the game from its European origins.

B. In 1905, a group called the Mills Commission declared that Civil War General Abner Doubleday had invented baseball. They claimed he had created the game in Cooperstown, New York in 1839, which the commission most likely knew wasn't entirely true, but they wanted to provide baseball with a uniquely American back-story to distance the game from its European origins.

C. In 1905, a group called the Mills Commission declared that Civil War General Abner Doubleday had invented baseball in Cooperstown, New York. They claimed it had happened in 1839, which the commission most likely knew wasn't entirely true, but they wanted to provide baseball with a uniquely American back-story to distance the game from its European origins.

D. In 1905, a group called the Mills Commission declared that Civil War General Abner Doubleday had invented baseball in Cooperstown, New York in 1839. The commission most likely knew this story wasn't entirely true, but they wanted to provide baseball with a uniquely American back-story to distance the game from its European origins.

13. Which sentence is least relevant to paragraph 3 and could be removed?

A. Sentence 13
B. Sentence 15
C. Sentence 16
D. Sentence 17

CONTINUE ON TO THE NEXT PAGE ➡

ENGLISH LANGUAGE ARTS
Practice Test 3

DIRECTIONS: Read the passage below to answer questions 14 to 20. The questions will focus on improving the writing quality of the passage to follow the conventions of standard written English.

Cribbage

(1) Cribbage is a popular two-person card game that is unique because it involves both a deck of 52 playing cards and a scoring board. (2) The object of the game is to reach a point total of either 61 or 121, depending on whether the players prefer a shorter or longer game. (3) Players can score points in a variety of ways, many of which are similar to scoring combinations in other card games, such as gin rummy. (4) Players can score by making pairs, creating runs of consecutive cards (5, 6, 7, for example), or making mathematical combinations of cards that add up to 15 (an 8 and a 7, for example). (5) Players keep track of their points by moving two pegs along the scoring board. (6) The board helps prevent players from forgetting their score.

(7) Each hand of cribbage is divided into three parts: the deal, the play, and the show. (8) The deal begins with one player dealing hands of six cards to each player. (9) The players then study their hands, analyzing them for scoring potential. (10) Each player must then discard two of his or her cards to form a third hand known as the "crib." (11) The player who is not the dealer then cuts the cards and reveals the top card of the deck. (12) This is a community card that either player can use later when scoring their hand. (13) The players begin the play by taking turns playing cards from their hands and stating the total value of all cards played. (14) If the first player puts down a nine, he or she would say, "Nine." (15) If the next player puts down a seven, he or she would say, "Sixteen." (16) During the play, players can score points by creating a total of exactly 15 or 31, or making pairs or runs of consecutive cards.

(17) Once players have used all the cards in their hands, the game moves into the show. (18) During the show, each player has another chance to score by counting all the possible pairs, runs of consecutive cards, and combinations of 15 made using their hand as well as the community card. (19) Each player has a distinct advantage during the show. (20) The player who is not the dealer counts their score first, so if they reach the goal of either 61 or 121, they win before the dealer even counts their points. (21) The dealer's advantage is that in addition to scoring his or her own hand, the dealer also counts the points made by the crib, which is made up of the cards players previously discarded. (22) After players count their points and move their pegs along the board accordingly, the next hand begins. (23) The player who dealt the hand gives the deck to the other player, who becomes the dealer for the next hand.

CONTINUE ON TO THE NEXT PAGE →

14. How could sentence 1 be revised to eliminate the use of "to be" verbs?

   A. Cribbage is a popular two-person card game unique because it involves both a deck of 52 playing cards and a scoring board.

   B. The popular two-person game cribbage involves both a deck of 52 playing cards and a scoring board, making it unique among card games.

   C. Cribbage, a popular two-person card game, is unique because it involves both a deck of 52 playing cards and a scoring board.

   D. Cribbage, unique due to the fact that it involves both a deck of 52 playing cards and a scoring board, is a popular two-person card game.

15. Which revision of sentence 4 correctly formats the use of numbers?

   A. Players can score by making pairs, creating runs of consecutive cards (five, six, seven, for example), or making mathematical combinations of cards that add up to fifteen (an eight and a seven, for example).

   B. Players can score by making pairs, creating runs of consecutive cards (5, 6, 7, for example), or making mathematical combinations of cards that add up to fifteen (an 8 and a 7, for example).

   C. Players can score by making pairs, creating runs of consecutive cards (five, six, seven, for example), or making mathematical combinations of cards that add up to 15 (an eight and a seven, for example).

   D. Players can score by making pairs, creating runs of consecutive cards (5, 6, 7, for example), or making mathematical combinations of cards that add up to 15 (an eight and a seven, for example).

16. Which of the following sentences could be removed from paragraph 1 without detracting from its main ideas?

   A. Sentence 3

   B. Sentence 4

   C. Sentence 5

   D. Sentence 6

17. Which edit is necessary to correct sentence 8?

   A. Change **begin** to **began**

   B. Change **dealing** to **deals**

   C. Change **hands** to a **hand**

   D. Change **six** to **6**

CONTINUE ON TO THE NEXT PAGE ➡

18. How could sentences 11 and 12 be combined to clarify the relationship between ideas?

A. The player who is not the dealer then cuts the cards and reveals the top card of the deck, which becomes a community card that either player can use later when scoring their hand.

B. The player who is not the dealer then cuts the cards and reveals the top card of the deck, and this card is a community card that either player can use later when scoring their hand.

C. The player who is not the dealer then cuts the cards and reveals the top card of the deck: this is a community card that either player can use later when scoring their hand.

D. The player who is not the dealer then cuts the cards and reveals the top card of the deck (this is a community card that either player can use later when scoring their hand).

19. Which edit is necessary to correct sentence 22?

A. Change **their** to **his** or **her**

B. Change **pegs** to **peg**

C. Change **according** to **accordingly**

D. Change **begin** to **will begin**

20. How could sentence 23 be revised to prevent reader confusion?

A. The player who dealt the hand that was just played gives the deck to the other player, who becomes the dealer for the hand that will be played next.

B. Players alternate taking the role of dealer each hand.

C. The other player who was not the dealer of the hand that was just played becomes the dealer for the next hand.

D. Players take turns being the dealer.

CONTINUE ON TO THE NEXT PAGE →

READING COMPREHENSION
Practice Test 3

DIRECTIONS: Analyze the passages below, and answer the commensurate questions. Only use information provided within the passage for your answers. There is only one answer for each question.

More than twenty-eight million school-age children have parents who are employed, and between seven and fifteen million children go home to an empty house on any given day. According to research conducted by the Urban ⁵ Institute, "an estimated 4 million 6-to-12-year-olds with employed mothers are regularly without adult supervision when not at school."

There are many risks associated with leaving children and youth without supervision during 10 afterschool hours. When children are in "self-care" rather than supervised, their personal safety as well as their emotional security can be compromised. For older youth, being unsupervised after school increases the likelihood that they 15 will become involved in criminal activity, develop a substance abuse problem, or engage in early sexual activity or other high-risk behaviors. Both juvenile crime and victimization of children and youth peak between the hours of 3 and 6 p.m.. 20

The younger children are when they are left alone, and the more hours they are unsupervised, the greater the probability they will be adversely affected.

In one study, sixth-graders who had been 25 unsupervised regularly between first and third grade were less socially competent and had lower grades than a control group. A study of nearly

5,000 eighth-graders found that those who took 30 care of themselves for eleven or more hours a week were twice as likely to smoke, drink, or use marijuana than those who were not in self-care after school.

21. What is the main idea of the passage?

A. Staying home increases an adolescent's chance of taking drugs.
B. Adolescents should participate in afterschool programs.
C. Being left self-monitored for extended periods of time can lead to adverse effects in adolescents.
D. It is never good for an adolescent to be left home alone.

22. The study in paragraph 4 is used to illustrate:

A. The impacts of being self-monitored at home for extended periods of time.
B. How likely sixth graders are to smoke or drink.
C. What is necessary to get good grades in school.
D. Fourth and fifth grades are not important to adolescent development.

CONTINUE ON TO THE NEXT PAGE →

23. According to the passage, which eighth grader is at greatest risk of criminal behavior.

   A. A student who was self-monitored from kindergarten through third grade, but who has been in afterschool programs since that time.

   B. Students who were in after-school programs regularly until sixth grade, but have been self-monitored for 20 hours a week since then.

   C. Students who are home-schooled.

   D. A student who's sibling was self-monitored growing up.

---

24. Which of the following is not listed as an issue associated with frequent self-monitoring amongst adolescents?

   A. Worse grades

   B. Higher crime rate

   C. Decreased intelligence

   D. Less safety

---

25. What may also be considered "high-risk behavior" according to its usage in the passage?

   A. Robbing a convenience store.

   B. Not studying for a test.

   C. Not eating vegetables.

   D. Playing the game "Risk."

26. Lines 21-23 is most likely used as an example of:

   A. Why afterschool programs are useful.

   B. A reason why cops should be on patrol between 3 and 6pm.

   C. Why school should start later and end after 6pm.

   D. Prove that being supervised is only critical during the hours of 3pm and 6pm.

CONTINUE ON TO THE NEXT PAGE ➡

There is a broad international agreement today on a minimal or threshold standard by which to judge whether or not a regime is a democracy. This minimal criterion is the regular occurrence of free, open, fair, and contested elections by which 5 an inclusive citizenry selects its representatives in government. Thus, there is government by consent of the governed in which the people's representatives are accountable to the people.

In 2002, 121 of the world's 192 sovereign states 10 could be recognized as democracies in terms of the minimal global standard for an electoral democracy. The collective populations of these electoral democracies accounted for 64.6% of the world's population. By contrast, in 1900 there 15 was not even one country in the world that met today's minimal global standard for democracy. In 1950, there were only 22 authentic democracies comprising 14.3% of the world's population. By the end of the twentieth century, however, there 20 was a dramatic global trend toward electoral democracy as communist regimes and other types of autocratic or authoritarian systems withered and died.

There is more to the content and process of 25 democracy than is entailed by the minimal electoral standard. An advanced or more fully developed conceptualization of democracy in today's world includes electoral democracy in concert with such core concepts as 30 representational government, constitutionalism, human rights, citizenship, civil society, and market economy. The idea of constitutionalism is the key to comprehending an advanced conceptualization of democracy. 35

Constitutionalism means limited government and the rule of law to prevent the arbitrary use of power, to protect human rights, to regulate democratic procedures in elections and public 40 policymaking, and to achieve a community's shared purposes.

Constitutionalism in a democracy, therefore, both limits and empowers the government of, by, and for the people. Through a constitution to which 45 they have consented, the people grant power to the government to act effectively for the common good. The people also set constitutional limits on the power of their democratic government in order to prevent tyranny and to protect 50 their rights. So, in an authentic constitutional democracy, the people's elected representatives in government are limited by the supreme law of the people's constitution for the primary purposes of protecting equally the rights of everyone in the 55 polity and thereby promoting the common good of the community.

27. This passage mostly serves to:

   A. Explain constitutionalism.
   B. Show that democracy is more prevalent today than in the past.
   C. Admonish non-democratic regimes.
   D. Outline the defining features of contemporary democracy.

CONTINUE ON TO THE NEXT PAGE →

28. What change to a country's election standards, since 1900, may have allowed it to now be considered democratic?

   A. Woman and minorities were granted enfranchisement.
   B. A single ruler was elected multiple times.
   C. Control changed from a Republican Party to a Democratic Party.
   D. A country enforced compulsory participation in elections.

29. What element of a democracy establishes election procedure, according to the passage?

   A. Whatever the ruler states
   B. International precedent
   C. Constitution
   D. Human rights

30. According to the passage, what would be covered by a constitution?

   A. Street parking regulations
   B. Human rights
   C. The Gross Domestic Product
   D. Education policy

31. What is true about democracies since 1950, according to the passage?

   A. On average , they are more democratic.
   B. On average, they possess more human rights.
   C. They are no more nor less democratic than democracies existing before 1950.
   D. On average, individual democratic countries in 1950 made up a larger percent of the global population than today.

32. What about constitutionalism, compared to basic election procedure, is necessary "to comprehending an advanced conceptualization of democracy?"

   A. Elections need to be free and open.
   B. Constitutionalism ensures that there will be multiple candidates in an election.
   C. Constitutionalism limits the power of the people, but ensures the democratic rights of all.
   D. Constitutions exclusively deal with election procedure.

CONTINUE ON TO THE NEXT PAGE ➡

The year 1000 was a turning point in the fortunes of western Europe. Within a decade of that date, Olaf had converted most of the Scandinavians to Christianity, and the Viking threat came to an end. King Stephen accepted Christianity for himself 5 and the Hungarian people, and the Magyars joined Christendom. The Muslim Caliphate of Cordoba collapsed into civil war, and the armed merchant vessels of the Italian city-states wrested control of the western Mediterranean from the Muslim 10 fleets of north Africa.

The Muslims who controlled the mountain passes between France and Italy made the mistake of capturing Majolus, abbot of Cluny, and holding him for ransom. After obtaining his freedom, 15 the Burgundian warrior class drove the Muslims from their fortresses and restored secure land communication between France and Italy.

Otto I, the German emperor, entered Rome and freed the papacy from the control of local Roman 20 political factions. He turned the papacy over to Gerbert of Aurillac, a learned and reform-minded monk and teacher, and the Cluniac reform movement finally reached the highest levels of the western Church. Meanwhile, the Guiscards 25 and Hautevilles, a family of adventurers from Normandy, began the reconquest of southern Italy and the establishment of the Norman Kingdom of Naples and Sicily.

Western Europe's economic fortunes began 30 to change just as quickly. The rulers of Kiev had destroyed the Khazar state to the east of them and, by so doing, removed a buffer that had protected the Varangian Route of Russian rivers from the peoples of central Asia. One of 35 these peoples, the Patchinaks (there are various

spellings of this name), settled around 1000 in those lands where the Varangian rivers entered the Black Sea. The Varangian route was blocked, 40 and merchants began once again to carry goods from the Baltic to Mediterranean markets by way of the Seine-Loire-Garonne/Rhone river routes of France. In turn, Eastern merchants in appreciable numbers began to appear once 45 again in the West.

33. What is this passage mostly about?

   A. How trade influenced Europe and Asia
   B. The rise of the Medieval Christian Church.
   C. The political, economic, and religious developments during 1000 AD.
   D. The developments of the Vikings and Germans during 1000 AD.

34. What is implied in the passage concerning Scandinavians prior to the actions of Olaf?

   A. Christianity was not the dominant religion.
   B. Scandinavians were Vikings.
   C. Scandinavia was not an important part of Western Europe.
   D. Scandinavia had more territory.

CONTINUE ON TO THE NEXT PAGE →

35. Otto I was responsible for assisting which reform movement in gaining power?

    A. Catholic reform movement
    B. Protestant reform movement
    C. Gerbert reform movement
    D. Cluniac reform movement

36. What does the author cite as a reason for economic success during the year 1000?

    A. Political reform
    B. Social reform
    C. Religious reform
    D. Change in trading routes

37. The "eastern merchants" were responsible for what development in the year 1000 AD?

    A. Economic prosperity
    B. Religious migration
    C. Population migration
    D. All of the above

38. According to the passage, what was true of King Stephen prior to the year 1000 AD?

    A. He was Christian, but not catholic.
    B. He practiced a pagan religion.
    C. He conquered Hungary.
    D. He was not Christian.

CONTINUE ON TO THE NEXT PAGE ➡

Let's first define heresy. The technical definition is "error, obdurately held," which meant, in the Middle Ages, that a person believed something that was contrary to the "revealed truth" offered by God to humanity through the Church, and that 5 the person continued to hold that belief even after it had been pointed out to him or her how that belief was contrary to "revealed truth." Heresy was both hated and feared.

People believed in physical Hell, in which 10 sinners would suffer the most excruciating pain imaginable forever and would be aware that their agony would never end. You would do well to think about that for a moment. The Church taught, and most people believed, that the only way to 15 avoid such a fate was by following the teachings and being protected by the rituals (sacraments) of the Church.

A heretic was doomed to Hell, but could also convince others of his or her wrong belief and 20 so lead them to Hell as well. So, a heretic was regarded as we might regard someone carrying a highly contagious and incurable disease. We would lock such a person up where they would not come in contact with anyone; the people of the Middle 25 Ages killed them. Moreover, they often killed them in public and horrible ways as a warning to everyone of how dangerous heretics were.

39. What is this passage mostly about?

    A. Contagious diseases in the middle ages.
    B. The judicial system in the middle ages.
    C. Reasons for execution in the middle ages.
    D. Defining heresy and explaining why it was publicly feared.

40. Why did people consider heresy a public, as opposed to purely private, concern?

    A. All people are connected religiously.
    B. Incorrect beliefs spread, corrupting others.
    C. Heresy was a contagious disease.
    D. People would discuss their heresy in public.

41. Based on the word's context, what is the meaning of "obdurate" as used in the passage?

    A. Refusing to change opinion, regardless of argumentation
    B. Non-religious
    C. Heretical
    D. Confident

CONTINUE ON TO THE NEXT PAGE ➡

42. According to the passage , what was a common penalty for heresy in the Middle Ages?

    A. Torture
    B. Exile
    C. Required to repent
    D. Execution

43. According to the passage, who offered the "revealed truth?"

    A. Priests
    B. Heretics
    C. Christians
    D. God

44. Gruesome execution standards were used as a means to both remove a heretic and ___?

    A. Provide disincentive to potential future heretics.
    B. Illustrate the Churches ultimate authority.
    C. Instill fear in the heart of believers.
    D. Heretics could be purified through pain.

CONTINUE ON TO THE NEXT PAGE ➡

You're probably surprised that I think that a stratified and status-ridden society like medieval Europe was the origin of the concept of equality. As I said, we often fall short of our ideals, but our ideal of the integrity of the individual was born in ⁵ medieval Europe.

The Greek Stoics, whose philosophy had a great effect on the early Christian Church, held that there was a Brotherhood of Man and that the highest calling of every person was to treat others ¹⁰ justly and compassionately. In the minds of the Stoics, however, this meant that people should be kind to their slaves, not that there shouldn't be any slaves at all.

Under the best of conditions, such as in a well- ¹⁵ run Benedictine monastery, medieval Europeans strove to achieve this ideal of equality. A tightly-run organization such as a monastery required some hierarchy, but the Benedictines based theirs solely upon seniority. Whoever had entered the ²⁰ monastery first held precedence over all those who had entered afterwards, regardless of what rank or status they might have held in secular life.

There is a neat story about this. A nobleman had decided to abandon secular life and enter a ²⁵ monastery that he had endowed with considerable wealth. When he rode up to the gate of the monastery, with his slave trotting along behind him and carrying his luggage, the abbot had the gates opened wide and greeted the noble with ³⁰ deference. When he was asked to step inside, the noble told his slave to take in his baggage. The slave did so and entered the monastery a couple of paces in front of his master.

For the rest of his life, the noble had to defer to his former slave since the slave had entered monastic life before he had.

45. What is this passage mostly about?

A. Medieval society may not have practiced ideals such as equality perfectly, but these ideals were important to the society.
B. The stoics preached equality.
C. Nobles and slaves were considered equals.
D. Nobles and slaves were treated the same by the church.

46. Based on the passage, the nobleman in paragraph four was most likely joining what kind of monastery?

A. Benedictine
B. Stoic
C. Medieval
D. Church

CONTINUE ON TO THE NEXT PAGE →

47. Which group believed that there was a "Brotherhood of Man," according to the passage?

    A. Nobleman
    B. Churches
    C. Medieval prophets
    D. Stoics

48. What is implied about medieval society?

    A. Medieval society was more advanced than contemporary society.
    B. Society was heavily stratified.
    C. There were no kings.
    D. Nobles owned slaves, but not by choice.

49. What is the purpose of the story in paragraph four?

    A. To illustrate that not everyone agreed with slavery.
    B. To illustrate how high-minded the Benedictines were.
    C. To illustrate how concepts of equality were enacted in medieval society.
    D. To illustrate how a slave could become free.

50. What would the author most likely agree with?

    A. Medieval society was more enlightened than contemporary society.
    B. An individual can have an ideal without necessarily following the ideal perfectly.
    C. The medieval period was the most important moment in the development of individualism as a concept.
    D. The nobleman in the story made the right choice to join the monastery.

CONTINUE ON TO THE NEXT PAGE ➡

My life has always been a continuous struggle with ill-health and ambition, and I have mastered neither. I try to reassure myself that this accursed ill-health will not affect my career. I keep flogging my will in the hope of winning through in the 5 end. Yet, at the back of my mind, there is the great improbability that I shall ever live long enough to realize myself. For a long time, my hope has simply been to last long enough to convince others of what I might have done – had I lived. That will be 10 something. But even to do that, I will not allow that I have overmuch time. I have never at any time lived with any sense of security. I have never felt permanently settled in this life - nothing more than a shadowy *locum tenens,* a wraith, a festoon 15 of mist likely to disappear any moment.

At times, when I am vividly conscious of the insecurity of my tenure here, my desires enter on a mad race to obtain fulfillment before it is too late… and as fulfillment recedes, ambition obsesses me 20 the more. I am daily occupied in calculating with my ill-health: trying to circumvent it, to carry on in spite of all. I conquer each day. Every week is a victory. I am always surprised that my health or will has not collapsed, that, by Jove! I am still 25 working and still living.

One day it looks like appendicitis, another stoppage, another threatened blindness, or I develop a cough and am menaced with consumption. So I go on in a hurricane of bad 30 dreams. I struggle like Laocoon with the serpents – the serpents. of nervous depression that press around the heart tighter than I care to admit. I must use every kind of blandishment to convince myself that my life and my work are worthwhile. 35 Frequently I must smother and kill (and it calls for

prompt action) the shrill voice that cries from the tiniest corner of my heart, "Are you quite sure you are such an important fellow as you imagine?" 40 Or I fret over the condition of my brain, finding that I forget what I read, I lose in acuteness of my perceptions. My brain is a tumefaction. But I won't give in. I go on trying to recollect what I have forgotten, I harry my brain all day to recall 45 a word or name, I attack other folk importunately. I write things down so as to look them up in reference books – I am always looking up the things I remember I have forgotten.

51. What is this passage mostly about?

   A. A writer's attempt to struggle through illness and self-loathing.
   B. An author's relationship to memory.
   C. The importance of friends.
   D. The impact of illness on one's career.

52. Why does the author never feel "settled?"

   A. He believes illness will kill him at any moment.
   B. He does not believe his work is very good.
   C. He is worried that others will not believe his work is very good.
   D. He is worried that he will never finish his work.

CONTINUE ON TO THE NEXT PAGE →

53. What is one impact of the author's bad health?

    A. It makes him a better author.
    B. It is sometimes the inspiration for his work.
    C. It makes him more intelligent.
    D. His work is always a study of his own health.

54. Why does the author always write down his thoughts?

    A. He is an author.
    B. As a way to fight off insanity.
    C. So that he may remember lost knowledge.
    D. To give himself purpose in life.

55. What does the author imply about himself?

    A. He is of good health.
    B. He does not always have confidence in himself.
    C. He is insane.
    D. He has never actually been ill.

56. *Locum tenens* most closely means:

    A. Locust
    B. Wraith
    C. Loco teen
    D. Local teen

57. What does the author mean when he says he is "vividly conscious of the insecurity of my tenure here" (lines 17-18)?

    A. He knows he will not live long.
    B. He knows his writing isn't actually good enough.
    C. He knows he will never get over his inner insecurities.
    D. He knows he will probably get fired from his job.

CONTINUE ON TO THE NEXT PAGE →

214

90 MINUTES • 57 QUESTIONS

Select the best answer from the choices given by carefully solving each problem. Bubble the letter of your answer on the answer sheet. Please refrain from making any stray marks on the answer sheet. If you need to erase an answer, please erase thoroughly.

Important Notes:

1. There are no formulas or definitions in the math section that will be provided.
2. Diagrams may or may not be drawn to scale. Do not make assumptions based on the diagram unless it is specifically stated in the diagram or question.
3. Diagrams are not in more than one plane, unless stated otherwise.
4. Graphs are drawn to scale, therefore, you can assume relationships according to the graph. If lines appear parallel, then you can assume the lines to be parallel. This is also true for right angles and so forth.
5. Simplify fractions completely.

Practice Test 3 (Questions 1-57)

1. $3[9 \div (-3)] + (-3 - (-8)] =$

   A. -20
   B. -4
   C. -2
   D. 2

2. If $\dfrac{2,000}{2x} = 10$, then what is $\sqrt{x}$

   A. $\sqrt{10}$
   B. 10
   C. $\sqrt{1,000}$
   D. 100

3. If $x = 9$, $y = -9$ and $z = -1$, what is the value of $yz + \sqrt{x} + yz - \sqrt{x}$?

   A. -24
   B. -18
   C. 0
   D. 18

CONTINUE ON TO THE NEXT PAGE →

4.

1 dollar = 0.5 pillets
4 coss = 1 dollar

Lindsey has $20 to spend. She needs to buy exactly 2 pillets. She spends the remaining amount buying coss. How many coss does Lindsey purchase?

A. 4
B. 5
C. 64
D. 72

---

5. $\sqrt{100} \div \sqrt{25} =$

A. $\sqrt{2}$
B. 2
C. 4
D. 10

---

6. If $x = -8$, what is the value of $\frac{1}{2}|4x - 4|$?

A. -18
B. -14
C. 14
D. 18

7.

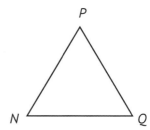

Triangle *NPQ* is an equilateral triangle. If its perimeter is 27, what is the length of *NP* + *NQ*?

A. 16
B. 18
C. 4
D. 32

---

8. If 40% of *x* is 160, what is *x*?

A. .0025
B. 64
C. 360
D. 400

---

9. When *d* is divided by 7, the remainder is 5. What is the remainder when *d* + 1 is divided by 7?

A. 0
B. 1
C. 5
D. 6

CONTINUE ON TO THE NEXT PAGE ➡

10.

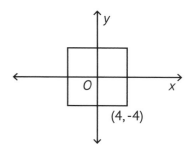

(4,-4)

In the figure above, *O* is the center of the square. What is the area of the square?

A. 8
B. 16
C. 32
D. 64

11.

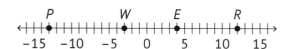

If *O* is the midpoint of $\overline{PW}$, then what is the distance of $\overline{OE}$?

A. 10
B. 11
C. 12
D. 13

12. The average of 7 consecutive even integers is 20. What is the median?

A. 18
B. 20
C. 20.5
D. 22

13. What is 0.003815 in scientific notation?

A. 3815×10^{-2}
B. 3.815×10^{-3}
C. 0.03815×10
D. 0.003815×10^{2}

14.

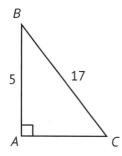

In the figure above, what is the length of $\overline{AC}$?

A. 8
B. 12
C. $2\sqrt{66}$
D. $2\sqrt{289}$

CONTINUE ON TO THE NEXT PAGE ➡

Explanations to each problem on:
Youtube.com/ArgoBrothers

MATHEMATICS
TEST 3

ARGO
BROTHERS
www.argobrothers.com

15. What time will it be 53 hours after 3:30 P.M. on Thursday?

   A. 8:30 A.M. Saturday
   B. 7:30 P.M. Saturday
   C. 8:30 P.M. Saturday
   D. 8:30 P.M. Sunday

16.

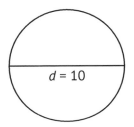

$d = 10$

If x represents the circumference of the above figure, and y represents the area, what is $\frac{x}{y}$?

Note: d is the diameter of the circle above.

   A. $\frac{10}{25}\pi$

   B. $\frac{5}{2}$

   C. $\frac{2}{5}$

   D. $\frac{25}{10}\pi$

17. A certain substance has a mass of 98 milligrams. What is the mass of this substance in kilograms?

   A. 9.8×10^5 kg
   B. 9.8×10^3 kg
   C. 9.8×10^{-3} kg
   D. 9.8×10^{-5} kg

18. Samuel scored a 72, 92 and 80 on his first three exams. What is the minimum score he needs to get on his next exam to get an average of 85?

   A. 85
   B. 90
   C. 93
   D. 96

19. Five out of 10 marbles in a bag are red. What percentage of the marbles are **not** red?

   A. 50%
   B. 55%
   C. 60%
   D. 75%

CONTINUE ON TO THE NEXT PAGE →

Explanations to each problem on:
Youtube.com/ArgoBrothers

MATHEMATICS
TEST 3

ARGO BROTHERS
www.argobrothers.com

20.

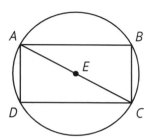

Figure not drawn to scale.

In the figure above, the rectangle *ABCD* is inscribed in the circle. Where *E* is the center and the radius is 5. If the length of *AD* is 6, what is the area of rectangle *ABCD*?

A. 30
B. 48
C. 60
D. 25π

21. $(\sqrt{81})\,(\sqrt{25}) + \sqrt{16} =$

A. 5
B. 40
C. 49
D. 56

22. It takes George 3 minutes to read 300 words. If each page in a book that he is reading has 750 words, how long will it take George to read 6 pages?

A. 30 minutes
B. 45 minutes
C. 60 minutes
D. 90 minutes

23. $(\frac{1}{2} - \frac{3}{4})^2 + \frac{5}{10} =$

A. $\frac{9}{16}$
B. $\frac{1}{2}$
C. $\frac{1}{16}$
D. $\frac{3}{4}$

24. If $x = 2^5 \cdot 3^2 \cdot 7$, then what is the value of *x*?

A. 1150
B. 2000
C. 2015
D. 2016

25.

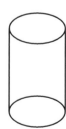

A right cylindrical can is being filled with water. At 1 P.M. it is half full. At 2 P.M. it is $\frac{3}{4}$ th full. At this rate, when was it empty?

A. 11:00 A.M.
B. 11:30 A.M.
C. 12:00 P.M.
D. 12:30 P.M.

CONTINUE ON TO THE NEXT PAGE →

26. If $x^8 = 2^{2^4}$, what is x^2?

    A. 2
    B. 4
    C. 8
    D. 64

27. James has yard work to finish. He finishes $\frac{1}{8}$ of the total work on the first day. What fraction of the work is left?

    A. $\frac{1}{8}$

    B. $\frac{3}{8}$

    C. $\frac{7}{8}$

    D. $\frac{3}{4}$

28.

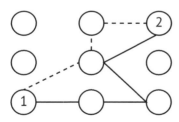

There are two different pathways connecting ① and ②. How many fewer steps is the solid-line path than the dotted-line path. (A step is defined as a line segment connecting 2 circles)?

    A. −4
    B. −1
    C. 1
    D. 4

29. Jackie and Jesse each solve the same problem a different way.

Problem: $\sqrt{a + b} = ?$
Jackie 's way: $\sqrt{a + b} = \sqrt{a} + \sqrt{b}$
Jesse's way: $\sqrt{a + b} = \sqrt{a + b}$

If $a = 9$ and $b = 25$, how much bigger is Jackie's way than Jesse's way?

    A. 0
    B. 2
    C. $\sqrt{36}$
    D. $8 - \sqrt{34}$

30. If $\theta\,(a, b, c, d, e, f, g, h, i\,) =$

$$\frac{(a)(b) - (c)(d) + (ef\,)^2(gh)^2}{i}$$

which cannot be a value of θ?

    A. $\theta(0, 0, 0, 0, 0, 0, 0, 0, 1)$
    B. $\theta(1, 1, 1, 1, 1, 1, 1, 1, 0)$
    C. $\theta(2, 2, 2, 2, 2, 2, 2, 2, 10)$
    D. $\theta(2, 3, 1, 4, 5, 6, 7, 0, 10)$

31. If James grows by 20 inches every day starting Monday, what is the difference in his height between Wednesday and Monday?

    A. 0 inches
    B. 20 inches
    C. 30 inches
    D. 40 inches

CONTINUE ON TO THE NEXT PAGE ➡

32. $(\frac{1}{2} - \frac{3}{4}) \div \frac{1}{2} =$

  A. $\frac{1}{2}$

  B. $\frac{3}{2}$

  C. $\frac{-1}{2}$

  D. $\frac{-3}{4}$

33.

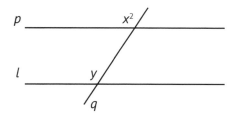

Line q intersects the parallel lines p and l. What is $\frac{y^3}{3}$?

  A. $\frac{x^4}{3}$

  B. x^9

  C. $\frac{x^4}{9}$

  D. $\frac{x^6}{3}$

34. Given the arithmetic sequence $x, y, 30, z, f$ find $x + y + z + f$?

  A. 60
  B. 80
  C. 120
  D. 130

35. If $(-1)^2 = 1$, then the value of $(-1)^{2023}$ is

  A. -2023
  B. -1
  C. 0
  D. 1

36. Caroline has two times as many marbles as Jake. Jake has 12 less than 7 times as many marbles James has. James has 14 marbles. How many marbles does Caroline have?

  A. 54
  B. 86
  C. 98
  D. 172

37. John is trying to escape a ditch. Every time he jumps 10 meters, he falls back 5 meters right after. The ditch is 19 meters long. What is the minimum number of jumps he needs to make to escape?

  A. 3
  B. 4
  C. 5
  D. 7

CONTINUE ON TO THE NEXT PAGE ➡

38. What is the largest number of digits the product of a 3 digit and a 2 digit number has?

   A. 4 digits
   B. 5 digits
   C. 6 digits
   D. 7 digits

39. If $F_n = 2F_{n-1} + 3F_{n-2}$, then what is F_3 if $F_1 = F_2 = 1$?

   A. 2
   B. 3
   C. 4
   D. 5

40. Sam walks 3m to the West, then 4m South, then 4m North. How far is he from his original location?

   A. 3m
   B. 5m
   C. 7m
   D. 8m

41. If $a = 3$, and $b = 5$, what is the value of $\dfrac{9a}{b - a} = ?$

   A. 9

   B. 27

   C. $\dfrac{13}{5}$

   D. $\dfrac{27}{2}$

42. The perimeter of a square is **four** times the circumference of a circle with radius of 1m. What is the area of the square?

   A. 4π
   B. 8π
   C. $4\pi^2$
   D. $8\pi^2$

43. If $\begin{array}{cc} a & b \\ c & d \end{array}$ means $bc + ad$, then what is the value of $\begin{array}{cc} 4 & 5 \\ 7 & 8 \end{array}$

   A. 24
   B. 66
   C. 67
   D. 68

44. Convert $\dfrac{3}{40}$ to a decimal.

   A. 0.0075
   B. 0.075
   C. 0.06
   D. .75

45. For what value of q is $6(q + 3) = 2(q + 4)$?

   A. $\dfrac{-1}{2}$

   B. $\dfrac{-4}{9}$

   C. $\dfrac{-5}{2}$

   D. -3

CONTINUE ON TO THE NEXT PAGE ➡

Explanations to each problem on:
Youtube.com/ArgoBrothers

MATHEMATICS
TEST 3

ARGO
BROTHERS
www.argobrothers.com

46.

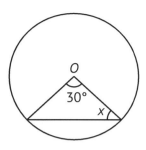

What is ∡ x if point O is the center of the above circle?

A. 45°
B. 60°
C. 75°
D. $\dfrac{\pi}{2}$

---

47. For how many values of x is, $\dfrac{-3x^2}{4} > 0$?

A. 0
B. 1
C. 3
D. 5

---

48. x is 40% of y and y is the square of x. What is the value of x?

A. $\sqrt{x}$
B. $0.4\sqrt{x}$
C. $0.4x^2$
D. $0.4x$

49. If $x = 7$; and $4x(3y - 2x) = 112$; what is the value of y?

A. 4
B. 6
C. 7
D. 28

---

50. If $x \, \partial \, y = \dfrac{x+y}{x-y}$, what is $a \, \partial \, (a - b)$?

A. $\dfrac{2a}{b}$

B. $\dfrac{2a-b}{2a}$

C. $\dfrac{2a-b}{b}$

D. $\dfrac{2a-b}{2b}$

---

51. A newly cleared tract of land has been designated for reforestation. The commission responsible for the project decided to plant 30 trees. 12 of the trees will be oak trees, one-fifth of the trees will be pine trees, 3 are weeping willows, and the rest of the trees will be fruit-bearing trees of a various types. What is the ratio of weeping willows to fruit-bearing trees?

A. 1:3
B. 1:2
C. 3:1
D. 3:12

CONTINUE ON TO THE NEXT PAGE →

52. The chart below reflects the total record sales (in thousands) for six major labels: Petra, Jams, AudioPro, Keynote, GSharp, and Lumia.

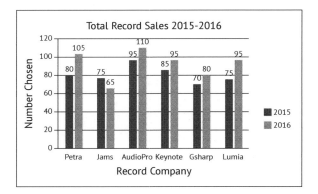

Which company experienced the greatest percentage increase in sales from 2015 to 2016?

A. Petra
B. Audiopro
C. Keynote
D. Lumia

GRID IN

Directions: The following five questions are grid-in problems. On the answer sheet, please be sure to write your answer in the boxes at the top of the grid. Start on the left side of each grid.

53. If Sarah scored an 80, 95, 75 and an 90 on her first four tests, what must she score on her fifth test if she wants an average of 88?

CONTINUE ON TO THE NEXT PAGE →

Explanations to each problem on:
Youtube.com/ArgoBrothers

MATHEMATICS
TEST 3

ARGO
BROTHERS
www.argobrothers.com

54. Solve for x

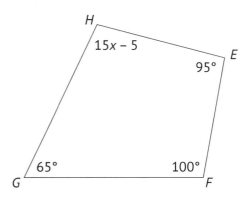

55. Lea's school is selling tickets for the upcoming choral performance. On the first day of ticket sales, the school sold 10 adult tickets and 10 child tickets for a total of $200. On the second day, the school sold 13 adult tickets and 2 child tickets for a total of $172 dollars. How much did each child ticket cost?

CONTINUE ON TO THE NEXT PAGE ➡

56. In a population of 10,000 geese the growth rate is 4% per year. What is the total increase in population over 4 years? Round your answer to the nearest whole number.

THIS IS THE END OF THE TEST. IF THERE IS TIME REMAINING, YOU MAY CHECK YOUR ANSWERS TO PART 1 OR PART 2.

57. $\dfrac{5.5}{0.1} \times .20$

SHSAT PRACTICE TEST 3
ANSWER KEY

Revising/Editing

1. **D**
2. **A**
3. **B**
4. **B**
5. **A**
6. **A**
7. **D**
8. **C**
9. **A**
10. **B**
11. **A**
12. **D**
13. **B**
14. **B**
15. **C**
16. **D**
17. **C**
18. **A**
19. **C**
20. **B**

Reading Comprehension

21. **C**
22. **A**
23. **A**
24. **C**
25. **A**
26. **A**
27. **D**
28. **A**
29. **C**
30. **B**
31. **D**
32. **C**
33. **C**
34. **A**
35. **D**
36. **D**
37. **A**
38. **D**
39. **D**
40. **B**

41. **A**
42. **D**
43. **D**
44. **A**
45. **A**
46. **A**
47. **D**
48. **B**
49. **C**
50. **B**
51. **A**
52. **A**
53. **B**
54. **C**
55. **B**
56. **B**
57. **A**

Math

1. **B**
2. **B**
3. **D**
4. **C**
5. **B**
6. **D**
7. **B**
8. **D**
9. **D**
10. **D**
11. **C**
12. **B**

13. **B**
14. **C**
15. **C**
16. **C**
17. **D**
18. **D**
19. **A**
20. **B**
21. **C**
22. **B**
23. **A**
24. **D**

25. **A**
26. **B**
27. **C**
28. **B**
29. **D**
30. **B**
31. **D**
32. **C**
33. **D**
34. **C**
35. **B**
36. **D**

37. **A**
38. **B**
39. **D**
40. **A**
41. **D**
42. **C**
43. **C**
44. **B**
45. **C**
46. **C**
47. **A**
48. **C**

49. **B**
50. **C**
51. **A**
52. **A**
53. **100**
54. **7**
55. **$8**
56. **1,699**
57. **11**

Practice Test 3 (Answers and Explanations)

1. **D** Passive voice occurs when the subject of a sentence is having action done to it rather than performing the action of the sentence. Answer D is correct because Sentence 4 contains the passive voice construction "acceptance speeches are given." Sentence 4 should be revised to say, "The winners of each award give elaborate, often memorable acceptance speeches." All the other sentences in the paragraph are written in active voice, so answers A, B, and C are all incorrect.

2. **A** Passive voice occurs when the main subject of a sentence is having action done to it rather than performing the action. The sample sentence is written in the passive voice because the subject "the ball" is being "hit" rather than hitting anything. Answer A corrects this error by restructuring the sentence to create a new subject ("two players") who are performing the action "hit," creating an active voice construction. Answer choices B and C both fail to correct the passive voice error, as both sentences still begin "the ball is hit…" Answer D restructures the sentence but is still incorrect because it contains the phrase "points are scored," which is a new example of passive voice in the sentence.

3. **B** Answer B is correct because Sentence 3 requires a comma to separate the introduction phrase "By the age of 20" from the rest of the sentence. Introductions that provide context such as this one should always be separated in this way. The sentence should read, "By the age of 20, Gershwin had written several hit songs." Answers A, C, and D are all incorrect because each of those sentences uses commas as appropriate to separate lists, introduction phrases, and nonessential clauses.

4. **B** Proper nouns (people, places, things, and ideas with specific names) are always capitalized. Answer B is correct because "Manhattan Project" was the specific name of the research in question, so both words in the name are capitalized. Answer D is incorrect because it takes a proper noun (World War II) and incorrectly reduces it to a common noun by removing its capital letters. Answers A and C are also incorrect because "government" and "nuclear weapons" are both common nouns with no specific names, so they do not need to be capitalized.

5. **A** Answer A is correct because Sentence 2 is the least thematically connected to the other sentences in the paragraph. Sentences 1, 3, 4, and 5 all deal specifically with memories of the author making a pie with his or her grandmother. Sentence 2 introduces the author's mother, who is not mentioned otherwise throughout the paragraph and whose involvement does little to enhance the main story. While this sentence could be the jumping-off point for a following paragraph, it is far less connected to this paragraph than any of the other sentences. Answers B, C, and D are all incorrect because each of those answers connects directly to the topic of the grandmother's pie making process.

6. **A** Sentence 2 is unnecessary because it is an expositional, declarative sentence that does little to develop the main ideas from Sentence 1 or transition into Sentence 3. If Sentence 2 is removed, the idea of baseball being an "international game" at the end of Sentence 1 transitions seamlessly

into the discussion of Europe in Sentence 3. Answer B is incorrect because Sentence 3 introduces the concept of baseball's European origins, which is central to the rest of the paragraph. Answer C is incorrect because Sentence 4 provides a key link in the logic that brings baseball from Europe to England in the time of colonization to the Americas. Answer D is incorrect because it introduces the idea of baseball in America, which is the main idea explored in Paragraph 2.

7. **D** This sentence requires two commas: one to indicate the fact that it's a compound sentence, and one to separate the introductory phrase "by the 1790s." Answer choice D includes both these commas and is therefore correct. Answer choice A is incorrect because it separates off the phrase "from Europe" as though it is parenthetical or nonessential information, which it is not. Answer choice B is incorrect because, while it correctly identifies the sentence as a compound sentence, it does not separate the introductory phrase from the second half of the sentence. Answer choice C is incorrect because it separates the introductory clause "by the 1790s" from the clause that follows but does not correctly place the comma before the conjunction that forms the compound sentence.

8. **C** Answer C is the best choice because it communicates the main ideas of both sentences (first, that early baseball was a game of local variations, and second, by providing some examples of those variations) while reducing the overall length of both. Answer choice A provides a solid effort to combine the sentences, but it does not adequately reduce wordiness by including both the phrases "local variations" and "different from town to town," which are redundant. Answer choice B is incorrect because the sentence is logically backwards, providing examples to support the point before making the point itself. This can create potential confusion for the reader. Answer choice D, while concise, is incorrect because it leaves out one of the important main ideas by not providing examples.

9. **A** The fact that Cartwright created a unified set of rules is contrary to the preceding idea (that the game had been built on local variation), so "However" (Answer A) is the best transition. Answer B is incorrect because "consequently" implies a causal relationship between the two ideas that is inaccurate. Answer choice C is incorrect because "moreover" implies that the content of sentence 8 is reinforcing the content of sentence 7, which it is not. Answer choice D is incorrect because there is nothing in the passage to suggest there were negative consequences to the creation of Cartwright's rules, so "unfortunately" would not be appropriate.

10. **B** From sentence 3 to sentence 16, the passage is consistently written in the past tense, so the sentence should read "The Knickerbocker Rules introduced the modern concept..." Also, since the content of the sentence refers to history, the past tense should be used to provide clarity for the reader, to prevent them from incorrectly assuming these events occurred very recently. Answer choice A is incorrect because, throughout the passage, the Knickerbocker Rules are referred to only in plural form. Answer choice C is incorrect because even though the rule change was made in the past, the author's explanation/interpretation of it is current and ongoing, so a progressive verb is appropriate. Answer choice D is also incorrect because "approaching" is a participle taking the role of an adjective in this sentence rather than a verb, so it cannot be put into the past tense.

11. A Answer A is the best choice to support sentence 11 because it provides two concrete examples of ways in which the Knickerbocker Rules differ from today's game (the main idea of sentence 11). Answer choice D is incorrect because it does the exact opposite, providing an example of a way the Knickerbocker Rules are similar to today's baseball. Answer choice D would better support sentences 8 and 9. Answer choices B and C are interesting facts that could fit in this passage, but they do not provide any material support to the idea laid out in sentence 11.

12. D Answer choice D is correct because it splits the overly long sentence 14 into two sentences with thematically connected elements. The first sentence establishes that the Mills Commission created the Doubleday Myth and gives some details about where/when the events supposedly took place. The second sentence establishes that this was most likely an intentional fraud and discusses the reasons why it was perpetrated. Answer choice A is incorrect because it creates an overly long first sentence that might seem confusing or contradictory to readers. Answer choice B is also incorrect because it does not group the content of the sentence in a logical way. The date and place of Doubleday's alleged creation of baseball make the most sense in the first sentence, alongside the introduction of the concept. Answer choice C similarly puts the date in the second sentence, when it is far more closely tied to the ideas in the first sentence.

13. B All the sentences in paragraph three are clearly and directly tied to the Doubleday myth except Sentence 15, which makes a broad, general statement about the nature of history. The same idea is also accessed in Sentence 17 ("...obscuring the incredible true history..."), making Sentence 15 completely unnecessary. Sentences 13, 16, and 17 all explore the same events and ideas, so they clearly belong grouped together in a paragraph.

14. B The "to be" verbs (am, is, are, was, were, will be, etc.) are often discouraged in formal writing, especially in the very first sentence of a piece, as is the case in this passage. Answer B is correct because it eliminates both appearances of the word "is" by reordering the sentence to describe cribbage as "a popular two-person game" rather than saying, "Cribbage is a popular two-person game," and creating a descriptive clause at the end of the sentence rather than just stating the game "is unique." Answer A is incorrect because it still maintains the first use of "is." Answer C is incorrect because it still maintains the second use of "is." Answer D makes an effort to reorder the sentence to eliminate one "to be" verb, but it leaves the second one ("...is unique").

15. C Writing style guides universally agree that numbers one through nine should be written out using letters rather than simply using their numeric symbol. Larger numbers can be written out numerically for the sake of length and clarity. Answer C is correct because it formats all the numbers under nine as words, and leaves 15 in numeric form. Answer A is incorrect because fifteen is written out longhand when it does not need to be. Answer B is incorrect because it leaves the numbers under ten in numeric form. Answer D is incorrect because it leaves some of the numbers under ten in numeric form and is inconsistent in its formatting (some are numerals, some are written out).

16. **D** Sentence 6 is essentially a statement of the obvious which fails to add anything meaningful to the ideas explored in Sentence 5. It is redundant and repetitive, and can therefore be removed, making Answer D correct. Sentence 3 cannot be removed because it introduces the basis of the game's scoring system, which is an important main idea. Sentence 4 builds on that idea, providing meaningful examples, so it should not be removed. Sentence 5 is essentially a clearer, stronger version of Sentence 6, so it should stay as well.

17. **C** The phrase "each player" in Sentence 8 communicates that the players are being treated as individuals. That means each one of them requires "a hand" of cards. As written in the passage, Sentence 8 could be interpreted to mean that each player receives multiple hands of six cards. Therefore, Answer C is correct. Answer A is incorrect because the use of a past tense verb would imply that cribbage was played exclusively in the past, which is not the case. Answer B is incorrect because the phrase "begins with" earlier in the sentence requires a progressive tense verb to following (as can easily be demonstrated by reading the sentence out loud). Answer D is incorrect because numbers one through nine should be written out longhand.

18. **A** Answer A is the best choice because it clearly communicates the role of the card in question while eliminating unnecessary words that could easily confuse the reader. Answer B is incorrect because it simply combines the sentences using basic means without eliminating any of the resultant repetitive wording ("...and this card is a community card..."). Answer C attempts to connect the two sentences with a colon, which is incorrect. Although semicolons can be used to connect to strongly linked sentences, a colon cannot. Answer D is incorrect because, by putting the explanation in parentheses, the author unfairly downplays the importance of this information to the overall meaning and clarity of the sentence.

19. **C** The adverb "accordingly" should be used in this sentence to communicate the relationship between the score of a player's hand and the manner in which the pegs are moved. The sentence as written is incorrect because "according" must always be followed by "to" (For example: "These are the rules according to Hoyle." "The neighbor's dog is vicious, according to Dad."). Answer A is incorrect because the sentence is referring to both players collectively (the opposite of the case in Question 4). In English, the plural pronoun "they" is gender neutral, so regardless of the gender makeup of the two players, "they" is an appropriate term to describe both of them. Answer B is incorrect for essentially the same reason: each player has two pegs, as was established in Sentence 5, so the plural form must be used. Answer D is incorrect because the sentence is written using present tense verbs (count and move), so the use of a future tense verb "will begin" would be grammatically inconsistent and possibly jarring to the reader.

20. **B** Answer B is the most straightforward, simplified way to present the content of Sentence 23. Answer A actually increases the wordiness of the sentence, creating additional places for a reader to become confused. Answer C uses repetitive language (player/played, dealer/dealer, the hand that was just played/the next hand) that could also provide stumbling blocks for many readers, especially those learning about the game for the first time. Answer D actually over-simplifies the

sentence in a way that could lead to additional reader confusion. By saying players take turns but not indicating what causes them to switch, Answer D fails to provide enough information to communicate the idea clearly to the reader.

READING COMPREHENSION

Passage 1 ("More than twenty-eight million...")

21. C Answer C is the best choice because it correctly identifies that the passage is exploring the risks of allowing adolescents to self-monitor after school. Answer A is not the best answer because, although drugs are introduced as one of the major risks for self-monitored children, the passage is about much more than simply the risk of drug abuse. Answer B is not the best answer because, while it is a logical takeaway from the passage, the importance of afterschool programs is not explicitly explored anywhere in the text. Answer D is also incorrect because it is an over-generalization, and the passage only finds fault with children who are habitually left in self-care.

22. A Answer A is the best choice because the study illustrates the adverse effects that children in self-care are more likely to experience than others. Answer B is incorrect because the study does not say how likely sixth graders are to smoke and drink, but rather demonstrates that 6th graders left home alone are more likely to smoke and drink than those who are supervised. Answer C is incorrect because the passage does not discuss academics or success strategies at all. Answer D is incorrect because the study does not make judgments about which grades are most important; it just happens that the study was done on 6th graders.

23. A Answer A is correct because Lines 21-24 clearly state: "The younger children are when they are left alone, and the more hours they are unsupervised, the greater they possibility they will be adversely affected." Therefore, the child at most risk would be the one who was left unsupervised from the earliest age, even if they later became more involved in afterschool activities. Answer B is incorrect because those children were older and more mature before they began self-monitoring, unlike those who were alone since kindergarten. Answer C is incorrect because the passage makes no mention of home schooling. Answer D is incorrect because the passage does not provide any data on how self-monitored siblings affect development.

24. C Answer C is correct because there is no mention of intelligence or IQ testing anywhere in the passage. Answer A is incorrect because low grades are clearly listed as an effect of self-monitoring in Lines 27-28. Answer B is incorrect because Lines 14-20 clearly indicate that self-monitored children are more likely to engage in crime. Answer D is incorrect because Lines 11-14 clearly state that safety is a major concern when children are left alone.

25. A Answer A is correct because robbing a convenience store is an example of committing a crime, which the author identifies as a high-risk behavior of unsupervised adolescents in Lines 14-20.

Answer B is incorrect because, while not studying on a test has negative effects, it is not "high-risk" because it doesn't pose a long-term risk to the health or safety of the student. Answer C is incorrect because the passage has nothing to do with food choices. Answer D is incorrect because the game Risk is unlikely to pose long-term negative effects for the health of students.

26.   **A**   Answer A is the best choice because, by illustrating that children who are left alone from early on are at the most risk, the author implies that afterschool programs would be useful to fight the problem. Answer B is incorrect because, while 3 to 6 is identified as the window when most youth crimes occur, Lines 21-23 don't include any content that would be affected by police involvement. Answer C is not the best answer because the author does not make any specific recommendations for schools or educators, and never suggests school should go later. Answer D is also incorrect because Lines 21-23 simply establish that the earlier and longer children are left alone, the more likely they are to suffer consequences – the specific hours of the day are not important.

Passage 2 ("There is a broad international agreement..."):

27.   **D**   Answer D is the best choice because democracy and its growth throughout the world are clearly the main topics of the passage. Answer A is incorrect because constitutionalism is only explained in the final two paragraphs, whereas democracy is discussed throughout the entire passage, making Answer D a better choice. Answer B is not the best choice because, while the passage does discuss democracy's relatively recent growth, the text does so much more than simply make that point. Answer C is also incorrect because, while the author of the passage clearly admires democracy, the text does not make outright calls to action against non-democratic regimes or even go into their flaws.

28.   **A**   Answer A is the best choice because Lines 4-9 establish that the most democratic concept is for a citizenry to elect leaders who represent them and their interests. By broadening the electorate to include women, minorities, and other groups, a country is becoming more democratic because it increases the chances that elected officials will actually represent the needs and goals of the full citizenry. Answer B is not correct because a single ruler maintaining power for a long time implies that there may not be "free, open, fair, and contested elections" (Line 5). Answer C is also incorrect because it is the will of the people, not the machinations of political parties that create a true democracy, according to the passage. Answer D is incorrect because forced voting would not be in the spirit of citizen-first democracy but rather the action of an oppressive government.

29.   **C**   Answer C is correct because Lines 36-41 establish that one of the goals of Constitutionalism is to "regulate democratic procedures in elections," placing the responsibility of determining how elections will be held on the Constitution. Answer A is incorrect because following the exact wishes of the ruler is contrary to the ideals of democracy laid out in Lines 1-9. Answers B and D are incorrect because elections are held within a country, so the international community or human rights advocacy groups have minimal involvement in organizing and carrying out elections.

30. **B** Answer B is correct because Lines 36-41 establish that one of the goals of Constitutionalism is to "protect human rights." Answers A, C, and D are all incorrect because neither parking, nor GDP, nor education is mentioned at all in the passage, meaning those answers have no textual basis.

31. **D** Answer D is correct because Lines 19-24 establish that the number of democracies in the world has actually shrunk since 1950. Answer A is incorrect because the author never lays out standards to determine "how democratic" a country is. Similarly, Answer B cannot be correct because, while the passage mentions human rights, it does not lay out specific milestones or human rights requirements for a country to be considered a democracy. Answer C is also incorrect because Lines 19-24 clearly state that the number has gone down.

32. **C** Answer C is the best choice because it is the only choice that pushes the reader to think beyond elections and consider the real-world implications of having a Constitution. Answers A and B comprise "basic election procedure," which the wording of the question establishes the reader must think beyond. Answer D is completely incorrect because Paragraphs 4 and 5 specifically discuss a number of Constitutional responsibilities beyond elections.

Passage 3 ("The year 1000 was a turning point..."):

33. **C** Answer C is the best choice because the passage discusses a variety of developments in European history and culture around the year 1000. Answer A is incorrect because trade is mentioned only in the passage's final paragraph, and a number of other important topics (particularly religion) are mentioned throughout the passage. Answer B is correct because, while the Church is mentioned, the passage does not explain how it rose to power. If anything, the Church is portrayed as weak and controlled by outside forces (Lines 19-29) in the passage. Answer D is also incorrect because the passage is not limited to the Vikings and Germans and mentions events around the Mediterranean and into the Baltic region.

34. **A** Answer A is the best choice because in Lines 2-4, the passage says, "Within a decade of that date, Olaf had converted most of the Scandinavians to Christianity." This language strongly indicates that they observed some other religion previously, since the verb "convert" implies a change from one state to another. Answer B is incorrect because the Scandinavians are outright described as Vikings in Line 4, so the author is not implying that fact at all, but rather stating it. Answer C is incorrect because the passage suggests the Scandinavians played a huge role in the changes that faced Europe around 1000 (Lines 1-11). Answer D cannot be correct because the passage makes no reference to the Scandinavians expanding their territory during the time in question.

35. **D** Answer D is correct because Lines 19-25 explain that "Olaf I, the German emperor, entered Rome and freed the papacy from the control of local Roman political factions... and the Cluniac reform finally reached the highest levels of the western Church." Answer A is not the best answer because, although it was the Catholic Church that was being reformed, the changes are specifically known as the Cluniac reform (Line 23). Answer B is incorrect because Protestants are not mentioned

anywhere in the passage (and the Protestant Reformation would not occur until the 16th century). Answer C is incorrect because Gerbert was the name of the pope, not the name of the reforms he instituted (Lines 21-25).

36.　**D**　Answer D is correct because Lines 30-45 explain how shifts in trade routes created prosperity. Lines 39-43 in particular describe how the shift in trade routes reconnected European merchants with Eastern goods they had not been able to access for many years. Answers A, B, and C are all incorrect because, although all of those topics are explored throughout the passage, the author clearly identifies trade routes as the main source of prosperity in the passage's final paragraph.

37.　**A**　Answer A is the correct choice because the section on Eastern merchants (Lines 43-45) falls in the paragraph that describes how changes in trade routes created economic prosperity. Answer B is incorrect because the passage clearly establishes in Lines 1-11 and 19-29 that Christianity was the default religion in Europe during this period and non-Christians were generally leaving – not coming – to Europe at this time. Answer C is incorrect because the Eastern merchants were traveling to trade and sell goods, not set up new homes in Europe. Answer D cannot be correct because B and C are both incorrect, so "All of the Above" is not an acceptable answer.

38.　**D**　Answer D is correct because the language of Lines 5-7 ("King Stephen adopted Christianity for himself and the Hungarian people...") indicates that becoming a Christian was something new for Stephen and his subjects. Answer A is incorrect because Line 5 specifically says he adopted "Christianity." Answer B is a reasonable answer but not the best choice because the passage does not provide any information about pre-Christian religious beliefs. Answer C is not the best answer either because it is possible that Stephen inherited the throne of Hungary, so it can't be assumed he conquered the country in a war without more details.

Passage 4 ("Let's first define heresy..."):

39.　**D**　Answer D is the best choice because the topic of heresy is introduced in the very first sentence of the passage and explored throughout. Answer A is incorrect and probably based on a faulty understanding of Lines 21-23, which explain that heresy was treated as if it was a disease. Answer B is incorrect because, while the passage mentions judicial punishments, all of those punishments were levied for heresy, which is the overarching subject of the whole passage. Answer C is also incorrect because there may have been many crimes for which people could be executed in the Middle Ages, but only heresy is mentioned in this passage.

40.　**B**　Answer B is correct because the passage establishes that people believed only official Church beliefs and teachings could help people avoid Hell (Lines 14-18). Lines 19-21 expand on this by explaining that people believed a heretic could "lead [others] to hell" (Line 21). Answer A is not the best answer because the text provides several passages (cited above) which point to the fuller, more specific Answer B. Answer C is incorrect and probably based on a faulty understanding of Lines 21-23, which explain that heresy was treated like a disease. Answer D is not the best

www.argobrothers.com

answer either because the problem of heresy is identified in the text as "corrupting" others. While people proclaiming their beliefs in public may have been a problem for some, the large issue is the fear of corruption, making Answer B a better choice.

41.   A   Answer A is the best choice because Lines 1-9 describe heretical beliefs as "obdurately held," which the text goes on to explain means, "...the person continued to hold that belief even after it had been pointed out to him or her how that word was contrary to the 'revealed truth'" (Lines 6-8). Answer B is not correct because the passage does not address atheism or secularism in any way. Answer C cannot be correct because heresy is characterized as being "obdurately held." Since the word "obdurate" is used to describe heresy, it can be assumed the words are not interchangeable. Answer D is incorrect because, while confidence is one aspect of obduracy, the text focuses on the idea that a heretic was someone who was stubborn in their beliefs.

42.   D   Answer D is correct because Lines 23-26 establish that "the people of the Middle Ages killed them." Answers A, B, and C are all incorrect because torture, exile, and repentance are never mentioned in the passage, meaning those answers have no textual basis.

43.   D   Answer D is correct because Lines 4-5 describe "the revealed truth, offered by God." Answer A is not the best choice because, although the passage touches on the power of the church, it asserts that the "revealed word" was supposed to have come directly from God, not any human intermediaries. Answer B is incorrect because, by definition, "heretics" were people whose beliefs were not in lock-step with the "revealed word." Answer C is also incorrect because the Christians didn't offer the revealed word; rather, they believed that God had revealed it to them.

44.   A   Answer A is the best choice because Lines 26-29 establish that "...they often killed them in public and horrible ways as a warning to everyone of how dangerous heretics were." While the use of executions as a psychological weapon or deterrent is not explicitly stated in the text, it is strongly implied that these executions were disincentive to those who might consider preaching heretical beliefs. Answer B is not the best answer because, while the executions could be seen as the Church flexing muscle, Answer A provides a more complete explanation of why the Church would want to flex its muscle publically, making Answer A the better choice. Similarly, Answer C is not the best choice because, while the Church was certainly trying to instill fear with grotesque public executions, Answer A still provides a more complete explanation of why the Church would want to act that way. Answer D has no textual basis because there is no mention of purification through pain anywhere in the passage.

Passage 5 ("You're probably surprised that I think..."):

45.   A   Answer A is the best answer because the author establishes in Lines 1-6 that he or she believes "our ideal of the integrity of the individual was born in medieval Europe," even though he or she knows the reader might find that fact surprising. Answer B is not the best choice because the Stoics are only mentioned in one paragraph, whereas the ideal of equality is explored in every

paragraph of the passage. Answer C is incorrect because, while the passage describes a specific scenario in which masters and slaves were treated equally, it makes it clear that this was a major reversal of the usual order. Answer D is similarly incorrect because, while the passage describes one situation in which a slave could ascend to be treated the same as a noble, it makes it clear that this would be a major reversal of the usual order.

46. **A** Answer A is the best choice based on the passage because Lines 15-23 describe how Benedictine monasteries used only seniority to determine rank (Lines 19-20). Answer B is incorrect because the Stoics lived in ancient Greece, as is established in Lines 7-14, which means it would be impossible for a medieval European nobleman to visit them. Answer C is not the best choice because any monastery existing during the time period in question would've been a "medieval" monastery, so that answer is not specific enough. Similarly, Answer D is incorrect because almost any monastery is associated with a church in some way, so saying "Church monastery" is neither specific nor descriptive.

47. **D** Answer D is correct because, according to Lines 7-10, "The Greek Stoics... held that there was a Brotherhood of Man and that the highest calling of every person was to treat others justly and compassionately." Answers A, B, and C are all incorrect and reveal a flawed or incomplete reading of Lines 7-14 of the text.

48. **B** Answer B is correct because the text suggests multiple times that medieval society was largely stratified and unequal. The author's words "You'd probably be surprised that I think that a stratified and status-ridden society like medieval Europe was the origin of the concept of equality," in Lines 1-3 should be one of the biggest hints, alongside the story of the nobleman and his slave told in Lines 24-37. Answer A is incorrect because there is no mention of technology or other advanced societal characteristics anywhere in the passage. Answer C is also incorrect because, while no kings are specifically mentioned in the passage, there is mention of nobles and slaves, suggesting a strict hierarchy. Answer D is incorrect because there's nothing in the text to suggest that nobles had mixed emotions about owning slaves. If anything, Lines 31-32 (in which the noble orders the slave to carry his bags) suggest European nobles were happy to have slaves.

49. **C** Answer C is correct because the story of the nobleman and his slave at the monastery serves to illustrate the author's point that life in medieval Europe actually had more elements of equality than people imagine. Answer A is incorrect because the author, while acknowledging the slavery issue in Lines 11-14, chooses to explore the roots of equality rather than focusing primarily on slavery, making Answer C a better choice. Answer B isn't the best answer either because the author is not writing about the progressiveness of the Benedictines, but rather using their monastery as a simple example of an environment in which stratified class boundaries did not exist. Answer D is similarly incorrect because, while the story does illustrate one example of a slave becoming free, the main focus of the passage is still equality in general, not slavery and

ARGO
BROTHERS
www.argobrothers.com

freedom.

50. **B** Answer B is the best choice because the author establishes in Lines 4-6 that "…we often fall short of our ideals, but our ideal of the integrity of the individual was born in medieval Europe." Throughout the passage, the author uses examples to show how people can have lofty ideals they don't quite live up to (the Stoics holding slaves in Lines 12-14, for example), making Answer B the best choice. Answer A is incorrect because, in the opening paragraph, the author admits that medieval society was very "stratified and status-ridden" (Line 2), strongly hinting that he or she prefers the society of today. Answer C is a good answer, but not the best answer because the author never assigns superlatives like "most important moment in the development of individualism." While the author clearly thinks medieval society was a key time and place for the development of individualism, he or she may think other times or places were slightly more important. Answer D is incorrect because the nobleman joining the monastery story is just a "neat story" used to provide an example for the concept. The author does not pass judgment on the nobleman or his slave one way or the other, so Answer B is a better choice.

Passage 6 ("My life has always been a continuous struggle…")

51. **A** Answer A is the best choice because, throughout the passage, the author attempts to describe navigating his or her own mortality and feelings of self-doubt. Answer B is incorrect because, although the author writes about memory in the final paragraph of the passage, the overall theme is still the writer's struggle with himself, making Answer A the better choice. Answer C is not correct because friendship is not one of the key ideas explored anywhere in the passage, let alone its overall theme. Answer D is not the best answer because, in addition to discussing illness, the author also discusses his self-loathing, making Answer A the better choice.

52. **A** Answer A is the best choice because in Lines 12-16, the author explains how he never feels settled because, "I have never felt permanently settled in this life – nothing more than a shadowy locum tenens, a wraith, a festoon of mist likely to disappear at any moment." Those term "wraith" and the phrase "likely to disappear at any moment" should be hints to the reader that the author is discussing mortality. Answers B, C, and D are all incorrect because, although they are concerns of the author's, he specifically identifies the inevitability of death as the reason he cannot feel settled.

53. **B** Answer B is the best choice because in Lines 17-20, the author explains, "…when I am vividly conscious of the insecurity of my tenure here, my desires enter on a mad race to obtain fulfillment before it is too late." These lines essentially state that he is sometimes motivated to work because he wants to achieve something more before dying. Answers A and C are both incorrect because the author never indicates he feels his sickness is the source of his talent or intelligence. Answer D is also incorrect because the author never states explicitly that he writes only about his health.

54. **C** Answer C is correct because in Lines 40-48, the author discusses his memory issues, saying "I forget what I read" (Line 41) and "I write things down so as to look them up in reference books"

(Lines 46-47). Answers A, B, and D are all incorrect and demonstrate a lack of understanding of Lines 40-48.

55. **B** Answer B is the best choice because the author frequently expresses self-doubt throughout the passage. Lines 34-35 provide a good example of this when the author writes, "I must use every kind of blandishment to convince myself that my life and my work are worthwhile." Answer A is incorrect and displays a lack of understanding of the passage, as the author talks at length about his health problems. Answer C is also incorrect because, while the author is self-conscious, sick, and sometimes depressed, he never suggests that he is insane in any way. Answer D is incorrect because the author presents his illness and physical maladies as being completely real. The reader could not know definitively that the author was not, in fact, ill based on the passage.

56. **B** Answer B is the best choice because "shadowy locum tenens" and "wraith" are positioned directly next to each other in Line 15, suggesting a very close connection between the two terms. Answer A is not the best answer because the author never describes any kind of insect or beetle, making "locust" and unlikely definition. Answer C is incorrect because, based on the overall tone of the passage, "Loco teen" does not seem like the kind of terminology the author would use. His preference for formal prose and flowery word choice make using "loco" highly unlikely. Answer D is incorrect because the author never self-identifies as a teen or even a young person, which, coupled with the proximity of "wraith" to "locum tenens," makes Answer B a much better choice.

57. **A** Answer A is correct because, using context clues, the reader can easily determine that the entire passage is talking about the issue of mortality and the idea that the author has limited time. Since the writer is indirect and uses euphemisms, however, this sentence can be confusing the first time for many readers. Answers B and C are both incorrect because they each misinterpret the use of the word "insecurity." Answer B interprets the sentence as being about insecurity over the quality of his work; while Answer C discusses insecurities in general. Answer D misinterprets the use of "tenure" and assumes the sentence is in some way talking about employment.

Practice Test 3 (Answers and Explanations)

1. **B** We must perform the operations inside the parentheses first and follow the order of operations:

Parentheses
Exponentiation
Multiplication
Division
Addition
Subtraction

$3[-3] + [5] = -9 + 5 = -4$, which is answer choice B.

2. **B** Simplify the expression to $\frac{1000}{x} = 10$, which when we solve, gives us, $x = 100$. If $x = 100$, then, $\sqrt{100} = 10$, which is the answer choice B.

3. **D** Plug in the values for x, y and z: $9 + \sqrt{9} + 9 - \sqrt{9} = 18$, which is answer choice D.

4. **C** If she needs to buy 2 pillets, that will cost $(\frac{2}{0.5})$ dollars = 4 dollars.
So, she will have $20 – $4 left, or $16.
With 16 dollars, she can buy $(16 \cdot 4)$ coss, or 64 coss, which is answer choice C.

5. **B** Simplifying gives us:

$\frac{\sqrt{100}}{\sqrt{25}} = \frac{10}{5} = 2$,

which is answer choice B.

6. **D** If $x = -8$, then $(4 \cdot -8) - 4 = -36$. Since we have an absolute value sign, we must take the positive of whatever number we have inside, which in this case, is -36.

So we have:
$(\frac{1}{2})(36) = 18$, which is answer choice D.

7. **B** Triangle NPQ is an equilateral triangle, which means all sides are equal. If the perimeter is 27, then the length of each side must be a third of the perimeter, or 9. Side lengths NP and NQ must add to $2(9) = 18$, which is answer choice B.

8. **D** 40% is equivalent to $(\frac{2}{5})$, so our expression is $(\frac{2}{5})(x) = 160$, and solving for x gives us 400, which is answer choice D.

9.   **D**   We know that the statement must hold for all numbers. We can substitute a number of our choosing such as 40. When 40 is divided by 7, we get a remainder of 5. Adding 1 to 40, we get 41, which when divided by 7, gives us a remainder of 6, which is answer choice D.

10.   **D**   The vertical distance (parallel to the y-axis) from the origin to a point on the square must be 4. Doubling that would give us the side Length of the square, which is 8. The area of the square is just the side length squared. 8 = 64, which is answer choice D.

11.   **C**   The points we are concerned with here are P, W, O and E. It is helpful to state the coordinates of those points. O is the midpoint of P and W. To find the midpoint , all we need to do is take the difference between points P and W, divide by 2, and subtract it from point P.

$P(-13)$
$W(-3)$
$O(-8)$
$E(4)$

So, therefore, the distance between O and E is $|-8 - 4| = 12$, which is answer choice C.

12.   **B**   The median of an odd number of even consecutive integers is actually just the average of those numbers. For example:

$\{2, 4, 6\}$

The mean of those numbers is 4, and the median is 4. So the answer here is 20, which is answer choice B.

13.   **B** 3.815×10^{-3} is the answer since we moved the decimal point three places to the right.

14.   **C**   Applying the Pythagorean Theorem, we get that the Length of AC is:

$(-17^2 - 5^5)^{\frac{1}{2}} = 2\sqrt{66}$,

which is answer choice C.

15.   **C**   53 hours from 3:30PM on a Thursday is composed of 2 sets of 24 hour days and 5 extra hours. This gives us Saturday at 8:30PM, which is answer choice C.

16.   **C**   The ratio of the circumference to the area of any circle is $(\frac{2}{r})$, where r is the radius. The radius of this circle is half of the diameter, which gives us 5. The answer is $(\frac{2}{5})$, which is answer choice C.

17. **D** To convert from milligrams to grams, we must divide by 1000. To convert from grams to kilograms, we must divide by 1000. So, to convert between milligrams to kilograms, we must divide by 1,000,000, which would give us, 9.8×10^{-5}, which is answer choice D.

18. **D** Let x be the minimum score he must get to get the desired average. The average equation can be expressed as:
$$\frac{244 + x}{4} = 85,$$
and solving for x, we get $x = 96$, which is answer choice D.

19. **A** If 5 out of 10 marbles in a bag are red, then 5 are not red, making the percentage 50%, which is answer choice A.

20. **B** If the radius is 5, then the diameter or length AC is 10 units. We know that length AD is 6, so then we must also know that length DC is 8 (3, 4, 5 special right triangle), which gives the rectangle an area of $6 \cdot 8 = 48$, which is answer choice B.

21. **C** $(9 \cdot 5) + (4) = 49$

22. **B** If it takes him 3 minutes to read 300 words, then it will take him 7.5 minutes to read 750 words. If there are 6 pages, each with 750 words, then it will take him $(6 \cdot 7.5)$ minutes to read the 6 pages.

$(7.5 \cdot 6) = 45$ minutes, which is answer choice B.

23. **A** If we simplify what is in the parentheses first, we get $(-\frac{1}{4})$.
$(-\frac{1}{4})^2 + (\frac{5}{10}) = (\frac{1}{16}) + (\frac{1}{2}) =$
$(\frac{1}{16}) + (\frac{8}{16}) = (\frac{9}{16})$, which is answer choice A.

24. **D** The only answer choice that is divisible by 7, is 2016, which is answer choice D.

25. **A** We can tell that each consecutive hour adds $\frac{1}{4}$th to the amount.
Let's say the units is gallons. So, if we work backwards, we can tell that the cylinder was empty 2 hours ago. So, the answer is 11AM, which is answer choice A.

26. **B** After simplifying, we get $x^8 = 2^8$, so we know that $x = 2$ and therefore $x^2 = 4$, which is answer choice B.

27. **C** If James finished $\frac{1}{8}$ of his total work, you can set up the following computation

to solve for this problem. $\frac{8}{8} - \frac{1}{8} = \frac{7}{8}$

28. **B** The solid line path takes 4 steps. The dotted line path takes 3 steps. So the solid line path is −1 steps fewer than the dotted line path, which is answer choice B.

29. **D** Jackie's way: $\sqrt{34}\sqrt{9} + \sqrt{25} = 8$
Jesse's way : $= \sqrt{9} + 25 = \sqrt{34}$
$8 - \sqrt{34}$, the answer choice is D.

30. **B** We need theta to be a real value. Since i, is in the denominator, if i ever equals to 0, it will make the value undefined. Answer choice B gives i the value of 0, and therefore using the values in answer choice B cannot give us a value for theta. Therefore, the answer choice is B.

31. **D** Every day, James grows by 20 inches. There is a difference of 2 days between Monday and Wednesday, which means the answer is 2(20) = 40 inches, which is answer choice D.

32. **C** Simplify and you will get $(-\frac{1}{2})$, which is answer choice C.

33. **D** We can tell that $x^2 = y$ since they are corresponding angles. So, $y^3 = x^6$, and x^2 and y are corresponding angles, meaning that they are equal.

*Note: Make sure you know the difference between corresponding, alternate interior, alternate exterior, and consecutive interior angles to help you with these types of problems.

Since x^2 and y are equal, and the question asks what is $\frac{y^3}{3}$, replace the y is x^2.

This gives you $\frac{x^{2^{(3)}}}{3}$, simplify to get $\frac{x^6}{3}$, which is answer choice D.

34. **C** Let, d, be the difference between consecutive terms. Each consecutive term differs by d. The values of x, y, z and f in terms of the differenced, is:
$x = 30 - 2d$
$y = 30 - d$
$z = 30 + d$
$f = 30 + 2d$

so when we add x, y, z and f, we get, 120, which is answer choice C.

35. **B** If a negative number in parentheses is raised to an even exponent, then the answer will always be positive. However, 2023 is an odd exponent, making the value of this expression −1, which is answer choice B.

36. **D** If Jake has X marbles, then Caroline has $2X$ marbles. If James has Y marbles, then:

$X = 7Y - 12$.

We know that James has 14 marbles, so $Y = 14$, so $X = 86$. Therefore, Caroline has $2X$ marbles or 172, which is answer choice D.

37. **A** The first jump he makes, he goes up 10 meters. Then he falls back 5 meters. Then he jumps again, reaching the 15 meter mark, then falls back 5 meters to the 10 meter mark. He only has to jump one last time to reach the 20 meter mark, which is past the 19 meter mark. In total, he jumped 3 times, so the answer is A.

38. **B** We can take the highest 3 digit number, 999, and the highest 2 digit number, which is 99. When we multiply them, we get a 5 digit number, 98901. The answer is B.

39. **D** We can plug in the initial values into the formula to get F_3.

$F_3 = 2 \cdot F_2 + 3 \cdot F_1 = 2 \cdot 1 + 3 \cdot 1 = 5$.

The answer is D.

40. **A** Sam moves 3 meters to the West. Since Sam walked 4 meters North after walking 4 meters South, he undid his vertical movement, making him end up 3 meters from his original location. The answer is A.

41. **D** Plugging in for the values of a and b, we get:

$\dfrac{9(3)}{5 - 3} = \dfrac{27}{2}$,

which is answer choice D.

42. **C** The circumference of a circle with a radius of 1m is 2π, which equals 4 times the perimeter of the square. The perimeter of a square is 4 times the length of one of its sides. If s is the side length of the square, then we can write:

$4s = 8\pi$, which means $s = 2\pi$ and the area is $s^2 = 4\pi^2$.

The answer is C.

43. **C** Following the pattern in the question, we know that $a = 4$, $b = 5$, $c = 7$ and $d = 8$. The question is asking what is the value of $be + ad$. Plug in the values, and you get $(4)(8) + (7)(5) = 32 + 35 = 67$, which is answer choice C.

44. **B** We know that $(\frac{3}{4})$ equates to 0.75 as a decimal. We simply multiply the denominator by 10 to get $(\frac{3}{40})$, which gives us 0.075 as a decimal, which is answer choice B.

45. **C** This requires us to solve for q.

$6(q + 3) = 2(q + 4)$
$3(q + 3) = (q + 4)$
$3q + 9 = q + 4$
$2q = -5$
$q = -\dfrac{5}{2}$

The answer is C.

46. **C** The two sides of the triangle that are adjacent to the angle of 30 degrees are equal since they make up two radii of the circle. All radii are equal. Therefore, the remaining two angles must be equal and must add up to 150° (180° − 30°).

This means that angle x is 75°, which is answer choice C.

47. **A** For this expression to be true, we must find a value of x that makes $\dfrac{-3x^2}{4}$ positive, which is impossible for real values of x since we are squaring x. When we square x, we return a positive value. So the answer is 0, which is answer choice A.

48. **C** We must equate the sentence into mathematical terms. We know that,

$x = 0.4y$ and
$y = x^2$ so,
$x = 0.4x^2$

which is answer choice C.

49. **B** Plugging in 7 for x in the equation, we get,

$4(7)(3y − 2(7)) = 112$, which gives us $28(3y − 14) = 112$ and solving for y, we get,
$(3y − 14) = 4$
$3y = 18$ so,
$y = 6$, which is answer choice B.

50. **C** Using the formula, we get,

$$\frac{a + (a − b)}{a − (a − b)} = \frac{2a − b}{b}$$

which is answer choice C.

51. **A** This problem tests your ability to understand fractional ratios as part of a whole. There are 30 trees in total, and you must find the ratio between fruit-bearing tress and weeping willows. There are 12 oak trees, while one-fifth are pine trees. This can be calculated: $\dfrac{30}{5} = 6$ pine trees. There are 3 weeping willows. The remainder must then be fruit-bearing.

Calculate: 30 − 12 − 6 − 3 = 9 fruit-bearing trees.

The ratio of weeping willows to fruit-bearing is therefore 3:9 or 1:3.

52. **A** You are asked to find the company which has experienced the greatest percentage increase in sales from 2015 to 2016. The strategy here is to use some reasoning to eliminate some choices so you do not waste time calculating each percentage. The percentage increase will use the difference in sales between the years divided by the sales in 2015.

$$\frac{\text{sales year 2016 − sales year 2015}}{\text{sales in 2015}} =$$
Percentage Increase

Keeping this in mind, you can save time by performing quick estimates without calculating the percentages. First start

with Petra. Petra sold 80 units in 2015 and 105 in 2016, for an increase of 25. Set up the fraction $\frac{25}{80} = \frac{5}{16}$.

Now compare this fraction with that of each company:

• AudioPro increased by 15 units while selling 95 units in 2015. $\frac{15}{95} = \frac{3}{19} < \frac{5}{16}$. Eliminate B.

• Keynote increased by 10 units while selling 85 units in 2015. $\frac{10}{85} = \frac{2}{17} < \frac{5}{16}$. Eliminate C.

• GSharp increased only 10 units but started from 70 units. $\frac{10}{70} = \frac{2}{14} < \frac{5}{16}$. Eliminate D.

• Lumia had an increase of 20 units and sold 75 units in 2015. $\frac{20}{75} = \frac{4}{15} \, ? \, \frac{5}{16}$. This ratio is close enough to that or Petra to justify calculating in order to verify.

If you are quick with fractions, you can see that $\frac{4}{15} < \frac{5}{16}$. Petra shows the greatest percentage increase, therefore the correct answer choice is A.

53. **100** This problem tests your ability to set up an average calculation. In order to find the average of the test scores, use the formula:

$$\frac{\text{sum of test scores}}{\text{number of tests}} = \text{test score average}$$

The number of tests is 5 and the desired average is 88. You have 4 of the test scores, and are asked to find the fifth to achieve this average. So let x be the fifth test score.

Now write your equation:
$$\frac{80 + 95 + 75 + 90 + x}{5} = 88$$
Cross multiply and solve for x.

$80 + 95 + 75 + 90 + x = 88(5)$

$340 + x = 440$

$x = 100$

54. **7** This problem tests your knowledge of geometry and your ability to set up a single variable equation. You are given three interior angles of a four-sided figure. The fourth side is defined by the expression $15x - 5$. First, find the value of the missing angle. Remember that the sum of the interior angles of a four-sided figure will always total 360. The missing angle calculates as $360 - 95 - 65 - 100 = 100$. Now solve the given expression using the missing angle:

$15x - 5 = 100$ write equation
$15x = 105$ add 5 to each side
$x = \frac{105}{15} = 7$ calculate

x is 7.

55. **$8** The school made $200 the first day by selling 10 adult tickets and 10 child tickets. Create an equation to solve.

$10a + 10c = 200$
$10c = 200 - 10a$
$c = 20 - a$

Now, you can plug in the value for c in terms of a.

$$13a + 2(20 - a) = 172$$
$$13a + 40 - 2a = 172$$
$$11a = 132$$
$$a = 12$$

Therefore, an adult ticket is $12 and a child ticket is $8.

56. **1,699**

If the population is 10,000 and the growth rate is 4% per year, to find the population after the first year, you simply multiply 10,000 × .04 to get 400. The population grew by 400 and therefore the total population at the end of the year was 10,400. The question asks you for the population increase over a period of 4 years. Second year the population increases by 416. Third year population increased by 432.64. Fourth year population increased by 449.95. The question asks for the total population increase over the span of four years, so add 400 + 416 + 432.64 + 449.95 = 1,698.59. The question asks you to round your answer to the nearest whole number which is 1,699.

57. **11** To make this computation easier, manipulate the denominator into a whole number. You can multiple the fraction by 10 to the numerator and denominator to get $\frac{55}{1}$. Now simply multiple 55 × .20 to get 11.

Practice Test 4
SHSAT

This exam is 3 hours long. Try to take this full exam in one sitting to simulate real test conditions.

While taking this exam, refrain from hearing music or watching T.V.

Please note, calculators are not permitted! You are permitted to answer questions in any order you see fit.

Allocate your test time accordingly.

Concentrate and GOOD LUCK!

SHSAT PRACTICE TEST 4
ANSWER SHEET

ENGLISH LANGUAGE ARTS

1. Ⓐ Ⓑ Ⓒ Ⓓ
2. Ⓐ Ⓑ Ⓒ Ⓓ
3. Ⓐ Ⓑ Ⓒ Ⓓ
4. Ⓐ Ⓑ Ⓒ Ⓓ
5. Ⓐ Ⓑ Ⓒ Ⓓ
6. Ⓐ Ⓑ Ⓒ Ⓓ
7. Ⓐ Ⓑ Ⓒ Ⓓ
8. Ⓐ Ⓑ Ⓒ Ⓓ
9. Ⓐ Ⓑ Ⓒ Ⓓ
10. Ⓐ Ⓑ Ⓒ Ⓓ
11. Ⓐ Ⓑ Ⓒ Ⓓ
12. Ⓐ Ⓑ Ⓒ Ⓓ
13. Ⓐ Ⓑ Ⓒ Ⓓ
14. Ⓐ Ⓑ Ⓒ Ⓓ
15. Ⓐ Ⓑ Ⓒ Ⓓ
16. Ⓐ Ⓑ Ⓒ Ⓓ
17. Ⓐ Ⓑ Ⓒ Ⓓ
18. Ⓐ Ⓑ Ⓒ Ⓓ
19. Ⓐ Ⓑ Ⓒ Ⓓ
20. Ⓐ Ⓑ Ⓒ Ⓓ
21. Ⓐ Ⓑ Ⓒ Ⓓ
22. Ⓐ Ⓑ Ⓒ Ⓓ
23. Ⓐ Ⓑ Ⓒ Ⓓ
24. Ⓐ Ⓑ Ⓒ Ⓓ
25. Ⓐ Ⓑ Ⓒ Ⓓ
26. Ⓐ Ⓑ Ⓒ Ⓓ
27. Ⓐ Ⓑ Ⓒ Ⓓ
28. Ⓐ Ⓑ Ⓒ Ⓓ
29. Ⓐ Ⓑ Ⓒ Ⓓ

30. Ⓐ Ⓑ Ⓒ Ⓓ
31. Ⓐ Ⓑ Ⓒ Ⓓ
32. Ⓐ Ⓑ Ⓒ Ⓓ
33. Ⓐ Ⓑ Ⓒ Ⓓ
34. Ⓐ Ⓑ Ⓒ Ⓓ
35. Ⓐ Ⓑ Ⓒ Ⓓ
36. Ⓐ Ⓑ Ⓒ Ⓓ
37. Ⓐ Ⓑ Ⓒ Ⓓ
38. Ⓐ Ⓑ Ⓒ Ⓓ
39. Ⓐ Ⓑ Ⓒ Ⓓ
40. Ⓐ Ⓑ Ⓒ Ⓓ
41. Ⓐ Ⓑ Ⓒ Ⓓ
42. Ⓐ Ⓑ Ⓒ Ⓓ
43. Ⓐ Ⓑ Ⓒ Ⓓ
44. Ⓐ Ⓑ Ⓒ Ⓓ
45. Ⓐ Ⓑ Ⓒ Ⓓ
46. Ⓐ Ⓑ Ⓒ Ⓓ
47. Ⓐ Ⓑ Ⓒ Ⓓ
48. Ⓐ Ⓑ Ⓒ Ⓓ
49. Ⓐ Ⓑ Ⓒ Ⓓ
50. Ⓐ Ⓑ Ⓒ Ⓓ
51. Ⓐ Ⓑ Ⓒ Ⓓ
52. Ⓐ Ⓑ Ⓒ Ⓓ
53. Ⓐ Ⓑ Ⓒ Ⓓ
54. Ⓐ Ⓑ Ⓒ Ⓓ
55. Ⓐ Ⓑ Ⓒ Ⓓ
56. Ⓐ Ⓑ Ⓒ Ⓓ
57. Ⓐ Ⓑ Ⓒ Ⓓ

MATHEMATICS

1. Ⓐ Ⓑ Ⓒ Ⓓ
2. Ⓐ Ⓑ Ⓒ Ⓓ
3. Ⓐ Ⓑ Ⓒ Ⓓ
4. Ⓐ Ⓑ Ⓒ Ⓓ
5. Ⓐ Ⓑ Ⓒ Ⓓ
6. Ⓐ Ⓑ Ⓒ Ⓓ
7. Ⓐ Ⓑ Ⓒ Ⓓ
8. Ⓐ Ⓑ Ⓒ Ⓓ
9. Ⓐ Ⓑ Ⓒ Ⓓ
10. Ⓐ Ⓑ Ⓒ Ⓓ
11. Ⓐ Ⓑ Ⓒ Ⓓ
12. Ⓐ Ⓑ Ⓒ Ⓓ
13. Ⓐ Ⓑ Ⓒ Ⓓ
14. Ⓐ Ⓑ Ⓒ Ⓓ
15. Ⓐ Ⓑ Ⓒ Ⓓ
16. Ⓐ Ⓑ Ⓒ Ⓓ
17. Ⓐ Ⓑ Ⓒ Ⓓ
18. Ⓐ Ⓑ Ⓒ Ⓓ
19. Ⓐ Ⓑ Ⓒ Ⓓ
20. Ⓐ Ⓑ Ⓒ Ⓓ
21. Ⓐ Ⓑ Ⓒ Ⓓ
22. Ⓐ Ⓑ Ⓒ Ⓓ
23. Ⓐ Ⓑ Ⓒ Ⓓ
24. Ⓐ Ⓑ Ⓒ Ⓓ
25. Ⓐ Ⓑ Ⓒ Ⓓ
26. Ⓐ Ⓑ Ⓒ Ⓓ

27. Ⓐ Ⓑ Ⓒ Ⓓ
28. Ⓐ Ⓑ Ⓒ Ⓓ
29. Ⓐ Ⓑ Ⓒ Ⓓ
30. Ⓐ Ⓑ Ⓒ Ⓓ
31. Ⓐ Ⓑ Ⓒ Ⓓ
32. Ⓐ Ⓑ Ⓒ Ⓓ
33. Ⓐ Ⓑ Ⓒ Ⓓ
34. Ⓐ Ⓑ Ⓒ Ⓓ
35. Ⓐ Ⓑ Ⓒ Ⓓ
36. Ⓐ Ⓑ Ⓒ Ⓓ
37. Ⓐ Ⓑ Ⓒ Ⓓ
38. Ⓐ Ⓑ Ⓒ Ⓓ
39. Ⓐ Ⓑ Ⓒ Ⓓ
40. Ⓐ Ⓑ Ⓒ Ⓓ
41. Ⓐ Ⓑ Ⓒ Ⓓ
42. Ⓐ Ⓑ Ⓒ Ⓓ
43. Ⓐ Ⓑ Ⓒ Ⓓ
44. Ⓐ Ⓑ Ⓒ Ⓓ
45. Ⓐ Ⓑ Ⓒ Ⓓ
46. Ⓐ Ⓑ Ⓒ Ⓓ
47. Ⓐ Ⓑ Ⓒ Ⓓ
48. Ⓐ Ⓑ Ⓒ Ⓓ
49. Ⓐ Ⓑ Ⓒ Ⓓ
50. Ⓐ Ⓑ Ⓒ Ⓓ
51. Ⓐ Ⓑ Ⓒ Ⓓ
52. Ⓐ Ⓑ Ⓒ Ⓓ

MATHEMATICS (GRID IN)

53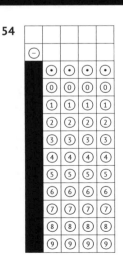
54
55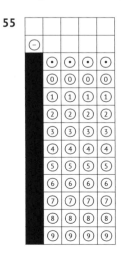
56
57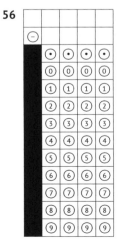

DIRECTIONS: For questions 1 to 5, you will be asked to recognize and correct errors in sentences or short paragraphs.

1. Read this paragraph.

> (1) Most American students read F. Scott Fitzgerald's *The Great Gatsby* at some point in high school. (2) The book which is sometimes recognized as the "Great American Novel" tells the story of two star-crossed lovers Jay Gatsby and Daisy Buchanan. (3) Many students find the novel hard to connect with because all of the characters seem to be profoundly unhappy. (4) Although not everybody loves *The Great Gatsby*, the fact that is so widely taught in schools makes it a common touchstone for many Americans.

Which answer provides a correct revision of Sentence 2?

A. The book which is sometimes recognized as the "Great American Novel," tells the story of two star-crossed lovers Jay Gatsby and Daisy Buchanan.

B. The book, which is sometimes recognized as the "Great American Novel," tells the story of two star-crossed lovers Jay Gatsby and Daisy Buchanan.

C. The book, which is sometimes recognized as the "Great American Novel," tells the story of two star-crossed lovers, Jay Gatsby and Daisy Buchanan.

D. The book, which is sometimes recognized as the "Great American Novel" tells the story of two star-crossed lovers, Jay Gatsby and Daisy Buchanan.

2. Read this paragraph.

> (1) Stan Lee revolutionized the comic book world as a writer for Marvel Comics. (2) In 1961, Lee and his partner Jack Kirby created the Fantastic Four, a team of four radioactive heroes who changed the way comics were written. (3) Within three years, Lee had also created the Hulk Thor Spider-Man and the X-Men all of whom are still major characters for Marvel more than 50 years later. (4) Lee's signature was creating deeply flawed characters who seemed like real people with real problems, even though they were fictional heroes with incredible powers.

Which revision would correct the comma use in Sentence 3?

A. ...Lee had also created the Hulk, Thor, Spider-Man and the X-Men all of whom are still major characters for Marvel more than 50 years later.

B. ...Lee had also created the Hulk, Thor, Spider-Man, and the X-Men all of whom are still major characters for Marvel more than 50 years later.

C. ...Lee had also created the Hulk Thor Spider-Man, and the X-Men, all of whom are still major characters for Marvel more than 50 years later.

D. ...Lee had also created the Hulk, Thor, Spider-Man, and the X-Men, all of whom are still major characters for Marvel more than 50 years later.

CONTINUE ON TO THE NEXT PAGE →

3. Read this sentence.

> I have three uncles: Mike who is my mother's brother, Steve who is my father's brother, and Henry who is my mother's half-brother.

Which revision uses proper punctuation to format the sentence?

A. I have three uncles: Mike who is my mother's brother; Steve who is my father's brother; and Henry who is my mother's half-brother.

B. I have three uncles: Mike, who is my mother's brother; Steve, who is my father's brother; and Henry, who is my mother's half-brother.

C. I have three uncles: Mike; who is my mother's brother, Steve; who is my father's brother, and Henry; who is my mother's half-brother.

D. I have three uncles; Mike, who is my mother's brother; Steve, who is my father's brother; and Henry, who is my mother's half-brother.

4. Read this paragraph.

> (1) Historians often cite the Seneca Falls Convention of 1848 as the beginning of feminism in America. (2) Throughout the two-day convention, women's conditions and rights were discussed by as many as 300 attendees. (3) At the conclusion of the convention, 100 people signed the Declaration of Sentiments, a document that set goals for the feminist movement moving forward. (4) Elizabeth Cady Stanton, the author of the Declaration of Sentiments, modeled the document on the structure of the United States Declaration of Independence.

In what way is Sentence 2 inconsistent with the rest of the paragraph?

A. Subject matter
B. Verb tense
C. Passive voice
D. "To be" verb use

5. Read this sentence.

> After school Gerry walked down the road to the park and played with Stephanie and Hunter.

Which edit should be made to correct the sentence?

A. Add a **comma** after **school**
B. Add a **comma** after **road**
C. Add a **comma** after **park**
D. Add a **comma** after **Stephanie**

CONTINUE ON TO THE NEXT PAGE ➡

ENGLISH LANGUAGE ARTS
Practice Test 4

DIRECTIONS: Read the passage below to answer questions 6 to 13. The questions will focus on improving the writing quality of the passage to follow the conventions of standard written English.

King Arthur

(1) Although historians cannot be sure that the legendary ruler of England, King Arthur, ever existed, his mythic importance to the English identity is undeniable. (2) According to legend, Arthur ruled around 500 AD and is considered an extremely brave and honorable king. (3) By the twelfth century, mythical stories were already being told about Arthur assembling the bravest knights of all time to serve at his heroic Round Table.

(4) In most versions of the story Arthur the secret son of King Uther Pendragon pulls a magical sword from a stone to prove that he is the rightful ruler of England. (5) The wizard Merlin mentors Arthur and teaches him how to be an effective leader as he assembles his Round Table of the bravest and best knights in the land. (6) The Knights of the Round Table go on a variety of quests to gather sacred relics (including the Holy Grail) and protect England from a variety of invading armies and magical monsters. (7) The Round Table and Arthur's idealized rule both end when his wife, the beautiful Queen Guinevere, engages in a relationship with one of his most trusted knights, Sir Lancelot. (8) These general elements are present in almost all versions of the Arthur myth.

(9) The Arthur myth has been central to English culture for over a thousand years. (10) Arthur exists as an ideal for English government: he is fair-minded, stands up for the weak, and always chooses the path of righteousness. (11) His emphasis on assembling a team of the best and brightest provides an example for business leaders and managers all over the world. (12) The myth of Arthur has even guided England's military policy over the years, emphasizing participation in just causes and decisive action. (13) For England's royal family, he and his Round Table stand as pillars of trustworthiness, responsibility, and public adulation that they can also aspire to. (14) King Arthur is one of the key figures in English history, even if he wasn't real.

6. Which edit is needed to correct Sentence 2?

   A. Change **ruled** to **rules**
   B. Change **is** to **was**
   C. Change **considered** to **considering**
   D. Changed **honorable** to **honored**

7. What kind of error does Sentence 3 contain?

   A. Subject-verb agreement
   B. Spelling
   C. Comma usage
   D. Passive voice

CONTINUE ON TO THE NEXT PAGE →

8. Which sentence would best precede Sentence 4 to serve as a topic sentence for the second paragraph?

   A. Although many versions of the Arthur myth have been told throughout history, most of them contain the same major characters and elements.
   B. The story of Arthur is packed with action, adventure, and betrayal.
   C. Arthur wields a mythical sword known as Excalibur.
   D. The story has a variety of interesting characters.

9. Which revision makes proper use of commas in Sentence 4?

   A. In most versions of the story, Arthur the secret son of King Uther Pendragon pulls a magical sword from a stone to prove that he is the rightful ruler of England.
   B. In most versions of the story, Arthur, the secret son of King Uther Pendragon, pulls a magical sword from a stone to prove that he is the rightful ruler of England.
   C. In most versions of the story Arthur, the secret son of King Uther Pendragon, pulls a magical sword from a stone to prove that he is the rightful ruler of England.
   D. In most versions of the story, Arthur, the secret son of King Uther Pendragon, pulls a magical sword from a stone to prove that he is the rightful ruler, of England.

10. Which transition should be added to the beginning of Sentence 7?

    A. Therefore
    B. However
    C. Ultimately
    D. Subsequently

11. Which sentence is least relevant to the content of the rest of the passage and should be removed?

    A. Sentence 9
    B. Sentence 10
    C. Sentence 11
    D. Sentence 12

12. Which revision of Sentence 13 best clarifies the use of pronouns?

    A. For England's royal family, Arthur and his Round Table stand as pillars of trustworthiness, responsibility, and public adulation that today's royals can also aspire to.
    B. For England's royal family, the king and his Round Table stand as pillars of trustworthiness, responsibility, and public adulation that other knights can also aspire to.
    C. For England's royal family, Arthur and his Round Table stand as pillars of trustworthiness, responsibility, and public adulation that all English people can also aspire to.
    D. For England's royal family, he and his Round Table stand as pillars of trustworthiness, responsibility, and public adulation that the Knights of the Round Table can also aspire to.

CONTINUE ON TO THE NEXT PAGE →

13. How could Sentence 14 be rewritten to eliminate the use of "to be" verbs?

   A. King Arthur is one of the key figures in English history, even if he was not real.

   B. King Arthur's one of the key figures in English history, even though he may be fictional.

   C. Even if he was fictional, King Arthur holds a key place in English history.

   D. King Arthur holds a key place in English history, fictional or not

CONTINUE ON TO THE NEXT PAGE ➡

ENGLISH LANGUAGE ARTS
Practice Test 4

DIRECTIONS: Read the passage below to answer questions 14 to 20. The questions will focus on improving the writing quality of the passage to follow the conventions of standard written English.

Flying

(1) From the dawn of humanity, people dreamed of flying like birds. (2) The ancient Greeks Egyptians, and Mesoamerican cultures all told myths and stories about people flying making use of either wings or machinery. (3) During the Renaissance, when knowledge of science was flourishing, Leonardo da Vinci created plans for a variety of flying machines for both warfare and adventure.

(4) The first confirmed manned flight took place in France during November of 1783. (5) On that day two pilots traveled about five miles in a hot air balloon. (6) While men could be transported upward by balloons, it was difficult to steer the devices in a controlled manner. (7) Now that people could travel up into the clouds, the next goal for scientists and engineers around the world was to create a steerable flying machine.

(8) At the turn of the twentieth century, many great minds are working on designing a manned flying machine. (9) Working separately but concurrently, Samuel Langley, the Wright Brothers, and German immigrant Gustave Whitehead attempted to build flying machines along the east coast of the United States. (10) The Wright Brothers became the first engineers to record a successful manned flight of a heavier-than-air flying machine in December of 1903. (11) The Wright Brothers became extremely wealthy and successful after their legendary flight. (12) Within seventy years of the Wright Brothers' flight, aviation had continued to grow to the degree that men were flown to the moon.

14. Which revision corrects the use of commas in Sentence 2?

   A. The ancient Greeks, Egyptians, and Mesoamerican cultures all told myths and stories about people flying making use of either wings or machinery.

   B. The ancient Greeks, Egyptians, and Mesoamerican cultures all told myths, and stories, about people flying making use of either wings or machinery.

   C. The ancient Greeks, Egyptians, and Mesoamerican cultures all told myths and stories about people flying, making use of either wings or machinery.

   D. The ancient Greeks, Egyptians, and Mesoamerican cultures all told myths and stories about people flying making use of either wings, or machinery.

CONTINUE ON TO THE NEXT PAGE →

15. Which sentence could be added after Sentence 3 to serve as a conclusion for the first paragraph?

   A. All of these historical figures would be amazed by today's commercial airliners.

   B. Although manned flight was not practical until relatively recently, it was one of mankind's main goals for millennia.

   C. Da Vinci is regarded as one of the great geniuses of all time, and working models have been created from many of his blueprints.

   D. As long as people have dreamed of soaring through the air, they have wanted to fly for military purposes.

16. Which revision is needed to correct Sentence 5?

   A. Insert a **comma** after **day**

   B. Change **traveled** to **travel**

   C. Change **five** to **5**

   D. Change **hot air balloon** to **hot-air-balloon**

17. Which revision corrects the use of passive voice in Sentence 6?

   A. While men could be transported upward by balloons, steering the balloons in a controlled manner often proved difficult.

   B. While men could be transported upward by balloons, the devices were seen as being difficult to steer in a controlled manner.

   C. While balloons could transport men upward, the devices were seen as being difficult to steer in a controlled manner.

   D. While balloons could transport men upward, steering the devices in a controlled manner often proved difficult.

18. What kind of error is present in Sentence 8?

   A. Subject-verb agreement

   B. Inconsistent verb tense

   C. Passive Voice

   D. Spelling

19. Which revision eliminates the dangling modifier in Sentence 9?

   A. Several researchers, working separately but concurrently along the east coast of the United States, attempted to build flying machines, including Samuel Langley, the Wright Brothers, and German immigrant Gustave Whitehead.

   B. Working separately but concurrently, several researchers along the east coast of the United States attempted to build flying machines, including Samuel Langley, the Wright Brothers, and German immigrant Gustave Whitehead.

   C. Including Samuel Langley, the Wright Brothers, and German immigrant Gustave Whitehead, several researchers attempted separately but concurrently to build flying machines along the east coast of the United States.

   D. Including Samuel Langley, the Wright Brothers, and German immigrant Gustave Whitehead, the east coast of the United States was an area where several researchers attempted to build flying machines working separately but concurrently.

CONTINUE ON TO THE NEXT PAGE ➡

20. Which transition should be added to the beginning of Sentence 10?

    A. However

    B. Eventually

    C. In conclusion

    D. Therefore

CONTINUE ON TO THE NEXT PAGE ➜

DIRECTIONS: Analyze the passages below, and answer the commensurate questions. Only use information provided within the passage for your answers. There is only one answer for each question.

Those enactments were called agrarian laws by the Romans which related to the public lands. The objects of these agrarian laws were various. A law (*lex*) for the establishment of a colony and the assignment of tracts of land to the colonists was 5 an agrarian law. The laws which regulated the use and enjoyment of the public lands and gave the ownership of portions of them to the commonalty (*plebes*) were also agrarian laws. Those agrarian laws which assigned small allotments to the 10 plebeians, varying in amount from two jugera to seven jugera (a jugerum is about three-fourths of an acre), were among the most important; but the agrarian laws, or those clauses of agrarian laws which limited the amount of public land which a 15 man could use and enjoy, are usually meant when the term agrarian laws is now used.

The origin of the Roman public land, or of the greater part of it, was this: Rome had originally a small territory but, by a series of conquests 20 carried on for many centuries, she finally obtained the dominion of the whole Italian peninsula. When the Romans conquered an Italian state, they seized a part of the lands of the conquered people; for it was a Roman principle that the 25 conquered people lost everything with the loss of their political independence; and what they enjoyed after the conquest was a gift from the generosity of the conqueror.

30 A state that submitted got better terms than one that made an obstinate resistance. Sometimes, a third of their land was taken from the conquered state, and sometimes two-thirds. It is not said how this arrangement was effected; whether each 35 landholder lost a third or whether an entire third was taken in the lump, and the conquered people were left to equalize the loss among themselves. But there were probably in all parts of Italy large tracts of uncultivated ground which were under 40 pasture, and these tracts would form a part of the Roman share, for we find that pasture land was a considerable portion of the Roman public land. The ravages of war also often left many of the conquered tracts in a desolate condition, 45 and these tracts formed part of the conqueror's share. The lands thus acquired could not always be carefully measured at the time of the conquest, and they were not always immediately sold or assigned to the citizens. The Roman state retained 50 the ownership of such public lands as were not sold or given in allotments, but allowed them to be occupied and enjoyed by any Roman citizen.

CONTINUE ON TO THE NEXT PAGE →

21. What is this passage mostly about?

  A. Roman conquest
  B. Roman imperial tactics
  C. The origin of agrarian laws and the public laws they created
  D. How Rome got so big

22. *Lex* is a Latin word for:

  A. Lawn
  B. Lord
  C. Lexicon
  D. Law

23. According to the passage, how did Rome acquire its public land?

  A. Laws turned private Rome into public land.
  B. Rome aquired land through conquest.
  C. Nobles gave up land to the *plebes*.
  D. Rome had public land since its inception.

24. According to the passage, what was one benefit to not defending yourself against an invading Roman army?

  A. You would not lose any of your land.
  B. You would not need to have war.
  C. You would not need to give up as much land to the Roman public.
  D. You would gain seats in the Roman Senate.

25. What kind of land was most likely to be Roman Agrarian land?

  A. Farms
  B. Cities
  C. Roads
  D. Pasture

26. All land not under Roman control, but in a state conquered by Rome, was:

  A. At one point controlled by Rome.
  B. Not inhabited by Romans.
  C. Off limits to Roman *plebes*.
  D. The less valuable land in a country.

CONTINUE ON TO THE NEXT PAGE ➡

It has been observed that the shortest man, standing on the shoulders of a giant, will see farther than the giant himself; and the moderns, standing as they do on the vantage ground of former discoveries, and uniting all the fruits of 5 the experience of their forefathers with their own actual observation, may be admitted to enjoy a more enlarged and comprehensive view of things than the ancients themselves. But by whom is antiquity enjoyed? Not by the ancients, 10 who did live in the infancy, but by the moderns, who do live in the maturity of things. Therefore, as regards the age of the world, we may lay a juster claim to the title of being the ancients even than our forefathers themselves; for they inhabited the 15 world when it was young, but we occupy it now that it is old.

Therefore, that precedent may not exert too despotic a rule over experience, and that the dead may not too strictly govern the living, may 20 I be pardoned in taking a brief and cursory view of the claims of the ancients to our veneration, so far as they are built on the only proper foundation - superiority of mind? But it is by no means my object to lessen our esteem for those 25 great men who have lived before us and who have accomplished such wonders, considering the scantiness of their means; my intention is merely to suggest that the veneration due to times that are past is a hind-sight focused veneration, the 30 moment it is paid at the expense of times that are present; for as these very ancients themselves were once the moderns, so we moderns must also become the ancients in our turn.

What I would principally contend for is that 35 the moderns enjoy a much more extended and comprehensive view of science than the ancients;

not because we have greater capacities, but simply because we enjoy far greater capabilities. For that 40 which is perfect in science is most commonly the elaborate result of successive improvements and of various judgments exercised in the rejection of what was wrong, no less than in the adoption of what was right. We, therefore, are profiting not 45 only by the knowledge, but also by the ignorance, not only by the discoveries, but also by the errors, of our forefathers. The march of science, like that of time, has been progressing in the darkness, no less than in the light.

27. What is this passage mostly about?

    A. Why past civilizations were ignorant.
    B. Why future societies will never surpass modern society.
    C. Why contemporary civilization is more knowledgeable than ancient civilization.
    D. The scientific beliefs of the ancients.

CONTINUE ON TO THE NEXT PAGE ➡

28. The author uses the metaphor of a short man and a giant to illustrate that:

A. A giant is capable of holding up a smaller man.
B. All of the past can be considered one entity.
C. Contemporary civilization cannot help being more advanced in science than ancient civilizations.
D. Contemporary civilizations are higher-minded than ancient civilizations.

29. Why does the author claim that contemporaries have a greater claim to being called ancient?

A. They live in a more ancient world than the ancients.
B. Because in the far future, they will be the ancient past.
C. The author believes contemporary civilization will invent time travel.
D. The phrase is used to indicate that all civilizations become ancient over time.

30. What would be an example of a "hind-sight focused" opinion?

A. Past cartographers were bad at making maps.
B. The first high jumper to jump laterally was a better jumper than current record-holders.
C. The inventor of an old technology was a genius.
D. A past movie was important to the development of cinema.

31. The author notes explicitly that contemporary civilization is better at ___ than ancient civilizations.

A. Nothing
B. Reading
C. Language acquisition
D. Science

32. What does the author mean by "The march of science, like that of time, has been progressing in the darkness, no less than in the light?"

A. It was not until modern times that science made real discoveries.
B. Past science was done poorly.
C. Science was not always conducted during day time.
D. Mistakes are as valuable to the furthering of science as discoveries.

CONTINUE ON TO THE NEXT PAGE ➡

Ralph Waldo Emerson

Some years ago, in company with an agreeable party, I spent a long summer day in exploring the Mammoth Cave in Kentucky. We traversed, through spacious galleries affording a solid masonry foundation for the town and county [5] overhead, the six or eight black miles from the mouth of the cavern to the innermost recess which tourists visit – a niche or grotto made of one seamless stalactite, and called, I believe, Serena's Bower. I lost the light of one day. I saw [10] high domes and bottomless pits; heard the voice of unseen waterfalls; paddled three quarters of a mile in the deep Echo River, whose waters are peopled with the blind fish; crossed the streams "Lethe" and "Styx;" plied with music and [15] guns the echoes in these alarming galleries; saw every form of stalagmite and stalactite in the sculptured and fretted chambers – icicle, orange-flower, acanthus, grapes, and snowball. We shot Bengal lights into the vaults and groins [20] of the sparry cathedrals, and examined all the masterpieces which the four combined engineers, water, limestone, gravitation, and time, could make in the dark.

The mysteries and scenery of the cave had the [25] same dignity that belongs to all natural objects, and which shames the fine things to which we foppishly compare them. I remarked, especially, the mimetic habit, with which Nature, on new instruments, hums her old tunes, making night [30] to mimic day, and chemistry to ape vegetation. But I then took notice, and still chiefly remember, that the best thing which the cave had to offer was an illusion. On arriving at what is called the "Star-Chamber," our lamps were taken from us by [35] the guide and extinguished or put aside, and, on looking upwards, I saw or seemed to see the night heaven thick with stars glimmering more or less brightly over our heads, and even what seemed [40] a comet flaming among them. All the party were touched with astonishment and pleasure. Our musical friends sung with much feeling a pretty song, "The stars are in the quiet sky," etc., and I sat down on the rocky floor to enjoy the serene [45] picture. Some crystal specks in the black ceiling high overhead, reflecting the light of a half-hid lamp, yielded this magnificent effect.

I own, I did not like the cave so well for eking out its sublimities with this theatrical trick. But [50] I have had many experiences like it, before and since; and we must be content to be pleased without too curiously analyzing the occasions. Our conversation with Nature is not just what it seems. The cloud-rack, the sunrise and sunset [55] glories, rainbows, and northern lights are not quite so absolute as our childhood thought them; and the part our organization plays in them is too large. The senses interfere everywhere and mix their own structure with all they report of. Once, [60] we fancied the earth a plane, and stationary. In admiring the sunset, we do not yet deduct the rounding, coordinating, pictorial powers of the eye.

33. What is this passage mostly about?

    A. The curiosity of man.

    B. The ignorance of man concerning nature.

    C. The importance of nature to man.

    D. The way human senses interact with our understanding of nature.

CONTINUE ON TO THE NEXT PAGE →

34. What is implied about the "star-chamber?"

   A. It was the only natural phenomenon of its kind.
   B. The stars were very bright.
   C. There was a comet.
   D. There were no actual stars on display.

35. Why does Emerson describe water as an engineer?

   A. Water is necessary for engineering.
   B. Water is one of the forces that created the cave.
   C. Water is the only force that created the cave.
   D. Water is the most important force in the creation of the cave.

36. Why did the party start singing under the "star-chamber?"

   A. They were tired after a long day of hiking.
   B. It is tradition to sing under the "star-chamber."
   C. They were moved by the beauty of the "star-chamber."
   D. They were always singing.

37. Why does Emerson note that we once believed the earth was flat?

   A. It is an example of when the senses led us to an incorrect belief.
   B. To show that humans are not capable of understanding nature.
   C. To show that nature is never understood.
   D. To show that it is best to avoid deeply considering the nature of the world.

38. In what state did Emerson's adventure take place?

   A. Maine
   B. North Dakota
   C. South Dakota
   D. Kentucky

CONTINUE ON TO THE NEXT PAGE ➡

There is a current impression that it is unpleasant to have to run after one's hat. Why should it be unpleasant to the well-ordered and pious mind? Not merely because it is running, and running exhausts one. The same people run much faster [5] in games and sports. The same people run much more eagerly after an uninteresting little leather ball than they will after a nice silk hat.

There is an idea that it is humiliating to run after one's hat; when people say it is humiliating, they [10] mean that it is comic. It certainly is comic; but man is a very comic creature, and most of the things he does are comic – eating, for instance. And the most comic things of all are exactly the things that are most worth doing. A man running [15] after a hat is not half so ridiculous as a man running after a job.

Now a man could, if he felt rightly in the matter, run after his hat with the manliest ardor and the most sacred joy. He might regard himself as a jolly [20] huntsman pursuing a wild animal, for certainly no animal could be wilder. In fact, I am inclined to believe that hat-hunting on windy days will be the sport of the upper classes in the future. There will be a meet of ladies and gentlemen on some [25] high ground on a gusty morning. They will be told that the professional attendants have started a hat in such-and-such a thicket, or whatever be the technical term.

Notice that this employment will in the fullest [30] degree combine sport with humanitarianism. The hunters would feel that they were not inflicting pain. Nay, they would feel that they were inflicting pleasure, rich, almost riotous pleasure, upon the people who were looking on. When last I saw an [35] old gentleman running after his hat in Hyde Park,

I told him that a heart so benevolent as his ought to be filled with peace and thanks at the thought of how much unaffected pleasure his every [40] gesture and bodily attitude were at that moment giving to the crowd.

The same principle can be applied to every other typical domestic worry. A gentleman trying to get a fly out of the milk or a piece of cork out [45] of his glass of wine often imagines himself to be irritated. Let him think for a moment of the patience of anglers sitting by dark pools, and let his soul be immediately irradiated with gratification and repose. Again, I have known [50] some people of very modern views driven by their distress to the use of theological terms to which they attached no doctrinal significance, merely because a drawer was jammed tight and they could not pull it out.

39. How best could this passage be described?

    A. A study of the aerodynamic tendencies of hats.

    B. An analysis as to why there persists a preference for traditional sports over futuristic sports.

    C. A list of ways that irritancies can give amusement.

    D. A satirical analysis of modern irritation.

CONTINUE ON TO THE NEXT PAGE →

40. Why does the author mention running for sport?

   A. To show that running alone is not a sufficient cause to be irritated.
   B. To assert the irritation associated with sports.
   C. To show that sports are as ridiculous as running after one's hat.
   D. To show that running after one's hat is already a sport.

---

41. Why did the author claim that the old man should be thanked?

   A. Because he was illustrating the athletic prowess of the elderly.
   B. Because he was not irritated, despite the situation.
   C. Because he was providing amusement to onlookers.
   D. Because he served in the past wars.

42. What "principle" does the author refer to in his final paragraph?

   A. Do not run after that which you cannot reach.
   B. Do not take mundane occurrences too seriously.
   C. Do not participate in sports that you do not enjoy.
   D. Do not swear.

---

43. What is not explicitly mentioned as a situation that makes people unnecessarily annoyed?

   A. Having your hat fly away in the wind.
   B. Chasing after a job.
   C. Having your desk drawer jam.
   D. Not doing well in school.

---

44. What does the author imply when he mentions that one could view chasing his or her hat as a hunt?

   A. Our irritation over mundane activities is rightfully placed.
   B. People are not overly irritated while hunting.
   C. Hunting in the woods makes even mundane tasks pleasurable.
   D. Only the wealthy hunt.

CONTINUE ON TO THE NEXT PAGE ➡

The attorney general of the United States, although his office was created by congress as early as Sept. 24, 1789, was not made the head of a department until June 22, 1870, when the department of justice was created. By this act, 5 the various law officers of the government, whose functions under previously existing laws were to interpret and apply the statutes governing the business of the various departments and bureaus and to prosecute violations of United States 10 laws in certain cases, were placed under the supervision of the attorney general. One leading reason for creating a department of justice was to bring about uniformity in the construction and application of the laws, which had not been 15 realized under the previously existing system, with half a dozen independent law officers, responsible to no common head.

The attorney general is made the head of the department of justice, being the chief law officer 20 of the executive branch of government. He is one of the members of the presidential cabinet, advising the president on questions of law, and, when required, renders opinions to the heads of any of the executive departments upon legal 25 questions arising as to the administration of any one of them. He is the representative of the United States in all matters involving legal questions. He has supervision of the United States district attorneys and marshals in the 30 United States courts of the states and territories. He sometimes appears in the Supreme Court of the United States to argue causes in which the government is a party, and even sometimes in a subordinate court of the United States. In all 35 other cases, the attorney general directs what officer is to appear and argue cases in which the United States is interested, in the Supreme

Court, the court of claims, or any other court, 40 providing special counsel for the United States when in his judgment it is required. Besides the conduct of law cases involving the interests or authority of the government, the department of justice is charged with the extensive and 45 complicated business connected with the judicial establishment, including some appointment (or recommendation for appointment) of judges, attorneys and marshals of the circuit and district courts of the United States. He or she is also 50 in charge of paying these various people and adjusting the salaries competitively.

45. What is this passage mostly about?

A. The history and role of the attorney general.
B. The origin of the first attorney general.
C. The nature of law in federal government
D. Moments where the federal government needs to be represented in court.

46. According to the passage, the attorney general is the lead legal counsel to the president and ___?

A. Appoints all judges.
B. Has the final say in all lower court decisions.
C. Is the head official of the department of justice.
D. Is the lead legal counsel to the house and senate.

CONTINUE ON TO THE NEXT PAGE →

47. What is one reason provided in the passage for why the department of justice was created?

    A. To give the president more power.
    B. To streamline the legal system.
    C. To add a cabinet post.
    D. To enlarge government.

---

48. What does the author imply was true prior to 1870?

    A. There was a simpler legal system.
    B. There was no attorney general.
    C. The attorney general was not a part of the federal government.
    D. The attorney general was not the ultimate legal officer.

---

49. What is not listed as a duty of an Attorney General?

    A. Prosecute cases at the supreme court.
    B. Manage the salaries of those working under the control of the department of justice.
    C. To represent the united states legally.
    D. To train judges.

---

50. Based on the passage, a successful attorney general must be outstanding at both ___?

    A. Law and management
    B. Law and politics
    C. Politics and governing
    D. School and law

CONTINUE ON TO THE NEXT PAGE →

When we read in history that Antigonus was very much displeased with his son for presenting him the head of King Pyrrhus, his enemy but newly slain fighting against him, and that seeing it, he wept; and that Rene, Duke of Lorraine, also 5 lamented the death of Charles, Duke of Burgundy, whom he had himself defeated, and appeared in mourning at his funeral; and that in the battle of D'Auray (which Count Montfort obtained over Charles de Blois, his competitor for the duchy of 10 Brittany), the conqueror meeting the dead body of his enemy, was very much afflicted at his death, we must not presently cry out (as did Petrarch): "And thus it happens that the mind of each veils its passion under a different appearance. 15 Melancholy beneath a smiling visage, happy beneath a somber air."

When Pompey's head was presented to Caesar, the histories tell us that he turned away his face, as from a sad and unpleasing object. There had been 20 so long an intelligence and society betwixt them in the management of the public affairs, so great a community of fortunes, so many mutual offices, and so near an alliance, that this countenance of his ought not to suffer under any misinterpretation, 25 or to be suspected for either false or counterfeit.

In judging of these accidents, we are to consider how much our souls are oftentimes agitated with diverse passions. And as they say that in our bodies there is a congregation of diverse humors, 30 so too is there in the soul. Thence, it is that we see not only children, who innocently obey and follow nature, often laugh and cry at the same thing, but not one of us can boast, what journey he may have in hand that he has the most set his heart 35 upon, but when he comes to part with his family

and friends, he will find something that troubles him within; and though he refrain his tears, yet he puts foot in the stirrup with a sad and cloudy countenance.

51. What is this passage mostly about?

   A. Reasons we distrust our enemies.
   B. Reasons that we love our enemies.
   C. Reasons why it is never wise to kill your enemy.
   D. Reasons why we may feel joy and sadness over the same occurrence.

52. According to the passage, who was victorious in the war between Antigonous and King Pyrrhus?

   A. King Pyrrhus
   B. Antigonous
   C. D'Auray
   D. Caesar

CONTINUE ON TO THE NEXT PAGE ➙

53. How best could the beliefs of Petrarch be described?

A. One should always take into consideration how someone feels.

B. It is unwise to kill one's enemy.

C. It is wise to lie about one's emotions.

D. A person's outward emotions rarely indicate their internal feelings.

54. What is not cited as a reason Caesar was upset about the death of his former foe?

A. Near alliance

B. Mutual offices

C. Similar managerial styles

D. Familial ties

55. The author's discussion most nearly relates to which of the following scenarios?

A. Someone is sad because they have been slighted by a friend.

B. Someone is happy because they have won a sporting championship.

C. Someone is glad, even though they were fired from their job.

D. Someone is angry, even though they normally do not get angry.

56. Tears are meant to represent what emotion throughout the passage?

A. Happiness

B. Sadness

C. Confusion

D. Determination

57. According to the final paragraph, how are the **body** and **soul** similar?

A. The body and soul are both efficient to keep mistakes from being made.

B. The body and soul are both pure and should be trusted above all things.

C. The body and soul are both filled with many thoughts and feelings, some of which may seem to contradict each other.

D. The body and soul are both untrustworthy because they contain weakness.

CONTINUE ON TO THE NEXT PAGE →

90 MINUTES • 57 QUESTIONS

Select the best answer from the choices given by carefully solving each problem. Bubble the letter of your answer on the answer sheet. Please refrain from making any stray marks on the answer sheet. If you need to erase an answer, please erase thoroughly.

Important Notes:

1. There are no formulas or definitions in the math section that will be provided.
2. Diagrams may or may not be drawn to scale. Do not make assumptions based on the diagram unless it is specifically stated in the diagram or question.
3. Diagrams are not in more than one plane, unless stated otherwise.
4. Graphs are drawn to scale, therefore, you can assume relationships according to the graph. If lines appear parallel, then you can assume the lines to be parallel. This is also true for right angles and so forth.
5. Simplify fractions completely.

Practice Test 4 (Questions 1-57)

1. What is the value of $\sqrt{25} + \sqrt{64}$?

- **A.** 10
- **B.** 13
- **C.** 14
- **D.** 89

2. What is the value of r in the equation: $2r = 10^2$?

- **A.** 10
- **B.** 25
- **C.** 50
- **D.** 100

3. What is the area of a square with a perimeter of 16?

- **A.** 8
- **B.** 12
- **C.** 16
- **D.** 24

4. What is 10% of a number whose square is 81?

- **A.** 0.81
- **B.** 0.9
- **C.** 8.1
- **D.** 9

CONTINUE ON TO THE NEXT PAGE →

Explanations to each problem on:
Youtube.com/ArgoBrothers

MATHEMATICS
TEST 4

ARGO
BROTHERS
www.argobrothers.com

5. What is the range of the set {1, 2, 5, 10, 6, 12}?

    A. −16
    B. −11
    C. 3
    D. 11

6. Nancy found a formula for the area of a square in terms of its perimeter. Let A stand for the area and P for perimeter. What is the formula Nancy found?

    A. $\dfrac{P^2}{8}$

    B. $\dfrac{P^2}{4}$

    C. $\dfrac{P^2}{16}$

    D. $4P$

7. Anayet is driving to work from home and realizes he left his wallet at home when he is at his workplace. He turns back to retrieve his wallet. His workplace and home are 45 miles apart and it takes him twice as long to get to workplace from his home than the other way around. It is a 30 minute drive from his workplace to home. What is the average speed for the round trip in miles per minute?

    A. 0.75
    B. 1.5
    C. 1
    D. 2

8. Given that, $\overleftrightarrow{a} = a^2 + a$, what is $\overleftrightarrow{a} \div a$?

    A. a
    B. $a + 2$
    C. 1
    D. $a + 1$

9. Sarah has a trick coin that has heads on both sides. She asks her friend John, who believes the coin is fair, to guess what face it will land on. If they flip the coin 100 times, how many times bigger is Sarah's expected probability of the coin landing on heads than John's expected probability of the coin landing on heads?

    A. 0.25
    B. 0.5
    C. 1
    D. 2

10. What is the square of a number that when added to any number does not change that number's value?

    A. 0
    B. 0.5
    C. 1
    D. undefined

11. How many nonzero numbers are between 3 and 5?

    A. 1
    B. 2
    C. 3
    D. ∞

CONTINUE ON TO THE NEXT PAGE →

Explanations to each problem on:
Youtube.com/ArgoBrothers

MATHEMATICS
TEST 4

ARGO
BROTHERS
www.argobrothers.com

12. The circle that is inscribed in the square below has a radius of 2. What is the length of the diagonal of the square?

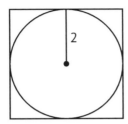

2

- **A.** 4
- **B.** 16
- **C.** $4\sqrt{2}$
- **D.** $2\sqrt{2}$

13. What is the absolute value of the difference between the number of integers between 0 and 5 inclusive and the number of integers between 1 and 6 exclusive?

- **A.** 0
- **B.** 1
- **C.** 2
- **D.** 3

14. Corey is walking on a path. Every three steps he takes, he makes a 30 degree rotation to counterclockwise. If he took 18 steps in total, how many full revolutions was he able to make all together?

- **A.** 0.25
- **B.** 0.5
- **C.** 1
- **D.** 2

15. What is 20% of 20% of 20?

- **A.** 0.2
- **B.** 0.8
- **C.** 2
- **D.** 8

16. What is the difference between the largest and lowest integer in the sequence of consecutive odd integers whose sum is 15?

- **A.** 2
- **B.** 4
- **C.** 5
- **D.** 9

17. The half life of a substance is the time it takes for a substance to decrease to half its initial amount. John has a pile of goo that decreases in amount at a constant rate. If John initially had 100 pounds of goo, and ten days later, he only had 25 pounds of goo, what is the half life of the goo?

- **A.** 10 days
- **B.** 5 days
- **C.** 7.5 days
- **D.** 20 days

18. What is the value of $\dfrac{9^4 - 8^4}{9^2 + 8^2}$?

- **A.** 1
- **B.** 16
- **C.** 17
- **D.** 18

CONTINUE ON TO THE NEXT PAGE →

19. Jackie fills a jug with water continuously. It takes her 2 minutes to fill up 50% of the empty space in the jug with water. After every 2 minutes, she puts a penny into a jar to celebrate. How many pennies will she have in the jar at the instant the jug has less than 30% empty space left?

A. 0
B. 1
C. 2
D. 3

20.

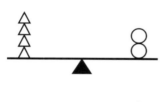

In the figure above, there are two balance beams that have triangles, circles and squares on them. Both beams are fully balanced. How many circles are needed to balance 70 squares?

A. 10
B. 12
C. 35
D. 70

21. $\overline{.7} + \dfrac{2}{9} = \overline{.6} +$ ___

A. $\dfrac{1}{2}$

B. $\dfrac{1}{3}$

C. $\dfrac{2}{9}$

D. $\dfrac{4}{9}$

22. The prime factors of 232 are

A. 2, 2, 2, 29
B. 116, 2
C. 2, 29
D. 2, 2, 58

23. If the pattern continues, what will be the 438th symbol?

$$\square \, \circlearrowleft \leftarrow \uparrow \rightarrow \nwarrow \square \, \circlearrowleft \leftarrow \uparrow \rightarrow \nwarrow \square \, \circlearrowleft$$

A. $\square$
B. $\uparrow$
C. $\nwarrow$
D. $\circlearrowleft$

CONTINUE ON TO THE NEXT PAGE ➡

24. Find the value of t if $\dfrac{t}{32} = \dfrac{x}{p}$

    A. $\dfrac{32p}{x}$

    B. $\dfrac{32}{px}$

    C. $\dfrac{32x}{p}$

    D. $32px$

25. What is the least integer greater than $\dfrac{52}{3}$?

    A. 16
    B. 17
    C. 18
    D. 19

26. If $5^5 + 5^5 + 5^5 + 5^5 + 5^5 = 5^{a+1}$, what is a?

    A. 3
    B. 4
    C. 5
    D. 6

27. If $(x + y)^2 = x^2 + y^2$, then what condition must be true?

    A. $x + y = 0$
    B. $2x = 0$
    C. $2y = 0$
    D. $xy = 0$

28. What is the maximum number points that two distinct circles can intersect at?

    A. 2
    B. 3
    C. 4
    D. ∞

29. A cumulative product of a set $\{a, b, c, ...\}$ is the sequence, $a, ab, abc, ...$ What is the mean of the terms in the cumulative product of $\{1, 2, 3, 0\}$?

    A. 0
    B. 2
    C. 2.25
    D. 3.5

30. How many integers are in the set of nonpositive, nonnegative integers?

    A. 0
    B. 1
    C. 2
    D. ∞

CONTINUE ON TO THE NEXT PAGE ➡

Explanations to each problem on:
Youtube.com/ArgoBrothers

MATHEMATICS
TEST 4

ARGO BROTHERS
www.argobrothers.com

31. How many chords are in the circle below?

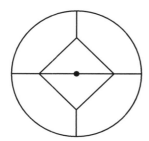

A. 1
B. 2
C. 3
D. 7

32. In the figure below, there is a function plotted and there are 5 points labeled *A* through *E* drawn. For how many points is *y(x)* equal to 0?

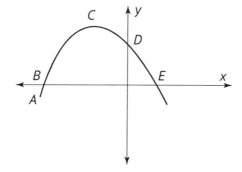

A. 0
B. 1
C. 2
D. 3

33. At what time on a clock will the hands form an acute angle formed of 60°?

A. 1:00 PM
B. 2:00 PM
C. 2:30 PM
D. 3:00 PM

34. A jar contains only red and blue marbles. The probability of picking a red marble is 20%. One blue marble is added to the jar. What is the probability of picking a blue marble?

A. $\dfrac{1}{2}$

B. $\dfrac{4}{5}$

C. $\dfrac{1}{6}$

D. Cannot be determined from the information given.

35. If $a = 35$, what is, $(-6)^2(-6)(-6) + 6(-6)$ in terms of *a*?

A. $a + 1$
B. a^2
C. $a^2 + 1$
D. $a^2 + a$

CONTINUE ON TO THE NEXT PAGE →

36. A circle and an octagon share the same perimeter (circumference for the circle). If the side length of the octagon is, a, and the radius of the circle is, r, then what is the radius in terms of the side length of the octagon?

A. $\dfrac{a}{\pi}$

B. $\dfrac{4}{\pi}$

C. $\dfrac{4a}{\pi}$

D. 4π

37. What is the least integer greater than the greatest integer less than 1.5?

A. 2
B. 1.5
C. 0.5
D. 1

38. What is the area of a semicircle in terms of tau (τ) with a radius of r. Tau is double the value of π.

A. $\tau^2 r$

B. τr^2

C. $\dfrac{\tau r^2}{4}$

D. $\dfrac{\tau r}{2}$

39. If $F = -kx$ and greater than 0, then what happens to the value of k if F triples in value and x remains constant

A. Increases
B. Doubles
C. Decreases
D. Cannot be determined from the information given.

40. If the length of the side of a square is, 7^a, what is the area?

A. 7^a
B. 49^a
C. 7^{2a}
D. $7a^a$

41. What is the circumference of the dotted section of the circle whose center is O below?

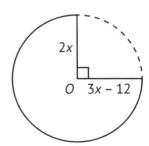

A. 6π
B. 12π
C. 24π
D. 48π

CONTINUE ON TO THE NEXT PAGE ➡

Explanations to each problem on:
Youtube.com/ArgoBrothers

MATHEMATICS
TEST 4

ARGO
BROTHERS
www.argobrothers.com

42. Given that $0 < x < 1$, and set $A = \{x, x^2, x^3, x^4\}$, what is the smallest value in set A?

  A. x^2
  B. x^3
  C. x^4
  D. Cannot be determined from the information given.

43. Sammy has a faulty clock. Every 15 degrees that one of the hands moves, 5 minutes passes. If a hand is initially 5:35 PM, in how long will the hand be at that same position?

  A. 65 minutes
  B. 2 hours
  C. 1 hour
  D. 45 minutes

44. If $(x - 2)(x + 2) = ax^2 + bx + c$, what is the sum of a, b and c?

  A. -4
  B. -3
  C. 0
  D. 1

45. Natalie walks in a special way. After every 2 steps, she takes 1 step in the opposite direction. She starts at point A and walks forward. When she is 7 steps away from point A, she has reached her destination, point B. How many steps in total did she take to get from point A to B?

  A. 7
  B. 8
  C. 17
  D. 15

46. If, $C_{m,n} = C(m + n)$, for what value of n is $C_{m,n}$ neither positive nor negative?

  A. $-C$
  B. $-m$
  C. $2m$
  D. 0

47. Two sides of a triangle are 6 and 8. What is the length of the third side?

  A. 2
  B. 4
  C. 5
  D. Cannot be uniquely determined.

CONTINUE ON TO THE NEXT PAGE →

48. $2 + \dfrac{1}{3} = \dfrac{14}{b}$, what is b?

   A. 3
   B. 6
   C. 7
   D. 9

49. In the formula $V = r^2h$, if h is doubled and r triples, then V is multiplied by?

   A. 6
   B. 9
   C. 12
   D. 18

50. Max A returns the largest value in the set A. Min A returns the lowest value in the set A. For example, max{1, 2, 3} = 3 and min{0, 4, 5} = 0.

   What is max{min{x, 2x, 3x}, max{$\dfrac{x}{2}, \dfrac{x}{4}, \dfrac{x}{8}$}}?

   A. $2x$

   B. $\dfrac{x}{2}$

   C. $3x$

   D. Cannot be uniquely determined.

Use the graph below to answers questions 51 and 52.

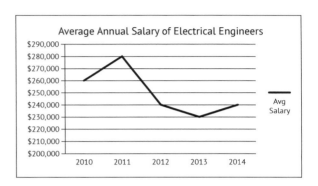

51. What was the approximate percentage decrease in average annual salary from 2011 to 2012?

   A. 14.3%
   B. 15.2%
   C. 50%
   D. 25%

52. What was the average salary in 2015 if it was 10% greater than the median salary for the previous five years?

   A. $253,000
   B. $264,000
   C. $275,000
   D. $286,000

CONTINUE ON TO THE NEXT PAGE ➡

MATHEMATICS
TEST 4

Explanations to each problem on:
Youtube.com/ArgoBrothers

ARGO
BROTHERS
www.argobrothers.com

GRID IN

Directions: The following five questions are grid-in problems. On the answer sheet, please be sure to write your answer in the boxes at the top of the grid. Start on the left side of each grid.

53. If $f(x) = x^2 + \sqrt[3]{x}$ and $g(y) = \sqrt{(y-2)}$, solve for $g(f(8))$.

54. The length of a rectangle is $3x - 1$ and the width is $3x + 9$, while the perimeter is 172. What is the area of the rectangle?

55. A fair coin is flipped 10 times. If the first 9 flips resulted in Heads, what is the chance the tenth flip will result in Heads? Make sure your answer is in decimal form.

CONTINUE ON TO THE NEXT PAGE ➡

284

56. A construction crane has a boom which extends 50 ft from the base. If the crane is stationed 30 ft from a building, how high up the building wall can the crane reach?

THIS IS THE END OF THE TEST. IF THERE IS TIME REMAINING, YOU MAY CHECK YOUR ANSWERS TO PART 1 OR PART 2.

57. If $\dfrac{x-8}{x+3} = 12$, solve for x.

SHSAT PRACTICE TEST 4
ANSWER KEY

Revising/Editing

1. **C**
2. **D**
3. **B**
4. **C**
5. **A**
6. **B**
7. **D**
8. **B**
9. **B**
10. **C**
11. **C**
12. **A**
13. **D**
14. **C**
15. **B**
16. **A**
17. **D**
18. **B**
19. **A**
20. **B**

Reading Comprehension

21. **C**
22. **D**
23. **B**
24. **C**
25. **D**
26. **A**
27. **C**
28. **C**
29. **A**
30. **B**
31. **D**
32. **D**
33. **D**
34. **D**
35. **B**
36. **C**
37. **A**
38. **D**
39. **D**
40. **A**

41. **C**
42. **B**
43. **D**
44. **B**
45. **A**
46. **C**
47. **B**
48. **D**
49. **D**
50. **A**
51. **C**
52. **B**
53. **D**
54. **D**
55. **A**
56. **B**
57. **C**

Math

1. **B**	13. **C**	25. **C**	37. **A**	49. **D**
2. **C**	14. **B**	26. **C**	38. **C**	50. **D**
3. **C**	15. **B**	27. **D**	39. **D**	51. **A**
4. **B**	16. **B**	28. **A**	40. **C**	52. **B**
5. **D**	17. **B**	29. **C**	41. **B**	53. **8**
6. **C**	18. **C**	30. **B**	42. **C**	54. **1824**
7. **C**	19. **B**	31. **A**	43. **B**	55. **0.5**
8. **D**	20. **D**	32. **C**	44. **B**	56. **40**
9. **D**	21. **B**	33. **B**	45. **C**	57. **-4**
10. **A**	22. **A**	34. **D**	46. **B**	
11. **D**	23. **C**	35. **D**	47. **D**	
12. **C**	24. **C**	36. **C**	48. **B**	

Practice Test 4 (Answers and Explanations)

1. **C** Answer C is correct because it inserts the three necessary commas into the sentence. The phrase "...which is sometimes recognized as the 'Great American Novel,'" needs a comma on each side of it because it is a nonessential clause. Nonessential clauses in the middle of a sentence are separated from the main text with two commas to provide clarity to the reader. The names of the two lovers at the end of the sentence are also technically nonessential information, which should also be preceded by a comma. Answer A is incorrect because it fails to insert commas to indicate the beginning of the first nonessential clause (after "book") as well as the second one (after "lovers"). Answer B correctly separates the first nonessential clause but not the second, making it incorrect overall. Answer D is incorrect because it neglects to indicate the end of the first nonessential clause by not putting a comma after "Novel."

2. **D** Answer D is correct because it separates all the items in the list using commas and separates the list from the nonessential clause "...all of whom are still major characters..." Answer A is incorrect because, while it puts commas between list items correctly, it fails to separate the end of the list from the nonessential modifier that follows. Answer B is incorrect because, while it puts commas between list items correctly (including the optional Oxford comma), it also fails to separate the list from the nonessential clause at the end. Answer C is incorrect because it does not put commas between Hulk, Thor, and Spider-Man.

3. **B** Semicolons can be used to separate list items that already contain commas. Since the description of each uncle contains a comma, the writer of this sentence can use semicolons to compartmentalize the sections of the sentence about each one of them. Answer B punctuates the sentence correctly, putting a comma after each name and a semicolon at the end of each section. Answer choice A is incorrect because it lacks the commas that separate each uncle's name from his describing clause. Answer choice C is incorrect because it incorrectly reverses the placement of commas and semicolons. Answer choice D is incorrect because it introduces the list which a semicolon, which is the job of a colon (as can be seen in the original sentence).

4. **C** Answer C is correct because Sentence 2 contains the passive voice construction "women's conditions and rights were discussed." Passive voice occurs when the subject of a sentence is having the action of the verb performed on it rather than being the actor in the sentence. Passive voice is generally discouraged in formal writing. Sentence 2 should be revised to create an active voice construction (for example: "Throughout the two-day convention, as many as 300 attendees discussed women's conditions and rights."). Answer A is incorrect because Sentence 2 is clearly about the Seneca Falls Convention, as are all the other sentences. Answer B is incorrect because the entire paragraph is consistently written in the historical past tense. Answer D is incorrect the "to be" verb "were" in the sentence is acting primarily as a helping verb as part of the passive voice construction. By correcting the passive voice, the author also eliminates the need for the "were" in the sentence, making Answer C a much better answer.

5. **A** "After school" should be separated from the rest of the sentence with a comma because it is an introductory phrase that only serves to provide context, making Answer A correct. Answers B, C, and D are all incorrect because they place commas at inappropriate places in the sentence. A comma after road (Answer B) would incorrectly break up the phrase "down the road to the park," reducing the clarity of the sentence. A comma after park (Answer C) would incorrectly identify the sentence as a compound sentence, which it is not since there is no second subject. A comma after Stephanie (Answer D) would incorrectly suggest a list at the end of the sentence, when there are only two names mentioned.

6. **B** The first verb of Sentence 2, "ruled," establishes that the events of this sentence occur in the past. Therefore, to prevent reader confusion, the present tense verb "is" later in the sentence should be made consistent by changing it to "was," making Answer B correct. Answer A is incorrect because a date of 500 AD is given in the sentence, demonstrating that Arthur could not possibly be ruling today and cementing the need for the past tense verb "ruled." Answer C is also incorrect because, again, the main verb of the sentence and date provided both establish that this sentence deals with events of the past. Answer D is incorrect because "honorable" and "honored" are two completely different adjectives with separate meanings. Substituting "honored" would change the fundamental meaning of the sentence, and is therefore incorrect.

7. **D** Passive voice occurs when the subject of the sentence is having action performed on or to it rather than being the actor of the main verb. Answer D is correct because Sentence 3 contains the passive voice construction "...mythical stories were already being told..." Sentence 3 should be revised to eliminate this use of passive voice. One example of a correct revision would be, "By the twelfth century, storytellers were already telling tales about Arthur assembling the bravest knights of all time to serve at his heroic Round Table." Answer A is incorrect because the given subject of the sentence ("stories") agrees in number with the verb. Answer B is incorrect because the sentence contains no spelling errors. Answer C is incorrect because the only necessary comma in the sentence (the one that separates the introduction "By the fifteenth century,") is placed correctly.

8. **B** Paragraph 2 contains a summary of the major features that most Arthur stories contain. This idea is summarized in the final (conclusion) sentence of the paragraph as well. Answer B is correct because it previews the main content of the paragraph and has a strong connection to Sentence 8, the conclusion. Answer B is incorrect because it is overly general and fails to address the idea of variation between different tellings of the story. Answer C is a relevant detail, but not a topic sentence because Sentences 4-8 do not all focus on Excalibur. Finally, Answer D is also incorrect because it is overly general and could be used at the beginning of a discussion of any story.

9. **B** Answer B is correct because it separates the introduction using a comma (by placing one after "story') and correctly separates out the nonessential modifier "the secret son of King Uther Pendragon"). Answer A is incorrect because, while it separates the introduction using a comma, it does not separate out the nonessential information. Answer C is also incorrect because it fails to separate the introduction phrase, even though it correctly identifies the nonessential modifier

in the middle of the sentence. Answer D is incorrect because even though it identifies all the necessary commas, it also adds a completely unnecessary one at the end (after "ruler").

10. **C**   Sentence 7 tells what happens at the end of a story, having skipped a large number of specific details and events. "Ultimately" is the best transition to indicate that the author is skipping to the end or conclusion of an idea, making Answer choice C correct. Answer A is incorrect because "Therefore" implies there is a clear, causal relationship between two events or ideas, which is not the case in this paragraph. Answer B is incorrect because "However" implies that the content of Sentence 7 is directly contrary to Sentence 6, which it is not. Answer D is incorrect because "Subsequently" is not the best answer choice. "Subsequently" implies that the events of Sentence 7 happened later after the events of Sentence 6, but "Ultimately" is still the best answer because it clearly communicates to the reader that many specific steps or events are being skipped over in order to discuss the end of the story.

11. **C**   Sentences 9, 10, 12, and 13 all connect clearly to Arthur's relevance to English culture and government. Sentence 11, however, is not thematically connected to the rest of the paragraph because it talks generally about businesspeople "all over the world," a phrase that should be a hint to the reader. Answer C is correct because removing Sentence 11 would not detract from the overall meaning of the paragraph and would create a clearer link between the other sentences. Answers A, B, and D are all incorrect because each of those sentence is tied directly to ways in which the Arthur myth is still culturally relevant in England today.

12. **A**   Answer A is the best choice because it clarifies the subject of the sentence as well as pinpoints the object of "they" towards the end of the sentence. Answer A correctly identifies Arthur as the first "he" of the sentence, eliminating any confusion that the author is discussing one of today's royals. By inserting "today's royals" for "they," however, the author can clarify the idea that Arthur and his knights are role models for today's leaders. Answer B is wrong because it misinterprets the object of "they," making it seem like there are still medieval knights today. Answer C is incorrect because it incorrectly attributes "they" to referring to all English people, destroying the original meaning of the sentence. Answer D is also incorrect because it misinterprets "they" as being the Knights of the Round Table, destroying the intended meaning of the whole sentence.

13. **D**   "To be" verbs (is, am, are, was, were, will be, etc.) are generally discouraged from formal writing, especially in a key situation like this conclusion sentence. Answer D is correct because it reorders the sentence to eliminate both the "is" and "was." Answer A is incorrect because it maintains both "is" and "was," changing only a few words. Answer B is also incorrect because it simply hides "is" in the contraction "Arthur's" and changes "was" to "may be," which is still a "to be" verb. Answer C is also incorrect because it only eliminates one of the two "to be" verbs while keeping the other ("was").

14. **C**   Answer C is correct because it includes the commas necessary to separate the list in the first half of the sentence and to separate the nonessential phrase "making use of either wings or machinery." Answer A is incorrect because it contains a comma-separated list but does not identify

the nonessential modifier at the end using a comma. Answer B is cannot be the answer because it incorrectly separates "and stories" with two commas as if it is a nonessential phrase. Answer D is also incorrect because it fails to separate the final nonessential modifier using a comma and incorrectly places one after "wings," as though the author was creating another list.

15. B Answer B makes the best conclusion sentence for the first paragraph because it sums up the main ideas of the first paragraph and previews the content of the next. The phrase "...it was one of mankind's goals for millennia" sums up Sentences 1-3 while "manned flight was not practical until relatively recently" introduces the ideas that will come next. Answer A is a poor conclusion because it makes an illogical jump from the earliest dreams of flying all the way to today's modern travel and is also written in passive voice. Answer C is incorrect because, while it provides additional information about Da Vinci, it does not address any of the content in Sentences 1-2 or preview upcoming ideas. Answer D is also incorrect because it introduces military use, which is not mentioned anywhere else in the passage.

16. A Answer A is correct because it inserts the necessary comma to separate the introduction "On that day" from the main body of the sentence. Answer B is incorrect because the passage is written consistently in the past tense, so using a present tense verb would be inconsistent with the rest of the paragraph. Answer C is incorrect because numbers one through nine should be written out longhand using letters rather than numerals. Answer D is also incorrect because "hot air balloon" is written as three words, not connected with dashes.

17. D Passive voice occurs when the subject of a sentence is having action done to them rather than being the actor of the main verb. The construction "...men could be transported..." is an example of passive voice because the subject ("men") is not the one doing the transporting. Answer D is correct because it reorganizes the sentence to make "balloons" the subject of the active voice construction "balloons could transport men..." Answers A and B are both incorrect because they maintain the original passive voice construction from the passage (Answer B even adds a second example of passive voice). Answer C is incorrect because, while it corrects the initial passive voice error at the beginning of the sentence, it actually creates another with the phrase "the devices were seen as..."

18. B The entire passage is written consistently in the past tense, but Sentence 8 uses the present progressive tense verb "are working," making Answer B correct. Sentence 8 should be revised to turn "are working" into "worked" to make the sentence consistent with the rest of the passage. Answer A is incorrect because there is no example of subject-verb disagreement in the sentence. Answer C is incorrect because the construction "minds are working" is written in the active voice. Answer D is also incorrect because all the words in the sentence are spelled correctly.

19. A A dangling modifier occurs when a sentence begins with a descriptive phrase whose object is unclear to the reader. "Working separately but concurrently" is an example of a dangling modifier because, at the time the reader reads those words on the page, it's unclear which people were working separately but concurrently. Answer A is the correct answer because it reorders the sentence to clarify that it was a variety of researchers who were working separately

but concurrently. Answer B maintains the original dangling modifier and is therefore incorrect. Answers C and D reorder the sentence in an attempt to eliminate the dangling modifier, but both answers inadvertently create a new dangling modifier: "Including Samuel Langley, the Wright Brothers, and German immigrant Gustave Whitehead…"

20. **B**   Answer B is correct because "Eventually" transitions the paragraph smoothly from the idea that many people were researching manned flight to the idea that the Wright Brothers became the first successful pilots. "Eventually" also communicates that there was a great deal of time and work put into this breakthrough and that it did not occur suddenly out of nowhere. Answer A is incorrect because the fact that the Wright Brothers were the first to fly is not contrary to the content of the previous sentence, as "However" would imply. Answer C is incorrect because "In conclusion" is always a weak, self-referential transition. Answer D is also incorrect because "Therefore" implies that Sentence 10 is the logical result of Sentence 9, which is not the case in the paragraph. For "Therefore" to be an acceptable transition, Sentence 9 should have set up the reader to expect that the Wright Brothers would eventually be the successful parties.

READING COMPREHENSION

Passage 1 ("Those enactments were called agrarian laws…")

21. **C**   Answer C is the best choice because the overall theme of the passage is agrarian law. Each paragraph explores this topic in some form or fashion. Answers A and B are not the best answer, even though they correctly identify Roman conquest as a key feature of the passage. Answer C is a better answer, however, because it identifies the agrarian laws that surrounded Roman conquest as the more specific focus of the text. Answer D is similarly incorrect because, while the expansion of Rome is a feature of the passage, the implementation of agrarian laws and allotments is clearly the main focus of each paragraph.

22. **D**   Answer D is correct because Line 4 defines the term, saying, "A law (lex) for the establishment of a colony…" Parentheses are used in the sentence to indicate that the author is providing the reader with a translation to Latin, the original Roman language. The use of italics should also be an indicator to the reader that the word "lex" is borrowed from another language, and therefore the word preceding it is a definition. Also, the visual similarities in length and letters between "lex" and "law" should be something of a hint to the reader. Answers A, B, and C are all incorrect and have minimal basis in the text, since lords and lexicons are never mentioned, and the idea of a lawn is only tangentially suggested by the fact that the author is discussing tracts of land.

23. **B**   Answer B is correct because Lines 19-30 describe the process by which Rome acquired land by conquest. Lines 20-23 in particular state: "Rome had originally a small territory, but by a series of conquests carried on for many centuries she finally obtained dominion of the whole Italian peninsula," providing a clearly stated explanation that Rome expanded through military conquest.

Answer A is incorrect because, while the passage makes reference to Rome repurposing private land as public in some cases, the answer itself presents a logical fallacy: if Rome "acquired" public land by converting it from private land, then how was that private land acquired? Answer C is incorrect because Lines 6-9 explain that Roman law provided allotments to plebes; the land was not given by nobles. Answer D cannot be correct because there is nothing in the text one way or the other that suggests whether or not public land had always been available in Rome.

24. **C** Answer C is correct because Lines 31-32 plainly state, "A state which submitted got better terms than one which made an obstinate resistance," explaining that surrender and cooperation could help people conquered by the Romans preserve more of their land. Answer A is incorrect because Lines 32-34 suggest that the Romans always took at least one-third of conquered land. Answer B cannot be correct because the passage never discusses peaceful acquisition of land, but rather focuses on how the Romans took land forcibly through warfare. Answer D cannot be correct because the passage never discusses Roman political representation, so there is no textual basis for the answer.

25. **D** Answer D is correct because Lines 39-45 explain, "But there were probably in all parts of Italy large tracts of uncultivated ground which were under pasture, and these tracts would form a part of the Roman share, for we find that pasture land was a considerable portion of the Roman public land." Answers A, B, and C are all incorrect with minimal basis in the text because the passage the words "farm," "city," and "road" never appear anywhere in the text.

26. **A** Answer A is correct because Lines 25-30 describe that "...it was a Roman principle that the conquered people lost everything with the loss of their political independence; and what they enjoyed after the conquest was a gift from the generosity of the conqueror." This means that all conquered land belonged to Rome, at least for some time, before being redistributed to the original owners. Answers B, C, and D are all incorrect because they fail to correctly identify Rome's policy of seizing all land and redistributing it, as is laid out in Lines 25-30. Answer C is particularly incorrect because plebes are only mentioned in the first paragraph of the passage and never discussed in connection to the conquered peoples.

Passage 2 ("It has been observed that the shortest man...")

27. **C** Answer C is the best choice because, throughout the passage, the author describes how scientific discoveries are better understood and put to use over time. Even the passage's first image (a man sitting on the shoulders of a giant in Lines 1-3) reinforces this idea that modern civilization is built on the foundation of achievement and knowledge established earlier by the ancients. This idea is explored in each paragraph of the passage. Answer A is not the best choice because the author explains in Lines 24-26 that "...it is by no means my object to lessen our esteem for those great men who have lived before us..." meaning he does not necessarily believe that the ancients were ignorant. Answer B is incorrect and represents a flawed reading of the text because, according to the author's perspective as laid out in the passage, future societies will absolutely surpass today's society because that is the nature of history. Answer D is incorrect because it fails to appreciate that the author is also writing about today's society, not just focusing on the ancients.

28. **C**   Answer C is the best choice because, in Lines 3-8, the author explains the metaphor of sitting on giant shoulders, saying, "…the moderns, standing as they do on the vantage ground of former discoveries… may be admitted to enjoy a more enlarged and comprehensive view of things…" Answer A is incorrect because the author is not discussing a literal giant, but rather using the image as a metaphor for the advancement of knowledge. Answer B is incorrect because the author does not group the entire past together, but presents it throughout the passage as a progression from era to era in which new discoveries are made each step of the way. Answer D is incorrect because, as the author explains in Lines 24-26, he does not believe the ancients were "less than" modern thinkers; they simply weren't equipped with the breadth of knowledge that people have today.

29. **A**   Answer A is correct because in Lines 9-14, the author explains, "But by whom is antiquity enjoyed? Not by the ancients… but by the moderns who do live in the maturity of things. Therefore, as regards the age of the world, we may lay a juster claim to the title of being the ancients," suggesting modern society is truly "ancient" because it is built on thousands of years of ancient knowledge and discovery. Answers B and C are both incorrect with no textual basis, since there is no suggestion of time travel or future societies in the passage. Answer D is also incorrect, even though it represents a traditional view of time and history, because it does not represent the author's perspective, as explained in Lines 9-14.

30. **B**   Answer B is the best choice because, in Lines 28-33, the author explains that "veneration due to times that are past is a high-sight focused veneration, the moment it is paid at the expense of times that are present…" This means that the author does not believe past accomplishments should be worshipped at the expense of appreciating the talents and knowledge of today's society. Answer B is the correct answer because it provides an example of somebody holding a high jumper of the past in such high esteem that they fail to appreciate the accomplishments of today's athletes. Answer A is incorrect because it doesn't demonstrate someone worshiping minds of the past – it actually shows them discounting them. Answer B is incorrect because, while it praises minds of the past, it does not do so in a way that denigrates today's inventors or minds. Finally, Answer D is also incorrect because it simply states a fact rather than making a judgment about the quality of that innovation as compared to today.

31. **D**   Answer D is correct because in Lines 35-37, the author plainly states, "What I would principally contend is that the moderns enjoy a much more extended and comprehensive view of science than the ancients…" Answers B and C are incorrect because there is no mention of reading or language anywhere in the text. Answer A is especially incorrect because the author clearly presents science as something moderns do and understand better than the ancients in Lines 35-37.

32. **D**   Answer D is the best choice because the quotation from the passage is immediately preceded by the following sentence: "We, therefore, are profiting not only by the knowledge, but also by the ignorance, not only by the discoveries, but also by the errors, of our forefathers" (Lines 44-47). By locating the quotation from the question in context, the reader can easily make this connection.

Answer A is incorrect because the passage repeatedly asserts that important discoveries were made by ancients in the past. Answer B is similarly incorrect because the author explains in Lines 40-43 that the main reason the ancients were not as good at science as us is that science is based on a foundation of knowledge that has to be built over time. The ancients cannot be characterized fairly as "bad at science," according to the author, because they simply didn't have the foundation of knowledge and discovery that moderns do. Answer C is incorrect and has no basis in the text, as scientific work can be done at any time of day or night.

Passage 3 ("Some years ago, in company with...")

33. **D** Answer D is the best choice because Emerson's sensory experience of nature is a feature of each paragraph of the passage. Lines 53-63 establish Emerson's main thoughts on this topic, stating, "Our conversation with Nature is not just what it seems... The senses interfere everywhere, and mix their own structure with all they report of." Answer A is incorrect because, while Emerson clearly views man as curious, the answer fails to take nature, which is one of the key features of the passage, into account. Answer B is not the best answer either because, although Emerson certainly believes man is in some ways ignorant towards nature (Lines 59-63), he mostly puts the blame on mankind's sensory experience of nature (Lines 58-59), making Answer D a better choice. Answer C is also incorrect because, while the connection between man and nature is clearly key to the passage, Answer D still represents a more complete, specific explanation of the passage by including the senses, which are also a key feature of the text.

34. **D** Answer D is correct because Emerson's repeated use of "seemed" (Lines 37 & 39) reinforces that what they are seeing is not in fact a starry sky, but rather a natural illusion that looks very much like the night sky. Emerson also describes the sight as a "magnificent effect" in Line 47, suggesting again that it's not a real sky. Answer A cannot be correct because Emerson never states whether or not the star-chamber was the only one of its kind. Answers B and C cannot be correct either because Emerson explicitly states that what "seemed" like stars and a comet appeared bright, but since both effects were illusions, Answer D remains the best choice.

35. **B** Answer B is the best choice because, in Lines 22-24, Emerson describes "four combined engineers, water, limestone, gravitation, and time," clearly establishing that water is one of the four main forces that created the cave. Answer A is incorrect because it is not tied to the text in any way. Answer C cannot be correct because Lines 22-24 establish that there were four engineers of the cave, not just water. Answer D is also incorrect because Emerson does not rank or grade the four engineers, he simply states what they are, so the reader has no way of knowing which (if any) was most important.

36. **C** Answer C is the best choice because Lines 40-45 state that "All the party were touched with astonishment and pleasure... I sat down on the rocky floor to enjoy the serene picture," indicating to the reader that the group was overcome by the beauty of the star-chamber. Answer A is incorrect because exhaustion is never mentioned and, if anything, Lines 40-45 suggest that the party

members were energized by the beauty of the star-chamber. Answer B cannot be correct because Emerson never establishes how many people have been in the star-chamber or any traditions associated with it. Answer D cannot be correct because the Emerson makes no mention of the party singing in any other circumstances and says they "sung with much feeling," suggesting that they had just begun.

37. A Answer A is the best choice because Lines 58-63 focus on how the senses' perception of nature cannot necessarily be trusted. Emerson provides "Once, we fancied the earth a plane and stationary" (Lines 59-60) as an example of how "The senses interfere everywhere" (Line 58). Answer B is incorrect because humans eventually realized that the earth was spherical, meaning that nature can be comprehended, at least on some level, eventually. Answer C is incorrect because people eventually understood the world was spherical, so the example of a flat earth is not proof that nature will never be understood. Answer D has no textual basis because, throughout the text, Emerson makes it clear that he believes people should deeply consider the nature of the world, so Answer D is completely contrary to his point.

38. D Answer D is correct because, in Lines 2-3, Emerson clearly identifies that he "spent a long summer day in exploring the Mammoth Cave in Kentucky." Answers A, B, and C are all incorrect with no textual basis because Maine and the Dakotas are never mentioned in the passage.

Passage 4 ("There is a current impression..."):

39. D Answer D is the best choice because the author establishes a satirical tone from the very first paragraph of the passage (Lines 6-8) and maintains it throughout as he discusses "typical domestic worry" (Line 33). Answer A is incorrect because the author does not make any scientific analysis of hats blowing in the wind but rather uses it as a metaphor and an amusing visual image. Answer B is incorrect and fails to recognize the author's sarcasm when he describes hat-chasing as a potential sport of the future in Lines 22-33. Answer C is incorrect because the author does not present a long list, but instead focuses on hat-chasing and expands on that at length.

40. A Answer A is correct because in Lines 4-5, the author writes, "Not merely because it is running, and running exhausts one" before using the example of sports to show why running cannot be the irritating problem with hat-chasing. Answer B is incorrect because the author does not characterize people as being irritated with sports, rather suggesting that they participate in sports "eagerly" (Line 7). Answer C is not the best answer because, although the author is certainly suggesting that sports are no less ridiculous than chasing a hat, the answer fails to connect either idea to irritation, which is one of the main points of the passage. Answer D is incorrect because hat-chasing is never identified as an actual sport in the passage and only provided as a sarcastic example.

41. C Answer C is correct because Lines 39-41 explain that the author wants to thank the old man because of "how much unaffected pleasure his every gesture and bodily attitude were at that moment giving to the crowd." Answer A is incorrect because the author is not amused by the man's athleticism, but rather the silly visual of watching him chase his hat through the park.

Answer B cannot be correct because the author never describes specifically whether the old man looked irritated or not. Answer D is also incorrect because there is absolutely nothing in the text to suggest whether or not the old man was a military veteran.

42. B Answer B is correct because immediately before saying "The same principle can be applied..." (Line 42), the author is describing the story of enjoying the old man chase his hat in the park. The "principle" in question is the ability to see the fun or amusement in activities that might be frustrating or irritating, such as chasing a hat in the wind. Answer A is incorrect because the author never states that the hat in the example got away or was uncatchable. Answer C is incorrect because it fails to identify the sarcasm of the author suggesting hat-chasing as an actual sport. Answer D is also incorrect because the passage makes no mention of swearing, profanity, or foul language in any way.

43. D Answer D is correct because the author does not mention school anywhere in the passage. Answer A cannot be correct because the example of a hat in the wind is used pervasively throughout the entire passage. Answer B cannot be correct because the author describes the annoyance of chasing a job in Lines 16-17. Answer C cannot be correct either because the author describes the frustration of a jammed drawer in Lines 53-54.

44. B Answer B is the best choice because in Lines 20-21, the author identifies hunting as a fun activity that people are not irritated by, but rather enjoy, saying, "He might regard himself as a jolly huntsman pursuing a wild animal." The author suggests that, by regarding their hat chase as a hunt, people might enjoy it more because they typically enjoy hunting. Answer A is incorrect because it is completely contrary to the author's main idea that people should be less irritated by mundane activities such as chasing a hat or getting a fly out of milk. Answer C incorrectly assumes that the author is suggesting people literally go hunting in the woods rather than imagining their hat chase as a "hunt." Answer D is incorrect because wealth or social class is irrelevant to the author's point and not mentioned in the passage.

Passage 5 ("The attorney general of the United States..."):

45. A Answer A is the best choice because the attorney general is the overarching topic of each paragraph in the passage. Answer B is not as good a choice as Answer A because the passage does much more than simply explain the origins of the job. Answer C is incorrect because the passage does not expound on the nature of the law, but rather introduces the idea of the attorney general. Answer D is incorrect because, while the passage states appearing before the court to represent the government is one of the attorney general's roles, the passage does not provide any examples of situations in which that would be necessary.

46. C Answer C is correct because Lines 19-21 clearly state, "The attorney general is made the head of the department of justice, being chief law officer of the executive branch of government?" Answer A is incorrect because Lines 46-49 establish that although the attorney general may have some role in appointing judges, it is not his or her primary responsibility. Answer B is incorrect because the attorney general is a lawyer, and it is the job of a judge, not a lawyer to make court decisions. Nowhere in the text does it claim the attorney general makes court decisions. Answer D is also incorrect because Line 25 establishes that the attorney general is head legal council to the executive branch, not the legislative branch.

47. **B** Answer B is the best choice because Lines 5-18 describe how the office of attorney general was created to make the legal system more consistent. Lines 12-16 state: "One leading reason for creating a department of justice was to bring about uniformity in the construction and application of the laws, which had not been realized under the previously existing system." Answer A is incorrect because, while the attorney general advises the president, the existence of the job does not give the president more power. Answer C is not the best choice because the office of attorney general was created for a clear purpose as outlined in Lines 5-18, not simply to fill out a new position. Answer D is incorrect because the "size" of government is never mentioned in the passage whatsoever.

48. **D** Answer D is correct because Lines 1-4 state "The attorney general of the United States, although his office was created by congress as early as Sept. 24, 1789, was not made the head of a department until June 22, 1870," communicating to the reader that the position existed, albeit not in as powerful a capacity, prior to 1870. Answer A is incorrect because Lines 5-18 establish that the legal system was actually more convoluted before the introduction of the attorney general. Answers B and C are also incorrect because the text plainly states the office was created as early as September 24, 1789, almost 90 years before 1870.

49. **D** Answer D is correct because, while Lines 46-49 state that the attorney general has some role in appointing judges, it says nothing about training them. Answer A cannot be correct because Line 32 identifies that the attorney general sometimes argues cases before the Supreme Court. Answer B is incorrect because Line 51 clearly states the attorney general is in charge of salaries for his or her subordinates. Answer C is also incorrect because Lines 27-28 establish that "He is the representative of the United States in all matters involving legal questions."

50. **A** Answer A is the best choice because Lines 27-28 establish that the attorney general is the legal representative of the United States, so he or she must understand the law, and Lines 41-50 describe the attorney general's responsibilities as a supervisor of a variety of professionals, so management experience is clearly necessary as well. Answer B is incorrect because, while law is crucial to the attorney general's job, the passage establishes that the attorney general is not a legislator, so politics would not be a key area of expertise. Answer C is incorrect because the attorney general does not govern in any way but simply advises the government on legal issues. Answer D is also incorrect because, while the attorney general certainly should be educated, they do not need any particular knowledge of school to do their job.

Passage 6 ("When we read in history that...")

51. **C** Answer C is the best choice because the first two paragraph tell the stories of people who felt regret or sadness when their enemy or rival was finally killed. The final paragraph explores and expands on this idea, making it the overall theme of the entire passage. Answers A and B are both incorrect because the passage does not address the relationship between rivals when both of them are alive; it simply focuses on what happens when one of them is permanently out of the picture. Answer D is not the best answer because it fails to identify what event the passage is saying can cause both joy and sadness: the death of an enemy.

52. **B** Answer B is correct because Lines 1-4 establish that the head of King Pyrrhus was given to Antigonous by his son. Answer A is incorrect because it completely reverses the events of the sentence, making Pyrrhus the victor rather than the loser. Answer C is incorrect because D'Auray is identified is identified in Line 8 as the name of a battle, not a person. Answer D is also incorrect because Caesar is represented in a struggle against Pompey, and the wording of the question indicates that only Pyrrhus or Antigonous (Answer A or B) can possibly be correct.

53. **D** Answer D is correct because Lines 13-16 quote Petrarch as saying, "And thus it happens that the mind of each veils its passion under a different appearance. Melancholy beneath a smiling visage, happy beneath a somber air," describing how people's outward appearance may hide ("veil") how they actually feel. Answer A is incorrect because Petrarch is describing someone's relationship to their own inner feelings, not anybody else's. Answer B is incorrect because the lines do not specifically mention killing one's enemy but simply reflect on the nature of our reactions to events. Answer C is incorrect because Lines 13-16 suggest that people cannot help but lie in this way. The phrase "thus it happens that the mind of each" suggests that this is a universal problem it's very difficult to avoid making.

54. **D** Answer D is correct because the passage never describes that Caesar and Pompey had family connections. Answer A cannot be correct because Line 23 mentions "so near an alliance" between the two. Answer B cannot be correct because Line 22 describes the two as having "so many mutual offices." Answer D cannot be correct because Line 21 mentions the two being similar in their "management of the public affairs."

55. **A** Answer A is the best choice because the examples of Pyrrhus and Antigonous, Montfort and de Blois, and Caesar and Pompey all contain situations in which the winner identified heavily with his rival. The passage explores the pain of eliminating somebody so close to oneself, much like the pain people endure when they are in conflict with a close friend. Answers B and C are both incorrect because the passage focuses on people who feel sad, not happy, at the events that unfold. Answer D is incorrect because the passage does not discuss anger at all, but rather focuses on melancholy.

56. B Answer B is the best choice because each anecdote in the passage identifies the winner as weeping tears of sadness at the news of his fallen rival. Lines 1-4 establish that Antigonous "wept" because he was "much displeased." Lines 5-13 establish that Montfort was "very much afflicted" at his rival's death. Lines 17-25 establish that Caesar felt Pompey's head was "a sad and unpleasing object." Each of these stories points to the idea that the winner of the rivalry was sad and distraught to see his opponent dead. Answer A is incorrect because the whole point of the passage is that none of these leaders felt the happiness people expected when their rival was dead. Answer C is incorrect because nobody is presented as confused in the passage; the leaders are simply heartbroken in spite of their victories. Answer D is also incorrect because the author never establishes what any of these leaders did after their victories over rival, so there is nothing in the passage that implies determination moving forward.

57. C Answer C is correct because paragraph 3 discusses how our bodies and souls can have a variety of competing, even contradictory, desires. Lines 26-30 of the original passage contain the best and clearest presentation of this key idea. Answer A is incorrect because the passage contains a variety of situations in which people experienced regret or felt that they had made a mistake. Answer B is incorrect because, as the passage illustrates, many people still experience sadness or feelings of dissatisfaction, even when they followed their gut and pursued their goals. Answer D is also incorrect because the existence of competing feelings is not proof that both viewpoints should be discounted. Throughout the passage, chasing palpable, competitive goals and having empathy for one's opponents are held up as equally important and valid, with neither representing weakness.

Practice Test 4 (Answers and Explanations)

1. **B** $\sqrt{25} + \sqrt{64} = 5 + 8 = 13$

2. **C** Simplifying this equation gives

$2r = 100$

$r = 50$

The answer is C.

3. **C** A square with a perimeter of 16 has a side length of a fourth of the perimeter. So the side length is 4. To find the area of that square, we must square the side length, giving us 16 again.

The answer is C.

4. **B** A number whose square is 81 is 9. 10% of 9 is 0.9 or answer B.

5. **D** The range is just the difference between the largest and smallest number. This is just 12 – 1 or 11. The answer is D.

6. **C** If P is the perimeter, and A is the area, we must find A in terms of P. We must divide P by 4 to get the side length of the square. Then we must square that value. This gives us $\frac{P^2}{16}$ or answer C.

7. **C** It takes Anayet 30 minutes to travel from his workplace to home. So it takes him 60 minutes to travel from his home to his workplace. In total, he spends 90 minutes traveling, and since the distance between his home to his workplace is 45 miles, the total distance for the round trip is 90 miles.

His average speed is 1 mi/ min. The answer is C.

8. **D** Dividing by a gives us answer choice D.

$$\frac{(a^2 + a)}{a} = a + 1$$

9. **D** Sarah knows that the coin is a trick coin with only heads on both sides. So her expected probability of the coin landing on heads is 1. John's expected probability is 0.5. 1 is two times bigger than 0.5.

The answer is D.

10. **A** 0 is the number that when added to any number, doesn't change that number's value. Squaring 0 gives 0 still.

The answer is A.

11. **D** Be careful. The question asks for how many nonzero numbers are between 3 and 5. There are an infinite number of numbers between those two integers.

The answer is D.

12. **C** We know that the diameter of the circle must be 4. So, the side length of the square is also 4. We can use the Pythagorean Theorem to find the length of the diagonal of the square. This gives us $4\sqrt{2}$ or answer C.

13. **C** There are 6 integers between 0 and 5 inclusive and 4 integers between 1 and 6 inclusive. The absolute value of the difference between 6 and 4 is 2. The answer is C.

14. **B** If every three steps he takes, he rotates 30°, then if he took 18 steps, he rotated 30° 6 times. 6 times 30° is 180 degrees, which is a half of a full revolution. The answer is B.

15. **B** We must find 20% of 20 first. That is 4. Then we must take 20% of 4, which is 0.8. The answer is B.

16. **B** The sequence, 3, 5, 7 adds up to 15. The difference between 7 and 3 is 4. The answer is B.

17. **B** In 10 days, the goo decreased by 2 half lives. So each half life is 5 days. The answer is B.

18. **C** Here, we must realize that the numerator is a difference of perfect squares. That allows us to write,

$$\frac{(9^2 - 8^2)(9^2 + 8^2)}{9^2 + 8^2} = 9^2 - 8^2 = 81 - 64 = 17$$

The answer is C.

19. **B** Jackie puts a penny away every 2 minutes. Right after the first 2 minutes, 50% of the jug is filled. She puts 1 penny in the jar at that moment. Then she starts to fill 50% of the empty space left. Well, there is 50% of empty space left, so she starts to reach the filling of 75% of the jug. But before she fills 75% of the jug, the jug already has less than 30% of empty space left. So, she is just left with 1 penny at that instant.

The answer is B.

Explanations to each problem on:
Youtube.com/ArgoBrothers

MATHEMATICS
ANSWERS & EXPLANATIONS

ARGO
BROTHERS
www.argobrothers.com

20. **D** We see that for every 4 triangles, we need 2 circles to balance it. In other words, we need 2 triangles for every circle. We also need 1 square for every 2 triangles. Therefore, there is a one to one ratio between the number of circles and squares. So we need 70 circles to balance 70 squares. The answer is D.

21. **B** $(\frac{2}{9})$ is the same as $.\overline{2}$. Solving for the missing number gives us. $\overline{3} = \frac{1}{3}$.
The answer is B.

22. **A** Factoring 232, gives us $2^3 \cdot 29$.
The answer is A.

23. **C** We can take note of the sequence that each symbol takes. The 6th symbol is also the 12th symbol and the 18th symbol and so on. The 438th symbol will be divisible by 6 as well. This means that the 6th symbol is also the 432nd symbol and therefore the 438th symbol as well.

The answer is C.

24. **C** Cross multiplying gives,
$32x = pt$ and solving for t gives,
$$t = \frac{32x}{p}$$
The answer is C.

25. **C** $(\frac{52}{3})$ equates to $17.\overline{3}$ and the least integer greater than that is 18.
The answer is C.

26. **C** $5^5 + 5^5 + 5^5 + 5^5 + 5^5 = 5(5^5) = 5^{a+1}$
so then:
$a + 1 = 6$ and $a = 5$.
The answer is C.

27. **D** We know that, $(x^2 + y^2) = x^2 + 2xy + y^2$ and if this is to equal $x^2 + y^2$, then $2xy$ must be equal to 0. In other words, $xy = 0$.

The answer is D.

28. **A** Two circles can intersect at 2 points at maximum.

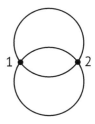

29. **C** The cumulative product of the set $\{1, 2, 3, 0\}$ is the sequence, 1, 2, 6, 0. The mean of this sequence is the sum of the terms divided by the number of terms in the sequence. This equates to $(\frac{9}{4})$ or 2.25. The answer is C.

30. **B** The only nonpositive, nonnegative integer is 0. So the answer is 1.

    The answer is B.

31. **A** A chord must touch the circle at two points. The only segment that does this is the diameter. The answer is A.

32. **C** $y(x) = 0$ at only 2 points, B and E, which are at the roots of the function.

    The answer is C.

33. **B** Using the fact that there is 30° between every two consecutive ticks on the clock, we can see that at 2:00, 60 ° is formed between the hands.

    The answer is B.

34. **D** The answer to this question depends on the number of marbles in the bag.

    The answer is D.

35. **D** The expression can be rewritten as, $(36)(36) - 36 = 36(36 - 1) = 36(35)$ and since $a = 35$, then we have,

    $(a + 1)(a) = a^2 + a$.

    The answer is D.

36. **C** Equating the two perimeters for the octagon and circle respectively gives, $8a = 2\pi r$ and solving for r gives,

    $$r = \frac{4a}{\pi}$$

    The answer is C.

37. **A** The greatest integer less than 1.5 is 1 and the least integer greater than 1 is 2. The answer is A.

38. **C** We know that, $\tau = 2\pi$ and the area of the semicircle is, $\frac{\pi r^2}{2}$.

    Solving for π and plugging in the area gives, $\frac{\tau r^2}{4}$.

    The answer is C.

39. **D** If $F = -kx$, then either k or x must be negative since F is greater than 0. We do not know which is negative, so we cannot determine a definite answer. The answer is D.

40. **C** We must square the side length to get the area.

    $(7^a)^2 = 7^{2a}$

    The answer is C.

41. **B** Set the two radii equal to each other and solve for x.

    Plug the value of x back into one of the expressions for the radius to solve for r. We have the expression $2x$. Plugging in the value of x gives us $12 \cdot 2 = 24$.

The radius of the circle is 24.

The dotted section represents a fourth of the whole circumference which is $\frac{2\pi(24)}{4} = 12\pi$.

The answer is 12π or answer choice B.

42. C The value of x must be a positive fraction, so the smallest value in the set would be the one that takes x to the highest power. The answer is C.

43. B There are 360° that the hands must move to complete a full revolution and to be at the same time of 5:35. If every 15°, 5 minutes passes, then (24 • 5) minutes will have passed by the time it is 5:35 again. This is 2 hours.

The answer is B.

44. B This equation simplifies to,

$x^2 - 4 = ax^2 + bx - c$ and,

$a = 1$
$b = 0$
$c = -4$

so the sum of a, b and c is -3. The answer is B.

45. C This question requires to count the steps. It is only after 17 steps does Natalie reach the 7 step distance from point A.

The answer is C.

46. B We must pick a value of n that makes the expression 0, since 0 is neither positive nor negative. This occurs when n is the negative of m. The answer is B.

$C(m + -m) = 0$

47. D The third side cannot be uniquely determined since we do not know if these two sides are legs of the hypotenuse or if one of the sides is a hypotenuse. The answer is D.

48. B $2 + (\frac{1}{3}) = (\frac{7}{3})$ and multiplying the numerator and denominator of $(\frac{7}{3})$ by 2 gives $(\frac{14}{6})$. Equating this with $(\frac{14}{b})$ gives that $b = 6$. The answer is B.

49. D If h doubles, then V gets multiplied by a factor of 2. If r triples, then V gets multiplied by a factor of 9 since we are squaring r. We multiply 2 and 9 to get 18. The answer is D.

50. D The answer cannot be uniquely determined since we do not know if x is negative or positive.

51. A Formula for percent decrease is:

$$\frac{\text{Original Number} - \text{New Number}}{\text{Original Number}} \times 100$$
= Percent Decrease

$$\frac{280,000 - 240,000}{280,000} \times 100 = 14.3\%$$

52. B To find the median, rearrange the numbers from lowest to greatest.

230000, 240000, 240000, 260000,

YouTube
Explanations to each problem on:
Youtube.com/ArgoBrothers

MATHEMATICS
ANSWERS & EXPLANATIONS

ARGO
BROTHERS
www.argobrothers.com

280000

The median value is 240,000 and by increasing it by 10% gives us 240,000 x 1.1 = 264,000. Therefore, the correct answer choice is B.

53. 8 You are given a composite function question where you first have to plug in the value of 8 to the function $f(x)$.

$f(8) = 8^2 + \sqrt[3]{8}$
$f(8) = 64 + 2$
$f(8) = 66$

$g(66) = \sqrt{66 - 2}$
$g(66) = \sqrt{64}$
$g(66) = \boxed{8}$

54. 1,824

You are given that the perimeter is equal to 172. The formula for finding the permitter of a rectangle is $2(l) \times 2(w) = P$. We are given both the length and width and plugging that into the formula gives us :

$2(3x - 1) + 2(3x + 9) = 172$.

Now simplify and solve for x.

$6x - 2 + 6x + 18 = 172$
$12x + 16 = 172$
$12x = 156$
$x = 13$

Plug the value of x back into the expression for length and width to find the respective measurements.

Length: $3(13) - 1 = 38$
Width: $3(13) + 9 = 48$

The question asks you to find the area. Formula for the area of a rectangle is length x width. The length is 38 and

width is 48. $38 \times 48 = 1,824$.

55. 0.5 This is a probability question. No matter how many times you flip a coin, you will always have a $\frac{1}{2}$ or 0.5 chance of getting Heads or Tails. Therefore, the answer is 0.5.

56. 40 If we draw a diagram for this question, it is easy to see that a right triangle is formed and the pythagorean theorem must be used to find the length of how high up the building wall can be reached by the crane.

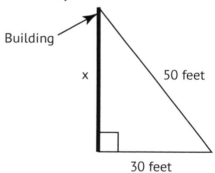

$x^2 + 30^2 = 50^2$
$x = 40$

You should know that 3, 4, 5 or any multiples of 3, 4, 5 in the same order is a Pythagorean triplet. Knowing this will save you time on the exam as calculations are not necessary.

57. −4 Cross multiply $(x + 3)$ and 12 to get $12x + 36$.

You now have the following equation.
$12x + 36 = x - 8$
Solve for x
$x = -4$

Practice Test 5
SHSAT

This exam is 3 hours long. Try to take this full exam in one sitting to simulate real test conditions.

While taking this exam, refrain from hearing music or watching T.V.

Please note, calculators are not permitted! You are permitted to answer questions in any order you see fit.

Allocate your test time accordingly.

Concentrate and GOOD LUCK!

SHSAT PRACTICE TEST 5
ANSWER SHEET

ENGLISH LANGUAGE ARTS

1. Ⓐ Ⓑ Ⓒ Ⓓ
2. Ⓐ Ⓑ Ⓒ Ⓓ
3. Ⓐ Ⓑ Ⓒ Ⓓ
4. Ⓐ Ⓑ Ⓒ Ⓓ
5. Ⓐ Ⓑ Ⓒ Ⓓ
6. Ⓐ Ⓑ Ⓒ Ⓓ
7. Ⓐ Ⓑ Ⓒ Ⓓ
8. Ⓐ Ⓑ Ⓒ Ⓓ
9. Ⓐ Ⓑ Ⓒ Ⓓ
10. Ⓐ Ⓑ Ⓒ Ⓓ
11. Ⓐ Ⓑ Ⓒ Ⓓ
12. Ⓐ Ⓑ Ⓒ Ⓓ
13. Ⓐ Ⓑ Ⓒ Ⓓ
14. Ⓐ Ⓑ Ⓒ Ⓓ
15. Ⓐ Ⓑ Ⓒ Ⓓ
16. Ⓐ Ⓑ Ⓒ Ⓓ
17. Ⓐ Ⓑ Ⓒ Ⓓ
18. Ⓐ Ⓑ Ⓒ Ⓓ
19. Ⓐ Ⓑ Ⓒ Ⓓ
20. Ⓐ Ⓑ Ⓒ Ⓓ
21. Ⓐ Ⓑ Ⓒ Ⓓ
22. Ⓐ Ⓑ Ⓒ Ⓓ
23. Ⓐ Ⓑ Ⓒ Ⓓ
24. Ⓐ Ⓑ Ⓒ Ⓓ
25. Ⓐ Ⓑ Ⓒ Ⓓ
26. Ⓐ Ⓑ Ⓒ Ⓓ
27. Ⓐ Ⓑ Ⓒ Ⓓ
28. Ⓐ Ⓑ Ⓒ Ⓓ
29. Ⓐ Ⓑ Ⓒ Ⓓ
30. Ⓐ Ⓑ Ⓒ Ⓓ
31. Ⓐ Ⓑ Ⓒ Ⓓ
32. Ⓐ Ⓑ Ⓒ Ⓓ
33. Ⓐ Ⓑ Ⓒ Ⓓ
34. Ⓐ Ⓑ Ⓒ Ⓓ
35. Ⓐ Ⓑ Ⓒ Ⓓ
36. Ⓐ Ⓑ Ⓒ Ⓓ
37. Ⓐ Ⓑ Ⓒ Ⓓ
38. Ⓐ Ⓑ Ⓒ Ⓓ
39. Ⓐ Ⓑ Ⓒ Ⓓ
40. Ⓐ Ⓑ Ⓒ Ⓓ
41. Ⓐ Ⓑ Ⓒ Ⓓ
42. Ⓐ Ⓑ Ⓒ Ⓓ
43. Ⓐ Ⓑ Ⓒ Ⓓ
44. Ⓐ Ⓑ Ⓒ Ⓓ
45. Ⓐ Ⓑ Ⓒ Ⓓ
46. Ⓐ Ⓑ Ⓒ Ⓓ
47. Ⓐ Ⓑ Ⓒ Ⓓ
48. Ⓐ Ⓑ Ⓒ Ⓓ
49. Ⓐ Ⓑ Ⓒ Ⓓ
50. Ⓐ Ⓑ Ⓒ Ⓓ
51. Ⓐ Ⓑ Ⓒ Ⓓ
52. Ⓐ Ⓑ Ⓒ Ⓓ
53. Ⓐ Ⓑ Ⓒ Ⓓ
54. Ⓐ Ⓑ Ⓒ Ⓓ
55. Ⓐ Ⓑ Ⓒ Ⓓ
56. Ⓐ Ⓑ Ⓒ Ⓓ
57. Ⓐ Ⓑ Ⓒ Ⓓ

MATHEMATICS

1. Ⓐ Ⓑ Ⓒ Ⓓ
2. Ⓐ Ⓑ Ⓒ Ⓓ
3. Ⓐ Ⓑ Ⓒ Ⓓ
4. Ⓐ Ⓑ Ⓒ Ⓓ
5. Ⓐ Ⓑ Ⓒ Ⓓ
6. Ⓐ Ⓑ Ⓒ Ⓓ
7. Ⓐ Ⓑ Ⓒ Ⓓ
8. Ⓐ Ⓑ Ⓒ Ⓓ
9. Ⓐ Ⓑ Ⓒ Ⓓ
10. Ⓐ Ⓑ Ⓒ Ⓓ
11. Ⓐ Ⓑ Ⓒ Ⓓ
12. Ⓐ Ⓑ Ⓒ Ⓓ
13. Ⓐ Ⓑ Ⓒ Ⓓ
14. Ⓐ Ⓑ Ⓒ Ⓓ
15. Ⓐ Ⓑ Ⓒ Ⓓ
16. Ⓐ Ⓑ Ⓒ Ⓓ
17. Ⓐ Ⓑ Ⓒ Ⓓ
18. Ⓐ Ⓑ Ⓒ Ⓓ
19. Ⓐ Ⓑ Ⓒ Ⓓ
20. Ⓐ Ⓑ Ⓒ Ⓓ
21. Ⓐ Ⓑ Ⓒ Ⓓ
22. Ⓐ Ⓑ Ⓒ Ⓓ
23. Ⓐ Ⓑ Ⓒ Ⓓ
24. Ⓐ Ⓑ Ⓒ Ⓓ
25. Ⓐ Ⓑ Ⓒ Ⓓ
26. Ⓐ Ⓑ Ⓒ Ⓓ
27. Ⓐ Ⓑ Ⓒ Ⓓ
28. Ⓐ Ⓑ Ⓒ Ⓓ
29. Ⓐ Ⓑ Ⓒ Ⓓ
30. Ⓐ Ⓑ Ⓒ Ⓓ
31. Ⓐ Ⓑ Ⓒ Ⓓ
32. Ⓐ Ⓑ Ⓒ Ⓓ
33. Ⓐ Ⓑ Ⓒ Ⓓ
34. Ⓐ Ⓑ Ⓒ Ⓓ
35. Ⓐ Ⓑ Ⓒ Ⓓ
36. Ⓐ Ⓑ Ⓒ Ⓓ
37. Ⓐ Ⓑ Ⓒ Ⓓ
38. Ⓐ Ⓑ Ⓒ Ⓓ
39. Ⓐ Ⓑ Ⓒ Ⓓ
40. Ⓐ Ⓑ Ⓒ Ⓓ
41. Ⓐ Ⓑ Ⓒ Ⓓ
42. Ⓐ Ⓑ Ⓒ Ⓓ
43. Ⓐ Ⓑ Ⓒ Ⓓ
44. Ⓐ Ⓑ Ⓒ Ⓓ
45. Ⓐ Ⓑ Ⓒ Ⓓ
46. Ⓐ Ⓑ Ⓒ Ⓓ
47. Ⓐ Ⓑ Ⓒ Ⓓ
48. Ⓐ Ⓑ Ⓒ Ⓓ
49. Ⓐ Ⓑ Ⓒ Ⓓ
50. Ⓐ Ⓑ Ⓒ Ⓓ
51. Ⓐ Ⓑ Ⓒ Ⓓ
52. Ⓐ Ⓑ Ⓒ Ⓓ

MATHEMATICS (GRID IN)

53.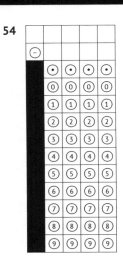
54.
55.
56.
57.

311

DIRECTIONS: For questions 1 to 5, you will be asked to recognize and correct errors in sentences or short paragraphs.

1. Read this sentence.

> The water cycle has three main steps evaporation, condensation, and precipitation.

Which of the choices below is the best revision of the sentence?

A. The water cycle has three main steps: evaporation, condensation, and precipitation.

B. The water cycle has three main steps (evaporation, condensation, and precipitation).

C. The water cycle has three main steps, and those steps are evaporation, condensation, and precipitation.

D. The water cycle has three main steps; evaporation, condensation, and precipitation.

2. Read this paragraph.

> (1) The First Amendment famously promises that the government will not limit the people's freedom of speech. (2) It also guarantees that the government cannot establish an official religion or limit the practice of any religions that citizens might believe in. (3) The First Amendment goes on to establish citizens also have the rights to assemble to spread ideas and petition the government to make changes. (4) Finally, a free press is legally protected to help ensure that the other rights are safeguarded.

Which sentence could be added before Sentence 1 as a topic sentence?

A. The Bill of Rights contains the first ten amendments to the Constitution of the United States.

B. The First Amendment provides five basic freedoms for citizens.

C. The Founding Fathers believed it was important for people to be protected from government.

D. The First Amendment is the most important part of the Bill of Rights.

CONTINUE ON TO THE NEXT PAGE →

3. Read this paragraph.

(1) The Charles River in Boston, Massachusetts is a haven for rowers from all around the world. (2) On any given day, amateur paddlers and collegiate competitors rows side by side. (3) Each October since 1965, the Head of the Charles Regatta has attracted the top rowers from the United States and beyond to compete in a variety of races. (4) Competitors are grouped into a variety of classes based on age, experience level, and number of rowers. (5) More than 11,000 rowers participate in the Head of the Charles over its two-day span.

Which sentence should be revised to correct a subject-verb agreement error?

A. Sentence 2
B. Sentence 3
C. Sentence 4
D. Sentence 5

4. Read this paragraph.

(1) Hockey is surprisingly popular in the United States in spite of the fact that most people consider football and baseball to be far more "American." (2) Even in warm weather cities like San Jose and Los Angeles, hockey has won over many American fans. (3) Conversely, some Americans think of hockey as being a Canadian sport. (4) In areas like New England and Minnesota, recreational hockey leagues dominate basketball and softball in popularity.

How could Sentence 2 and Sentence 3 best be combined to clarify the relationship between ideas?

A. Even in warm weather cities like San Jose and Los Angeles, hockey has won over many American fans, but conversely, some Americans think of hockey as being a Canadian sport.
B. Even in warm weather cities like San Jose and Los Angeles, hockey has won over many American fans even though some still think of hockey as being a Canadian sport.
C. Even in warm weather cities like San Jose and Los Angeles, hockey has won over many American fans; some still think of hockey as being a Canadian sport.
D. Even in warm weather cities like San Jose and Los Angeles, hockey has won over many American fans, although some still think of hockey as being a Canadian sport.

5. Read this paragraph.

(1) Every Fourth of July, people across the nation celebrate the birth of the United States of America. (2) Familes around the country practice a variety of traditions including backyard barbecues, frolicking in public parks, and coming together at night for fireworks. (3) Americans never lost sight of what July Fourth is all about, though. (4) People still take time to recognize the wisdom of the Founding Fathers and the bravery of early patriots.

Which sentence should be revised to correct an inconsistent verb tense?

A. Sentence 1
B. Sentence 2
C. Sentence 3
D. Sentence 4

CONTINUE ON TO THE NEXT PAGE →

ENGLISH LANGUAGE ARTS
Practice Test 5

DIRECTIONS: Read the passage below to answer questions 6 to 13. The questions will focus on improving the writing quality of the passage to follow the conventions of standard written English.

School Segregation

(1) Slavery in the United States officially ended with the Emancipation Proclamation of 1863. (2) Even though they were no longer slaves, black southerners were still discriminated against in many fundamental ways. (3) One example of this prejudiced treatment is the segregation of public schools throughout the South. (4) School segregation meant that black and white students had to go to separate schools. (5) The system lasted from about 1877 until 1954.

(6) In 1896, the Supreme Court ruled that racial segregation of schools was legal as long as the conditions were "separate but equal." (7) Conditions in black schools were consistently worse throughout the history of segregation. (8) The white public school system, on the other hand, was propped up with millions of dollars of additional taxpayer funding and had preferential access to the best teachers, materials, and facilities.

(9) Formal segregation was ruled illegal by the Supreme Court in 1954 in the famous decision *Brown vs. Board of Education of Topeka*. (10) The court explained in their majority decision that having separate educational facilities for each race was inherently unequal. (11) While *Brown vs. Board* ended government-sanctioned school segregation, the issue did not disappear instantly. (12) Schools throughout the South dragged their feet on integration for years, making it a drawn out, painful process for many southerners, black and white. (13) Today, education cannot be legally segregated, but schools in historically black neighborhoods are still some of the most underserved in the nation.

6. Which revision eliminates the use of passive voice in Sentence 2

   A. Black southerners were discriminated against in many fundamental ways, even though they were no longer slaves.
   B. Black southerners, no longer slaves, were discriminated against in many fundamental ways.
   C. White southerners continued to discriminate against their black neighbors, even though they were no longer slaves.
   D. Black people were discriminated against throughout the South, even though they were no longer slaves.

CONTINUE ON TO THE NEXT PAGE →

7. Which revision is necessary to correct Sentence 3?

   A. Change **this** to **these**

   B. Change **is** to **was**

   C. Change **throughout** to **in**

   D. Change **South** to **south**

---

8. What is the best way to combine Sentence 4 and Sentence 5 to clarify the relationship between ideas?

   A. School segregation, which lasted from about 1877 to 1954, meant that black and white students had to go to separate schools.

   B. From 1877 to 1954, school segregation existed, which meant that black and white students had to go to separate schools.

   C. White and black students had to go to separate schools from about 1877 to 1954, and that system was known as segregation.

   D. The system that lasted from about 1877 to 1954 was called school segregation, and that meant that white and black students had to go to separate schools.

---

9. Which transition should be added to the beginning of Sentence 7?

   A. Therefore

   B. Consequently

   C. For example

   D. However

10. Which sentence would best follow and support Sentence 7?

   A. Imagine how the students in segregated schools must have felt when they saw the huge differences between black and white schools.

   B. Black schools were faced with a shortage of qualified teachers, a lack of quality textbooks, and minimal government funding to maintain their facilities.

   C. This lack of institutional support made many people in black communities around the country feel neglected and rejected.

   D. Overall, this shabby treatment reduced African Americans' chances to better their lives.

---

11. Which sentence would best follow Sentence 8 to serve as a conclusion sentence for the second paragraph?

   A. Many people felt something had to be done to fix these conditions.

   B. Seventeen different states had formal school segregation programs.

   C. These disparities were clearly unequal, meaning that segregation was not only cruel but also illegal.

   D. Several organizations, including the United Nations, realized that this system was unjust.

CONTINUE ON TO THE NEXT PAGE ➞

12. What kind of error needs to be corrected in Sentence 10?

   A. Pronoun Agreement

   B. Subject-Verb Agreement

   C. Passive Voice

   D. Dangling modifier

---

13. Which revision eliminates the use of "to be" verbs in Sentence 13?

   A. Segregation is illegal today, but schools in historically black neighborhoods are still some of the most underserved in the nation.

   B. Today, education cannot be legally segregated, but schools in historically black neighborhoods are still some of the most underserved in the nation.

   C. Legal racial segregation is over, but schools in historically black neighborhoods still have some of the most underserved schools in the nation.

   D. Today, even without a legal framework for school segregation, historically black schools remain some of the most underserved in the nation.

CONTINUE ON TO THE NEXT PAGE ➡

ENGLISH LANGUAGE ARTS
Practice Test 5

DIRECTIONS: Read the passage below to answer questions 14 to 20. The questions will focus on improving the writing quality of the passage to follow the conventions of standard written English.

The Hero's Journey

(1) The best stories are all unique, but many of them are also very similar. (2) Created by Joseph Campbell in 1949, the Hero's Journey explores how stories throughout history, from ancient times to today, almost always follow the same general structure. (3) According to Campbell most stories involve a hero, going on a journey, to resolve a conflict in their life or world. (4) Throughout the course of the journey, the hero faces challenges that cause him or her to grow and change.

(5) The Hero's Journey is broken into very specific steps. (6) First; the hero receives a "call to adventure" then the hero gets advice from a wise mentor, usually an older character, before beginning his or her journey. (7) As the hero journeys into the unknown, he or she must overcome a series of increasingly changing obstacles. (8) At some point in the story, the hero experiences a heartbreaking loss, such as the deaths of a friend, which he or she must overcome. (9) When the hero reaches the climax of his or her journey, he or she experiences a fundamental change, either physically, emotionally, or personally. (10) This change empowers the hero to resolve the conflict that drove him or her since the beginning of the story.

(11) While Campbell created the Hero's Journey to help analyze ancient stories, it is still relevant to writers today. (12) The Hero's Journey has been used to write many successful books and movies. (13) George Lucas, the creator of Star Wars and the character Indiana Jones, sights Campbell as one of his biggest influences. (14) Without the Hero's Journey, our understanding of stories, both new and old, would be significantly different.

14. Which revision of Sentence 2 eliminates the dangling modifier?

- **A.** Created by Joseph Campbell in 1949, the Hero's Journey explores how the same general structure has almost always been used from ancient times to today.
- **B.** The Hero's Journey, created by Joseph Campbell in 1949, explores how stories throughout history, from ancient times to today, almost always follow the same general structure.
- **C.** Following the same general structure, most stories from ancient times to today are very similar, according to the Hero's Journey, created by Joseph Campbell in 1949.
- **D.** Created by Joseph Campbell in 1949, stories from ancient times to today always follow the same general structure, called the Hero's Journey.

CONTINUE ON TO THE NEXT PAGE →

15. Which revision of Sentence 3 corrects the use of commas?

   A. According to Campbell most stories involve a hero going on a journey to resolve a conflict in their life or world.
   B. According to Campbell most stories involve a hero going on a journey, to resolve a conflict in their life or world.
   C. According to Campbell, most stories involve a hero, going on a journey, to resolve a conflict in their life or world.
   D. According to Campbell, most stories involve a hero going on a journey to resolve a conflict in their life or world.

16. Which sentence would best follow Sentence 4 to serve as a conclusion for paragraph 1?

   A. By the end of the story, the hero becomes a new person who can help his or her community better than ever before.
   B. The Hero's Journey is often depicted using a circle.
   C. Joseph Campbell died in 1987, but his ideas live on through other scholars.
   D. Not all stories follow the Hero's Journey, though.

17. Which revision of Sentence 6 corrects the use of semicolons and commas?

   A. First; the hero receives a "call to adventure," then the hero receives advice from a wise mentor, usually an older character, before beginning his or her journey.
   B. First, the hero receives a "call to adventure," then; the hero receives advice from a wise mentor, usually an older character before beginning his or her journey.
   C. First, the hero receives a "call to adventure," then the hero receives advice from a wise mentor; usually an older character, before beginning his or her journey.
   D. First, the hero receives a "call to adventure;" then, the hero gets advice from a wise mentor, usually an older character, before beginning his or her journey.

18. Which edit is needed to correct Sentence 8?

   A. Eliminate the **comma** after **story**
   B. Change **experiences** to **experience**
   C. Change **deaths** to **death**
   D. Change **must overcome** to **overcame**

CONTINUE ON TO THE NEXT PAGE ➡

19. Which revision of Sentence 12 corrects the use of passive voice?

    A. Many successful books and movies have been written using the Hero's Journey.

    B. Many successful writers have used the Hero's Journey to create books and movies.

    C. The Hero's Journey is used to create books and movies, many of which are successful.

    D. Books and movies are often created with the Hero's Journey in mind, and many of those stories become successful.

20. Which edit is needed to correct Sentence 13?

    A. Change **sights** to **cites**

    B. Change **creator** to **creater**

    C. Change **sight** to **site**

    D. Change **influences** to **influence**

CONTINUE ON TO THE NEXT PAGE ➞

READING COMPREHENSION
Practice Test 5

DIRECTIONS: Analyze the passages below, and answer the commensurate questions. Only use information provided within the passage for your answers. There is only one answer for each question.

Long ago, when you were a little boy or a little girl – perhaps not so very long ago, either – were you never interrupted in your play by being called in to have your face washed, your hair combed, and your soiled apron exchanged for a clean one, 5 preparatory to an introduction to Mrs. Smith, or Dr. Jones, or Aunt Judkins, your mother's early friend? And after being ushered into that august presence and made to face a battery of questions which were either above or below your capacity, 10 and which you consequently despised as trash or resented as insult, did you not, as were gleefully vanishing, hear a soft sigh breathed out upon the air, "Dear child, he is seeing his happiest days?" In the concrete, it was Mrs. Smith or Dr. Jones 15 speaking of you. But going back to general principles, it was Commonplacedom expressing its opinion of childhood.

There never was a greater piece of absurdity in the world. I thought so when I was a child, and now 20 I know it; and I desire here to brand it as at once a platitude and a falsehood. How the idea gained currency, that childhood is the happiest period of life, I cannot conceive. How, once started, it kept afloat, is equally incomprehensible. I should 25 have supposed that the experience of every sane person would have given the lie to it. I should have supposed that every soul, as it burst into flower, would have hurled off the imputation.

30 I can only account for it by recurring to Lady Mary Wortley Montague's statistics, and concluding that the fools are three out of four in every person's acquaintance.

I, for one, lift up my voice emphatically against the 35 assertion and do affirm that I think childhood is the most undesirable portion of human life, and I am thankful to be well out of it. I look upon it as no better than a mitigated form of slavery. There is not a child in the land that can call his soul, or his body, 40 or his jacket his own. A little soft lump of clay, he comes into the world and is moulded into a vessel of honor or a vessel of dishonor long before he can put in a word about the matter. He has no voice as to his education or his training, what he shall 45 eat, what he shall drink, or wherewithal he shall be clothed. He has to wait upon the wisdom, the whims, and often the wickedness of other people. Imagine, my six-foot friend, how you would feel to be obliged to wear your woollen mittens when you 50 desire to bloom out in straw-colored kids, or to be buttoned into your black waistcoat when your taste leads you to select your white, or to be forced under your Kossuth hat when you had set your heart on your black beaver: yet this is what children are 55 perpetually called on to undergo. Their wills are just as strong as ours, and their tastes are stronger, yet they have to bend the one and sacrifice the other; and they do it under pressure of necessity.

CONTINUE ON TO THE NEXT PAGE →

21. What is this passage mostly about?

  A. Why it is great to be a child.
  B. Why being told what to do is bad.
  C. To prove that people are fools.
  D. To illustrate that, contrary to popular belief, childhood is the worst time of life.

22. What does the author imply about the belief that childhood is the happiest time of one's life?

  A. It is a commonly held belief.
  B. It is a lie we tell ourselves.
  C. It is never true.
  D. It is always true.

23. What do we know about the author's childhood?

  A. She was never allowed to decide what she would wear.
  B. She was never allowed to leave the house when she wanted.
  C. She did not prefer it to her adult life.
  D. She was happier at the time of her childhood.

24. What is one reason listed as to why childhood is considered by the author to be the worst time in one's life?

  A. You need to focus too much on school.
  B. You do not get to play as much as when you are an adult.
  C. You do not get to boss people around as much as when you are an adult.
  D. Many important decisions are not in your control.

25. Why does the author ask the six-foot friend to imagine needing to wear mittens?

  A. To illustrate how distasteful mittens are.
  B. To illustrate that we take for granted our right to decide mundane actions.
  C. The illusion requires a cold habitat.
  D. The author believes her friend would look good in mittens.

26. What, if true, would most strongly weaken the author's main claim?

  A. Children are given some decision making.
  B. Adults are not entirely free to decide everything.
  C. Making decisions can be tiresome.
  D. People are happiest when others decide what is good for them.

CONTINUE ON TO THE NEXT PAGE →

If you asked a group of people which verb they would use to describe how their favorite foods are made, many people would say, "They're cooked!" However, a strong percentage of people would also say, "They're baked!" Although the [5] two processes may seem very similar at first blush, cooking and baking are actually markedly different methods of creating food. Many people even say that cooking is an art, while baking is a science. Even in the culinary world, bakers [10] and chefs are prepared separately and learn completely different techniques.

Since eating is a daily necessity, cooking's clear goal is to make food that is tasty and nutritious. In order to accomplish this, chefs can call on a [15] variety of ingredients and flavor combinations to create a near infinite smorgasbord of delicious treats. By switching just a few local ingredients or incorporating a signature technique, chefs can reinvent a classic dish with a fresh, personal spin. [20] Once chefs have a clear understanding of cooking fundamentals, they are free to experiment to create bold new flavor combinations and innovative techniques.

Bakers create breads, cakes, and other treats that [25] rival the flavors of the world's finest chefs, but their road to creating delicious food is a more disciplined one. Baking involves creating dough, which must rise to be tasty and digestible. Getting that dough to rise involves facilitating specific [30] chemical reactions that require a leavening agent, such as yeast or baking soda. For the dough to rise correctly, the ratio of ingredients must be in proper proportion, or the cake, bread, or other delicious baked good will not have an appealing [35] taste, texture, or appearance.

Many great chefs are utterly terrified of baking. Since they have been trained to experiment and make adjustments on the fly, the idea of putting [40] something in an oven and walking away for half an hour can be very intimidating for them. On the other hand, many bakers find cooking to be overwhelming because there is such a wide variety of ingredients that somebody must know how to [45] use to become a great cook. Bakers love that they can create dozens of different delectable treats from a few basic ingredients like sugar, flour, salt, and water.

Baking and cooking are both crucial for mankind [50] to survive and thrive. Creating food to feed the world is a key responsibility, which cooks and bakers around the world all work hard each day to accomplish. By creating food, they are also culinary caretakers of their ethnic, regional, and [55] cultural heritage. Bakers and cooks both make the world a better place, but don't mistake them for each other!

27. Which of the following best tells what this passage is about?

   A. Baking is better than cooking because it is more scientific.

   B. Cooking is better than baking because it is more artistic.

   C. Cooking and baking are very different processes, even though they seem quite similar.

   D. Cooking and baking are both rewarding hobbies that many people enjoy.

CONTINUE ON TO THE NEXT PAGE ➡

28. Based on context clues, what is a "smorgasbord?"

   A. A regional specialty dish unique to a certain part of the world
   B. A restaurant that serves the most exotic food on earth
   C. A European cooking competition
   D. A wide array of hot and cold snacks.

29. Based on the passage, why might somebody believe that cooking is "an art?"

   A. Chefs have a great deal of freedom when they cook and can adjust to incorporate new ingredients and techniques as they work.
   B. When they cook, chefs create a plate of food that can rival the beauty of the works of famous painters.
   C. Food is a daily necessity, and without cooks, many people around the world would starve.
   D. Cooks have different individual styles and passions, whereas baking is the same all around the world.

30. Based on the passage, why might somebody believe baking is "a science?"

   A. Bakers make complex creations out of very simple, basic elements.
   B. Baking relies on creating specific reactions in proper proportion, so recipes and measurements must be precise.
   C. Baking involves using and heating a lot of glassware, as does laboratory science.

   D. Bakers have to worry about mastering the taste, texture, and appearance of their goods, which means they need a lot of complex knowledge.

31. Based on the passage, which of these processes would probably be hardest for a chef who wasn't familiar with baking?

   A. Frosting a cupcake
   B. Writing properly spaced and sized text on a cake
   C. Choosing herbs to season an herb bread
   D. Making cinnamon roll dough

32. How are cooks and bakers both "culinary caretakers of their ethnic, regional, and cultural heritage?"

   A. They create food that makes people happy and reminds them of home, family, and traditions.
   B. Cooks and bakers can get jobs at museums where they recreate food that people ate in different locations and eras.
   C. The most important part of a cook or baker's identity is their ethnic, regional, and cultural heritage.
   D. Cooks and bakers work together to feed the world, so they are unsung cultural heroes.

CONTINUE ON TO THE NEXT PAGE →

Golf is popular around the world with people of all ages, nationalities, and athletic backgrounds. Although uninitiated television viewers often assume golf is boring, millions of enthusiasts appreciate the rewarding thrill of a shot well 5 played. People enjoy golf because it provides hundreds of individual opportunities for strategizing and success. While golf may have a reputation as an exclusive game reserved for elites, it's actually one of the most straightforward 10 sports to play and understand.

The object of the game in golf is to get a small, white ball into a hole that's typically between 100 and 500 yards away. Players hit the ball with a long club, counting the number of hits, or "strokes," 15 it takes them to get from the starting point to the hole. A "round" of golf is consists of playing either nine or 18 of these holes and then tallying strokes at the end. In competitive play, the player with the lowest score wins the game; however, 20 many people also like to play golf individually and simply try to break their personal best score.

Each player is allowed to carry up to 14 different clubs to help them hit the ball different distances. Those clubs are broken into four basic groups: 25 woods, irons, wedges, and putters. Woods have bulbous metal heads (although, as their name suggests, they were once made from wood) and hit the ball the farthest, although at the lowest trajectory, of all the clubs. The biggest and longest 30 wood is called the driver, and it is typically used for the first shot of each hole. Irons are used for distances under 200 yards and are numbered in ascending order from one to nine, with higher numbers counterintuitively representing shorter 35 potential distances. Wedges are used near the green (the target area around the hole) to help players get into position to finish the hole. Each player has one putter, which is the club used 40 to actually knock the ball into the hole from short distance.

During a round of golf, players are constantly strategizing, making decisions, and attempting to put their plans into action. Before each stroke, 45 players must approximate their distance to the hole, decide which club would best fit their needs, determine the angle at which they need to line up to hit the ball, and settle on how far down they will choke on their grip. Once they've made 50 these considerations, a player must decide how full a swing to execute, since hitting the ball the maximum possible distance is not always the best decision. Of course, all this decision-making can be complicated when the mind is filled with 55 competitive anxieties, frustration, or feelings of self-doubt. For this reason, golfers must focus, clear their head, and focus on playing in the moment.

Of course, there are also a variety of external 60 factors that golfers must consider. Courses are loaded with small bodies of water, which players must keep their ball out of or suffer a penalty stroke added to their score for that hole. Sand traps, also known as bunkers, are pits of sand 65 around the course that players must hit their ball out of without letting their club touch the ground. If a player's club touches the sand, they must add a penalty stroke to their score also. These physical obstacles only add to the challenge that is golf's 70 mental game.

CONTINUE ON TO THE NEXT PAGE →

33. Which answer best describes the purpose of this passage?

   A. To show the reader why golf is better than other sports
   B. To convince the reader to try golf
   C. To provide the reader with a brief explanation of golf
   D. To tell the reader a story about golf

34. Based on the passage, why might "uninitiated television viewers often assume golf is boring?"

   A. Golf is primarily a game of internal strategizing and disciplined execution.
   B. The rules of golf are highly complex and difficult to explain to new fans.
   C. Golf requires too much athletic skill for most people to appreciate.
   D. Televised golf has commercial breaks, which slow down the action.

35. Based on the passage, which iron could potentially hit a golf ball the farthest?

   A. Seven
   B. Five
   C. Two
   D. Four

36. If A, B, C, and D played a competitive round of golf together, which score would win the game?

   A. 120
   B. 79
   C. 84
   D. 102

37. Based on the passage, which of these scenarios is the worst outcome in terms of score?

   A. Dennis hit his ball into the water once.
   B. Dennis hit his ball into two sand traps, but he kept his club from touching the ground as he got it out both times.
   C. Dennis hit his ball into the water once, and then into two sand traps, but he kept his club from touching the ground both times as he got out of the bunkers.
   D. Dennis hit his ball into two sand traps, and he allowed his club to touch the ground both times that he hit the ball out.

38. Based on the passage, which is the best explanation of why golf can be frustrating?

   A. All the equipment you need to play golf is very expensive.
   B. When you're having a bad day on the golf course, you often have nobody to blame but yourself.
   C. Golfers are highly competitive and often give each other a hard time about past failures and embarrassing moments.
   D. Playing golf involves highly complex math.

CONTINUE ON TO THE NEXT PAGE ➡

People have caught fish for food since the earliest days of hunter-gatherer society. In the middle ages, however, sport fishing, also known as angling, became a popular hobby for nobles in the royal courts of Europe. The first documented 5 text on sport fishing, "Treatise on Fishing with an Angle," was published in 1388 and attributed to Dame Juliana Berners, an English nun and sports enthusiast. The attribution to Berners is now considered dubious by many historians, though. 10

Following the publication of "Treatise on Fishing with an Angle," sport fishing became increasingly popular with the upper classes throughout Europe. Many of these aristocrats did not want to share angling with the common people, however, 15 as they assumed hungry peasants would overfish lakes and rivers to the point where the stock of fish would be exhausted. There were even attempts in England to pass laws to "protect" the rivers so that only the rich could fish them. 20

Throughout the seventeenth century, fishing exploded in popularity with military officers, and an increasing number of middle class anglers emerged. In 1653, Izaak Walton published his first edition of *The Complete Angler*, which immediately 25 became the definitive book on recreational fishing. Coupled with the commercialization of fishing in England, *The Complete Angler* turned sport fishing from a growing trend to a booming leisure industry. Due to the increased popularity 30 of fishing and the regard anglers held for Walton's text, *The Complete Angler* was one of the most revised, republished, and widely sold books of its time.

As railways expanded throughout the nineteenth 35 century, sport fishing experienced another boom as innovations in travel could bring more people to the water than ever before. As the middle class continued to grow and leisure time 40 expanded, anglers around England, Europe, and the United States could be found waist-deep in rivers or dangling a line off the back of a boat every weekend. Specialized recreational bait and tackle shops began to open near popular fishing 45 spots to service the increasing number of people who were drawn to the water to fish. When the automobile became commonplace in the early twentieth century, another wave of freshly mobile anglers appeared again, flocking to previously 50 unreachable ponds, lakes, rivers, and streams around the world.

Statistics indicate that the popularity of recreational fishing peaked in the 1920s. When the Great Depression hit, much of the rising middle 55 class that had been enjoying fishing for the last few centuries briefly disappeared. With money, food, and work all scarce, the idea of going down to the water no longer seemed fun or feasible for many people. After World War II, however, sport 60 fishing began to grow again throughout England and the United States as economic prosperity returned. Today, people all around the world enjoy recreational fishing, and the sport continues to grow.

CONTINUE ON TO THE NEXT PAGE →

39. Which of the following best describes what this passage is about?

   A. An explanation of why sport fishing is popular with an emphasis on the rich historical tradition
   B. A defense of sport fishing with an emphasis on its rich history and environmental sustainability
   C. An essay arguing for sport fishing to be recognized as one of the world's great sports
   D. A brief history of angling with an emphasis on times the sport grew in popularity

---

40. What does the author mean in Paragraph 1 when he or she writes, "The attribution to Berners is now considered dubious by many historians, though"?

   A. Historians aren't sure if Juliana Berners ever existed.
   B. Most experts now believe Juliana Berners did not actually write "Treatise on Fishing with an Angle."
   C. Historians aren't sure if the book ever really existed.
   D. Most experts now believe the "Treatise on Fishing with an Angle" wasn't nearly as popular as was previously believed.

41. Based on the passage, why did aristocrats initially want to keep common people from adopting the hobby of angling?

   A. They were concerned with the environmental impact that overfishing might have and wanted to protect the health of lakes and streams.
   B. They were jealous because, on average, peasants were much better fishermen than royalty.
   C. They believed peasants were too greedy and stupid to handle the responsibility of fishing and wanted to keep the waterways for themselves.
   D. Their religious and social beliefs told them that peasants were unclean and would foul the rivers.

---

42. Which of these best explains the meaning of "commercialized" in Paragraph 3?

   A. Fishing to supply food for England had mostly been taken over by large businesses, so rod and reel angling had turned almost completely into a hobby.
   B. At this time, there were a large number of technological innovations that meant that amateur anglers could catch fish as effectively as professionals.
   C. The government set strict limits on how many fish people could catch during this period, so anglers always had to worry about government regulations and taxes.
   D. During the seventeenth century, the cost of fishing tackle exploded, so many poor anglers were priced out.

CONTINUE ON TO THE NEXT PAGE →

43. Based on the passage, how did the train and automobile help the growth of fishing?

   A. They provided anglers with more leisure time to spend on the water.

   B. They simplified transportation, allowing fisherman to find and access more fishing spots than ever before.

   C. They carried fishing supplies like rods, reels, and lures to anglers all around the world.

   D. People were intimidated by the expansion of technology, so they returned to nature in reaction.

44. Based on the passage, why did fishing shrink in popularity during the Great Depression?

   A. Many of the men who enjoyed fishing had to go serve in the war.

   B. The stock market crash had caused all the bait and tackle shops to close.

   C. Most people lacked either the time or the money for leisure activities because economic conditions were so poor.

   D. President Hoover was an avid angler, and many people blamed him for the Great Depression.

CONTINUE ON TO THE NEXT PAGE →

When the ground shakes under your feet, pictures bang against the wall, trees fall, and buildings crumble, you know something serious is happening. Earthquakes are devastating natural disasters that kill 10,000 people on average each 5 year and cause billions of dollars in property damage. Depending on where you are in the world, you might be very familiar with earthquakes, or you may not know anybody who's ever felt one. That's because earthquakes are created by specific 10 geological conditions that only exist in certain parts of the world.

Earthquakes are typically caused by the movement of tectonic plates, the hundred kilometer thick pieces of the planet's crust that drift just on top 15 of the earth's upper mantle. These plates have been moving a tiny distance (between 40 and 100 millimeters) each year for all of history, subtly reshaping the planet over time. The areas surrounding the boundaries of these tectonic 20 plates are exponentially more earthquake prone than other parts of the planet. That's because the results of the plates' tiny movements can be felt most dramatically where they come together. Plates can slam into each other, pull away from 25 each other, or slide under one another, each of which can cause an earthquake.

One of the most important tectonic plates for people who study earthquakes is the Pacific Plate, which forms most of the area between North 30 America and Asia. One of the plate's boundaries runs right down the western coastline of the United States, running near key cities including Seattle, Portland, San Francisco, San Jose, and Los Angeles. On the other side of the Pacific 35 Plate, it bumps up against the Filipino, Australian, and Eurasian plates near Indonesia, Japan, the

Philippines, and South Korea. These are some of the most densely populated areas on earth, 40 meaning a huge number of people on both sides of the Pacific live at increased risk for earthquakes.

While the Pacific Rim is known for its impressive geological activity (volcanoes are also common along the plate's edges), there are other places in 45 the world that are highly seismically active as well. The Mediterranean sees regular seismic tremors because three plates (the African, Arabian, and Eurasian) all come together around the region's famous sea. On the other hand, areas like the 50 American Midwest and Central Europe are snugly located near the center of large tectonic plates, where the collisions and movements that occur along the boundaries cannot be felt. For many of those people, the idea of moving to an area 55 where they'd have to worry about earthquakes seems ridiculous.

More recently, earthquakes have become prevalent in Texas, Oklahoma, and Kansas because of human activity. Hydraulic fracturing (fracking) 60 and similar oil and gas extraction methods require injecting massive amounts of wastewater down into subterranean wells. This additional water creates pressure beneath the surface of the earth, which can build up over time and cause 65 tremors. The United States Geological Survey, which tracks earthquakes for the government, calls these "induced earthquakes." Although the American South has not historically been an area of high seismic activity, these manmade 70 earthquakes have made Oklahoma a hotspot for house shaking.

CONTINUE ON TO THE NEXT PAGE ➡

45. Which of the following best describes the passage?

   A. An in-depth scientific examination of the causes of earthquakes

   B. Instructions on where to live to avoid being affected by an earthquake

   C. A narrative providing accounts of several famous earthquakes

   D. A general explanation of why earthquakes are largely regional phenomena

---

46. Based on the passage, which areas are most prone to earthquakes and why?

   A. Areas in the middle of tectonic plates are most prone to earthquakes because that's where vibrations can be felt the most.

   B. Areas in the middle of tectonic plates are most prone to earthquakes because inward pressure builds at the center point of each plate.

   C. Areas near the edges of tectonic plates are most prone to earthquakes because the interactions between nearby plates create the motion that causes earthquakes.

   D. Areas near the edges of tectonic plates are most prone to earthquakes because the plates are gradually eroding, which causes them to vibrate and shake.

47. Based on the passage, which of these scenarios would be unlikely to cause an earthquake?

   A. The Pacific Plate and the Filipino Plate smash into each other

   B. The Arabian Plate slides under the Pacific Plate

   C. The African Plate and the Eurasian Plate pull slightly apart from each other

   D. The Australian Plate and the Pacific Plate smash into each other

---

48. Based on the passage, which of these cities would probably be least prone to earthquakes?

   A. London, England

   B. Santa Cruz, California

   C. Tokyo, Japan

   D. Palermo, Italy

---

49. Based on the passage, which of these statements is <u>not</u> true about the Mediterranean?

   A. Three plates come together in the area.

   B. It is located safely in the middle of a tectonic plate.

   C. The region contains a famous sea.

   D. The area sees high seismic activity.

---

50. What does the word "induced" in Paragraph 5 mean?

   A. Accidental or unintended

   B. Highly hazardous or dangerous

   C. Silly or stupid

   D. Forced or caused to happen

CONTINUE ON TO THE NEXT PAGE ➡

People who live in American suburbs and cities often take home heating for granted. They live in apartment buildings filled with radiators and central air and assume that people only build fires when they're camping or experiencing an [5] electrical outage. The truth is that people all over rural American, especially in snowy regions, still have to make serious choices about how to heat their homes during the winter. Many of those people live in older homes without central air [10] systems as well, meaning they must think beyond built-in electrical climate control.

Home heating in cold climates is not optional; it's necessary. As temperatures approach 20 degrees Fahrenheit, household plumbing can be [15] badly damaged, and pipes can even burst. Frozen pipes are a major inconvenience and can cost thousands of dollars to repair. A heating system of some sort is required to keep the thick metal pipes that run under and throughout the house [20] a safe temperature. Additionally, cold conditions can pose a variety of health concerns, especially for young children and the elderly.

Heating oil and propane are two popular fuels that people in cold, rural areas use to heat their houses [25] during the winter. These traditional fossil fuels are effective and widely available through delivery companies, who contract with homeowners to keep their reserves full throughout the winter. Fossil fuel markets are prone to price fluctuations, [30] meaning that the cost of oil and propane can (and usually does) jump up during the winter months, when people need it the most. A lot of people find these fuel company practices frustrating, but the abilities of heating oil and propane to keep a [35] house warm are undeniable.

One of the best-kept secrets about rural life is that people still regularly burn wood for heat. In Maine, Vermont, and New Hampshire, for [40] example, wood-burning stoves are commonly used to bring serious warmth right into the living room. For this reason, good, dry wood is one of the main currencies of the informal swap-and-trade economy that often exists in rural towns. [45] Pellet stones, which burn preprocessed chunks of concentrated wood, are also growing in popularity to bring some natural heat to the home without the cost of oil.

The fact of the matter is that very few Americans [50] in cold, rural areas rely on just one fuel source. Since oil is so expensive, many people use oil sparingly to keep their pipes warm but also install a wood-burning stove to comfortably heat living spaces. These complex heating decisions are a [55] part of the yearly cycle in the wintry, rural parts of America but still remain completely foreign to many of those who grew up in the country's vast population centers.

51. Which of the following best tells what this passage is about?

A. How people in the city do not appreciate how people live in rural areas

B. How people in rural areas are innovative and always finding ways to save money

C. How heating a home through the winter is often complex for people in rural areas.

D. How alternative, clean energy is better for heating that traditional fossil fuels.

CONTINUE ON TO THE NEXT PAGE ➡

52. Why does the author of the passage explain the process of pipes freezing?

  A. Because without pipes, there can be no heat

  B. To provide background knowledge that the reader requires to understand ideas later in the passage

  C. To illustrate why home heating in cold climates is necessary

  D. To build credibility by proving that he or she is an expert on heating.

53. Based on the passage, which of these statements is most likely to be true about the author?

  A. The author lives in a rural area where alternative heating is commonplace.

  B. The author lives in the suburbs where most houses have central air.

  C. The author lives in the city where apartment buildings are filled with radiators.

  D. The author lives in another country and is writing an essay about how people live in the United States.

54. Based on the passage, why can fossil fuels be expensive?

  A. Fossil fuels exist in limited supplies within the earth, and we will run out of them, one day.

  B. The people who sell oil frequent change the cost, increasing it when people need it most.

  C. Gathering wood is very inconvenient, so fuel companies know they can charge high prices.

  D. Fossil fuel is only available at certain times throughout the winter, so people have to buy it when it's available.

55. What does the author mean when he or she writes, "For this reason, good, dry wood is one of the main currencies of the informal swap-and-trade economy that often exists in rural towns"?

  A. People in cold, rural areas have a different economy where they use wood as money.

  B. Wood is valuable in rural areas because people who live there don't have access to heating oil.

  C. People prefer dry wood over wet wood for heating because it burns better.

  D. People in cold, rural areas value wood highly because it is an inexpensive way to heat their homes.

CONTINUE ON TO THE NEXT PAGE ➡

56. Based on the passage, why might people use multiple fuel sources throughout the winter?

  A. To avoid being boring
  B. To avoid relying too much on any one method
  C. To heat their house in a way that balanced cost and reliability
  D. To heat their house in a unique way that would interest people

57. Which best explains the meaning of the phrase "vast population centers" in Paragraph 5?

  A. Expensive, high-end neighborhoods
  B. Areas in the developing world where people live in poverty
  C. Poor, high-crime neighborhoods
  D. Areas like cities where a lot of people are concentrated

CONTINUE ON TO THE NEXT PAGE →

MATHEMATICS
INSTRUCTIONS

ARGO
BROTHERS
www.argobrothers.com

90 MINUTES • 57 QUESTIONS

Select the best answer from the choices given by carefully solving each problem. Bubble the letter of your answer on the answer sheet. Please refrain from making any stray marks on the answer sheet. If you need to erase an answer, please erase thoroughly.

Important Notes:

1. There are no formulas or definitions in the math section that will be provided.
2. Diagrams may or may not be drawn to scale. Do not make assumptions based on the diagram unless it is specifically stated in the diagram or question.
3. Diagrams are not in more than one plane, unless stated otherwise.
4. Graphs are drawn to scale, therefore, you can assume relationships according to the graph. If lines appear parallel, then you can assume the lines to be parallel. This is also true for right angles and so forth.
5. Simplify fractions completely.

*THIS EXAM IS MORE DIFFICULT

Practice Test 5* (Questions 1-57)

1. Find the next term in the series:
0, 1, 1, 2, 4, 7, 13, 24...

A. 28
B. 37
C. 44
D. 48

2. Which is true about *A* and *B*?

$A = \sqrt{65} - 9$
$B = \sqrt{50} - 8$

A. $A = B$
B. $A > B$
C. $A > 1$
D. $B > A$

CONTINUE ON TO THE NEXT PAGE →

335

3. Which is a solution of the following equation?

$$\frac{(x^2 + x - 6)}{(x - 2)} = 0$$

- **A.** -2
- **B.** -3
- **C.** 0
- **D.** 2

---

4. John is stacking boxes directly upon each other. He stacks at 1 box per minute initially and every minute after that, his stacking rate increases by 1 box per minute. If each box is 5 inches tall, in how many minutes will the stack be 30 inches tall.

- **A.** 2 min
- **B.** 3 min
- **C.** 5 min
- **D.** 6 min

---

5. A Dilob has a mass of 20.2 milligrams. What is the Dilob's mass in grams?

- **A.** 0.0202 g
- **B.** 0.202 g
- **C.** 2.02 g
- **D.** 20.2 g

6. Jesse goes to the store. He buys a magazine for $8. Then he sells it for $10 and buys it back again for $11. He finally sells it for $12. What was his profit?

- **A.** $-$1$
- **B.** 0
- **C.** 2
- **D.** 3

---

7. If $f(\gamma) = 2f(\delta)$ and $\gamma = 2\delta$, what is a possible function for f?

- **A.** x
- **B.** x^2
- **C.** $2x^2$
- **D.** $\sqrt{x}$

---

8. A substance's length doubles every hour. At 2PM it was 3 meters. What was the length at 11AM that same day?

- **A.** 0.375 meters
- **B.** 0.5 meters
- **C.** 0.75 meters
- **D.** 1 meter

---

9. Which is true of these three functions?

$$f = x^{x^4}$$
$$g = (x^x)^4$$
$$h = x^{4^x}$$

- **A.** $f = g$
- **B.** $h = g$
- **C.** $f = g + h$
- **D.** $f \neq g$

CONTINUE ON TO THE NEXT PAGE →

10. Linda scored a 66, 82, 81, and 92 on her English exams. What score must Linda obtain on the next english test to have an average of exactly 84?

   A. 84
   B. 87
   C. 95
   D. 99

11. If today is Saturday, what day of the week will it be in 365 days from now?

   A. Tuesday
   B. Thursday
   C. Friday
   D. Sunday

12. What is the remainder of
7,700,000,000,202 divided by **9?**

   A. 0
   B. 1
   C. 2
   D. 3

13.

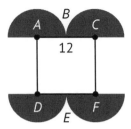

In the figure above $\overline{AB} = \overline{BC} = \overline{DE} = \overline{EF}$ and the side of the square is 12. Points B and E are the midpoints of the square. Find the area of the shaded region.

   A. 12π
   B. 24π
   C. 36π
   D. 72π

14. $8^{x+3} = 64^{3x}$, what is the value of x?

   A. $\dfrac{1}{2}$

   B. $\dfrac{3}{5}$

   C. $\dfrac{5}{3}$

   D. 2

CONTINUE ON TO THE NEXT PAGE →

15. If $A \blacktriangleright \blacktriangleleft B = AB\left(\dfrac{A}{B}\right) - 2^3$

then what is the value of $3 \blacktriangleright \blacktriangleleft 2$?

A. 1

B. $13\dfrac{3}{7}$

C. $14\dfrac{3}{7}$

D. $13\dfrac{7}{4}$

16. If the average of 11 numbers is 15, then what is the sum of these 11 numbers?

A. 26
B. 121
C. 165
D. 225

17. What is the average of
$(9b - 7) + (7 - 3b) - (-3 - 3b) + (6 + 3b)$

A. $3b + \dfrac{9}{4}$

B. $\dfrac{9}{4}b + 3$

C. $3b + 2$

D. $2b + 3$

18. $\dfrac{y^{-1} \cdot y^3 \cdot y^4 \cdot y^5 \cdot y^6}{y^6 \cdot y^5 \cdot y^4}$

A. y^{-4}
B. y^{-2}
C. 1
D. y^2

19. If the pattern continues, what will be the 50ᵗʰ symbol?

★ ♥ → ← * ↑ ★ ♥ → ← ...

A. ←
B. *
C. ★
D. ♥

20. A trapezoid has base lengths in the ratio of 2:6. If the area of a trapezoid is 260 and the altitude is 5, then what is the length of the longer base?

A. 20
B. 26
C. 65
D. 78

CONTINUE ON TO THE NEXT PAGE ➡

21. $\frac{4}{9}$ is the square root of what number?

   A. $\frac{1}{2}$

   B. $\frac{2}{3}$

   C. $\frac{8}{18}$

   D. $\frac{16}{81}$

22. In the following system of equations,
$3x + 7y = 24$
$9x + 4y = 21$

What is (x, y)?

   A. $(1, 1)$
   B. $(1, 3)$
   C. $(3, 1)$
   D. $(2, 4)$

23. If a trapezoid with a, b on top and c, d on bottom means $\sqrt{abcd}$, then

what is the value of a trapezoid with 1, 12 on top and 3, 4 on bottom?

   A. 3
   B. $\sqrt{12}$
   C. $\sqrt{24}$
   D. 12

24. Which of the following is bigger, the first or the second? Assume X does not equal Y.

First: $\frac{X}{X - Y}$ Second: $\frac{Y}{Y - X}$

   A. They are equal
   B. First
   C. Second
   D. Not enough information

25.

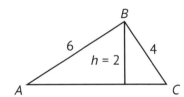

Figure not drawn to scale

In the figure above, triangle ABC has an area of 20 square inches, where the height is 2 inches. If a square has the same perimeter as the triangle above, then what is the area of the square?

   A. 56 sq.in
   B. 56.15 sq.in
   C. 56.25 sq.in
   D. 56.50 sq.in

CONTINUE ON TO THE NEXT PAGE →

26. The following table shows the class test average score in Ms.Jones' Biology class over the years she has been teaching for. What is the median class test score for the years shown?

Average Test Score in Ms. Jones' Biology Class

Year	2007	2008	2009	2010	2011	2012	2013	2014	2015
Avg. Test Score	74	83	74	71	92	84	69	89	91

A. 74
B. 83
C. 84
D. 89

---

27. The wheels of a car have a diameter of 10 meters. If the speed of the car is 50 meters per hour, how many revolutions does one wheel make in **one hour?**

A. 5

B. $\dfrac{50}{\pi}$

C. 10

D. $\dfrac{5}{\pi}$

28. A circle is inscribed in a square. What is the probability that a penny, if thrown, will fall in the shaded region below?

A. 1

B. $\pi - 2$

C. $1 - \dfrac{\pi}{4}$

D. $\left(\dfrac{\pi}{2}\right)$

---

29. What is: $\dfrac{(10\%) \cdot (10\%)}{100\%}$?

A. 1%
B. 10%
C. .001
D. 1

---

30. The greatest integer function of x, gives the largest integer that is less than x and is represented by: $\lfloor x \rfloor$, what is $\lfloor 10\% \rfloor + 1$?

A. 1
B. 1.1
C. 11
D. 11%

CONTINUE ON TO THE NEXT PAGE →

31. Sara is stuck in a circular field. She knows that the area of the circular field is 100 square meters. She walks at a speed of 10 meters per minute. How long will it take her to walk from one end of the circular field to the other end assuming she must cross through the center.

A. $\sqrt{\dfrac{100}{\pi}}$

B. $2\sqrt{\dfrac{100}{\pi}}$

C. $10\sqrt{\dfrac{100}{\pi}}$

D. $0.2\sqrt{\dfrac{100}{\pi}}$

32. The Fibonacci Sequence involves taking two previous numbers and adding them together to get the next. If the first two Fibonacci numbers are 0 and 1, what is the mean of the first 5 Fibonnaci numbers?

A. $\dfrac{5}{6}$

B. $\dfrac{7}{6}$

C. $\dfrac{7}{5}$

D. 1

33. If
1 slack = x vaks
9 vaks = 12 hips,

How many slacks are in 24 hips?

A. 2

B. $\dfrac{9}{x}$

C. $\dfrac{18}{x}$

D. $\dfrac{x}{9}$

34. What is the value of $\dfrac{11^2}{10^2}$?

A. 12.1
B. 121
C. .121
D. 1.21

35. If $(a\check{}b) = a + b - b^2$, then what is the value of this expression when $a = 5$ and $b = 2$?

A. 2
B. 3
C. 4
D. 5

36. How many nonpositive integers are **between** -3 and 5, inclusive?

A. 1
B. 3
C. 4
D. 6

CONTINUE ON TO THE NEXT PAGE ➡

37. A number is squared and added to its reciprocal. If that number is represented by x, what is the expression?

   A. $x^2 + 1$

   B. $x^2 + \dfrac{1}{x}$

   C. $x^2 + \dfrac{1}{x^2}$

   D. $\dfrac{x^4 + 1}{x^2}$

---

38. If I increase the size of a ball by 50% two times in a row, what is the percent increase assuming that the initial size of the ball was 20.

   A. 25%
   B. 50%
   C. 75%
   D. 125%

39.

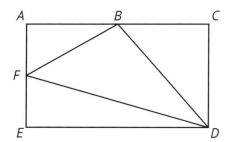

In the figure above, the rectangle *ACDE* has an area of 440 square meters. The points *B* and *F* are the midpoints of the sides *AC* and *AE* respectively. What is the area of the triangle, *BCD?*

   A. 56
   B. 110
   C. 200
   D. 220

---

40. The least common multiple of two numbers, x and y can be represented by:

$LCM(x, y)$. The following is true for the concept of the least common multiple:

If we can find integers, a and b for both x and y respectively such that $ax = by = LCM(x, y)$, then ax or by is the least common multiple of x and y.

What is the least common multiple of $\sqrt{2} \bullet \pi$?

   A. $2\pi\sqrt{2}$
   B. 2π
   C. $2\pi^2$
   D. Does not exist

CONTINUE ON TO THE NEXT PAGE ➡

Explanations to each problem on:
Youtube.com/ArgoBrothers

MATHEMATICS
TEST 5

ARGO
BROTHERS
www.argobrothers.com

41. For how many values of x is the function not equal to 1?

$$f(x) = \frac{x - 3}{x - 3}$$

A. 0
B. 1
C. 2
D. 3

42. If today is Monday, what day will it be in 49^2 from now?

A. Tuesday
B. Wednesday
C. Thursday
D. Monday

43. If $f(x) = x^3$, then how many times greater is $f(4)$ than $f(2)$?

A. 2
B. 3
C. 4
D. 8

44. Convert $\frac{3}{40}$ to a decimal.

A. 0.0075
B. 0.075
C. 0.06
D. .75

45. How many prime numbers are between 4 and 16 inclusive?

A. 2
B. 3
C. 4
D. 5

46. How many perfect squares are between 9 and 25 exclusive?

A. 0
B. 1
C. 2
D. 3

47. An octagon, a triangle and a circle all have the same perimeter (circumference for the circle). Which is true of the areas of these shapes? (O = area of octagon, T = area of triangle, and C = area of circle).

A. $O < C < T$
B. $O = T = C$
C. $C > T = C$
D. $C > O > T$

48. If $(\frac{x}{y}) = x^2$, then what is $(\frac{x}{y}) - (\frac{x}{y})^2$?

A. x^2y
B. x^4
C. $x^2(1 - x^2)$
D. $x^2(1 + x^2)$

CONTINUE ON TO THE NEXT PAGE →

49. In a scaled drawing, 1 millimeter represents 150 meters. How many square millimeters on the drawing represent 1 square meter?

    A. $\dfrac{1}{150}$

    B. $\dfrac{1}{22,500}$

    C. $\dfrac{1150}{22,500}$

    D. 22,500

50. A rectangle is drawn on a coordinate plane. If the coordinates of one corner of the rectangle is $(0, -5)$ and the coordinates of the opposite corner is $(7, 3)$, then what is the area of the rectangle?

    A. -21
    B. 21
    C. 56
    D. 105

51. Which one of the following is equivalent to the expression

$$\frac{(xy)^3(z)^0}{x^3y^4}, \text{ when } xyz \neq 0?$$

    A. xyz

    B. xz

    C. $\dfrac{1}{y}$

    D. 1

52. How many distinct prime factors does 2,520 have?

    A. 3
    B. 4
    C. 7
    D. 48

GRID IN

Directions: The following five questions are grid-in problems. On the answer sheet, please be sure to write your answer in the boxes at the top of the grid. Start on the left side of each grid.

53. Given $p @ t = \dfrac{p}{4}(1 - t^2)$, calculate $7 @ 3$.

Explanations to each problem on:
Youtube.com/ArgoBrothers

MATHEMATICS
TEST 5

ARGO
BROTHERS
www.argobrothers.com

54. Solve $-7(3n + 5) = -6n + 25$ for n.

55. Bob is making mini fondant cakes for the next bake sale. Each cake costs Bob $1.80 to make. If he sells the cakes for $3.00 each, how many will he have to sell to make a profit of exactly $36.00?

56. A car travels for 3 hours at a speed of 55 miles per hour and then for the next 2 hours travels at a speed of 65 miles per hour. Find the average speed of the car for the entire journey.

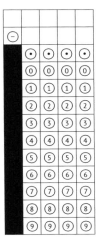

57. If $x = -1$ and $y = 2$, what is the value of the expression $2x^3 - 3xy$?

THIS IS THE END OF THE TEST. IF THERE IS TIME REMAINING, YOU MAY CHECK YOUR ANSWERS TO

SHSAT PRACTICE TEST 5
ANSWER KEY

Revising/Editing

1. **A**
2. **B**
3. **A**
4. **D**
5. **C**
6. **C**
7. **B**
8. **A**
9. **D**
10. **B**
11. **C**
12. **A**
13. **D**
14. **B**
15. **D**
16. **A**
17. **D**
18. **C**
19. **B**
20. **A**

Reading Comprehension

21. **D**		41. **C**	
22. **A**		42. **A**	
23. **C**		43. **B**	
24. **D**		44. **C**	
25. **B**		45. **D**	
26. **D**		46. **C**	
27. **C**		47. **B**	
28. **D**		48. **A**	
29. **A**		49. **B**	
30. **B**		50. **D**	
31. **D**		51. **C**	
32. **A**		52. **C**	
33. **C**		53. **A**	
34. **A**		54. **B**	
35. **C**		55. **D**	
36. **B**		56. **C**	
37. **D**		57. **D**	
38. **B**			
39. **D**			
40. **B**			

Math

1. **C**	13. **D**	25. **C**	37. **B**	49. **B**
2. **D**	14. **B**	26. **B**	38. **D**	50. **C**
3. **B**	15. **A**	27. **D**	39. **B**	51. **C**
4. **B**	16. **C**	28. **C**	40. **D**	52. **B**
5. **A**	17. **A**	29. **A**	41. **B**	53. **-14**
6. **D**	18. **D**	30. **A**	42. **D**	54. **-4**
7. **A**	19. **D**	31. **D**	43. **D**	55. **30**
8. **A**	20. **D**	32. **C**	44. **B**	56. **59**
9. **D**	21. **D**	33. **C**	45. **C**	57. **4**
10. **D**	22. **B**	34. **D**	46. **B**	
11. **D**	23. **D**	35. **B**	47. **D**	
12. **A**	24. **D**	36. **C**	48. **C**	

Practice Test 5 (Answers and Explanations)

1.   **A**   Answer A is the best choice because a colon is the correct punctuation mark to introduce a list. Answer B is incorrect because, by placing the steps in parentheses, the author downplays the importance of that information, making it seem almost unnecessary when it is actually the main idea of the sentence. Answer choice C is incorrect because it adds the unnecessary, wordy phrase "...and those steps are..." Answer choice D is incorrect because it uses a semicolon to introduce the list, which is the job of the colon.

2.   **B**   Answer B would make the best topic sentence because it clearly states the overarching topic that Sentences 1 through 4 are all about. Answer A is a true statement of fact that is related to paragraph, but it is not specific enough to be the best topic sentence. Answer C is similarly a related fact, but not a clear statement of the main idea of Sentences 1 through 4. Answer D is not a strong topic sentence because it is a statement of opinion (as it could be reasonably disagreed with). Since the rest of the paragraph is clearly explanatory, rather than argumentative, it should have a topic sentence that is a clear statement of fact.

3.   **A**   Answer A is correct because Sentence 2 contains the subject-verb agreement error "...amateur paddlers and collegiate competitors rows side by side." Since "paddlers and... competitors" is a plural subject, the plural verb "row" is required. Answers B, C, and D are all incorrect because "Regatta has attracted," "Competitors are grouped," and "rowers participate" all make correct use of subject-verb agreement.

4.   **D**   Answer D combines the sentences in a way that clarifies the logical relationship between the two, making it the correct answer. By using the comma and the word "although," Answer D connects the two sentences in a grammatically correct way that shows the relationship between the two sentences better than the original passage. Answer A is incorrect because it simply combines the two sentences using the conjunction "and," doing little to enhance the complementary relationship of the two ideas. Answer B is incorrect because it uses the word "even" in a repetitive manner and fails to insert a comma before "even" to ease flow for the reader. Answer C is also incorrect because it simply combines the two sentences using a semicolon, which does not demonstrate the connection between the two ideas as well as the "although" in Answer D.

5.   **C**   This paragraph is consistently written in the present tense, so Answer C is correct because it contains the past tense phrase "Americans never lost sight..." The addition of the modifier "Americans have never lost sight..." would bring the sentence into the present tense to make it consistent with the rest of the paragraph. Answers A, B, and D are all incorrect because they contain only present tense verbs.

6.   **C**   Passive voice occurs when the subject of a sentence is having action done to them rather than being the actor of the verb. Sentence 2 contains the passive voice construction "black southerners were still discriminated against." Answer C is correct because it restructures the sentence to

make "White southerners" the new subject of an active voice construction ("White southerners continued to discriminate..."). Answers A, B, and D are all incorrect because they all fail to identify and correct the passive voice construction "...were discriminated against..."

7. **B** The first two paragraphs of this passage are consistently written using past tense verbs, which is appropriate since historical information is the theme. Answer B is correct because it makes the tense of Sentence 3's verb consistent with the rest of the paragraph and clarifies the timeline of events for the reader. Answer A is incorrect because "these" is a plural pronoun, which would disagree in number with its object "treatment." Answer C is incorrect because "throughout" is a more specific, descriptive preposition than "in." By using "throughout," the author communicates that this was a wide-ranging, systematic problem rather than something that happened in a few places. Answer D is also incorrect because when speaking of the American South, particularly as it relates to issues of the Civil War and segregation, "the South" is treated as a proper noun and should therefore be capitalized.

8. **A** Answer A is the best combination of Sentences 4 and 5 because it combines all of their main ideas in a grammatically correct way while also significantly reducing wordiness. Answers B and D are both incorrect because, although they include the main ideas of both sentences, they are essentially jumbles of comma-separated clauses, which could easily confuse the reader. Answer C is also incorrect because it uses the unnecessarily wordy statement "...and that system was known as," which hurts the flow of the sentences and paragraph.

9. **D** Answer D is correct because the content of Sentence 7 (that black schools were subject to worse conditions) is directly contrary to the ideas laid out in Sentence 6 (that schools should be "separate but equal"). The transition "However" is used to indicate unexpected or contrary information, making it the perfect fit for Sentence 7. Answers A and B are both incorrect because "Therefore" and "Consequently" both suggest that the content of Sentence 7 is the logical conclusion of Sentence 6, which it is not. Answer C is also incorrect because the author is not presenting information in Sentence 6 that supports Sentence 7.

10. **B** Answer B is the best choice because it provides concrete examples that support the claim made in Sentence 7. By providing evidence, an author can strengthen their point and clarify ideas to the reader. Answer A is incorrect because it doesn't match the tone of the rest of the passage (as the author speaks directly to the reader). Answer C is provides a valuable detail that would fit in the overall passage, but it is not the best choice to provide direct support to Sentence 7 because it doesn't provide any examples or directly elaborate on the conditions laid out in Sentence 7. Answer D is also incorrect because, while it is a true statement that could have a place in this passage, it does not directly support Sentence 7.

11. **C** Answer C is the best conclusion sentence because it continues to develop the ideas that came before it (that conditions were clearly unequal in the different schools) while also calling back to the topic sentence (by referencing the "separate but equal" doctrine). Wrapping up ideas and reminding the reader of the paragraph's purpose are the two main roles of a conclusion sentence,

so Answer C is an excellent choice. Answers A and D are both incorrect because they abruptly transition into talking about solutions rather than concisely summarizing the problem that had been laid out in the paragraph (as Answer C does). Answer B is also incorrect because, while it is an interesting and relevant fact, it does not serve any of the purposes of a conclusion (summarizing, transitioning, signposting for the reader, etc.).

12. **A** "Court" is a collective noun, meaning it takes the singular possessive pronoun "its" rather than the plural "their." Answer A is correct because it identifies this pronoun issue. Answer B is incorrect because "court... explained" agrees. Answer C is incorrect because "court... explained" is an active voice construction in which the subject performs the action of the sentence. Answer D is incorrect because there is no modifier whose subject is confusing within the sentence.

13. **D** The "to be" verbs (am, is, are, was, were, will be, etc.) are generally discouraged from use in formal writing. These kind of conventions are especially important in key portions of the essay, such as its final sentence. Answer D is correct because it eliminates the "to be" verbs "be" an "are" from the sentence while maintaining the original meaning by rearranging ideas. Answer A is incorrect because it includes both "is" and "are." Answer B is incorrect because it includes "be." Answer C cannot be correct because it includes "is."

14. **B** A dangling modifier occurs when a sentence begins with a descriptive phrase whose object may be unclear to the reader. "Created by Joseph Campbell in 1949" from Sentence 2 is an example of dangling modifier because the reader has not yet been introduced to the concept of the Hero's Journey, so they have no way of knowing what the modifier is describing. Answer B reorganizes the sentence to eliminate the dangling modifier by placing "The Hero's Journey" clearly at the beginning of the sentence. Answers A and D are both incorrect because they do nothing to correct the dangling modifier. Answer C is also incorrect because it actually creates a new dangling modifier "Following the same general structure," which would probably be even more confusing to the reader.

15. **D** Answer D is correct because it uses a comma to separate the introduction "According to Campbell" from the rest of the sentence, which is the only necessary comma in the sentence. Answer A is incorrect because, while it eliminates unnecessary commas, it does not add the comma at the beginning of the sentence to separate the introduction. Answer B is incorrect because it incorrectly separates the dependant clause "to resolve a conflict in their life or world" from the rest of the sentence. Answer C is also incorrect because, while it includes the necessary comma at the beginning of the sentence, it also incorrectly separates out "going on a journey" as a nonessential modifier, which it is not.

16. **A** Answer A is correct because it wraps up the main ideas of paragraph 1 by describing the last set of steps in the process of the Hero's Journey. Without the information in Answer A, the reader does not have a full overview of the process before moving on to the specifics contained in paragraph 2. Answer B is incorrect because, while it could be relevant somewhere in the passage, it is not closely related to the sentences that preceded it. Also, introducing the idea of the circle diagram would require more sentences than simply Answer B to provide an adequate explanation.

Answer C is incorrect because the passage is about the Hero's Journey, not biographical details on Campbell. Answer D could have a place somewhere in the passage, but it is not an adequate conclusion sentence for the first paragraph because it does not connect directly to Sentences 3 and 4, which immediately precede it.

17. **D** Answer D is correct because it uses the semicolon to transition between two closely related sentences and uses commas as appropriate to separate words and phrases within each of the two sentences. Answer A is incorrect because it inappropriately uses a semicolon to separate the introduction "First" and creates a comma splice by using the comma without a conjunction to transition from one sentence to the next. Answer B is also incorrect because it reverses the placement of the comma and the semicolon leading into the transition between the two sentences. Answer C is in incorrect as well because it also contains a comma spliced transition between sentences and places the semicolon incorrectly.

18. **C** Answer C is correct because each (singular) character can only have one death. Answer C corrects the sentence by making the two related nouns agree in number. Answer A is incorrect because a comma is needed after story to separate the introduction from the main body of the sentence. Answer B is incorrect because the singular verb "experiences" matches in number with the singular subject "hero." Answer D is incorrect because the paragraph is written consistently in progressive verb tenses. Using a past tense verb would be inconsistent.

19. **B** Passive voice occurs when the subject of a sentence is having the action of the verb performed on it rather than being the actor. "The Hero's Journey has been used" at the beginning of Sentence 12 is a passive voice construction. Answer B reorders the sentence to create an active voice construction by adding "writers" to create a subject that can perform the verb "use." Answer A is incorrect because "...books and movies have been written..." is passive voice. Answer C is incorrect because it does nothing to correct the original example of passive voice. Answer D is also incorrect because it includes the passive voice construction "Books and movies are often created."

20. **A** Site, sight, and cite are three homophones with very different meanings. The original "sight" means the ability to see. Answer A is correct because to "cite" is to reference, which George Lucas is doing in the sentence. Answer C is incorrect because a "site" is a location. Answer B is incorrect because "creator" is the correct, while irregular, spelling of the word. Answer D is also incorrect because the phrase "one of" earlier in the sentence communicates that Lucas has multiple influences, necessitating the plural.

READING COMPREHENSION

Passage 1 ("Long ago, when you were a little boy..."):

21. D Answer D is the best choice because, throughout the text, the author vehemently disagrees that childhood is the best part of life and resents the assertion by adults that it is. Lines 34-36 articulate this point clearly by saying, "I for one lift up my voice emphatically against the assertion, and do affirm that I think childhood is the most undesirable portion of human life." Paragraph 1 introduces the idea that adults overrate and over-sentimentalize childhood, Paragraph 2 explains that the author disagrees, and Paragraph 4 contains a fleshing out of the author's point featuring several examples as evidence. Answer A is incorrect because it represents the exact opposite of the author's point of view. Answer B is incorrect because being told what to do is only one of the many problems the author identifies with childhood. Answer C is also incorrect because, while the author would probably agree that adults who romanticize childhood are fools, the main argument of the passage is about the nature of childhood, not the foolishness of adults.

22. A Answer A is correct because, throughout the passage, the author addresses the idea that childhood is the happiest time in life as if it is a commonly held belief. By associating this idea with "Commonplacedom" (Line 17), the author establishes that he or she believes the romanticism of childhood is very commonplace. Answer B is incorrect because the author makes this point explicitly in Lines 19-58 rather than implying anything. Answers C and D are both incorrect because the author does not use absolutes like "always" or "never" in the passage, and never makes the claim that nobody has a happy childhood.

23. C Answer C is correct because in Lines 35-37, the author clearly states, "I think childhood is the most undesirable portion of human life, and I am thankful to be well out of it." These words clearly display that the author prefers her adult life to her childhood. Answer A is incorrect because, while the author identifies clothing as a realm in which children have minimal freedom (Lines 45-55), she never says outright that she was never allowed to pick her own clothes. Similarly, Answer B is incorrect because the author never explicitly states that she herself was not allowed to leave the house. Answer D cannot be correct because the author clearly states in Lines 35-37 that she prefers her adulthood over childhood.

24. D Answer D is the best choice because Lines 40-58 all provide examples of ways in which children are not in control of the major decisions surrounding their lives. Answer A cannot be correct because schools are never mentioned in the passage. Answer B is incorrect as well because the passage never makes any reference to adults having the freedom to play. Answer C cannot be correct because the passage suggests that children are powerless and adults are the ones who do the bossing around, while Answer C asserts the exact opposite.

25. B Answer B is the best choice because in Lines 48-55, the author describes to the "six-foot friend" that children often have choices made for them, even in situations that don't really matter, such as how to dress. The author asks the adult to "imagine... how you would feel, to be obliged to

wear your woolen mittens when you desire to bloom out in straw-colored kids, or to be buttoned in your black waistcoat when your taste leads you to select your white... yet this is what children are perpetually called to undergo." Answer A is incorrect because the author does not make any judgement about the fashionableness of mittens in the passage. Answer C is incorrect because the author asserts throughout the passage that children everywhere are treated this way, and uses other examples besides just warm gloves (such as being forced to wear the black waistcoat over a white one). Answer D cannot be correct because the author is not suggesting their friend wear mittens; rather, she suggests "Imagine if you were forced to wear mittens."

26. **D**   Answer D is the best choice because if people prefer not to make decisions, then being told what to do would actually make them very happy. Answer A is not the best answer because, the author would probably argue, that making "some" decisions is not enough. Answer B is not the best answer because, while true, the fact that adults don't have total freedom doesn't forgive putting overly stringent limits on the freedom of children. Answer C is not the best answer either because the fact that decision-making is hard does not mean that people would prefer to have all their decisions made for them.

Passage 2 ("If you asked a group of people which verb they would use"):

27. **C**   Answer C is correct because it provides the best summary of the main ideas of the passage. The reader could easily infer this by reading the first (introduction) paragraph and the final sentence of the final (conclusion) paragraph. Answers A and B are incorrect because they both assume that the writer is arguing that one style is superior to the other, which is untrue. The passage compares the two, but it does not make judgments about their value. Answer D is also incorrect, although it is a true statement. While Answer D correctly identifies the subjects of the passage (cooking and baking), it fails to identify what the passage is saying about them (that they are surprisingly different).

28. **D**   Answer D is correct because it is nearest to the dictionary definition of "smorgasbord," which is: "a buffet offering a variety of hot and cold meats, salads, hors d'oeuvres, etc," or, "a wide range of something; a variety." Readers could easily determine that Answer D is correct based on the words "variety," "combinations," and "infinite" appearing in the same sentence. Answers A through C are all incorrect. There is no textual basis for Answer C. Answers A and B suggest a partial, but incomplete, understanding of the sentence.

29. **A**   The ability of chefs to adjust and make changes on the fly is emphasized in the second and fourth paragraphs, making Answer A correct. Like artists, chefs can tweak their food as it cooks - unlike bakers, who are constrained within their recipes and must patiently wait while their goods bake in the oven. Answer B is a reasonable conclusion, but not the best answer as supported by the passage. Answer C demonstrates that the reader is trying to connect the answer to the passage (as "Food is a daily necessity" closely mirrors the beginning of paragraph 2). However, Answer C is still incorrect because preventing people from starving is not considered one of the artistic aspects of food. The first half of Answer D ("Cooks have different individual styles and passions") is the beginning of a good answers, but the second half ("baking is the same all around the world") is an untrue and oversimplified statement. Although it accesses one of the passage's key ideas, Answer D is not the best answer.

30. **B** Paragraphs 3 and 4 emphasize the precise and repeatable nature of baking, making Answer B correct. Answer A is incorrect, but it does show the reader trying to connect the answer to the text, as the phrase "very simple, basic elements" mirrors the content of the final sentence of Paragraph 4. Answer C is incorrect and has no basis in the passage because glassware is never mentioned. Answer D is incorrect because needing to master the taste, texture, and appearance of food is not exclusive to bakers, and therefore, cannot be the reason why baking is more scientific than cooking.

31. **D** Answer D is the best answer because Paragraph 3 emphasizes that creating dough is one of the hardest (and most scientific) processes that bakers must master. Given what the reader has been told about chefs (that they enjoy flexibility and making adjustments), the regimented approach required to make dough is most likely to be difficult for a chef. Answers A and B are incorrect with no textual basis. Answer C is incorrect because, due to their need to master a variety of ingredients and flavors, chefs might actually be good at selecting herbs for a bread.

32. **A** Answer A is the best answer because it combines the idea of making food for the world (one of the main ideas of the final paragraph) with ideas that relate to culture (home, family, and tradition). Answer B is incorrect and most likely suggests the reader misinterprets the use of the word "caretaker." Answer C is not the best answer because it could be reasonably disagreed with, and many chefs and bakers might not agree that their ethnic, regional, and cultural heritage are the most important parts of their identities. Answer D is incorrect because, while it hits on the main idea of the last paragraph, it does not address the actual elements of culture (home, family, and traditions) in the way that Answer A does.

Passage 3 ("Golf is popular around the world..."):

33. **C** Answer C is the best answer because this passage provides a general explanation of the rules of golf, the procedure of playing, and the challenges most often faced by players. Answer A is incorrect because the author never directly addresses other sports and only talks about golf on its own merits. Answer B is incorrect because, while the passage clearly has a favorable view of golf, it does not actively attempt to persuade anybody in include any calls to action. Answer D is also incorrect because the passage does not contain any distinct narrative or story, as it is purely explanatory.

34. **A** Answer A is correct because the passage repeatedly emphasizes that golf is a game of mental strategizing and planning, which are internalized activities that can't be appreciated through a television. Answer B is incorrect because, as Paragraph 2 demonstrates, the fundamental rules of golf are fairly straightforward. Answer C is incorrect because the passage mentions twice that golf

is accessible to people of all ages and body types, contradicting this assumption. Answer D, while somewhat factual, is not the best answer because, as the passage details, fast-paced "action" is not the most important or intriguing part of golf.

35. **C** Paragraph 3 explains that irons "are numbered in ascending order from one to nine, with higher numbers counter intuitively representing shorter potential distances." Using either knowledge of the term "counter intuitively" or by using context clues such as "shorter potential outcomes," readers can can determine that smaller numbered irons actually hit the ball farther, making Answer C correct. Answers A, B, and D are all incorrect because the two iron, the club represented by the lowest number, has the potential to hit the ball the longest distance.

36. **B** The final sentence of Paragraph 2 clearly establishes that "the player with the lowest score wins the game." Since 79 is the lowest of the available numbers, Answer B is correct. Answers A, C, and D are all incorrect because none of those numbers represent the lowest (winning) score.

37. **D** Based on Paragraph 5, hitting a ball into the water adds one stroke to a player's score, as does grounding a club in a sand trap. Answer D is the correct choice because it is the only scenario that portrays Dennis racking up two penalty strokes. Each time he grounds his club in the sand trap accounts for one additional stroke, giving him a score of +2. Answer A is incorrect because it shows Dennis incurring only one penalty stroke (for hitting the ball into the water). Answer B actually shows Dennis committing no penalty strokes because he avoided grounding his club in the sand trap. Answer C shows Dennis receiving only one penalty stroke (for hitting his ball into the water) because he did not ground his club either time he was in a sand trap.

38. **B** Answer B is correct because the passage repeatedly emphasizes the individualistic, internalized nature of golf. Answer B is closely aligned with the passage because it demonstrates the "dark side" of the main point of Paragraphs 3-5. Answer A is incorrect and has no textual basis because the passage never mentions cost or expense in any way and, if anything, works to dispel the stereotype that golf is a rich person's game in Paragraph 1. Similarly, Answer C has no textual basis because, if anything, the passage stresses golf as a casual game that is often played with no stakes at all. Answer D is incorrect because the scoring of the game is described and demonstrated as being simple in the passage itself.

Passage 4 ("People have caught fish for food since the earliest days..."):

39. **D** Answer D is correct because the passage provides a summary of the history of sport fishing and also emphasizes key moments that influenced the sport's growth. Answer A is incorrect because the passage does little to explain what the actual appeal of fishing is. Answer B is incorrect because the passage is in no way defensive or answering to any criticisms and sustainability is mentioned only once tangentially (in Paragraph 2) in the passage. Answer C is also incorrect because the author is not making an effort to try to argue for or convince anybody of anything in the essay; it is simply explanatory.

40. **B**   Answer B is correct because it correctly identifies that "dubious attribution" means "there is a high probability that she didn't write it." Answer A is incorrect because it mistakenly believes it was Juliana Berners who historians believe to be dubious rather than the attribution of authorship. Answer B is similarly incorrect because it mistakenly believes it was the book itself that historians believe to be dubious rather than the attribution of authorship. Answer D is incorrect because it mistakes that the popularity of the book was dubious rather than the authorship.

41. **C**   Answer C is the right answer because it correctly identifies the motivations of the nobility that are heavily implied (although not said outright) in Paragraph 2. The phrases "...did not want to share...," "they assumed," and the use of quotation marks for irony around "protect" are all strong implications by the author that the nobles' motivations were untrustworthy. Answer A is incorrect because it fails to identify the use of sarcasm and irony in the passage, particularly the use of "protect" in quotation marks. Answer B is incorrect because it has no textual basis in the passage, as skills are never compared. Answer D is also incorrect because the passage does not mention religious or social beliefs (outside of the existence of a nun) at any point.

42. **A**   Answer A is correct because it best explains and clarifies what the author means when they say that the professional fishing business had been "commercialized." Answer B shows some general knowledge about the early industrial revolution but has no basis in this passage. Answer C is incorrect because regulation and taxation are not mentioned at all in passage, and the answer mistakes "commercialization" with "regulation." Answer D is incorrect but attempts to tie the term to economic struggle, which is an ongoing theme in the passage.

43. **B**   Answer B is correct because, throughout Paragraphs 4 and 5, the expansion of transportation is closely tied to people going further from home to fish in scenic, new locations. Answer A accesses the idea of leisure time, which is mentioned in the passage, but incorrectly assumes that it was the trains themselves that created it. Answer C is incorrect because, while the statement is partially true, the idea of fishing equipment being complex or in short supply is not mentioned. On the contrary, the passage suggests that many local bait shops existed. Answer D is incorrect because the idea of people fearing technology is not explored anywhere in the passage.

44. **C**   Answer C is correct because Paragraph 5 explains that the Depression reduced people's economic ability and desire to fish. Words and phrases like "middle class...disappeared," "money, food, and work all scarce," and "no longer seemed fun or feasible," should have all served as clues to the reader. Answer A is incorrect and shows a fundamental misunderstanding of 20th century history. Answer B is incorrect but at least attempts to connect the answer to the concept of bait and tackle shops, which were mentioned in Paragraph 4. Answer D is incorrect and has no basis in the passage.

Passage 5 ("When the ground shakes under your feet..."):

45. **D**   Answer D is correct because it best articulates the form and function of the passage. Answer A

is incorrect because the passage is very general and informal, making it far from an "in-depth, scientific examination." Answer B is also incorrect because the passage does not contain any specific advice or recommendations of any sort. Answer C is incorrect because the passage is not a narrative or story in any way.

46. C   Answer C is correct because the content of Paragraphs 2 and 4 explains that it is interactions between nearby plates that cause the majority of seismic activity. Answer D correctly says the edges are the most active areas, but provides an explanation with no textual basis. Paragraphs 2 and 4 also both explain that areas where plates come together are the most seismically active, making answers A and B completely incorrect.

47. B   Even without a map, the reader can use the passage to determine that Answer B is an impossible situation, and therefore the correct answer. The Arabian Plate is established in Paragraph 4 as being in the Mediterranean, whereas the Pacific Plate is established in Paragraph 3 as being between North America and Asia. Answer B is correct because those two plates are on opposite sides of the world and, consequently, could not possibly interact with each other to cause an earthquake. Answers A, C, and D are all incorrect because each of them represents a plausible scenario that might cause an earthquake.

48. A   Answer A is correct because the Pacific Rim (where California and Japan are both located) and the Mediterranean (where Italy is located) have both been established in Paragraphs 3 and 4 as hotspots of seismic activity. Since London and England are not mentioned at all throughout the passage, the reader can infer that England is not an area of significant earthquake activity. Answers B, C, and D are all incorrect because they all fall within established earthquake regions.

49. B   Answer B is the only detail about the Mediterranean not supported by details from Paragraph 4, making it the correct answer. Answer A is the wrong answer because the paragraph explains that the Arabian, Eurasian, and African plates all come together in the regions. Answer C is incorrect because the paragraph particularly mentions the "famous sea." Answer D is also incorrect because the second sentence of the paragraph clearly states that the region experiences regular activity.

50. D   Answer D is correct because it best defines the word "induced" as used in Paragraph 5. The phrases "human activity" and "manmade" in the paragraph should have been key context clues for the reader. Answer A is incorrect, but at least demonstrates the reader is searching within the paragraph. Answer B similarly shows the reader looking to the paragraph for answers but ultimately misunderstanding the use of "induced." Answer C is also incorrect because manmade earthquakes are clearly portrayed as serious issues throughout the paragraph.

Passage 6 ("People who live in American suburbs and cities..."):

51. C   Answer C is the best answer because the passage primarily discusses how people in cold, rural areas use a variety of home heating techniques that people who live in the suburbs and city often don't need to think about. Answer A is incorrect because, even though the passage hints at this idea, it clearly focuses primarily on heat. Answer B is incorrect because, again, the primary topic of the passage is clearly heating. Answer D is also incorrect because "clean" energy is not explored anywhere in the passage.

52. **C**   Answer C is correct because the explanation of pipes freezing is used as evidence that directly supports Paragraph 2's first sentence "Home heating in cold climates is not optional; it's necessary." Answer A is incorrect because the passage goes on to talk about methods of heating that don't require piping (such as a fire). Answer B is incorrect because the idea of pipes freezing is never referred to again after Paragraph 2. Answer D is incorrect because, while the example does build authority, its primary function is to support the topic sentence, making Answer C the best choice overall.

53. **A**   Answer A is the best inference that the reader can make based on a variety of phrases throughout the passage. The first two sentences of Paragraph 1 strongly imply that the speaker is not him- or herself a dweller of the city or suburbs, writing from an outsider's perspective. Additionally, the author's knowledge of pipes freezing in Paragraph 2 and general understanding of heating solutions throughout Paragraphs 3-5 indicate that he or she probably has firsthand experience with this topic, making it most likely that the author lives in one of the cold, rural areas described in the text. Answers B, C, and D are all incorrect because there is nothing in the text to suggest that the author is from a city, suburb, or other country, while there is at least some evidence pointing at the author being from a rural area.

54. **B**   Answer B is correct because the fluctuating price of fossil fuel is cited as a major drawback in Paragraph 3. The phrases and words "prone to price fluctuations," "jump up," and "...find these practices frustrating," should have all been context clues to the reader. Answer A, while true, does not connect to the passage in any way. Answer C, while perhaps partially true, is not the best answer because nothing in the passage suggests accessing wood is a problem for most people. Answer D is also incorrect because Paragraph 3 clearly establishes that oil and propane are delivered "throughout the winter."

55. **D**   Answer D is correct because the sentence in question's main function is to illustrate that people in cold, rural areas find burnable wood especially valuable. Answer A is incorrect and suggests that the reader misinterprets the phrase "informal swap-and-trade economy." Answer B is incorrect because the facts of Paragraph 3 prove it to be false. Answer C, while a true statement, does not address the idea of why wood is a "currency."

56. **C**   Answer C is the best answer because it reflects the overall content of Paragraphs 3-5. The author establishes the benefits and drawbacks of fossil fuels and also describes the use of wood as a supplement in depth. The second sentence of Paragraph 5 should provide a significant hint to the

reader. Answers A and D are incorrect because the main motivation described the passage has simply been to heat a house, not to be exciting or fashionable in any way. Answer B is a decent answer, but not the best, because it does not touch specifically on the best aspects of wood (cost) and fossil fuel (reliability).

57.   **D**   Answer D is the correct answer because it contains the best explanation for the term "vast population center." The use of the words "city" and "rural" throughout the passage should have provided context clues for the reader. Answers A, B, and C are all incorrect because there is no textual basis for any of them, since living conditions (outside of temperature) have not been mentioned at any point in the passage.

Practice Test 5 (Answers and Explanations)

1. **C** After inspection, it can be seen that if you sum the first three terms, you get the next term. If you continue this pattern of adding the previous three terms to get the next, you can find the next term in the series to be,
7 + 13 + 24 = 44.

The answer is C.

2. **D** To make this problem easier, you can square all the numbers for A and B to get rid of the square root to help you see which value is greater.
$A = (\sqrt{65})^2 - 9^2$
$B = (\sqrt{50})^2 - 8^2$
A = 65 - 81 = -16
B = 50 - 64 = -14
As you can see the value of B is greater than A. Therefore, the correct answer is D.

3. **B** This equation can be factored as,
$$\frac{(x-2)(x+3)}{(x-2)} = (x+3) = 0,$$
so $x = -3$. The answer is B.

4. **B** During the first minute, he stacks one box. During the second minute, he stacks 2 more boxes on that 1 box he had originally. During the third minute, he stacks 3 more boxes on everything making the total 6 boxes, and since each box is 5 inches tall, that is 30 inches in total. It took 3 minutes

to reach 30 inches.

The answer is B.

5. **A** We simply must divide by 1000 to convert from miligrams to grams. 0.0202g is the answer or answer choice A.

6. **D** If we assume negative values for costs and positive values for profit, we can write, -$8 + $10 - $11 + $12 = +$3, so his profit is $3 or answer choice D.

7. **A** Substituting $\gamma = 2\delta$ into the function gives us, $f(2\delta) = 2f(\delta)$ which only happens for a non-constant linear function. The only non-constant linear function shown is, x, or answer choice A.

8. **A** 11AM is 3 hours before 2PM. If the length doubles every hour, then three hours before, it was $\frac{1}{2^3}$ the length at 2PM or $(\frac{3}{8})$ = 0.375 meters.
In other words, we have to cut the length in half three times.

The answer is A.

9. **D** None of these functions are equal to each other. The answer is D.

10. **D** Using the definition of averages and

YouTube

Explanations to each problem on:
Youtube.com/ArgoBrothers

MATHEMATICS
ANSWERS & EXPLANATIONS

ARGO BROTHERS

www.argobrothers.com

using x as the score for the next test, we have:

$$\frac{66 + 82 + 81 + 92 + x}{5} = \frac{321 + x}{5} = 84,$$

which simplifies to $x = 420 - 321 = 99$, or answer choice D.

11. **D** Every 7 days from Saturday, it will be Saturday again. 7 can go into 365, 52 times with a remainder of 1 day. So it will be 1 day after Saturday, which is Sunday.

The answer is D.

12. **A** A number is divisible by 9 if all of the digits of that number sum up to a number divisible by 9, which in this case, does. The answer is 0 or answer choice A.

13. **D** The length of AB is 6, since B is the midpoint of AC. The radius of each semicircle is then, 6 and there are 4 identical semicircles, which is equivalent to 2 circles. The area of 1 circle is 36π, so the area of both circles is 72π, or answer choice D.

14. **B** This equation can be simplified to, $8^{x+3} = (8^2)^{3x} = 8^{6x}$, so $x + 3 = 6x$, or $x = (\frac{3}{5})$.

The answer B.

15. **A** The right hand side of the equation simplifies to $A^2 - 8$. So, we only need to worry about the value of A. The value of A is 3 and we can plug that in to our expression.

$3^2 - 8 = 1$. The answer is A.

16. **C** We simply have to multiply 11 by 15 to find the sum. The answer is 165 or answer choice C.

17. **A** Adding all of the terms and dividing by 4 gives,

$$\frac{12b + 9}{4} = 3b + \frac{9}{4}$$

The answer is A.

18. **D** This simplifies to, $\frac{y^{17}}{y^{15}} = y^2$.

The answer is D.

19. **D** Each symbol repeats every 6 symbols Later. For example, the first symbol appears at position 1, 7, 13 and so on. So, the second symbol will appear at 2, 8, 14, ..., 50. The answer is D.

20. **D** The area of a trapezoid with bases a and band altitude, h, is:

$A = \frac{(a + b)h}{2}$ and we know what h is and we know what A is. Plugging those in and solving for $a + b$ gives us, $a + b = 104$. We also know the ratio of the base lengths if $(\frac{2}{6})$ which means, or $3a = b$. Plugging this into $a + b = 104$ and solving for b gives us a value for b

of, $b = 78$ or answer choice D.

21. **D**   The square root of $(\frac{16}{81})$ is $(\frac{4}{9})$.
The answer is D.

22. **B**   Multiplying the first equation by -3 and adding it to the second equation gives, $-17y = -51$ or $y = 3$. If $y = 3$, then we can plug that value into the first equation and solve for x to give us $x = 1$. The solution is $(1, 3)$.

The answer is B.

23. **D**   Multiplying all of the numbers in the trapezoid and taking the square root of that gives us, $\sqrt{144} = 12$

The answer is D.

24. **D**   This answer depends on the signs of X and Y so the answer is D.

25. **C**   If we call the unknown side, AC, x, we have that the perimeter of the triangle is, $P = 10 + x$ and the area is $(\frac{2}{2})x = 20$.

We can solve for x to get $x = 20$, which means the perimeter of the triangle is, 30, which is also the perimeter of the square. All of the sides of a square are equal and the area is the side length squared. So, the area of the square is $(\frac{30}{4})^2$ square inches $= 56.25$ square inches.

The answer is C.

26. **B**   To solve this problem, we must align the scores in order from least to greatest (or greatest to least) and find the middle number. The middle number is 83, so the answer is B.

27. **D**   In one hour, the car travels 50 meters and the circumference of the wheel is $2\pi r = 10\pi$, with a radius of 5 meters. Given this, we can find the number of revolutions that occur in one hour. This will be 50 meters divided by 10π which is $\frac{5}{\pi}$.
The answer is D.

28. **C**   To find this probability, we must divide the area of the shaded region by the area of the square. Let's say that the radius of the circle is r. Then, the side length of the square is $2r$. The area of the square is then, $4r$. The area of the circle is πr^2 and the area of the shaded region is the difference between these two areas, $r^2(4 - \pi^2)$, and once we divide this by $4r^2$, we get:

$$\frac{r^2(4 - \pi^2)}{4r^2} = 1 - \frac{\pi}{4}$$

which is answer choice C.

29. **A**   We know that 100% = 1, so we can simplify this to just 10% times 10%, which is 0.01 or 1%. The answer is A.

30. **A**   10% = 0.1. The greatest integer less than 0.1 is 0. 0 + 1 = 1.

The answer is A.

MATHEMATICS
ANSWERS & EXPLANATIONS

Explanations to each problem on:
Youtube.com/ArgoBrothers

www.argobrothers.com

31. D We know that the area is 100 square meters, so we can find the diameter (2 times the radius, r) by equating, $\pi r^2 = 100$, which gives a diameter of, $2\sqrt{\dfrac{100}{\pi}}$ and dividing this by her speed gives us the time it takes for her to traverse the diameter which is, $0.2\sqrt{\dfrac{100}{\pi}}$. The answer is D.

32. C Using this formula of adding the previous 2 terms to get the next, we have for the first 5 terms,

0, 1, 1, 2, 3 which sums to 7.
The mean is $(\dfrac{7}{5})$ or answer choice C.

33. C If there are 9 vaks in 12 hips, then there are 18 vaks in 24 hips. There are $(\dfrac{18}{x})$ slacks in 24 hips or 18 vaks.
The answer is C.

34. D This simplifies to,
$(\dfrac{11}{10})^2 = (1.1)^2 = 1.21$,
or answer choice D.

35. B Plugging in the values for a and b into the equation gives us, $5 + 2 - 2^2 = 3$. The answer is B.

36. C The integers that are nonpositive within that range are, $-3, -2, -1$ and 0. There are 4 non positive integers. So the answer is C.

37. B A number squared is x. It's reciprocal is $(\dfrac{1}{x})$. The sum is,
$x^2 + \dfrac{1}{x}$. The answer is B.

38. D If the original size is 20, then it increases by 50%, the size will be 30. Then the size will be 45 if we increase it by 50% again. The percent increase from 20 to 45 is 125%.

The answer is D.

39. B Labeling the sides AB and BC as x, respectively and the sides, AF and FE as y, respectively, we can represent the area of the rectangle as, $4xy = 440$. This means that $xy = 110$. x represents the base of triangle BCD, and y represents only half of the height. In order to represent the height, we need to multiply y by 2, and we get $2xy$. Since we doubled y, 110 is also doubled so we have $2xy=220$. $2xy$ represents base times height and the formula for the area of the triangle is A = $\dfrac{1}{2}$bh. Since we know bh is 220, we have A = $\dfrac{1}{2}(220) = 110$. The area of triangle BCD is 110. The answer is B.

40. D Since $\sqrt{2}$ and π are both irrational, there are no integers, a and b that can satisfy the definition of $LCM(x, y)$.

The answer is D.

41. B This function is undefined and not

equal to 1 when the denominator is 0, which occurs when $x = 3$. The answer is 1, or answer choice B.

42. D Since 49^2 is divisible by 7, the answer is still Monday. The answer choice is D.

43. D $f(4)$ can be written as 4^3 or 2^6.
$f(2)$ can be written as 2^3.
The question becomes, how much greater is 2^6 than 2^3. The answer is 2^3 greater, or 8 times greater. The answer is D.

44. B $(\frac{3}{40}) = 0.075$. The answer is B.

45. C There are four prime numbers between 4 and 16 inclusive. They are: 5, 7, 11, 13. The answer is C.

46. B The only perfect square between 9 and 25 exclusive is 16.

The answer is B.

47. D The more sides the figure has, the bigger the area, holding the perimeter constant. So, an octagon would have a bigger area than a triangle, and a circle would have the largest area. The answer is D.

48. C Plugging in what the formula tells us gives us,

$x^2 - x^4 = x^2(1 - x^2)$ or answer C.

49. B If 1 mm represents 150 m, then 1 sq.

mm represents 22,500 sq. m. So then, 1 sq. m. is simply $(\frac{1}{22,500})$ sq. mm.

The answer is B.

50. C If we draw the two points that represent the corners of the rectangle, we see that the rectangle would look like this:

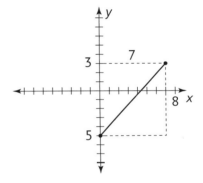

The area is $8 \cdot 7 = 56$. The answer is C.

51. C Simplify the following expression. x^3 cancels out and z^0 is simply one. $\frac{y^3}{y^4}$ results in y^1 and we are left with $\frac{1}{y}$.

52. B The prime factors of 2520 are $2 \cdot 2 \cdot 2 \cdot 3 \cdot 3 \cdot 5 \cdot 7$. There are 4 distinct prime numbers making the answer 4 or answer choice B.

53. **-14** Plug in your given values:

$$= \frac{7}{4}(1 - 3^2)$$

$$= \frac{7}{4}(-8)$$

$$= -\frac{56}{4}$$

$$= -14$$

54. **-4** $-7(3n + 5) = -6n + 25$
$-21n - 35 = -6n + 25$
$-15n = 60$
$n = -4$

55. **30** If Bob sells the cake for $3.00 and it costs him $1.80 to make one, his profit for each cake sold is $1.20. The question asks how many cakes Bob needs to sell in order to make a profit of exactly $36.00. We can divide $36 by $1.2 to get 30. Bob will need to sell 30 cakes to make a profit of $36.00.

56. **59** To solve this problem we need to know the average speed formula which is:

Average Speed = Total Distance Covered / Total Time

First calculate the total distance covered. For the first 3 hours the car traveled 55 miles per hour, so (55 • 3) = 165 miles. For the remaining 2 hours the car travels 65 miles per hour, so (65 • 2) = 130 miles. 165 miles + 130 miles = 295 miles. The total distance covered by the car is 295 miles. The total time taken is 5 hours. Divide 295

miles by 5 hours to get your average speed which is 59 miles per hour.

57. **4** $2x^3 - 3xy$
$2(-1)^3 - 3(-1)(2)$
$(2 \cdot -1) - (-3 \cdot 2)$
$-2 + 6$
$= 4$